Classical
Music Insights

Understanding and Enjoying Great Music

❧ Betsy Schwarm

classical radio announcer, concert speaker, music
historian, college professor of music

 www.trafford.com

North America & international
toll-free: 1 888 232 4444 (USA & Canada)
phone: 250 383 6864 ♦ fax: 812 355 4082

Author's Note

For whom is this book intended? Quite likely for you, but more generally speaking, anyone who is curious about classical music, where it comes from, and what it's trying to achieve. Here are stories about the people who created great music and why we still enjoy it.

If you happen to have some technical background in music, that can be useful, but it isn't required. In all my years in classical radio, we never presumed that a technical background was necessary to enjoy great music. So whether or not you can read music, please proceed.

Persons new to the world of great music have often said to me words to the effect of: "I'm too busy in my professional life to go back to school, but I'm looking for a better understanding of music that gives me more than pop music does. I want to make sense of what I hear when I go to concerts, especially if I go with the boss (or a new romantic interest)."
This book is for you.

We'll explore reasons why, for centuries, people have been fascinated by this field, and continue to find it fulfilling as composers, as performers, and most crucially, as listeners. After all, without us in the audience, they'd have little reason to do what they do.

Betsy Schwarm

TABLE OF CONTENTS

Chapter Five: Chamber Music 149

Chapter Eight: Opera and Operetta 239

Cover Art by Wayne Rigsby of Gearbox Creative, Inc. Running counter-clockwise from upper right of the front cover, the images are Beethoven, Mozart, Clara Wieck Schumann, JS Bach, and Schubert.

Author Photo by Mark Kiryluk.

Chapter One
Sublime Noise

Those first four notes of Beethoven's Symphony no. 5 – immediately repeated slightly lower in pitch – are likely the most famous small sample of music ever conceived by the human mind. In substance, they are simplicity itself; in concept and execution, they become a sonic world. As EM Forster put it at the opening to the fifth chapter of *Howard's End*, "It will be generally admitted that Beethoven's Fifth Symphony is the most sublime noise that has ever penetrated into the ear of man." Being a novelist, not a musicologist writing only for other musicologists, Forster would not have bothered to say so had he not believed that much of his readership was familiar with the music and would agree with the statement.

The purpose of this book is to help casual interested listeners gain an understanding as to how Beethoven came to create that "sublime noise" and what was happening in his life and in the world at that time to cause it to sound that way. We'll also give similar insights into a great many other composers — both influential names of the past and figures of today — to find out how classical music has come to be what it is.

Classical music: the term means many things to many people. To some, it is anything with an orchestra, to others anything over a century old. The uninitiated may think of classical music as elitist and beyond their comprehension. Scholars in the field insist that the term "classical" refers only to Mozart and his contemporaries, preferring other, more specific terms for other times in history.

None of those views is completely useful. Orchestras are part of the field, but not its sum total. Besides, sometimes, orchestras appear in pop music, and there is plenty of fine music that manages without an orchestra. Age, too, is not a defining factor: folk music and even some drinking songs have been around for centuries without becoming "classical," and there are great composers currently working in the twenty-first century. As for charges of elitism, classical music is accessible to anyone with ears, a brain, and an open mind, particularly if that mind is armed with some background information, which this book hopes to provide. To the scholars in the field, one can observe that indeed, they have defined the "Classical Era" as roughly 1750 to 1820, and prefer the term "art music" if something more all-encompassing is needed. However, if society as a whole wishes to call all this range of expression "classical music," it seems petty to quibble. Moreover, quibbling only reinforces ideas of elitism. So though our subject matter for these twelve chapters is broadly speaking "art music," it is the word "classical" that appears in the title.

To begin our discussion, the word "art" is worth remembering, for there is a connection. It is not merely that a composition may be inspired by an artistic style borrowed from painting, although that is sometimes the case. More to the point, this is music written to artistic standards by men and women who hope to master those standards and prove that they have something to say within the expected framework, something that will outlast the present moment and still speak to future generations. After all, Michelangelo did not paint the ceiling of the Sistine Chapel merely because there was a paycheck involved; the paycheck was a nice bonus to his artistic expression. Similarly, Monet's water lilies did pay the rent, but also allowed him to preserve and share his vision of the world. Let us emphasize that, though both Michelangelo and Monet were expressing themselves with colors and shapes, the resulting works are radically different from each other because styles had changed over time. The same is true in music: Bach does not sound like Beethoven, nor do they sound like Brahms, and none of those three sounds like Bernstein. One cannot judge them by each other's standards. So in order to know what to expect from great music, it is best to begin with a quick overview of what those standards (and expectations) would have been at various times.

Great music of artistic value was composed even in the Middle Ages and the Renaissance. However, back then, the vast majority of it was composed for the church, first the Catholic Church, and then (after the Reformation of 1517) also the Protestant. The simple fact was that power and money were largely in the hands of the church, as was the education that one would need to compose anything beyond the simplest peasant tunes. So most music from this time — at least, that which anyone bothered to write down and preserve — tended to be religious in nature. By the Renaissance, there were powerful monarchs seeking musical diversion. Yet even their music often echoes what the church music was seeking to do: emphasizing singing with instruments in a supporting role at best. Often, music was written in an "a cappella" fashion, meaning for singers with no instruments at all. Of the great music of this time, it is the church music that is still performed with any frequency (excepting entertainment at Renaissance fairs).

Around 1600, scholars draw a line and declare a new time, the Baroque Era, in which secular (non-religious) music first comes to the fore as do works for instruments without singers, rather than singers without instruments. The latter trend was encouraged by new and improved techniques for instrumental

3

construction, epitomized by the master builder Antonio Stradivari (1644-1737), whose unsurpassed artistry has yet to be fully explained. Wishing to keep his techniques secret, he wrote no handbook on instrument construction. Therefore, the magic behind his method remains a mystery, yet is sufficiently magical that a Stradivari instrument in mint condition and of proven provenance can sell for several million dollars.

At this time in history, there was an increase in power and wealth of the royal courts, determined to indulge in ever more extravagant entertainment, thereby making a statement about their power and influence. Much music of the time was composed for such royal houses. However, one also finds cities, notably London, Paris, and Venice, investing in musical diversion for their citizens of non-noble birth. Even five-hundred years ago, people from all walks of life liked to listen to music and did not want it to be always religious in nature.

Baroque music tends to be rather busy, highly detailed with lots of notes: hard to play, but not hard on the ears. Repetition of phrases was considered important for making a piece cohesive; thus, a Baroque piece may start to sound familiar even before it is quite over. In this so-called "Age of Reason," strict, logical structures for music were the norm with emotions generally understated. Favored instruments were strings (violin, viola, cello, bass), usually with the harpsichord, a keyboard instrument that was a more delicate predecessor of the piano. Wind instruments were used less frequently and generally lightly, and some winds, notably the clarinet and the tuba, had yet to be invented.

Up next, after 1750, is what the scholars call Classical, and classic it is: the origin of many of the most lasting and influential ideas still in use today. Here, one finds even greater popularity of public concerts, with all of the great composers earning a significant percentage of their income through ticket proceeds and publishing contracts. With the French Revolution of 1789 on the horizon, the royalty and aristocrats are beginning to decline in influence, though it is a very gradual process. For decades, composers will still be encouraged — sometimes driven — to seek employment as director of music for some aristocratic house.

Although fine music was found throughout Europe, the center of focus was Vienna, as Hollywood now is for films; one can pursue a career in the field elsewhere, but one likes to be in the heart of activity if at all possible. Classical works tend to be somewhat less detailed than Baroque ones, with more focus upon grace and flow than upon intricate energy. Balance and orderly contrast are greatly admired, so that a melody of one character is often offset by another of different personality. Emotions, though still restrained, are allowed rather freer rein than in the Baroque. Strings are still favorite instruments; however, the harpsichord is being displaced by the piano. Woodwinds and brass, valued for the role they can fill in that search for contrast, enjoy greater prominence. New inventions (the clarinet) and new technologies (refinements to the trumpet and the French horn) further improve the tools at a composer's disposal.

By the early 1800s, one begins to find styles moving toward what will be called "Romantic." This is not to say that music must be about love; rather, "romantic" was an ideal that promoted deep, heartfelt expressions and stronger emotions than had formerly been popular. The stylistic name for this trend was "Sturm und Drang," German for "storm and stress," with the idea that the more turbulence, the better. Compositions are often quite personal, sometimes autobiographical in nature. Furthermore, composers begin to move away from the thought of music as abstract expression, often preferring their works to have some kind of plot content, even when there are no singers, speakers, or narrators to tell that story but rather only instrumental colors.

No longer are composers and performers expected to obtain regular employment in some aristocratic house. Rather, they write their music and arrange for its public performance and publication, often supplementing their income by conducting and teaching, or perhaps with journalistic work. Greater ease of transportation makes travel for concerts more practical, and some of the greatest names in music become international stars, some of them even traveling to the United States.

Many composers tend toward writing grand, dramatic works of strongly emotional character with colorful and boisterous orchestral sounds. At the other extreme, some composers prefer shorter, smaller, more delicate moods, often for a single pianist, or one pianist with a singer. This latter category catered to increased popularity of music-making for entertainment in middle class homes, particularly homes possessed of daughters who aspired toward refinement. Compared to the Classical composers, and even more so to those of the Baroque, Romantic composers put themselves heart and soul into their music, and insight into their lives and personalities grants insight into what to make of their music.

With the approach of the end of the nineteenth century, new ideas begin to develop which will turn away from past practices in favor of innovations. Rules are bent, even broken, but the challenge in summarizing what happens is that there are many ways in which one can bend a rule. One might be amongst the first to bring formlessness and exotic Asian sounds into one's music, in place of techniques that Mozart would have used: such were the Impressionists. One might look to one's own roots, showcasing folk rhythms that to an earlier generation might have sounded disorderly; such were the Nationalists. By the early 1900s, some composers, often under the influence of Sigmund Freud, began to look at the darker side of life, expressing in their music harsh states of mind so intense that the result was far from easy listening. These so-called Expressionists did not enjoy great popularity with the public, but were still influential as they explored ideas that had not been tried previously and proved that there are many voices of musical expression.

Even as all these new ideas came to the fore, there were still some composers who sincerely felt that the old models were not yet played out and still had something to offer; these composers blended some of the older elements with some of the newer ones. Taken all in all, one cannot predict how early twentieth century music will sound, other than that, to varying degrees, it will sound at least partially more progressive than that of the previous century. Public performances, publishing, and teaching continue as professional fields, joined soon by recordings and radio.

The trend toward increasing diversity of influence continues through the twentieth century and into the twenty-first, with composers drawing upon whatever various inspirations suit some facets of their interests. New media allow new methods of reaching out to audiences, though not always with a corresponding increase of income, for the internet has proved to be a mixed bag. Thanks to broadcasting, and, for that matter, to jet-setting composers and performers, new music can reach new audiences incredibly quickly, with some current composers' individual works getting more performances in a single year than Beethoven's did in his entire life.

Styles are too varied to be effectively summarized, but of particular influence are two American creations: jazz and minimalism. Jazz began in the 1920s as a pop music style, but by the '30s, its sassy syncopations had begun to appear even in works of some great European masters. Minimalism appeared first in the late '60s as a trance-like idea based on short melodic fragments frequently repeated and only subtly varying. Straight minimalism can seem to some ears like too much of a good thing, but some composers have found that it makes a good foundation to more substantial and colorful melodic/harmonic structures. Art music is not just a European/North American interest; it is popular everywhere, and skilled composers come from every continent except Antarctica.

Who fits where? Here is a list of prominent names in classical music appearing in this book:

Renaissance: Thomas Tallis (c. 1505-1585)
               Giovanni da Palestrina (c. 1525-1594)
               Michael Praetorius (1571-1621)
               Gregorio Allegri (c. 1573-1648)

Baroque: Johann Pachelbel (1653-1706)
               Arcangelo Corelli (1653-1713)
               Antonio Vivaldi (1678-1741)
               Georg Philipp Telemann (1681-1767)
               Johann Sebastian Bach (1685-1750)
               George Frideric Handel (1685-1759)
               Dominico Scarlatti (1685-1757)

Classical: Leopold Mozart (1719-1787)
               Franz Joseph Haydn (1732-1809)
               Luigi Boccherini (1743-1805)
               Antonio Salieri (1750-1825)
               Wolfgang Amadeus Mozart (1756-1791)
               Ludwig van Beethoven (1770-1827)
                 (also an early Romantic)

Early Romantic: Johann Nepomuk Hummel (1778-1837)
               John Field (1782-1837)
               Nicolo Paganini (1782-1840)
               Carl Maria von Weber (1786-1826)
               Gioacchino Rossini (1792-1868)
               Franz Schubert (1797-1828)
               Gaetano Donizetti (1797-1848)
               Vincenzo Bellini (1801-1835)
               Hector Berlioz (1803-1869)
               Adolphe Adam (1803-1856)
               Felix Mendelssohn (1809-1847)
               Frederic Chopin (1810-1849)
               Franz Liszt (1811-1886)
               Robert Schumann (1810-1856)

Mid Romantic: Giuseppe Verdi (1813-1901)
Richard Wagner (1813-1883)
Charles Gounod (1818-1893)
Jacques Offenbach (1819-1880)
Clara Wieck Schumann (1819-1896)
Cesar Franck (1822-1890)
Bedrich Smetana (1824-1884)
Anton Bruckner (1824-1896)
Johann Strauss Jr. (1825-1899)
Louis Moreau Gottschalk (1829-1869)
Alexander Borodin (1833-1887)
Johannes Brahms (1833-1897)
Amilcare Ponchielli (1834-1886)
Camille Saint-Saëns (1835-1921)
Leo Delibes (1836-1891)
Emil Waldteufel (1837-1915)
Georges Bizet (1838-1875)
Max Bruch (1838-1920)
Modest Mussorgsky (1839-1881)
Peter Tchaikovsky (1840-1893)
Antonín Dvořák (1841-1904)
Jules Massenet (1842-1912)
Sir Arthur Sullivan (1842-1900)
Edvard Grieg (1843-1907)
Pablo de Sarasate (1844-1908)
Nicolai Rimsky-Korsakov (1844-1908)
Gabriel Fauré (1845-1924)

Late Romantic: Vincent d'Indy (1851-1931)
Charles Stanford (1852-1924)
Englebert Humperdinck (1854-1921)
(the original one, not the pop star)
John Philip Sousa (1854-1932)
Sir Edward Elgar (1857-1934)
Cecile Chaminade (1857-1944)
Giacomo Puccini (1858-1924)
Hugo Wolf (1860-1903)
Gustav Mahler (1860-1911)

Isaac Albeniz (1860-1909)
Claude Debussy (1862-1918)
Frederick Delius (1862-1934)
Richard Strauss (1864-1949)
Carl Nielsen (1865-1931)
Paul Dukas (1865-1935)
Jean Sibelius (1865-1957)
Erik Satie (1866-1925)
Amy Beach (Mrs. HHA) (1867-1944)
Franz Lehar (1870-1948)
Louis Vierne (1870-1937)
Alexander Scriabin (1872-1915)
Ralph Vaughan Williams (1872-1958)

Early 20th Century: Sergei Rachmaninoff (1873-1943)
Gustav Holst (1874-1934)
Charles Ives (1874-1954)
Arnold Schoenberg (1874-1951)
Maurice Ravel (1875-1937)
Reinhold Gliere (1875-1956)
Manuel de Falla (1876-1946)
Ottorino Respighi (1879-1936)
Joseph Canteloube (1879-1957)
Ernest Bloch (1880-1959)
Béla Bartók (1881-1945)
Zoltan Kodaly (1882-1967)
Igor Stravinsky (1882-1971)
Alban Berg (1885-1935)
Rebecca Clark (1886-1979)
Heitor Villa Lobos (1887-1959)

Mid 20th Century: Sergei Prokofiev (1891-1953)
Arthur Honegger (1892-1955)
Darius Milhaud (1892-1974)
Douglas Moore (1893-1969)
Carl Orff (1895-1982)
Paul Hindemith (1895-1963)
Howard Hanson (1896-1981)
Virgil Thomson (1896-1989)

Eric Korngold (1897-1957)
George Gershwin (1898-1937)
Carlos Chávez (1899-1978)
Silvestre Revueltas (1899-1940)
Francis Poulenc (1899-1963)
"Duke" Ellington (1899–1974)
Randall Thompson (1899-1984)
Kurt Weill (1900-1950)
George Antheil (1900-1959)
Aaron Copland (1900-1990)
Gerald Finzi (1901-1956)
Joaquin Rodrigo (1901-1999)
Sir William Walton (1902-1983)
Aram Khachaturian (1903-1978)
Dmitri Kabalevsky (1904-1987)
Dmitri Shostakovich (1906-1975)
Miklós Rózsa (1907-1995)
Olivier Messiaen (1908-1992)
Samuel Barber (1910-1981)
Bernard Herrmann (1911-1975)
Nino Rota (1911-1979)
Jean Françaix (1912-1997)
John Cage (1912-1992)
Morton Gould (1913-1996)
Benjamin Britten (1913-1976)
Alberto Ginastera (1916-1983)
Leonard Bernstein (1918-1990)
Astor Piazzolla (1921-1992)

Current and Recent Names: Elliott Carter (b. 1908)
Alan Hovhaness (1911-2000)
Gian Carlo Menotti (1911-2007)
Ariel Ramirez (1921-2010)
György Ligeti (1923-2006)
Ned Rorem (b. 1923)
Carlisle Floyd (b. 1926)
Einojuhani Rautavaara (b. 1928)
John Williams (b. 1932)

Arvo Pärt (b. 1935)
Philip Glass (b. 1937)
Joan Tower (b. 1938)
John Corigliano (b. 1938)
Morton Lauridsen (b. 1943)
John Tavener (b. 1944)
Karl Jenkins (b. 1944)
John Rutter (b. 1945)
Peter Lieberson (1946-2011)
Howard Shore (b. 1946)
John Adams (b. 1947)
Daniel Catán (1949-2011)
Libby Larsen (b. 1950)
Michael Daughtery (b. 1954)
Philip Feeney (b. 1954)
Tan Dun (b. 1957)
James MacMillan (b. 1959)
Osvaldo Golijov (b. 1960)
Edgar Meyer (b. 1960)
Jake Heggie (b. 1961)
Michael Torke (b. 1961)
Jennifer Higdon (b. 1962)
Christopher Theofanides (b. 1967)
Eric Whitacre (b. 1970)
Gabriela Montero (b. 1970)
Jay Greenberg (b. 1991)

Most of these composers are featured in this book with detailed essays about specific works. A few appear the end of each of the main chapters in a list of further recommendations which, for reasons of space, didn't make it in for an in-depth essay but are still worth discovery. These lists of further recommendations also include a few other composers who are not on this introductory list.

Chapters Two through Eleven are organized according to type of music, with items appearing chronologically according to the composer's birth years. The first time a featured composer appears, there is biographical background in addition to information about the particular composition. If that person appears again in later chapters (as may be the case with especially influential names), the biographical material is not repeated. The index can readily refer you to other references to that person, so as to find more biographical data.

In the chapters that follow, you'll often see that the title of a composition is followed by an opus number (op.), or some similar designation. These derive from the order in which a composer's work was published, and may or may not represent a strict order of composition. Sometimes, something might sit on the shelf for years awaiting publication, and thus earn a misleading number. At other times, a composer might give something a number whether or not he has yet arranged publication.

There are also a few important composers who, for various reasons, didn't always publish their works with opus numbers, or didn't publish their works at all. For the most prominent of these composers, later music historians have compiled catalogs to organize that person's works, and those catalogs carry their own designations. With Johann Sebastian Bach, the catalog of record is the so-called Bach Werke Verzeichnis (Catalog of Bach's Works), routinely abbreviated as BWV. For Wolfgang Amadeus Mozart, it's the Köchel catalog, the work of one Ludwig Köchel, and abbreviated as K. For Franz Schubert, it's the Deutsch catalog, compiled by Otto Deutsch, and abbreviated as D.

The average listener has no pressing need to memorize these numbers; even for this author, who knows many of them by heart, they are more useful than seriously required. However, they are valuable as designations of the approximate order in which a composer's works came into being. The exception with the BWV catalog is that, as specific data on chronology is limited, it does not pretend to specify dates, and instead organizes works by type.

With the extensive (and continuing) history of classical music, it is impossible in any single volume of manageable size to discuss — or even list — every significant composer and composition ever to exist. So it has been necessary to make choices. Repertoire was chosen first by placing in each of the thematically organized chapters composers who absolutely could not be ignored in that particular area. Thus, the names of Mozart and Beethoven appear frequently, though not under film music. With those names in place, I then selected representative works from that person, knowing that one could not include everything. Choices amongst several otherwise similar works were based upon how familiar an individual composition is to the general public and how frequently it is performed.

Once these not-to-be-overlooked items were on the list, I added other composers who might be less famous than Mozart and Beethoven (who isn't?), but still made significant contributions in that field, and whose music is readily encountered, either in recordings or in live performance. A few markedly avant garde composers were included because, though their music is not often presented in live concerts, it is yet influential and helps to demonstrate the various ways in which music might be used.

I took especial care to bring the various chapters up to the present day, as far as practical including composers who are still at work, so as to make clear that classical music is not only of the past. It is a timeless and living art, and will outlive all of us, a fact that would please Mozart, Beethoven, and all the others.

Chapter Two

Symphonies

When one hears it, it's familiar even to those who know little classical music: the main theme from the so-called "Ode to Joy" from Beethoven's Symphony no. 9. This chapter will explore not only that specific work, but also other prominent and interesting symphonies, as well as the idea of what exactly a "symphony" is supposed to be. Some follow Beethoven's model; others explore new realms.

The word "sinfonie," deriving from Greek roots meaning "sounding together," was first used for an instrumental introduction to or interlude in a larger work. By the early eighteenth century, however, it had come to mean a free-standing orchestral composition in several separate and contrasting movements. A movement of a composition is comparable to a chapter in a book: a self-contained section within a larger whole. Early symphonies tended to have three movements (first a fast one, then a slow one, then concluding with another fast one); later, the trend changed to four or sometimes more.

Those early symphonies were usually ten to fifteen minutes in length, which at the time was relatively expansive, compared to earlier music. By the late 1700s, a symphony was more likely to be about half an hour in length, and after another century, works twice that long were not unknown. In theory, the different movements would contrast with each other for the sake of variety, yet still have enough resemblance to each other so that together they made up a cohesive whole. Some composers liked to repeat themes from one movement to the next so as to create a firm link. Others enjoyed bringing some narrative element into the flow of music, so that it was not simply a pleasant rush of sound, but rather sound that had some specific ideas to convey. Whichever approach a composer preferred, principal was using the varied timbres (voices) of the different instruments to create varied effects.

It's worth remembering that, although this chapter deals with the symphony as a type of composition, the word also applies to a large group of instrumental players. In that context, a symphony is comparable to an orchestra or a philharmonic; in fact, some prominent performing groups, notably the Chicago Symphony Orchestra, use several of those same synonyms in their names. Having said that a symphony can be a large group of instrumental players begs a question as to how large is large. The answer depends upon the historical period. When Mozart was a boy in the 1760s, a symphony orchestra had about thirty players. Sixty years later, the number had doubled, and in another sixty years, symphony orchestras of a hundred players were not uncommon. Most modern orchestras have about seventy to eighty players on regular salary. Depending on the music to be played, weeks will occur in which some of those players get time off; at other times, extra support players will be needed.

Now, let us return to the symphony as a type of composition. If this book attempted to detail every symphony every written, there would be space for nothing else, even if one limited the discussion to the most important and influential composers. Instead, we shall consider a range of representative works by those great names, giving consideration to how the perspective of what constituted a symphony changed over the years, and the role these works played in their composers' lives. That this is the longest chapter in this book serves as evidence of how important symphonies are.

- Haydn: Symphony no. 94 in G major, "Surprise"

Throughout most of the eighteenth century, nearly all composers worked for the courts or the church, in which capacity, they were little more than servants. They wrote as they were told, performed when they were ordered, and had little of the freedom that one might wish for an artist. Franz Joseph Haydn (1732-1809), for example, spent nearly thirty years working for the aristocratic Esterhazy court. It was a secure life, but Haydn was so isolated from the world that he little realized how far his fame had spread. He was nearly sixty before he had an opportunity to discover it for himself.

Haydn's chance for freedom came in 1790 with the death of his long-time employer, Prince Nikolaus Esterhazy. Nikolaus had been devoted to music, especially Haydn's, but his successor, Prince Anton, had little interest in the arts. Anton valued Haydn only for the prestige which he brought to the Esterhazy court. The music itself held no attraction for him, and he never gave Haydn any real duties, so, when the composer asked for permission to visit London, Anton easily agreed. Haydn was gone for a year and a half. Then, after checking back briefly with the Esterhazys in Vienna, he returned for a second eighteen month stay in the British capital.

Haydn's London visit was spurred by an invitation from Johann Peter Salomon, a German-born violinist and impresario, who presented six months of concerts in London each year. Well aware of how popular Haydn's symphonies had become, Salomon imagined that the master himself would be an even bigger attraction, and he was right. Londoners turned out by the thousands to watch Haydn conduct premieres of his new works. Critics and audiences alike were generous with their praise, which must have been a gratifying experience for someone who had labored so long as a servant. Haydn's entries in his diary during these tours exult in his popularity, the attendance at his concerts, the frequent dinner invitations, and the impressive concert receipts. "I made 4000 Gulden on this evening," the composer once observed to his diary. "Such a thing," he continued, "is possible only in England."

Among the new works heard at these concerts were twelve new symphonies, the last symphonies Haydn ever wrote. One of the most popular of the collection, the Symphony no. 94, premiered in London March 23, 1792. The piece gained notoriety at a later performance, when the composer himself, serving as conductor, impulsively altered the dynamics of the second movement. As the story is told, Haydn had already given the downbeat to begin the movement when the gentle snores of a front-row patron attracted his attention and piqued his sense of humor. He and his musicians forged ahead with the whimsical little theme until reaching its final chord, for which Haydn cued an immense fortissimo, bringing the drowsy patron to his feet. The episode earned for the symphony its ever-lasting nickname, "Surprise," at least in English-speaking lands. In German, it is known as the symphony "mit dem Paukenschlag," that is, with the drum stroke.

Beyond that colorful anecdote, the symphony does exactly what symphonies were supposed to do at this time: it begins with a mostly lively movement in which several melodies are offered to contrast with one another, its second movement offers a gentler pace — though with the moment of "surprise", the third movement is dance-flavored (specifically resembling the then-popular minuet, a predecessor of the waltz), and the last movement is the liveliest of all, with brisk and scurrying ideas that bring the piece to an energetic conclusion. Such a pattern had become the norm for symphonies over the course of decades, a situation that was a credit to Haydn himself. He had pioneered the plan, and his popularity was such that other composers chose him as their model as to how a symphony should be written.

- Mozart: Symphony no. 41 in C major, K. 551

One often hears of the neglect in which Wolfgang Amadeus Mozart (1756-1791) labored during the last years of his life: fewer concerts to give, fewer paychecks to collect, all too many creditors at the door. The stories are largely true, yet one must remember that he had begun his career in triumph. Only surviving son of Leopold Mozart, a respected violinist/composer, Wolfgang was composing by the age of six and performing in public on international tours by the age of eight. He astonished audiences with his youthful genius and the ease with which he had mastered compositional ideas with which many adult composers were still struggling.

At age twenty-five, Mozart abandoned his native Salzburg in favor of the imperial capital of Vienna. There, all went well for several years, as he found more piano students than he wanted and as many concert opportunities as he could manage, with the emperor himself applauding Mozart's works. However, before the 1780s ended, the situation was less favorable. By 1788, his opera *Don Giovanni*, after a successful run in Prague, had failed in Vienna, and the Viennese public, seeking something new and different in their entertainment, no longer flocked to support his concerts. In addition, cultural activities as a whole were sharply limited by the Austrian Empire's new war with Turkey.

As a consequence, Mozart's income dropped; he and his family were forced to seek less expensive lodgings in the suburbs of Vienna. Attempting to put a good face on this move, the composer boasted in a letter that the distance he now lived from the city's heart was actually beneficial, claiming "I have greater leisure to work now since I am not bothered by so many visitors." Unfortunately, a distraction or two might have been more therapeutic, for Mozart was troubled by a lack of commissions for new compositions, and by the recent death of his six-month-old daughter, Theresia. One letter to a lodge brother refers to "dark thoughts which I must force from my mind," and apparently those thoughts interfered in his ability to compose. During this summer, Mozart completed very few compositions. The only significant works were three symphonies, written in a mere seven weeks: the final symphonies of his career.

Mozart rarely composed on a whim. Generally, his works were written on commission, or for his own concerts, or as gifts for friends. Such transactions were usually cataloged in the composer's letters and writings. However, in this case, the historical record is silent. Music scholars have found no evidence of a commission; that is, no one paid for these symphonies to be written. Perhaps Mozart composed them on speculation, in hopes of selling them or presenting them in a Viennese concert. If so, he was disappointed, for they were not published during his lifetime, and there is no clear evidence of a performance. Nevertheless, the sudden burst of activity does suggest that the composer had some objective in mind, and it now seems that his goal may have been a London tour. As a child, Mozart had spent over a year living in London, absorbing the musical ambience. Even in adulthood in Vienna, he had several close English friends, and since at least 1786, he had spoken of traveling to London to present a concert series. In the event of such a tour, it was customary for composers to bring new works, preferably a set of three or six symphonies. Haydn would do exactly that when he came to London in the 1790s. Scholars now suggest that, several years before Haydn's journey, Mozart wrote these three symphonies while dreaming of a similar excursion, though he never embarked upon the adventure.

The Symphony no. 41 — last of all Mozart's symphonies — is known as the *Jupiter* Symphony, a title not granted it by its creator. Rather, the title seems to have originated, ironically enough, in London, thanks to the impresario Johann Peter Salomon, who would later bring Haydn to England. The nickname was apparently inspired by a sense of Olympian grandeur in this, Mozart's largest and most complex symphony. It is a long step beyond the angelic grace usually associated with Mozart's name. Here, he calls upon a more robust spirit, hinting at the grand Romantic symphonies that would come with Beethoven. The symphony is Jupiter-like in another way, too, for it is frequently jovial, as if the Roman god himself were laughing heartily in the celebratory key of C major.

Mozart's Symphony no. 41 proved inspirational to many composers, especially Haydn, who modeled his 95th and 98th symphonies on the *Jupiter*. Yet the most succinct reflection on the work's importance is found in the critiques of composer/ journalist Robert Schumann (1810-1856), who in 1835 wrote "about many things in this world there is simply nothing to be said — for example, about Mozart's C-major symphony with the fugue, much of Shakespeare, and some of Beethoven." It is perhaps significant that Schumann does not merely equate the *Jupiter* with Shakespeare and Beethoven. Rather, he places this piece *above* many of those master's efforts.

- Beethoven: Symphony no. 5 in c minor, op. 67

Born in Bonn, Germany, Ludwig van Beethoven (1770-1827) would become the most famous member of a musical family, for both his father and his grandfather pursued professions in music. It was his father who first encouraged Ludwig's inclination, though nothing further positive can be said of the elder Beethoven, who was by all accounts of those who knew him, an abusive drunk who compelled his son to practice endlessly at the piano and, once the child was old enough to work (age eleven), was happy to let his eldest son support him. Young Ludwig left Bonn in favor of Vienna as soon as he could, making the move permanent at the age of twenty-one, and, for the remainder of his life, would spend most of his time in the Austrian capital. The first years were times of personal joy and professional triumphs. The triumphs would last until his death in 1827, but the joy was of shorter duration, as Beethoven's hearing began to fail when he was barely thirty, and he was profoundly deaf before completing his famed Symphony no. 5.

On December 22, 1808, Viennese devotees of new music made their way to the Theater-an-der-Wien for the most significant concert of the year, one of the most significant concerts in all of music history. The program, consisting entirely of Beethoven premieres, began with the Symphony no. 6, followed, in order, by the concert aria, "*Ah, perfido*", two movements from the Mass in C major, the Piano Concerto no. 4, the Symphony no. 5, and, last but not least, the *Choral Fantasy*. It was four hours of music, new music to their ears.

Those pieces all premiered together because Beethoven habitually worked on several compositions simultaneously. He began the work now known as the Symphony no. 5 around 1804, just after finishing the Symphony no. 3. Many other projects intervened, however, including what became the Symphony no. 4, pushing this one a bit further down the list. In fact, it nearly moved down even more. Beethoven completed this c minor symphony at nearly the same time he finished the Symphony no. 6 in F major, the "*Pastorale*," and, at that first concert, it was the *Pastorale* that bore the number five. Somewhere between performance and publication, Beethoven renumbered the two. The c minor became the Fifth, and the F major became the Sixth, as they are known today.

At its premiere performance, music critics had little to say about Beethoven's Symphony no. 5. However, a year and a half later, the *Allgemeine musikalische Zeitung* (General Musical Journal) gave a highly favorable review of another performance. The reviewer described the work this way: "Glowing beams shoot through this realm of deep night, and we become aware of immense shadows, that rise and fall, closing in closer and closer on us, wiping us out, but not the ache of unending longing, in which every desire, rising quickly in the sounds of celebration, sinks and goes under, and only in this aching, in which love, hope, and joy are consumed but not destroyed." Few reviewers today write with such descriptive energy, perhaps because few reviewers are novelists and few are composers. ETA Hoffmann, author of that particular review, was both.

The Symphony no. 5 has undergone much analysis since Hoffmann's attempt, and those first four notes have drawn much of the attention. Beethoven himself allegedly described them as "Fate knocking at the door". It's an evocative image, but the source on that statement, Beethoven's sometime friend Anton Schindler, was known for not letting facts get in the way of a good story. Furthermore, the supposed conversation took place years after the symphony was finished, and Beethoven had been known to say nearly anything to relieve himself of questioning pests, such as Schindler. Whether or not there is a symbolic meaning to the notes, their musical meaning is clear: the pitches of those first notes — G and E-flat — are two of the three pitches that make up a c minor chord. Thus, with this opening motif, Beethoven bellows at his listeners the key of his symphony, and then hammers the point home by repeating the rhythm throughout the work. Sometimes ominous, sometimes triumphant, the four-note pattern remains the recurring element that unites the symphony's four movements.

- Beethoven: Symphony no. 9 in d minor, op. 125, "Choral"

It's a familiar tale: an aging Beethoven, ill and deaf, conducting the orchestra and chorus in the premiere of his Symphony no. 9, conducting even after they had ceased to perform, after they had reached the end of the stunning new work, after the audience had already begun to applaud, continuing to conduct until a singer turned him around so that he could see the thunderous cheers that were resounding throughout the hall. The image is deeply moving, so much so that more cynical historians would like to discount it; it is, they feel, too perfect to be true. Yet this once, the cynics are apparently wrong, for several eyewitnesses tell the same tale of that fateful performance in Vienna on May 7, 1824. Their stories vary somewhat in detail. Some place the dramatic moment at the symphony's conclusion. Others maintain it occurred at the end of the second movement scherzo. This difference of opinion might merely be credited to the passage of years between the incident itself and the day long after when those observers at last spoke to a biographer. Whenever the applause occurred, the fact that it passed unheard by Beethoven makes clear that he could never have heard a note of this most magnificent composition. Think about that bitter fact, and then wonder that a man so crossed by fate could still demand a choir to sing rapturously of joy.

Beethoven had first encountered Schiller's poem "An die Freude" ("To Joy") over thirty years before he completed the Ninth Symphony. The poem had first appeared in print in 1785, and from that time on was quite popular in the German states. Evidence suggests that Beethoven may have initially set the text to music as early as 1792. Other attempts were made in 1808 and 1811, when Beethoven's notebooks include remarks to himself concerning possible settings for the familiar text.

These years of toying with Schiller's ode were also years of personal and professional growth. When he first came to know the poem, he was an optimistic young artist who had not yet composed his Symphony no. 1, yet Beethoven's definitive approach to the poem, in 1812, came with the completion of the Symphony no. 8. Perhaps the professional experience he had gained in those decades led him to consider that a poem of such spiritual power required an equally powerful setting, for he soon embarked on the creation of his Symphony no. 9, the work in which Schiller's words would take glorious flight.

Ten years would pass before this final symphony's completion, ten years in which Beethoven virtually shed blood over every note, considering and rejecting over two-hundred different versions of the "Joy" theme alone. At the end of that time, he offered to the public a radically new creation that was part symphony and part oratorio, a hybrid that proved puzzling to his less daring observers. The conductor Louis Spohr, who knew Beethoven, asserted privately that the piece was "tasteless," and Giuseppe Verdi, who, as one of the greatest masters of opera, knew a thing or two about how to blend music and words, lamented that the grand finale was "badly set."

Others have better understood Beethoven's final symphonic work, and have defended it eloquently. Let us give the French Impressionist Claude Debussy the last word: "It is the most triumphant example of the molding of an idea to the preconceived form; at each leap forward there is a new delight, without either effort or appearance of repetition; the magical blossoming, so to speak, of a tree whose leaves burst forth simultaneously. Nothing is superfluous in this stupendous work . . . Beethoven had already written eight symphonies and the figure nine seems to have had for him an almost mystic significance. He determined to surpass himself. I can scarcely see how his success can be questioned."

- Schubert: Symphony no. 9 in C major, D. 944, "Great C Major"

The year was 1828, the final year of Franz Schubert's tragically abbreviated life. Neglected, debt-ridden, and in failing health, the thirty-one year old composer was already glimpsing the closure of his days without having achieved any real success. A shy man who felt uncomfortable promoting himself, he had never achieved much prominence in Vienna, though as a native Viennese, he ought to have been familiar to all. Instead, he labored away on his music in private, and the vast majority of his compositions were heard only by private gatherings of friends. Therefore, he wrote a great many songs for performance at those gatherings (see Chapter Seven).

At last, however, there seemed cause for optimism. The month of January 1828 had seen two well-received performances of his chamber music; at a later concert in March, Schubert himself, despite chronic timidity, dared to appear on stage and came home with his pockets pleasantly full of cash. Viennese critics were still taking little notice of his skills, a visit by the superstar violinist Nicolo Paganini (1782-1840) being deemed of greater interest than the progress of a home-grown artist. However, Schubert remained generally upbeat and impressively productive. In these waning months, he completed a variety of works that would have made a career for any other man. Yet even the most significant of these late scores would be overshadowed by his last and most magnificent symphony.

Schubert had begun his Symphony no. 9 in the summer of 1825, while vacationing with friends in the Austrian countryside near Gmunden. The beauty of his surroundings proved inspiring, as did the enthusiasm with which he was received, for here, in these scenic little towns, he found an eager audience for his music. Perhaps driven by this enthusiasm, Schubert planned a new symphony of glorious extent, grander even than Beethoven's Symphony no. 3, "Eroica," itself nearly an hour in length. A marathon to play as well as to compose, this newest work would not be completed for over two years.

It was not until 1828 that Vienna's Gesellschaft der Musikfreunde (Society of the Friends of Music) agreed to premiere the new work. Rehearsals began, but the piece was fiendishly difficult. Its opening French horn theme required almost as much luck as skill, and some of the four individual movements were as long as entire symphonies by Schubert's predecessors. At last, the orchestra rebelled. It refused the play the new symphony, and Schubert, with little choice, acquiesced. He brought out instead a shorter work in the same key, his Symphony no. 6, which also had not yet been heard publicly, but even that piece reached the stage too late. By the time of its premiere December 14, 1828, the composer, laid low, it seems, by the combined effects of typhoid and syphilis, had been dead for nearly a month.

The still-unperformed Symphony no. 9 might have vanished, except for the timely intervention of German born Robert Schumann (1810-1856). At the time better known as a journalist than as a composer, Schumann traveled to Vienna on business and while there, made a point of visiting Schubert's grave. Later, in his newspaper, the *New Journal for Music*, he reported on the bewildering emotions that had overwhelmed him, and the sudden notion that while in the area, he might visit Schubert's brother, Ferdinand. "I looked him up," Schumann wrote. "He knew me as one of his brother's unreserved admirers, told me much and finally showed me . . . those of Franz Schubert's compositions still in his hands . . . He showed me, among other things, the scores of a number of symphonies, some never heard, some studied, then put aside as too difficult and extravagant."

Eagerly, Schumann persuaded Ferdinand Schubert that the music, and in particular the unheard grand Symphony in C major, would be better off in Leipzig, where, with his Gewandhaus Orchestra, Felix Mendelssohn (1809-1847) was actively championing new music. Mendelssohn, a friend of Schumann, agreed, and the work (not then known as the Symphony no. 9, as some of its predecessors were missing) received its belated premiere March 21, 1839. Three subsequent performances were offered in Leipzig that fall and the following spring, by which time the work had found publication with the respected firm of Breitkopf und Härtel. As to continued allegations that the hour-long symphony was too much to be endured, Schumann had no patience. It is, he declared, a symphony of "heavenly length," and, after all, the longer heaven lasts, the better.

- Berlioz: *Symphonie fantastique, op. 14*

In the fall of 1827, French composer Hector Berlioz (1803-1869), age twenty-four and son of a doctor who tried determinedly but unsuccessfully to divert the young man into medical studies, encountered the two loves of his life when an English theatre company came to Paris to present a full season of Shakespeare in English. Berlioz understood almost none of the language, for his liberal arts education had exposed him only to Latin and Greek. Yet he attended the opening night of *Hamlet,* mostly for the novelty of the experience. In his memoirs, he would recall the experience: "Shakespeare, coming upon me unaware, struck me like a thunderbolt."

In addition to his new fascination for the Bard, he also fell for the young lady inhabiting the role of Ophelia. She was Harriet

Smithson, a minor player with the company, who on this evening was making her debut in a major role. Berlioz became obsessed. He haunted the stage door and inundated her with love letters, most in French that she could not read, some in fractured English that made all too clear his intentions. Lacking the power of a restraining order, Harriet did the only thing she could do: she ignored him. Undismayed, Berlioz continued the assault on his dream girl for three years, but by 1830, even he had to admit that the romance existed only in his imagination. Lacking any other outlet for his passions, he instead poured his tortured soul into composition, spinning an elaborate symphonic fantasy of a disconsolate lover driven to the brink of suicide by his lady's indifference. This work would become the *Symphonie fantastique*.

The musical milestone that arose from this thwarted relationship is a grand, five-movement symphony portraying Berlioz's concept of an epic romance, as distilled through an overdose of opium that the composer imagines his love-sick protagonist has consumed. The first movement, titled "Dreams, Passions" is intended to depict the delights and despairs of love. In the second, the scene shifts to a waltz ball where the lover again encounters the woman he can never possess. He attempts to escape his passions by traveling to the countryside, but, as portrayed in the third movement, her image follows him, evoked by a shepherd's pipe. The composition then takes a highly dramatic turn as the young lover imagines that he has murdered his beloved and is about to be executed for the crime. The fourth movement shows him dreaming of the scaffold where he faces the guillotine; in the fifth, he is in hell at a witches' sabbath over which the beloved herself presides. Throughout the entire work, a single musical theme persists, representing in its varying moods the ever-changing image of his lady love. It is essentially Harriet's tune, and it unites the massive program symphony.

Nowhere in *Symphonie fantastique* are the lover and the beloved united, yet, against all odds, Berlioz ultimately achieved that denouement. Three years after the December 5, 1830, premiere, when the composer was planning another performance of the massive work together with its new sequel titled *Lelio, or Return to Life*, he arranged for an English newspaper correspondent to attend the concert with Harriet as his guest. The unsuspecting actress was not warned about what music was on the program, nor was she aware that Berlioz himself would be there. But she took the shock reasonably well, and was observed to be closely reading the composer's descriptive program notes and paying keen attention to the music. Soon afterward, she consented at last to meet him, and on October 3, 1833, Hector Berlioz and Harriet Smithson were married, with composer/pianist Franz Liszt and poet Heinrich Heine as witnesses.

It seems, however, that the lady's initial resistance might have been well-considered. The marriage was neither happy nor long, though thanks to the initial fascination, this most remarkable work had come into being. Not only had it won Berlioz the girl, it also ensured his reputation, both inside France and outside it, as one of the most original figures of the Romantic, someone whose favorite topics for his compositions were literature and himself.

- Mendelssohn: Symphony no. 4 in A major, op. 90 "Italian"

Felix Mendelssohn (1809-1847) chose his parents well. Wealthy patrons of the arts in Berlin, they supported numerous activities throughout the city, and brought much of that culture home to their family, giving dinners for musicians, composers, and philosophers, and hosting regular Sunday morning concerts in their private recital hall. Their efforts brought young Felix into close contact with Rossini and Goethe, among others, but his intensive training did not stop with social exposure. The Mendelssohns also hired the best teachers for their talented son. He studied piano, violin, and composition, and his parents ensured that the pieces he produced would be performed in public. Stimulated by such attentions and surrounded by the culture of a continent, young Mendelssohn quickly polished his talents. At an age when most musicians today are still in school, he was conquering the concert stage.

In 1830 and '31, young Mendelssohn, barely into his twenties, toured Italy. He had come south to enjoy the climate and the art, both of which he apparently found to be satisfactory. The region's music, though, was a different story. In letters to friends and relatives, Mendelssohn gave his view of the situation. "I have not heard a single note worth remembering," he wrote. "In Naples, the music is most inferior." Later, he described the orchestras in Rome as "unbelievably bad." Despite these negative reactions, or perhaps in hopes of erasing them, Mendelssohn began his *Italian Symphony* while still on tour. The piece was completed in the fall of 1832, on a commission from the London Philharmonic Society, and the composer himself conducted the premiere in London. The symphony was a tremendous success, and Mendelssohn himself called it "the jolliest piece I have so far written . . . and the most mature thing I have ever done." It has remained as one of his most endearing and enduring compositions.

Despite the audible delights of the piece, the *Italian Symphony* did not have an easy birth. Even its creator admitted that it had cost him, in his words, "some of the bitterest moments I have ever endured." Most of those trying times seem to have been spent with an editor's pen in hand, for though the piece was well received, Mendelssohn remained unsatisfied. In 1834, over a year after the work's public premiere, the composer began extensive revisions on the second, third, and fourth movements. The following year, he reworked the first movement, and was sufficiently satisfied with the results to allow another London performance in 1838. Yet Mendelssohn still withheld it from publication, and refused to permit its performance in Germany. He continued tinkering until his death in 1847. Another four years would pass before his colleague Ignaz Moscheles, who had conducted the 1838 London performance, edited a so-called "official" edition that finally appeared in print.

Musicologists have offered many interpretations of this symphony, none of which bear the composer's stamp of approval. However, despite Mendelssohn's reticence on the subject, the symphony's changing moods do suggest possibilities. The extroverted opening movement, suffused with radiant conviviality, calls to mind a lively urban scene, perhaps of Venice. The reverent second movement is almost certainly Rome during Holy Week, for Mendelssohn's letters reveal that he was impressed by the religious processions he witnessed. The third movement, a graceful minuet distantly reminiscent of Mozart, might be an elegant Florentine Renaissance palace, but the fourth movement needs no speculation. It is, without a doubt, a rural scene in southern Italy, for it blends two frantic folk dance styles: the saltarello and the tarantella. The dances, different in rhythmic structure, are alike in general character. Both are wild and swirling, abundantly energetic, almost frenetic, and utterly, irrepressibly Italian. In this uninhibited finale, Mendelssohn, so deeply displeased with Italian concert music, showed his lasting delight in the nation's folk music. He also proved to Italians that their native music could be used to great effect in an orchestral composition, even though it might take a German to prove the point.

- R. Schumann: Symphony no. 1 in B-flat major, op. 38, *"Spring"*

Few artistic partnerships are more endearing than that of Robert and Clara Schumann. The beginning, at least, of their relationship, might have been imagined by a novelist, and indeed, once inspired a film starring Katharine Hepburn in the role of Clara. Robert (1810-1856) was an up-and-coming composer and influential music journalist, publisher of the *New Journal for Music*, which would first bring international attention to Schubert, Chopin, and Brahms. Clara (1819-1896) was a greatly renowned pianist who, even in childhood as Clara Wieck, was famed across the continent for her style and interpretations. Robert composed for Clara; Clara played for Robert. Out of this symbiotic relationship arose many of the greatest masterpieces of the piano and chamber repertoires. Although their later years were darkened by tragedy with his failing emotional health, the optimism of their early marriage is preserved in Robert's effervescent compositions.

After years of opposition from her father, this musical couple married September 12, 1840, one day before Clara's twenty-first birthday. The inspiration provided by having this gifted musician in his daily presence sent Schumann into a torrent of productivity, leading to the composition of dozen of songs and piano pieces, a one-movement piano fantasy (that would ultimately mature into a full concerto), and two symphonies, the first of which courses with the joy of a blissful bridegroom. The work, he once observed, was "born in one fiery hour," and indeed, from start to finish, the piece required only two months of the composer's effort. By March 31, 1841, it was ready for its premiere with the Leipzig Gewandhaus Orchestra with its conductor, Schumann's friend, Felix Mendelssohn. The piece was published later that same year.

Despite the winter months in which it was composed, this buoyant symphony carries the subtitle "Spring," and was inspired by an Adolf Boettger poem, the last line of which reads, "In the valley, spring is bursting out all over!" For Schumann, it seems, spring bursts with a glorious brass fanfare that broadens into a majestic orchestral theme rather reminiscent of Beethoven at his grandest. As the work progresses through its standard four movements, there are gentle chorales, sprightly dances, and exuberantly flowing melodies that easily communicate the "vivace" mood that the composer often specifies. Though the composer's disgruntled father-in-law, Friedrich Wieck, dismissed the work as the "Symphony of Contradictions," a less biased listener can only conclude that here is a work suffused with grace and good cheer. For Schumann, here in the springtime of his career, the season conveys a mood of optimism rarely surpassed in his compositions.

- Bruckner: Symphony no. 4 in E- flat major

To be a composer, it would seem that one would need extraordinary self-confidence, absolute faith in the worth of what one has created and total belief that it will also be of value to others. Without that assurance, it is difficult to imagine that anyone would dare to complete a symphony and have it performed in public. After all, if the composer doubts the quality of his own work, how could he possibly bear to face hostile critics or perplexed audiences? History has shown that most of the greatest composers have been noted for their belief in themselves. Mozart, Beethoven, Verdi, and Wagner all come to mind as examples of men who refused to alter their compositions because, despite criticism, they were sure of their work's perfection. Other composers were less fortunate. Throughout his career, Brahms destroyed works which he felt were unworthy, and Tchaikovsky filled his diaries with entries doubting the value of even his most successful pieces. Yet even those men, when compared to Anton Bruckner, would be the very picture of self-confidence, for Bruckner, as long as he lived, never learned to believe in himself.

Anton Bruckner (1824-1896) was born near Linz, Austria. Although his father was a school-master and organist, the family had only recently risen from the peasantry, and those humble beginnings may have played a part in Bruckner's lack of confidence. He always felt awkward and provincial when surrounded by Viennese sophistication, and even Linz, a good-sized city, but hardly a cultural center, seemed somewhat intimidating. Left to his own slender initiative, Bruckner would have remained organist and teacher at the neighborhood monastery where he had attended services as a child. His friends, however, pushed him toward broader horizons, forcing him to apply for more ambitious positions, first in Linz, and later in Vienna. He may not have believed in himself, but they were convinced that Bruckner had contributions to make to the musical world.

As a devoutly Catholic village boy, Bruckner devoted his early compositional attention to choral and organ music. He was past forty when he completed his Symphony no. 1; one earlier piece he himself labeled the Symphony no. 0, and it would not premiere until long after his death. His first successful symphony was number four, which gained the nickname "Romantic" when the composer's friends suggested that anything attached to Romanticism would have a pre-made audience. He completed the symphony's first version in 1874, but almost immediately began revisions, as the less-than-successful premiere of his Symphony no. 2 in 1873 had led him to think of new structural approaches. The subsequent premiere of his Symphony no. 3 led to further revisions of poor no. 4. Not until 1881 would Bruckner declare himself to be pleased with the work and allow its premiere in Vienna February 20. For the amusement of his friends who liked music with plot content, the composer sketched out a program for the work concerning chivalric adventures with knights and damsels, but the story was solely an after-thought and cannot be said to have been a driving force behind the music. It is Bruckner at his best, with forthright, dramatic brass themes driving the piece forward amidst almost folk-like string melodies. His tempo instructions repeatedly specify a need for motion without excessive urgency. He seems to wish for the symphony to have energy but not frenzy.

- Brahms: Symphony no. 1 in c minor, op. 68

One can only pity the English playwrights who lived in the years shortly after Shakespeare. Born in the shadow of the ultimate achiever in their field, they must have despaired at the inevitable comparisons, for beside Shakespeare, their greatest creations, which might have been admired in any other age, would appear woefully inadequate. Their careers might even seem unworthy of pursuit. Exactly what those unfortunate playwrights had to say on the subject is uncertain, but we do have the testimony of another man who faced a similar situation. Johannes Brahms (1833-1897) dreamed of writing symphonies, even though a generation earlier, Beethoven had proven himself to be master of that genre. "You don't know," Brahms once observed, "what it means to the likes of us when we hear his footsteps behind us." What it meant to Brahms was years of hesitation and preparation before he dared to publicly present a post-Beethoven symphony.

Initially a pianist, the Hamburg-born Brahms became interested in composition and began his first symphony in the early 1860s. His long-time friend Clara Wieck Schumann (she and her husband Robert had been early fans and promoters of the young German's work) recalled seeing some sketches of it and a nearly-completed first movement, yet it wasn't until September of 1876 that Brahms finished the piece. It premiered November 4 of that year in Karlsruhe. Many observers were surprised that the first symphony of such an important composer was not premiered in Vienna where Brahms now lived, but the composer had good reasons for his choice. Leery of Vienna's notoriously stern music critics and its equally opinionated audiences, who worshipped Beethoven, he felt that the work would have a better chance outside of Vienna. This same logic leads Broadway producers to open new productions somewhere other than Broadway itself; if there are bugs to be worked out, don't do it in front of a big city audience or big city critics.

The Karlsruhe premiere went rather well, with the only discouraging words coming from Brahms himself, who described the new symphony as "long and not especially amiable." Brahms then arranged for a Vienna performance, and it was on this occasion, in Beethoven's backyard, that the Beethoven parallels at last emerged. Critic Eduard Hanslick compared the styles of the two masters, suggesting that Brahms had relied rather heavily on the serious side of Beethoven at the expense of what he called "heart-warming sunshine." Furthermore, he insisted that the regal string melody of the fourth movement was strikingly similar to the *Ode to Joy* in Beethoven's Symphony no. 9. Conductor/pianist Hans von Bülow, a student of Liszt, agreed with Hanslick's assessment, and memorably tagged the piece "Beethoven's Tenth".

Such comparative remarks could not have pleased Brahms, who had fought to be considered on his own merits, but if he read further in the reviews, he would have found high praise for the piece. Hanslick, for all his reservations, lauded it as "one of the most individual and magnificent works of the symphonic literature." He closed his review with these enthusiastic words: "The new symphony of Brahms is something of which the nation may be proud, an inexhaustible fountain of deep pleasure and fruitful study." Over a century later, that assessment still holds.

- Saint- Saëns: Symphony no. 3 in c minor, op. 78, *"Organ"*

Camille Saint-Saëns (1835-1921) was one of history's greatest musical prodigies. Born in Paris to a government clerk and a carpenter's daughter, the future composer had perfect pitch, that is, any pitch played to him, he could name flawlessly just from hearing it. Indeed, the boy was known to stand at the elbow of the local piano tuner, correcting that gentleman whenever necessary, a stunt which can't have gone down well with the poor piano tuner. Young Saint-Saëns wrote his first composition at the age of three, and began formal study of composition and organ performance at the age of seven. At his formal debut, a concert given when he was ten, young Saint-Saëns performed concertos by Mozart and Beethoven, then as an encore, offered to play any of Beethoven's thirty-two piano sonatas from memory. That he could even play them — let alone have them memorized — would have been an achievement worthy of adults.

Many child prodigies fail to find ultimate success, reaching an early limit to their talents. Yet Saint-Saëns' potential could not have been more fully realized. As an adult, he composed over three-hundred works, producing music, to use his own words, "as naturally as a tree produces apples," working so effortlessly that he could even orchestrate a new piece while conversing with friends. Yet music was not his only interest. Saint-Saëns was also devoted to archaeology, astronomy, literature, and philosophy. Occasionally, this latter-day Renaissance man would even drop in at local universities, take over a classroom, and start lecturing on diverse subjects. His rich and varied life spanned over eighty years, from the height of Mendelssohn to the early days of Stravinsky, yet it is the earlier styles that one hears in his bright and spirited works.

Over the years, Saint-Saëns began eight symphonies, although only five were completed and only three were published with numbers. Thus, the last of his large-scale symphonic works carries the number three. The piece was written in 1886 on a commission from the Royal Philharmonic Society of London, which had been impressed by the composer's opera *Henry VIII*. For the new work, Saint-Saëns was awarded the paltry sum of thirty pounds; his reputation alone would have dictated far more generosity, but the composer apparently felt that the prestige of a London premiere was sufficient reward. Saint-Saëns himself led the first performance May 19, 1886, in a St. James Hall concert that also featured the composer as soloist in his Fourth Piano Concerto. Such multi-faceted talents led composer Charles Gounod (1818-1893), who was in attendance, to remark, "There goes the French Beethoven."

Although the work's early movements have their charms — Saint-Saëns was always a fine melodist — it is to the last movement that the symphony owes its reputation, for here, after a dramatic pause, we hear at last the instrument from which the work takes its name: the organ entering with all the glory of a gothic cathedral. The composer, formerly organist at the Church of the Madeleine in Paris, was well familiar with the instrument's ability to astonish, and here he draws upon that ability to magnificent effect. The beloved theme that follows, first heard gently in the strings as the piano flutters in the background, develops soon into a majestic march complete with organ, brass, and percussion, reminiscent in its striding energy of the finale of Brahms' Symphony no. 1. This is music for a victory parade, music conceived by a man who had scored many victories of his own in the course of a triumphant career.

Those who know the film *Babe* will recall the grand final theme of this symphony as that of a lullaby that the farmer sings to Babe the pig. That Saint-Saëns did not intend it for such usage is beside the point; he lived long enough to know of the existence of film and to understand that music could be a powerful part of that experience. In fact, Saint-Saëns was the first important composer to write for film, as we'll discover in Chapter Nine.

- Tchaikovsky: Symphony no. 4 in f minor, op. 36

Nearly every major composer has endured a watershed year in which personal crises affected the future development of his music. For Ludwig van Beethoven (1770-1827), that year was 1802, when encroaching deafness drove him to the verge of suicide. For Richard Wagner (1813-1883), it was 1848 when the Dresden Revolution forced him to rethink his political convictions. For Peter Tchaikovsky (1840-1893), the year of turmoil was 1877. Though his greatest masterworks still lay in the future, the composer had already proven his mettle with three symphonies, several operas, and the ballet *Swan Lake*. He was also benefiting from the recent acquisition of a patron, Nadezhda von Meck, whose financial support had allowed him to concentrate more fully upon composition.

Those were positive influences upon Tchaikovsky's life; the crisis lay in a sudden and very ill-considered marriage. A former student of the composer's had become deeply infatuated with him, and swore that, if he did not marry her, she would take her life. Concerned for the young lady's well-being and believing that having a wife in his possession would be useful social camouflage (as Tchaikovsky's diaries reveal, he was homosexual), he agreed to the marriage, even though taking a woman into his home was the last thing his own inclinations would have led him to do. They married in the summer. His nervous breakdown came in the fall, at which point his doctors recommended that he never see the young woman again. Soon, the composer and his brother Anatoly had left Russia for

Switzerland in hope of finding solace for poor Peter's battered spirit.

As so often happened, Tchaikovsky sought consolation in composition, plunging back into his sketches for the opera *Eugene Onegin*, and beginning orchestration of his new symphony, the fourth of what would ultimately be six numbered works in the genre. By late in the year, he was able to give an optimistic report to Madame von Meck, writing, "Never yet has any of my orchestral works cost me so much labor, but I've never yet felt such love for any of my things . . . Perhaps I'm mistaken, but it seems to me that this Symphony is better than anything I've done so far." Such enthusiasm was rather unusual for the composer, who more often expressed a loathing for his works, but here, it seems, he knew that he had exceeded even his own demanding standards. He completed the new symphony on Christmas Day, by the Russian calendar, in 1877 (January 7, 1878 by the Western calendar). The piece bore a dedication "to my best friend," a reference to Madame von Meck, who agreed to accept the honor only on the grounds of anonymity.

The Symphony no. 4 premiered in Moscow that same winter, with the composer's mentor Nikolay Rubinstein conducting. A few months later, a colleague of Tchaikovsky's criticized the piece for being programmatic, that is, for having a plot. Tchaikovsky defended his creation, declaring, "I don't see why you consider this a defect. On the contrary, I should be sorry if symphonies that mean nothing should flow from my pen, consisting solely of a progression of harmonies, rhythms and modulations . . . As a matter of fact, the work is patterned after Beethoven's Fifth Symphony, not as to musical content but as to the basic idea."

Tchaikovsky's statement referring to Beethoven begs a question as to what this "basic idea" might be. After all, the answer to that question would not only help us to interpret the Russian master's creation; it would also shed light on what Tchaikovsky saw as the central concept of the Beethoven piece. Fortunately, Tchaikovsky provides us with an answer in a letter to Madame von Meck in which he outlined what he viewed as the program for his Symphony no. 4. According to the composer himself, the ominous opening theme for horns and bassoons represents fate hanging over one's head like a sword. This all-consuming gloom devours the few, brief glimpses of happiness, appearing mostly in the form of waltz themes. The second movement, Tchaikovsky asserted, expresses the melancholy felt at the end of a weary day. Then, in the third movement, he imagined what he called "fleeting images that pass through the imagination when one has begun to drink a little wine." The fourth movement holds Tchaikovsky's prescription for happiness. Here's how he described it: "If you cannot find reasons for happiness in yourself, look at others. Get out among the people . . . Oh, how gay they are! . . . Life is bearable after all." So, to summarize Tchaikovsky's view, this is a symphony that brings listeners from gloom to melancholy to slow recovery to life-affirming energy. It is a progression from darkness to light, a progression that one can sense in Tchaikovsky's Fourth as well as in Beethoven's Fifth.

- Dvořák: Symphony no. 9 in e minor, op. 95, "From the New World"

Few composers have worked harder for their fame than Antonín Dvořák (1841-1904). The Bohemian (Czech) composer was the son of a country butcher and innkeeper, himself an amateur musician who taught his son to love music, but perhaps did not mention what a tough living it would be. As a young man, Dvořák eked out a meager existence in Prague playing coffee-house music and acting as section violist in the Prague orchestra, which was led for much of Dvořák's tenure by the Czech nationalist composer Bedrich Smetana (1824-1884), creator of Bohemia's pseudo-anthem, *The Moldau* (see Chapter Three). It was steady work, but less than profitable. In fact, Dvořák's marriage to Anna Cermakova was delayed because the prospective bride's father insisted, not without reason, that the young man could not support her. Perhaps most tellingly, for three out of four years in the 1870s, Dvořák won an Austrian State scholarship award. This would seem to be good news, except that to be eligible for the award, he had to meet two criteria: be both talented and poor. The talent was unquestionable; unfortunately, so was the poverty. All was not lost, however, for that state competition brought Dvořák to the attention of Brahms, who then brought the young composer to the attention of the world. Before long, all music lovers knew Dvořák's name.

In 1891, a noted American patron of the arts, Jeannette Thurber, was seeking a director for the school she had founded, the National Conservatory of Music in New York City. Many American teachers or composers would have begged for such a position, particularly given the $15,000 annual salary, but Mrs. Thurber was determined to find a person of global reputation, someone whose own prestige would boost that of the conservatory. Since such persons were not to be found in the United States, where classical music was still in its adolescence, Mrs. Thurber focused her search upon Europe, ultimately choosing a Bohemian composer and music professor whose Prague Conservatory salary was only one-twenty-fifth of what Mrs. Thurber was offering. The offer was too good to resist. Thus, Antonín Dvořák was on his way to America.

Dvořák was an unlikely candidate to lead a New York musical conservatory. Certainly, he was a marvelously skilled composer of international renown, a conservative late Romantic who specialized in lush symphonic works and chamber music rather like that of his mentor Brahms. He had much to share with aspiring composers, and, according to his colleagues in Prague, a definite flair for teaching. Yet he was far less suited to America itself. A self-confessed country boy, Dvořák disliked cities and abhorred being absent from his homeland. His new address of 327 East 17th Street in New York City seemed a poor substitute for the rolling hills of Bohemia. Thus, though his American years were professionally successful, Dvořák was personally dissatisfied and terminated his contract after three years, returning with relief to Prague.

Although Dvořák's American sojourn had been brief, it was also productive as the unhappy composer consoled himself with composition, producing choral works, chamber pieces, and one remarkable symphony, his Ninth, subtitled "From the New World." The work premiered with the New York Philharmonic in Carnegie Hall December 16, 1893, sharing the program with Brahms' Violin Concerto (see Chapter Four) and Mendelssohn's music for *A Midsummer Night's Dream* (see Chapter Nine). Having attended the last rehearsal before that premiere, a reporter for the New York Herald observed that the new symphony was "a noble composition . . . . of heroic proportions," and compared the work favorably to the efforts of Beethoven, Schubert, Schumann, Mendelssohn, and Brahms. The review, illustrated with drawings of the composer and of the orchestra and conductor Anton Seidl in action, continues for several thousand more words of highly insightful musical description, which clearly presupposes a readership familiar with musical vocabulary

Legend has it that the symphony's melodies were inspired by Native American legends, or perhaps by spirituals of the Old South. Supposedly, the gently lyrical second movement was an orchestral setting of the slave song "Goin' Home." However, the song remembered as "Goin' Home" has no tie to plantations. It is Dvořák's own melody, written specifically for this piece; the words its now evokes were set to it later by one of Dvořák's students, Harry Burleigh. As for other folk tunes supposedly echoed in the new symphony, the composer denied it, writing to one quizzical European conductor. "I tried to write only in the spirit of those national American melodies." Thus, this most American of symphonies was wholly written by a European.

- Mahler: Symphony no. 5

Austrian born Gustav Mahler (1860-1911) wrote his Symphony no. 1 in 1888, his second in 1894. His remaining eight symphonic works appeared every few years thereafter until his death in 1911, in the midst of completing one more symphony. Producing ten-and-a-half symphonies in twenty-four years might not seem impressive at first; after all, Mozart wrote about fifty symphonies in a similar time period, and Haydn wrote nine in 1766 alone. However, their symphonies lack the all-embracing ambitions of Mahler's compositions. Their symphonies are conventionally structured. Their symphonies don't include choruses and religious/dramatic scenes. Their symphonies are perhaps twenty to thirty minutes long, about one-third the length of Mahler's shortest symphonies. Their works *were* ambitious for their day; Mahler's were ambitious for *his* day, and his was a day in which many composers, Mahler firmly amongst them, strove for the stars.

At the dawn of the twentieth century, the composer was thoroughly enmeshed in his duties as conductor of the Vienna Opera. A demanding rehearsal and performance schedule, combined with frequent quarrels with musicians and singers, as well as contentious debates over programming choices and stylistic decisions, absorbed all of Mahler's attentions for three-quarters of the year. Only during summer vacations could he relax into composition. His wife Alma (nearly twenty years his junior) remembered blissful summers at Maiernigg an der Wörthersee, where the couple would retreat with their young daughters, and Mahler would fill his days with swimming, rowing, hiking, sunbathing, swimming, and composing. In this setting, Alma claimed, her husband was like "a tree in full leaf and flower" and at the height of his powers.

Of his Symphony no. 5, dating from 1901, Mahler once observed, "There is nothing romantic or mystical about it; it is simply an expression of incredible energy. It is a human being in the full light of day, in the prime of his life." One might imagine that the composer, who was only forty-one at the time, might have intended this powerful and virile work as a reflection of himself, but in fact, he was enduring difficult times, struggling through serious health problems (a newly diagnosed heart condition) and artistic quarrels with his orchestra, the Vienna Philharmonic. Soon, he would be forced to resign his conducting post with the ensemble, though he would continue to be associated with the Vienna Court Opera. So it was in Cologne, Germany, not Vienna, that Mahler would premiere this new symphony October 18, 1904.

By this time, the symphony had lain complete for three years, but only in the days leading up to the premiere did the composer begin to sense clouds on the horizon. After the first rehearsal, he wrote to Alma, "The public, oh heavens, what are they to make of this chaos, of which new worlds are forever being engendered, only to crumble in ruin the moment after? What are they to say to this primeval music, this foaming, roaring, raging sea of sound?" Indeed, the premiere did not go particularly well, and Mahler soon set about revising the symphony. He would conduct it nine more times in the seven years that remained to him, and each time he would revise the work anew. The last revision was in 1911, in the final months of his life, before his heart condition (medical evidence suggests subacute bacterial endocarditis, which even now, a century later, cardiologists admit is a hard one to beat) brought his days to an end.

As was Mahler's usual practice, the symphony uses a grand orchestra, with healthy doses of brass and percussion supplementing the strings and woodwinds. The variety and number of instruments gave him many tonal colors on which to draw, allowing him to craft a marvelously varied tapestry of sound. Much of the score is bold and dramatic, beginning with the trumpet solo of military mood in the opening moments. Energy and determination, if not always optimism, are the dominant images, and the music might suit a story in which the brave, young hero sets out against a formidable foe. The famed fourth movement Adagietto is a gentle break from the action, with a lyrical, love-scene like attitude. By the symphony's end, one feels sure the young hero has triumphed, for the final movement opens cheerfully, and then builds to a spirit of victory. Mahler has crafted an epic journey that, after many trials, culminates in a happy ending.

- R. Strauss: *An Alpine Symphony*, op. 64

Son of the principal French horn player at the Munich Court Orchestra, Richard Strauss (1864-1949) was exposed to music from his earliest years. He began studying piano at the age of four, started composing at six, and soon was permitted to sit in on his father's rehearsals and performances, provided that music of the dreaded radical, Richard Wagner, was not on the program. By the time he was in his teens, young Strauss was developing the skills and perceptions necessary for a career in music. His letters to family and friends reveal tastes strongly shaped by his ultra-conservative father. Mozart and Beethoven, Schubert and Mendelssohn: all were held up for admiration, and when it came to German opera, it was Weber's *Der Freischütz* that was praised. Wagner's *Ring Cycle* simply did not exist. Both are profiled in Chapter Eight.

As he matured, Strauss would rebel against his father's preferences, developing a marked appreciation for Wagner and conducting that master's operas frequently throughout a long career on the conductor's podium. Yet though he himself began to move in the direction of modernism, Strauss never lost his fondness for at least one of his father's favorites. Throughout his long life, Strauss would always adore the works of the man he called "the immortal Mozart." He would eventually become one of the founders of the Salzburg Festival, launched with the particular purpose of bringing greater glory to Mozart's birthplace. Most of a century later, that festival is still prominent.

Strauss' *An Alpine Symphony* takes his listeners on a musical mountain climb. The composer himself was no mountaineer, but during the time at which the piece was composed, Strauss' primary home was in the Bavarian town of Garmisch, at the foot of Germany's highest peak, the Zugspitze. Perhaps he observed ambitious climbers beginning their assaults or overheard their conversations in the streets. Conversely, he may have recalled a schoolboy adventure when, at age fourteen, he and a group of friends set out at 2am to climb a mountain, reaching the summit five hours later, only to be repelled from the peak by thunder and lightning. After his safe return, Strauss recounted the day in a letter, noting that, once the boys were again within reach of a piano, he had seated himself at the keyboard to improvise a musical version of their experience. Perhaps, with this composition, Strauss was seeking to recapture a youthful memory. If so, he achieved his goal in grand fashion, calling upon an enormous ensemble of 123 players, with a percussion section that includes implements for wind and thunder effects. "I have finally learned to orchestrate!" he declared once the piece was in rehearsal. It premiered October 28, 1915 in Berlin.

An Alpine Symphony is written in one uninterrupted flow of music not quite an hour in length, portraying twenty-two distinct episodes, each of which was described in the score. It begins in the hours before sunrise, painted in dark and somber tones. After the brassy emergence of the sun, the climbers set forth to a rhythmic, rising theme. Horns and clarinets, perhaps representing hunters and birds, carry them into the forest, where they pass by a brook and a waterfall. The mists of that cascade lead one of the climbers to imagine that he has seen an Alpine fairy. Leaving the forest, the climbers ascend to a sunny alpine meadow filled with flowers, then to a mountain pasture, where shepherds call to one another. The clangor of cowbells is heard. The adventure next takes an ominous turn, as the climbers become lost in a thicket, then must traverse a glacier and a perilous precipice before finally reaching the summit. Here, a grand trombone fanfare followed by rich orchestral passages reveal to the listener the glorious panorama, brought to a close by darkness and turmoil. Clouds cover the sun, as a tremendous thunderstorm breaks over the climber's heads. Now the adventurers are in full flight, their descent represented by the inverted (moving up where it formerly moved down and vice versa) repetition of the "climbing" theme heard earlier. Each of the previous sights — the glacier, the pasture, and the waterfall — passes by in reverse order, as the climbers hasten down the slopes. By the time the base is reached, it is sunset. The storm has passed, night has come, and they are enfolded in the darkness. Musically and dramatically, Strauss has brought his listeners full circle.

Strauss called it a "symphony," though earlier generations might have debated the point. Since it is one protracted sweep of music rather than being organized into defined separate movements of distinctly different tempos and forms, it doesn't act like a symphony as Mozart or even Beethoven or Brahms would have defined it. However, by Strauss's time, musical concepts were taking on freer forms, often (as in this specific case) driven more by plot content than by any pre-existing rule book. It isn't exactly what Mozart would have called a symphony, but it is certainly a grand work for symphony orchestra, and if Strauss, who conducted many of the finest orchestras of the day, wished to call it a symphony, one ought not question him.

The sections: Night — Sunrise — The Ascent — Entering the Forest — Wandering by the Brook — Waterfall — Apparition — In Flowery Meadows — In a Mountain Pasture — Through Thicket and Undergrowth on the Wrong Path — On the Glacier — Dangerous Moments — On the Summit — Vision — Mists Rise Up — The Sun Grows Dark — Elegy — Calm Before the Storm — Thunderstorm—Descent—Sunset—Night

- Nielsen: Symphony no. 4, op. 29, "The Inextinguishable"

The career of Carl Nielsen (1865-1931) is a rags-to-riches to story. He was seventh of twelve children of a village housepainter on the Danish island of Funen. The family lived a Spartan life, with all those bodies sharing a two-room cottage. Yet within those cramped quarters was a door to broader horizons, for Father Nielsen supplemented his income by playing violin in local bands. Thus, there was always music in the house, and young Carl showed an early interest in the field, progressing from tapping out rhythms on the domestic firewood to learning violin and cornet from his father.

At age fourteen, he became a military bugler. Soon thereafter, he took up piano, tackling the intricacies of Bach's *Well-Tempered Clavier* (see Chapter Six), before earning a scholarship to the Copenhagen Conservatory at age eighteen. Only after graduating from the Conservatory in 1886 did he step away from keyboard lessons to give serious attention to composition, pursuing advanced studies in Germany where he developed affection for both the blood-stirring grandeur of Wagner and the well-ordered structures of Brahms. Both inspirations can be heard in his own orchestral scores.

By 1901, Nielsen was well enough regarded in his homeland to earn a state pension for the rest of his life, enabling him to devote most of the next thirty years to composition, producing five more symphonies (for a total of six), three concertos (violin, flute, and clarinet), dozens of songs, much stage music, and various other works. Of all these pieces from the last half of his career, the most famed is his Symphony no. 4, begun in 1914. Having recently stepped down from the post of opera conductor at Copenhagen's Royal Theater, Nielsen found himself with sufficient time for a major project, which became this symphony, finished only two weeks before he conducted its premiere February 1, 1916. Well received both by audience members and by critics, the new work earned Nielsen a reputation as the greatest of Scandinavia's living composers.

Although the fine music of the Symphony no. 4 would be enough to attract favorable attention, its fame is further boosted by the imaginative subtitle that the composer granted it: "The Inextinguishable." In a letter to a friend, Nielsen himself described the intention as follows: "It is meant to express the appearance of the most elementary forces among men, animals, and even plants . . . man's aspiration and yearning would be felt. These forces, which are inextinguishable, I have tried to represent." It is a lofty goal, but one to which the composer would prove equal, producing a score marvelously varied in melodic content and musical structure alike. It does not wear out its welcome, but rather draws the listener's attention further with its vivid evocation of the changeable life spirit that inspired Nielsen.

- Sibelius: Symphony no. 5 in E- flat major, op. 82

Brace yourself for the truth: Jean Sibelius (1865-1957), the great musical patriot of Finland, grew up in a Swedish-speaking family. Until he was eight years old, he spoke scarcely a word of Finnish, had no schooling in the language until he was eleven, and did not become fluent until early adulthood. His situation was not unique. When Sibelius was growing up, Finland was dominated linguistically, politically, and culturally by its western neighbor Sweden. In later decades, the reins would be handed from west to east, and Russia would take the position of control. For nearly all of Sibelius' ninety-one years, Finland could only dream of freedom. Yet lack of independence is not the same as lack of pride. Whatever the language of their government, the Finns always remembered their heritage. For Sibelius, this recollection served as inspiration for many evocative and nationalistic works. Even his pure symphonies, having no specific patriotic content, bear the richness and breadth of the Finnish landscape.

One of the most popular of all his grand orchestral compositions, Sibelius' Symphony no. 5 dates from the middle of his long life. The work premiered under the composer's baton on a concert December 8, 1915, given on the occasion of his fiftieth birthday, which was being treated as a national holiday in Finland. He had just returned from a successful American concert tour, but otherwise the years of the First World War were quiet for him, in part because his usual publishing house, Breitkopf und Härtel, was out of reach in Germany. Perhaps in part due to having time on his hands, Sibelius set about revising the new symphony, and in the years that followed would present three more versions of the piece in concert.

The last premiere, November 24, 1919, took place during a tumultuous period in Finnish history in which the region's attempt to break free of the new Communist regime in Russia came to a bitter end. Yet there is none of that bitterness in this music. From a serene and stately opening, the music builds to a majestic conclusion centered upon a proud three-note pattern that strides firmly toward its regal conclusion. The stern self-possession of this music seems to speak of the Finnish people's determination to persevere through these dark days. Although the Finns would not find their independence in this particular battle, Sibelius' music sings with hope for the future.

- Rachmaninoff: Symphony no. 2 in e minor, op. 27

Sergei Rachmaninoff (1873-1943) was born to what had been a wealthy family. Unfortunately, his spendthrift father squandered the family's wealth, forcing sale of estates and a move to St. Petersburg. The change of locale at least bore the advantage of bringing the musically inclined young boy to the most musical of Russia's great cities. Early piano lessons expanded into formal study of piano and composition at the St. Petersburg Conservatory, and later at the Moscow Conservatory, from which he graduated in 1892. He scored various early successes, both as a pianist and as a composer, but the 1897 premiere of his Symphony no. 1 was, in the composer's own words, "a fiasco," thanks to a conductor who was judged to be intoxicated. The traumatic experience gutted Rachmaninoff's confidence. Giving up composition entirely, he determined to support himself only as a pianist. Only in 1899, after treatment by hypnotist Dr. Nikolay Dahl, did he agree to try his hand again. The triumphant 1901 premiere of his Piano Concerto no. 2 renewed the young composer's faith in his abilities, and the Symphony no. 2 soon followed.

Rachmaninoff wrote most of his Symphony no. 2 in Dresden, Germany, where he had gone in 1906 with his wife and young daughter seeking respite from the political conflicts inherent in his conducting post at the Bolshoi Theatre. There at the Bolshoi, the composer had been entrenched in opera, not only conducting it, but also composing it. One might imagine that taking on a symphony would have been a refreshing change. In fact, his letters reveal that the composer found it tedious to compose music without dramatic content. Perhaps the evil experience with his Symphony no. 1 contributed to this reluctance. As it is, fifteen months were needed to bring the work to completion. Yet perhaps the delay served him well, for during the Dresden excursion, he had opportunity to hear a performance of Richard Strauss' opera *Salome*. The dark, sometimes violent story itself left him cold, but Strauss' use of the orchestra he found enthralling. Here, for perhaps the first time, Rachmaninoff sensed the full palette of possibilities in terms of orchestral tone color, a concept he would explore to impressive effect in this newest symphony.

The composer himself conducted the work's St. Petersburg premiere January 26, 1908; a Moscow premiere was given the following week. Of the piece, one entranced reviewer noted, "After listening with unflagging attention to its four movements, one notes with surprise that the hands of the watch have moved forward sixty-five minutes. This might be over-long for the general audience, but how fresh, how beautiful it is!" Both verdicts would win general acceptance: that it was beautiful, and that it was long. Later performances, particularly those in the US, were often abbreviated, much against the composer's will. "You don't know what cuts do to me," he lamented to conductor Eugene Ormandy. "It is like cutting a piece out of my heart." More recent conductors — and audiences as well — generally find greater patience for Rachmaninoff's lyric expansiveness. If the symphony is lengthy, that is simply because the composer had much to say, all of which is worth hearing. Like an epic novel or film, it is an adventure painted in broad strokes, one in which the listener is swept along on the tide of expression.

Much of the symphony is lush and spacious in mood, like a strong river in full flow. Although strings are frequently prominent, Rachmaninoff does not neglect woodwinds and brass, and even percussionists, ranging from timpani to cymbals to xylophone, have their impact. Throughout, the music has a determined sense of energy and motion that draws its listeners along on a journey of epic proportion, with moods that shift from melancholy to triumph. Particularly in the last two movements, melodies are of such lyrical and song-like beauty as to beg for words, and in days gone by, some performers obliged by adapting his themes into popular songs. Some melodic fragments recur in later movements, tying the whole symphony together and reminding the listeners of where they have been. Though the symphony's title suggests a dark minor key, that somberness is gradually dismissed; by the closing pages, the composer has moved on to a scene of powerful victory.

- Hanson: Symphony no. 2, "Romantic"

In general, this country's most influential composers have been from the East Coast, where the long existence of thriving musical organizations has facilitated their development. Relatively few Westerners have earned leading positions in American classical music, but there is one prominent example: Howard Hanson (1896-1981), born in Wahoo, Nebraska. In that prairie community not far from Omaha, he learned music first at the local Lutheran school and by his high school years was serving occasionally as conductor of the orchestra, when the regular teacher was otherwise occupied. From his frontier origins, Hanson went on to study at Northwestern University. After graduating at the age of eighteen, he accepted a post as theory professor at the College of the Pacific, of which he would serve as dean from the ages of twenty-one through twenty-four. In 1921, he won the prestigious Prix de Rome and spent several years in Italy working closely with the respected Italian composer Ottorino Respighi (1879-1936). Then in 1924, still not yet thirty, Hanson began a forty year term as director of the prestigious Eastman School of Music in Rochester, New York, where he is credited with developing one of the finest conservatories on the continent. In addition to his educational influence, Hanson was also a conductor known for advocating American music, and was a prolific composer in his own right, with seven symphonies, various short orchestral, chamber, and choral works, and the opera *Merry Mount*, which premiered in 1933 at the Metropolitan Opera to impressive acclaim.

That Hanson achieved an early international reputation is proven by the fact that, when the Boston Symphony decided to commemorate its fiftieth anniversary with a large number of newly commissioned works, those composers granted the honor included most of the international stars of the day, as well as Hanson himself, then still in his early thirties. The work he produced for the occasion, his Symphony no. 2, premiered November 28, 1930 with Serge Koussevitzky conducting. Of the broadly-flowing, three-movement score, the composer observed, "My aim in this symphony has been to create a work young in spirit, Romantic in temperament, and simple and direct in expression." He later added that he saw it as "a protest against the growing Schoenbergism of the time." Indeed, Schoenberg-style edgy dissonances and unstructured musical progress are nowhere to be found in Hanson's lyrically conservative score. Here, it becomes clear that he learned much from his time with Respighi, who after all had learned his own approach to orchestration directly from the Russian master Nicolai Rimsky-Korsakov (1844-1908). Hanson understood well how to produce orchestral colors that would be dramatic but still pleasant to the ear.

- Chávez: *Sinfonia India*

Born in Mexico City, Carlos Chávez (1899-1978) was raised by his widowed mother, a teacher who supported six children on her modest salary. It was from his elder brother that Chávez received his first music lessons. Nearly all his formal training would be as a pianist; as a composer, he was self-taught, largely through study of scores and through actual practice. In 1924, having spent a few years studying in Europe, he returned home to become music and arts writer for the Mexico City newspaper *El universal*, and in 1928 was appointed director of the National Conservatory and of the Orquesta Sinfónica de México (Mexico

Symphony Orchestra). He was then not yet thirty years old. Through these diverse employments, Chávez encouraged investigations into indigenous music and performances of works by Latin American composers, without neglecting masterpieces from the European and North American repertoires. As a conductor at home and abroad, and through his own rhythmically dynamic scores, Chávez proved that Mexico had arrived on the classical music scene.

Chávez cherished a lasting interest in Mexican Native American music, thanks to his maternal grandfather (himself a Native American) and family holidays spent in the region of Tlaxcala, where he was exposed to indigenous music of several cultural traditions, particularly those rooted in Aztec heritage. In pre-Columbian times, music served mostly ritualistic purposes for the Aztecs, with singers and players given the most rigorous training lest a flawed performance offend the deities. There is no evidence of written musical notation; rather, music was composed and communicated only in the oral tradition. Thus, there are no written commentaries upon Aztec music prior to the arrival of the Spaniards in the sixteenth century. Observers remarked upon the variety of drums, some played with mallets, others with bare hands. They further noted that, unlike European percussion instruments, the Aztec versions tended to be tuned to specific pitches, allowing for intricate melodic and tonal combinations, in addition to the rhythmic energy that one would more typically expect in percussive works.

The most frequently performed of his compositions, Chávez' *Sinfonia India* is chronologically second of his six symphonies, though he decided against giving it a specific number. Instead, its title pays tribute to the native cultures whose music is echoed throughout the compact, single movement score. The first of its two main themes, strongly rhythmic in nature, is borrowed from the Huichol Indians, the more lyrical second from the Yaqui. Musicians and conductors alike must pay close attention to their work, as the meter (patterns of beats) shift continually. The composer himself insists that the work follows the old Classical idea of sonata form, in which a pair of melodies are stated at the beginning, toyed with and varied through the middle, then restated at the end. Although it is rather freer in structure than any sonata form by the great European masters of earlier centuries, it still shows what happens when a European idea is transplanted to the New World and takes on adventurous and imaginative flavors.

- Copland: Symphony no. 3

Aaron Copland (1900-1990) was the quintessential twentieth century American composer. A first generation American and son of Eastern European immigrant Jewish stock, he was born in 1900 in Brooklyn, and rose from humble roots to become one of the most respected names in the nation's music. Copland later attested that his family was not particularly musical. Although the boy had had some piano lessons, it surprised all when, upon finishing high school, he declared that he wished to become a composer.

At the time, American music schools were not highly regarded. Any ambitious young music student would head to Paris for advanced training, and that's exactly what Copland did, basing himself in that city from 1920 to 1924. By the time he returned to the US, he had acquired the professional polish he needed to tackle a composing career, but had also spent four years immersed in European stylistic ideas. Such experience might have turned him into a copy of his French instructors, but instead, Copland came home determined to pursue a distinctly American voice in his music. Soon, he developed his own musical voice: broad and spacious like the great outdoors, heroic and optimistic as one would wish of the future. It was a voice that won him a devoted following at home and abroad.

Often considered to be Copland's masterpiece, the Symphony no. 3 was begun in Mexico which the composer was visiting as part of a cultural tour in the summer of 1944. Two years would pass before its completion only shortly before rehearsals for the premiere were scheduled to begin. That first performance could not easily be put off, as Copland was writing the work at the specific request of the conductor of the Boston Symphony, who already announced the new work's pending appearance, so more determined effort was required. "A mad dash," the composer called it, but the finish line was reached in time. Serge Koussevitzky and the Boston Symphony premiered the piece October 18, 1946.

In preparing his own program notes for the premiere, Copland reflected upon the serious mission inherent in creating such a large-scale composition: "Inevitably the writing of a symphony brings with it the question of what it is meant to express. I suppose if I forced myself I could invent an ideological basis for my symphony. But if I did I'd be bluffing — or at any rate adding something ex post facto." So any specific meaning is left at the discretion of the listener, but on one point the composer was clear: that the piece was not based on any folk or popular melodies, as he sometimes did in other works, such as his ballet *Appalachian Spring* (see Chapter Ten).

Instead of presenting conscious bits of Americana, Copland intended the work as pure music, its various themes arising from the composer's inspiration, not from research into folk tunes. Nonetheless, in the final movement arises a melody that nearly every listener will recognize and to which most will give patriotic connotations. It is the theme of Copland's own *Fanfare for the Common Man*, written a few years previously as part of a public morale campaign during World War II. The familiar theme is whispered at first, but soon is proclaimed in glorious tones. It is a mighty ending for one of the composer's finest works.

- Shostakovich: Symphony no. 5 in d minor, op. 47

Dmitri Shostakovich (1906-1975) labored throughout his life under a Soviet system that placed a premium on ideology. The Russian Revolution was already two years in the past when the thirteen-year-old prodigy was admitted to what had been renamed as the Petrograd Conservatory; even as the teenager supported his mother and sisters by playing piano in the cinema, the films shown there had been chosen by a Soviet authority. Those in power roundly rejected Western ideals, including Western approaches to composition, which were judged to be corrupt and degenerate. A true Soviet composer, it was alleged, would write only music that endorsed the Soviet point of view, works that communicated accepted ideals or endorsed accepted behaviors. Any composer who did not publicly endorse this party line could expect to find himself and his music silenced.

Faced with this inauspicious environment, many notable Russian composers, amongst them Stravinsky, Prokofiev, and Rachmaninoff (all detailed elsewhere in this book), chose to emigrate. But young Shostakovich remained in his homeland and continued his education with every indication of a prosperous future. The premiere of his Symphony no. 1, written in 1926 as a graduation project, was so well received, that within two years, the work had been heard in Vienna, Berlin, and Philadelphia, and had entered the repertoires of the great conductors Bruno Walter and Leopold Stokowski. His Symphonies no. 2 and 3 were both commissioned in commemoration of Marxist anniversaries (of the October Revolution and May Day, respectively), and other compositions, including ballets, operas, film scores, and a set of piano preludes, were well-received by public and press alike. Along with the compositional triumphs, Shostakovich's career as a pianist also stood on firm footing, and it seemed that the young man might come to dominate Soviet musical society as Tchaikovsky had dominated his milieu forty years earlier.

Unfortunately, even the artistic community was not immune to cultural purges. Shostakovich's turn came in 1936. In that year, Joseph Stalin attended a performance of Shostakovich's opera, *Lady Macbeth of Mtsensk*. The opera was not particularly new. Since its premiere January 22, 1934, the piece had had eighty performances in Leningrad, one-hundred in Moscow, and had reached the stage in London, New York, Zurich, Copenhagen, and Stockholm. However, Stalin found the work's overt sexuality unsettling, and his single dissenting opinion was all that was needed to destroy the composer's reputation. In an article titled "Chaos Instead of Music," the newspaper *Pravda* launched a violent attack upon Shostakovich, denouncing him as "coarse, primitive, and vulgar" and branding him "an enemy of the people." The article continued in that virulent vein, ultimately proclaiming, "The danger to Soviet music is clear." Shostakovich had no defenders, and soon, no audience. His Symphony no. 4, already in rehearsal for its scheduled premiere, was abruptly withdrawn.

In the face of such opposition, many composers would have surrendered or emigrated. Yet Shostakovich did not emigrate, and whether or not he surrendered is a matter of opinion. He remained in his homeland, continuing to compose music, despite the fact that his works were unlikely ever to be heard in public. Over a year passed before he responded to the official criticism. The occasion was a concert commemorating the twentieth anniversary of the 1917 revolution; the composition was Shostakovich's Symphony no. 5. Shortly before the symphony premiered, the composer declared in a published article that he was reformed by the government's judgment, that, in his words, "I cannot think of my further progress apart from the socialist structure, and the goal that I set for my work is to contribute at every point toward the growth of our remarkable country." He even went so far as to allow the symphony to be subtitled, "A Soviet artist's answer to just criticism." Such apparent contrition convinced Soviet authorities to look favorably upon the new work and its creator. At its premiere November 21,

1937, the symphony won official approval, and the composer was welcomed back to the artist's community.

If there is irony in Shostakovich's fall from grace being caused by the opinions of one disgruntled autocrat, it is even more ironic that his rebirth was due to the strength of this one mighty symphony, for clearly whoever passed the official judgment had not listened closely to the music. This piece is, by no stretch of the imagination, a song of repentance. It is, rather, the voice of stubborn rebellion, with its opening measures steeped in anger and its conclusion only comparably more optimistic. Moreover, the elements of Western style — its forms and patterns and structures — are even more strictly applied than in his earlier works. Shostakovich does not turn away from the West, as his rulers wished him to do. Rather, he seizes the essence of the German/Austrian tradition and makes it work for him, giving it his own particular voice, one of unending determination, and its impact on the public was intense. According to the composer himself, many people in that first audience wept openly because they understood what the music was saying, whereas others, stunned by what they had heard, filed silently out of the hall after the performance, overwhelmed by its powerful message.

Clearly, Shostakovich wanted the Soviet authorities to imagine that the symphony was the product of acceptance of the Soviet system, but later in his life, when the purges were distant history and artistic expression a matter of more personal taste, he presented a more pointed insight. "I think that it is clear to everyone what happens in the Fifth," he wrote. "It's as if someone were beating you with a stick, and saying, 'Your business is rejoicing, your business is rejoicing,' and you rise shakily, and go off muttering, 'Our business is rejoicing, our business is rejoicing.'" It is music that still has great power most of a century after its premiere.

- Hovhaness: Symphony no. 50, "Mt. St. Helens"

Born in Massachusetts, Alan Hovhaness (1911-2000) was of Armenian and Scottish descent; his compositions are equally diverse in influence. Although educated in mainstream classical ideals, Hovhaness was strongly influenced by Asian and Middle Eastern techniques, from which he borrowed unusual rhythms and harmonies. The diversity of his inspirations led to a catalogue containing both works that are edgy and dissonant and those that are serene and soaring. It seemed to vary according to his mood of the day and his specific task at hand. Over a career which would last until the end of the century, Hovhaness composed dozens of symphonies, short orchestral pieces, choral works on sacred texts, much chamber works, and several chamber operas, though it is his symphonies that have received the most attention.

In 1972, the Easterner and his Japanese-born wife Hinako settled near Puget Sound in Washington State, where they would live until his death in 2000. There, he found himself more than ever struck by the spiritual power of nature, which he delighting in expressing in his music. In 1983, his publisher C. F. Peters asked for a new symphony, which would be Hovhaness' fiftieth. He decided to flavor the work with impressions of the recent cataclysmic explosion (on May 18, 1980) of Mt. St. Helens, no great distance from his home. Fortunately for Hovhaness, the volcano was located downwind, so the force of the blast and its huge subsequent ash-fall did not impact him directly, but, knowing the mountain well and regretting its loss, he was sure that this was the perfect subject for a symphony of rare and impressive power.

The work is structured in three movements. The calm and soaring first movement seeks to capture the beauty and majesty of this remarkably symmetrical peak before the blast. Here, an intricate fugue locks the various groups of instruments together into a complicated melodic structure. The mystical second movement recalls Spirit Lake, which before the blast lay serenely on the mountain's flank, reflecting its slopes and the surrounding pine forests. Its music is suffused with South East Asian bell sounds and woodwind solos, lending a rather unearthly feel. In the third movement, "Volcano," the music opens at dawn, before the mid — morning blast that sheared a thousand feet from the peak and flattened forests for miles around. Percussion and brass bring the eruption fearsomely to listeners' ears. Yet the symphony does not end with this disastrous vision. Rather, Hovhaness segues into a rapturous fugue of stupendous loveliness, recalling what he termed "the vitality of our beautiful planet, the living earth." Here, the volcano is not the end, but rather a new beginning.

- Bernstein: Symphony no. 2 "The Age of Anxiety"

He was the most charismatic figure in American music of the twentieth century, attracting crowds no less fervent than those who, in these same years, came to see the Beatles. He was Leonard Bernstein (1918-1990), a first generation American, son of Eastern European Jewish immigrants, and nearly denied a music education by his father Samuel, who preferred that this elder son should follow him into the family business. Leonard only got his way by persuading his father that if the first year of college music studies didn't go well, he'd then consent to go into business. However, his Harvard professors were so impressed that they convinced Samuel to let his son stay at the university. After graduation, Bernstein became assistant conductor at the New York Philharmonic, where he might have spent years honing his skills in the background, had not conductor Bruno Walter fallen suddenly ill, thrusting the young American into the spotlight of Carnegie Hall November 14, 1943, only months after Bernstein had taken the job. The Sunday matinee concert was also broadcast on radio, so that millions of music lovers knew of the debut. The next morning, Bernstein was front page news in the *New York Times*, and for the rest of his career, was rarely off the front page.

Although Bernstein was most often busy travelling the world as a conductor, he also found time to compose, writing not just the famed *West Side Story* (see Chapter Nine), but also songs, chamber music, orchestral pieces, a mass for Jackie Kennedy (in memory of JFK), and three symphonies. Bernstein's three symphonies were composed at wide intervals: the first "Jeremiah" in 1942, the second "The Age of Anxiety" in 1949, and the last "Kaddish" in 1963. Yet each deals with the question of man's search for faith, though from very different angles. The Symphony no. 2 is the most secular of the three, drawing both title and inspiration from W.H. Auden's text of the same name. Bernstein first read the Auden, which he later described as "fascinating and hair-raising," in the summer of 1947 and felt compelled to convey it in music. Possessing a commission from the Koussevitzky Foundation for a new piece, he set to work and had the score ready (if only barely) in time for its premiere April 8, 1949, with the Boston Symphony and conductor Serge Koussevitzky, to whom it is dedicated. As the work includes a prominent role for pianist, Bernstein, too, performed in the premiere.

Auden's text deals with four lonely young adults — three men and a woman — seeking meaning in their lives. Failing to find it in a bottle of whiskey, they next explore the Seven Ages and Seven Stages of life, and though they begin to draw closer to one another, they still feel adrift. Taking a cab together to the young woman's apartment (the movement called "The Dirge"), they lament the lack of a great leader. In the succeeding Masque, alcohol-flavored revelry again erupts to little avail. Only with the concluding epilogue do they come to understand that what they need is faith.

Bernstein insisted that he was experimenting with musical responses to ideas and was not attempting to portray specific scenes literally. Yet he came to discover that, in his own words, details had "written themselves." In the drunken Masque late in the symphony, inspired by fiendishly late revelries, one hears the celesta ring four o'clock, which the composer says occurred quite by accident. Moreover, that entire scene is strongly flavored with jazz, as many a New York City bacchanal would have been in 1949. Curiously, the epilogue, when the young people finally find truth, abandons jazz in favor of grand, rich orchestral statements, as if Bernstein secretly felt that were the answer to all dilemmas. As for the other movements, the Prologue is a brief if somewhat surreal glimpse into their troubled souls. The Seven Ages and Seven Stages are each a set of variations, not upon a single central theme but rather upon elements borrowed from earlier variations. The gloomy Dirge scene, in which hope seems most distant, draws upon twentieth century "serialist" techniques, refusing to rely upon a tonal center in the same way that the characters have failed to find a center for their lives. It becomes music as psychological expression, apropos for a composer who admired the theories of Sigmund Freud.

- Glass: Symphony no. 7 "A Toltec Symphony"

Mathematics, philosophy, and Ravi Shankar: with those diverse interests on the resume, the subject can only be Philip Glass (b. 1937). Born in Baltimore, the future king of minimalism gained his first exposure to classical music through his father's record collection and early lessons on the violin and the flute. Despite a strong aptitude in the field, young Glass chose mathematics and philosophy as his majors when he enrolled at the University of Chicago, from which he graduated at age nineteen. Only then did he begin composition studies, first at the Juilliard School, and later in Paris with Nadia Boulanger, whose former students had included both Copland and Bernstein. It was during this Paris sojourn that Glass was engaged to transcribe Shankar's sitar music into Western notation, a task that triggered within the young composer a lasting fascination for things Asian. Before long, he would reject the strict serialism so popular at the time in favor of a new style drawn from ancient roots. It would be the beginnings of minimalism.

In addition to film scores (which include *Koyaanisqatsi, Mishima, The Thin Blue Line,* and *The Hours*), concertos (see Chapter Four), piano pieces, and small ensemble works, Glass has also composed several symphonies. The Seventh — not his last; another has followed — was commissioned in 2004 by the National Symphony Orchestra for the sixtieth birthday of its musical director Leonard Slatkin. The Toltec connection was Glass' own idea, for he says he had long been intrigued by that pre-Columbian Mesoamerican culture. Subtitles for the symphony's three movements are drawn from the composer's understanding of that culture's spiritual values.

As Glass tells it, "Corn" represents the link between humans and the Earth, as well as the human responsibility to nurture the Earth. "The Sacred Root," subtitle of the second movement, he views as "the doorway to the world of the Spirit." Of this second movement, Glass says its progress was inspired by an anthropologist's field recording of an old Mexican Indian singing while playing the drum. Of the last movement's subtitle, "The Blue Deer," Glass describes it as evocative of "the holder of the Book of Knowledge," to which a worthy person might aspire. Glass says he thought the image was apt for Maestro Slatkin, given his long service to musical knowledge. Thus, the whole symphony builds gradually to this image of the keeper of truth.

All three movements make use of Glass' trademark pulsing beat and brief melodic fragments, haunting in mood, with subtle changes wrought in part through contrast of instrumental timbres as well as slight shifts in how those melodic fragments develop. It is a style that has long been described as "minimalism." Of the overall effect, Glass, speaking in an interview in 2005 with National Public Radio's Scott Simon, compared it to an experience that most listeners have had and nearly all can imagine, saying: "Lie on the beach. Watch the waves come in. They're not the same. It's the differences that are so beautiful. That's why we sit there." It only seems unchanging if one is not paying attention. Attend to the details and the music gradually evolves.

"A Toltec Symphony" premiered January 20, 2005, at the Kennedy Center in Washington D.C, with the National Symphony Orchestra joined by the Master Chorale and led by Maestro Slatkin. The work is scored for chorus and an orchestra with abundant woodwinds (including piccolo, English horn, E-flat clarinet, and bass clarinet), brass, timpani, percussion (including rattle, tom-tom, wood block, and glockenspiel), strings, harp, piano, and organ). Given those varied performing forces, Glass can call for a varied tapestry of orchestral sound, varying subtly from one moment to the next, as those waves on the beach vary.

Further Recommendations:

Here is a selection of other interesting symphonies for which there was not space in the main body of the chapter:

- Johann Christian Bach (1735-1782): This youngest son of Johann Sebastian Bach represents the earliest generation of symphony composers. His several dozen symphonies are shorter than those of his successors, but no less finely crafted. Christian — nearly all his brothers also had "Johann" as a first name, so they generally went by their middle names — spent most of his career in London, where the residents tended to prefer foreign-born composers to native born Englishmen.

- Leopold Mozart (1719-1787): Father of the revered Wolfgang, Leopold is often overlooked in favor of his offspring. In his time, however, the elder Mozart was a respected composer and violinist. His light-hearted *Toy Symphony* brings sundry toy instruments — including ratchets and bird-calls — into the ensemble.

- Ludwig van Beethoven (1770-1827): Consider also his Symphony no. 3, known as "Eroica" for its heroic scale; no.

6, known as "Pastorale" for its views of the countryside; and the jovial no. 7.

- Felix Mendelssohn (1809-1847): Consider also his Symphony no. 3, known as "Scottish," since its inspiration arose from his visit to the Highlands, and even uses Scottish rhythms in places.

- Cesar Franck (1822-1890): Born in Liege and long based in Paris, Franck wrote only one symphony, but did so at a time when writing symphonies was largely a German/ Austrian endeavor. In this rich and lyrical score, he managed to prove that one could master the field even without speaking German.

- Peter Tchaikovsky (1840-1893): Symphony no. 6 in b minor, op. 74 — his last symphony, known as "Pathetique" and completed only shortly before his death, and ending with music that seems to speak of unavoidable sorrow. Evidence strongly suggests that the composer took his life in the days following the symphony's premiere.

- Vincent d'Indy (1851-1931): A contemporary of Camille Saint-Saëns and like him of moderately conservative musical tastes, d'Indy was inspired by French folk songs to compose his *Symphony on a French Mountain Air*, beloved by fans of the English horn (lower pitched cousin to the oboe), which gets the first statement of the main theme.

- Amy Cheney Beach (1867-1944): *Gaelic Symphony* — Long resident in Boston, Mrs. HHA Beach (as she always declared herself in her music) was inspired by the Irish element in that city's heritage. Prior to this work, American composers had not generally bothered to write symphonies, and American women composers not at all.

- Ralph Vaughan Williams (1872-1958): The Englishman composed nine symphonies. Of these, the Symphony no.

2, known as "London," is a grand abstract vision of that magnificent city. His Symphony no. 7, known as "Sinfonia Antartica," is based on his film music for "Scott of the Antarctic." Incidentally, the slightly divergent spelling of the continent's name was intentional on the composer's part, as he wished it to match the Italianate spelling of the word "sinfonia."

- William Grant Still (1895-1978): Raised in Little Rock, Arkansas, Still composed his Afro-American Symphony in New York in 1931. The jazz-tinged work went on to become the first symphony by an African-American composer to gain wide-spread favorable attention.

- George Antheil (1900-1959): The American composer, a self-described bad boy of music, was bringing jazz rhythms into the classical concert hall long before Gershwin got around to doing it. His vibrant *Jazz Symphony* premiered not in New York but in Berlin, where Antheil had gone to pursue a career as a concert pianist.

- Wynton Marsalis (b. 1961): The masterful jazz trumpeter also possesses Grammy awards for his classical recordings, and some of his compositions bridge those worlds. Late in 2010, he and his ensemble joined the New York Philharmonic for the premiere of his *Swing Symphony*, which immediately went on to international performances.

- Jay Greenberg (b. 1991): Symphony no. 5 — This young American had a recording contract with Sony Classical while still in his teens and twice has been profiled on *Sixty Minutes*; his music, imaginative and energetic, modern but not particularly dissonant, may be one of the voices of the future.

Chapter Three
Other Symphonic Works

It is the main theme to *The Moldau*, Bedrich Smetana's beloved musical excursion along his Bohemian nation's most important river: played by a symphony orchestra, but not exactly a symphony. As noted in the introduction to the previous chapter, that which is called a "symphony" is generally a work in several chapters or "movements" that are seen as portions of a greater whole. *The Moldau* and the other works in this chapter have another purpose.

Sometimes, a composition may use an entire orchestra and still not be a symphony. If there are also singers, props, costumes, and plot, it's an opera or at least a part of an opera (see Chapter Eight). If there are dancers, it's a ballet or ballroom music (see Chapter Ten). If there is a featured soloist or two with that orchestra, it's a concerto (see Chapter Four). Even if there are no soloists, singers, or dancers, the composition may be shorter or more free-form than the concept of a symphony implies. Moreover, sometimes an orchestral work may be a collection of somewhat related movements, perhaps based upon a central idea but linked by no specific musical structures; such compositions are often called suites.

Especially during the 1800s, these not-quite-symphonies tended to have plot content, portraying scenes from literature or art or even one's ethnic heritage. Give instrumental music a plot, and it's considered "program music," a "concert overture," a "tone poem," or a "symphonic poem." Always, there would be a descriptive title detailing the subject matter. So *Short Ride in a Fast Machine* is exactly that, and *Night on Bald Mountain* is similarly descriptive, as long as one knows who's gathering that night at that mountain. More on that one (and others) ahead.

- Handel: *Water Music* suites

There are a few stories in the history of music which, whether or not they are true, will nonetheless live forever. For example, there is the tale of Salieri conspiring against the life of Mozart, and the legend of Beethoven too deaf to hear the applause for his Symphony no. 9, continuing to conduct even after the music had ended. Of equal longevity is the spurious story behind the creation of George Frideric Handel's *Water Music*. According to a biographer writing one year after the composer's death, German-born Handel (1685-1759) was an employee of the Elector of Hanover when, in 1712, he left for a London vacation from which he never returned. He was not a victim of foul play. Rather, the composer was so enjoying himself at the London courts that he no longer wished to live in Hanover, and basically went "absent without leave." The plot thickened when, two years later, England's Queen Anne died and, having survived all her children, was succeeded on the throne by her cousin, who happened to be the man of all men on earth whom Handel would not have wished to see: the Elector of Hanover, now King George I of England. That much of the story is historical. However, supposedly, Handel so feared the wrath of his once-and-future employer that he composed the *Water Music* as a kind of peace offering, and the new king was so delighted that he forgave his truant music master, from which point they all lived happily ever after — at least according to legend.

Such a charming story might persuade one that music has extraordinary persuasive powers (which, of course, it does) but in this case, those powers are at least somewhat exaggerated, for the *Water Music* played no role in Handel's redemption. At the time of its composition, three years had passed since King George arrived, and Handel had long since resumed his duties. In addition, there was no evidence that the King had ever been particularly annoyed with Handel, of whose whereabouts he had never been in doubt. Furthermore, the King, who spoke scarcely a word of English, was likely pleased to have a fellow German-speaker at the London court. Thus, a beloved legend is dismissed, but the facts remain, and in this case, the facts themselves are sufficiently interesting as to not require such embroidery. So, in the interest of historical truth, what follows is the actual story of the *Water Music*.

It was July 17, 1717. The King and his aristocratic friends had planned a water party on the Thames. They were to ride barges from Whitehall to Chelsea where they would have a late supper before returning. Entertainment would be provided by an orchestra of about fifty musicians, including, according to one observer, "trumpets, horns, hautboys [oboes], bassoons, German flutes, French flutes [that is, both recorders, which Germans preferred, and transverse flutes, more to French tastes], violins and basses." No mention was made of the timpani that are now customarily included, but percussion may have been added later once the limiting factor of a barge-borne performance was eliminated. On this first excursion, the musicians played all the way to Chelsea, and their performance of Handel's new work so delighted the King that he asked to hear the music again and again and again, a total of four performances, lasting an hour apiece.

Selections from this extended suite were published during Handel's lifetime, but the entire score did not come into print until 1788, nearly three decades after the composer's passing. Thus, it cannot be certain in which order he wished the various dance-style movements to be played. It is customary, however, to group the movements according to their keys and instrumentations, creating three shorter suites, one in F major, one in D major, and one in G major. Although many listeners will recognize the almost waltz-like lilt of a minuet, the bourrée and the hornpipe may be less familiar. Of the two, both lively in mood, the bourrée developed in France as a light-footed dance, usually in a duple meter with two beats per measure, known both in boisterous folk forms and more elegant courtly circles. By contrast, the hornpipe originated in the British Isles and is similar to a jig with intricate, often syncopated rhythms. Although the name also appears in the context of sailor's music, the hornpipe Handel would have known was a social dance for one or more persons, with no sails in sight.

- Handel: *Music for the Royal Fireworks*

A "Grand Overture of Warlike Instruments:" such was the original title of the composition now known as Handel's *Music for the Royal Fireworks*. It was April, 1749. The previous fall, a treaty had been signed to bring to a close the War of the Austrian Succession. Now, with the return of warmer weather, King George II was determined to present a festival to celebrate the peace. The festival, to be held outdoors in Green Park, just west of Buckingham Palace, would include both fireworks and music. In fact, in the weeks leading up to the event, there was fireworks over the music itself. The king, a man whose musical tastes ran strongly to the military, wanted only a military band, whereas Handel was advocating the addition of string instruments. Although Handel defended his point of view, when a king is involved, there is no real debate.

George got his way. Strings were excluded from the composition, and were only added on a later occasion. The original instrumentation, in accordance with the king's demands, was nine trumpets, nine horns, twenty-four oboes, twelve bassoons, one contrabassoon (an extra-large and extra-low-pitched bassoon, even lower in pitch than the tuba), one serpent (not a reptile, but rather a low pitched wind instrument), six kettledrums, and two side drums. It was a hearty blend guaranteed to resonate throughout the spaces of Green Park, and reach most of the way to the Tower Bridge.

Six days before the festival itself, a public rehearsal of the music was presented in the Spring Gardens at Vauxhall. Handel opposed the idea of public rehearsals, but Londoners approved earnestly. So strong was their anticipation of the upcoming event that 12,000 people arrived for the rehearsal, overflowing from the Gardens and causing a three hour traffic jam on London Bridge. If such was the crowd for the rehearsal, imagine how many celebrants arrived in Green Park for the festival itself on April 27. Festivities began at six in the evening with Handel's music, followed after dark by an elaborate fireworks display, launched from 101 brass cannons. The evening was not without mishaps. At one point in the festivities, a rocket went astray and set fire to a decorative pavilion. Although no one was injured, the pavilion's designer, an apparently excitable Frenchman, took personal offence at the incident and threatened the fireworks master with his sword. Fortunately, the quarrel was quickly concluded. It would be tragic indeed if, at the celebration of one international peace treaty, another international conflict were to be launched.

- Mendelssohn: *The Hebrides* Overture, op. 27

Felix Mendelssohn loved to travel. Whether in the ancient cities of Italy or the high mountain valleys of Switzerland, he delighted in meeting new people and hearing new styles of musical expression. His journals and letters home were often filled with these chance discoveries, much as other people would write of a memorable meal or a striking view, and, along with such musical souvenirs, Mendelssohn would note down original melodies which occurred to him during his travels. These melodic ideas often reappeared in later compositions, uncannily evoking the source of their inspiration. Such works are the musical voices of Mendelssohn's travels.

Mendelssohn was twenty when he visited Scotland in the summer of 1829. Traveling with a childhood friend, he roved amongst the lakes and moors of the highlands, writing colorful letters about his adventures. He described the "comfortless, inhospitable solitude," which stood in contrast to the entrancing beauty and brilliance of the countryside. Here was a place very different from Berlin, where the young composer had grown up. Mendelssohn loved the highlands, and closely observed its native music, yet also found within himself melodic expression for the sights and sounds he encountered. While on a ferry voyage in western Scotland, Mendelssohn was so struck by the misty scene and the rolling waves that a melody came into his mind, a melody with all the surge and power of the sea itself. In an exuberant letter, he described the experience to his sister Fanny, and wishing to convey to her how deeply he was moved, he noted in the letter a few bars of this magical melody. It is the same melody heard at the beginning of *The Hebrides Overture*.

Although Mendelssohn began the overture while in mid-voyage, he was so busy with traveling that he set the piece aside, only continuing work on it the next year, when he was visiting Rome. He revised the overture several times, changing its title as the work progressed. What began as *Overture for a Lonely Isle* became *The Hebrides*, then *Fingal's Cave*. By the time of its London premiere in 1832, Mendelssohn had returned to *The Hebrides* as a title, a geographically inaccurate decision. At the time of his original inspiration, he was on his way to Fingal's Cave on the Isle of Staffa, a tiny and arguably lonely isle. However, Staffa is not, properly speaking, in the Hebrides, but rather is closer to the mainland and further to the south. A resident would not have made that mistake. In modern editions, the overture is often given two titles: *Hebrides* and *Fingal's Cave*.

- Liszt: *Les Préludes* (Symphonic Poem no. 3)

Hungarian born Franz Liszt (1811-1886) was an extraordinary pianist. The popular music idol of his day, he built a thriving career by offering flamboyant recitals to adoring audiences, largely female. Most observers found Liszt's musical charisma inescapable. Less sympathetic critics took Liszt to task, accusing him of being all glitter and no gold, but regardless of his extravagant public image, the man himself was far more substantial. Deeply introspective, Liszt read widely, demonstrating a preference for religious and philosophical texts, and published many essays based upon these and other readings. Gradually, his ideas began to influence his music both in terms of style and inspiration. Liszt's compositions, like the man himself, offer an intricate blend of showmanship and idealism. We'll have more about his piano music in Chapter Six, but first the orchestral side of his musical voice.

Les Préludes serves as a perfect example of Liszt's metaphysical approach to music. The third and most familiar of his thirteen tone poems, the piece draws its title from a line in Alphonse de Lamartine's "Poetic Meditations," which reads, "What is life but a series of preludes to that unknown hymn whose first solemn note is intoned by death?" The philosophy inherent in those words has led generations of critics to draw parallels between that line and the poem's other lines to the particular melodies of Liszt's work. However, such attempts are off the mark, for though the title is indeed of the composer's own choosing, it was not his first choice. This composition had been written, and was premiered, as an overture to a choral setting of a completely different text. When that work found little popularity, Liszt decided to refit the overture as a tone poem, and chose Lamartine's words for the program it would supposedly portray. Although he undertook some revisions of the score, the piece remains substantially the same as it was in its previous incarnation. Thus, any relation between *Les Préludes* as a composition and "Les Préludes" as life preceding death is largely coincidental.

In its final form, *Les Préludes* received its premiere in 1854, with the composer himself conducting a performance in Weimar, where since 1844 he had served as Grand Ducal Director of Music Extraordinary. At its publication two years later, the work was dedicated to Liszt's lady-love of the time, Polish-born Princess Carolyne Sayn-Wittgenstein, who had proved instrumental in persuading this genius of the piano to devote more serious attention to composition. Thus, it is perhaps thanks to her that *Les Préludes* exists at all.

- Wagner: *Siegfried Idyll*

In the first months of his marriage to his second wife Cosima (daughter of composer Franz Liszt), German opera specialist Richard Wagner (1813-1883) decided to write a new work as a surprise gift for her thirty-third birthday, which they would celebrate on Christmas Day, 1870. He completed the piece in secret. Then early on that special morning, he admitted a small group of musicians into their home. What happened next is best conveyed in Cosima's own words, for she detailed the event in her diary. "As I awoke, my ears caught a sound which grew fuller and fuller. I could not tell myself that I was dreaming. Music was sounding, and what music! As it died away, Richard came into my room with the children and offered me the score of the symphonic birthday poem — I was in tears, but so was the whole household." Twice more that day, the new composition, which they dubbed the "Staircase Music," was performed. Cosima came to treasure it as proof of her new husband's love. In fact, she was so attached to the work that, eight years later, when Wagner announced that he was planning to publish it, she protested vigorously. It was hers, she said, and ought not be sold. But the family needed money, and Wagner won the debate.

Cosima's birthday music was published under the new name of *Siegfried Idyll*, after her husband's recent opera; it is worth noting that their son, at this time only eighteen months old, was also named Siegfried. In its original form, the work was scored for a very small orchestra of fewer than sixteen players. Those numbers were dictated by the circumstances of the first performance, for the stairs at Tribschen could not accommodate more musicians. A year later, Wagner rescored the work for a larger orchestra, and it is this version that is usually performed today.

In either setting, Wagner's musical sources remain clear. One is his opera *Siegfried*, from which he borrowed the horn motif and the melody of the forest bird, as well as the major love theme, a theme that is sung with great force and exuberance on stage, but here takes on a far more gentle character. Wagner also quoted melodies from an uncompleted string quartet he had sketched some years before, and he gave to the oboe a solo based upon a lullaby that Wagner had composed in 1868. Combined, the two themes comprise a domestic portrait, lyrically depicting the love of the parents for each other and also for their children.

It is a softer side of Wagner than one is accustomed to hearing from this composer of the grandest of grand operas (see Chapter Eight), one that brings out a far more endearing side of an otherwise problematic persona. By all evidence, he was an anti-Semitic opportunist who would take any chance to promote his music and his goals at the expense of all else, but he adored Cosima. That he had taken her away from her first husband, conductor Hans von Bülow, who had been one of Wagner's greatest supporters did not apparently bother Wagner in the least.

- Smetana: *The Moldau*, from *Ma Vlast (My Fatherland)*

Eastern Europe has long been a hotbed of musical nationalism, with music used to express dreams of independence. Few composers from this region have been more devoted to the cause than Bedrich Smetana (1824-1884), a man who spent five years in Swedish exile for revolutionary activities in support of Bohemian freedom. The composer had grown up speaking German, the language of those who controlled his homeland, but over the years, developed a strong love for all things Czech. He learned the language and the legends, and soon began setting both to music. Smetana's first efforts were in the field of opera. His comic masterpiece, *The Bartered Bride*, is a celebration of Czech culture, and other operas continued that theme in more serious terms. As the heroine of one opera, *Libuse*, declares, "My beloved Czech nation will not perish; gloriously she will vanquish the terrors of Hell." It was a battle Smetana was fighting in musical terms.

Some years after these operas were written, Smetana turned to the concert stage for his nationalist expression. He had in mind a cycle of symphonic poems, with topics drawn from the legends and landscapes of his homeland, what the composer called "musical pictures of Czech glories and defeats." In eloquent terms, he portrayed chivalrous deeds at a medieval castle, a river journey with scenes of rural life, the legendary revenge of a spurned maiden, the fields and woods along the Elbe River, the perseverance of Czech warriors, and the reminder of their eventual return in victory. It was an ambitious effort, one that would require five years to complete, by which time Smetana was completely deaf. He called his epic *Ma Vlast* (*My Fatherland*), and it would become his most enduring composition. It premiered in Prague November 5, 1882, to a rapturous reception.

Of the six pieces, the most popular is the second, *Vltava*, named for the river which in English and German is called The Moldau. It is a musical river trip, showing listeners the sounds and emotions along the course of this river, as it flows through the nation's heart. Smetana begins in the mountains where a pair of springs emerge, one warm and one cold, both flowing downhill until they come together to create what will be a mighty river. It is this theme that appeared in musical notes at the head of this chapter. As the journey continues, one passes a scene of jubilant hunters (French horns), then a village wedding (polka rhythms), then a gorge where according to legend, water nymphs come out to bathe in the moonlight (serene and mysterious phrases). With the morning light, the main river theme returns, though it soon breaks into drama, as the river enters the rapids. When the tumult of the white water is safely passed, the river, both geographically and musically, reaches the city of Prague and flows past the castle Vyšehrad, once the seat of power for Bohemian kings, by this time long deposed. Passing the castle to the strains of a regal hymn, the river flows on and the music begins to fade away, punctuated at its close with a pair of strong chords that seem to declare "the end."

- Brahms: *Academic Festival Overture, op. 80*

No doubt it was intended to be a solemn occasion. The University of Breslau had conferred an honorary doctorate of music upon Johannes Brahms, arguably Germany's greatest living composer, and had invited him to write a new work that he might conduct at the award ceremonies. He agreed, and arrived in Breslau with a new overture. Yet Brahms, never an ivory-tower intellectual, had provided a work different from anyone's expectations. Rather than composing a Germanic equivalent of *Pomp and Circumstance* (see Chapter Ten), he produced instead what he described as a "rollicking potpourri of student's songs," in this case, mostly drinking songs. It is easy to imagine the laughter of the assembled students, as well as the forced smiles on the faces of the dignitaries, when this light-hearted caprice premiered January 4, 1881.

Academic Festival Overture showcases four songs that were popular at the time on college campuses throughout the various German states. The first was "Wir hatten gebauet ein stattliches Haus," proclaimed in the trumpets. "Der Landesvater" followed in the strings, and then the bassoons took the lead for "Was kommt dort von der Höh." Lastly, the entire orchestra joined together for a grand rendition of "Gaudeamus igitur," beloved by operetta lovers for its appearance in Sigmund Romberg's

The Student Prince, but it was the first melody which was most notorious in the composer's day. "Wir hatten gebauet" was the theme song of a student organization that advocated the unification of the dozens of independent German principalities. This cause was so objectionable to authorities that the song had been banned for decades, and although the proscription was lifted in most regions in 1871, it was still in effect in Vienna at the time that Brahms completed this overture. Due to the ban, police ordered the Viennese premiere of the *Academic Festival Overture* delayed by two weeks, for fear of student protests.

- Tchaikovsky: *Romeo and Juliet Fantasy Overture*

The writings of Shakespeare may have inspired more classical music than by those of any other author. Over three hundred years, composers from Henry Purcell (1659-1695) through David Diamond (1915-2005), have found in the Bard's stage works characters and situations well-suited to musical expression. Consistently attracting the most attention is the familiar tragedy of *Romeo and Juliet.* The star-crossed lovers have found life in operatic, balletic, and symphonic conceptions, among many other versions, but of all those numerous settings, Tchaikovsky's has become the most beloved.

The *Romeo and Juliet Fantasy-Overture* arose from a consultation between Tchaikovsky and his more experienced colleague, the composer Mily Balakirev (1837-1910). In 1869, Tchaikovsky complained to his friend that he was lacking ideas for new pieces. At the time working on a *King Lear Overture,* Balakirev suggested a Shakespearean solution: *Romeo and Juliet.* He even proposed possible themes and a general outline for the work. Tchaikovsky agreed, and soon set to work, sending the composition-in-progress to Balakirev for commentary. Apparently irked that Tchaikovsky had not followed his suggestions to the letter, Balakirev was somewhat critical of the results, yet expressed cautious approval, declaring, "It is the first of your compositions that contains so many beautiful things one does not hesitate to pronounce it good as a whole." The completed score premiered in Moscow in March, 1870. Two revisions followed; the final edition was first heard in 1886.

Rather than setting out to portray the play's events in the order in which they occur, Tchaikovsky's score instead concerns itself with a variety of characters and moods whose melodies offer effective musical contrast. The work opens with a serene clarinet-and-bassoon melody that represents the lover's ally, Friar Laurence, shown in a somber and reflective state of mind. The scene then shifts to one of violence, with a chaotic theme for the feuding Montagues and Capulets. Yet before long, Tchaikovsky introduces a new melody: the soaring love theme of Romeo and Juliet themselves, one featured in many a film of television commercial when a romantic mood was required. As the piece progresses, love and violence share the stage with a sense of growing urgency until the climax is reached and the lovers lie dying in the tomb. With a hint of Friar Laurence's melancholy theme, as if he has arrived on the scene too late to help his young friends, the *Fantasy-Overture* concludes.

- Mussorgsky: *Night on Bald Mountain*

Youngest son of a wealthy landowning Russian family, Modest Mussorgsky (1839-1881) learned music in boyhood, but as a social skill, not a potential profession. It was his family's expectation that he would join the military, and so by the time he was in his teens, he had headed off to cadet school. Upon graduation at age seventeen, he took a post with the Preobrazhensky Guards, but devoted most of his spare time to playing piano and composing. Before he reached his twentieth birthday, he would resign from the guards and make music his career.

Only after his premature death (his friends had long remarked upon his heavy drinking, which ultimately ruined his health) did most of Mussorgsky's music re-emerge, thanks to the intervention of Nicolai Rimsky-Korsakov (1844-1908). Himself a composer and a long-time friend of Mussorgsky's, Rimsky-Korsakov took it upon himself to revise Mussorgsky's unpublished works and prepare them for publication, granting much of his attention to his late friend's masterpiece, the opera *Boris Godunov*, but not neglecting other works. He took up the tone poem *Night on Bald Mountain*, rearranging and re-orchestrating it with more conservative choices; then, rejecting his friend's original conclusion of crashing dissonance, created instead an ending in which dawn and church bells disperse the gathered demons. In this form, the piece first reached an international audience when Rimsky-Korsakov himself conducted it in concert at the Paris Exhibition of 1887. Mussorgsky's original version did not come to print until 1968.

Rimsky-Korsakov's familiar version allows the violins to carry much of the motion, with driving, almost minimalistic rhythms. Brass and percussion have assertive declamatory statements, and for lyrical passages, the choice generally leans toward the woodwinds, especially the clarinet. Rimsky-Korsakov civilized his friend's music, particularly in its harmonies, but the orchestral parts are still rife with 'allegro feroce' markings. Fast and ferocious: that's *Night on Bald Mountain* in a nutshell.

Incidentally, thanks to its subject matter dealing with a nocturnal assembly of demonic spirits, *Night on Bald Mountain* has come to be associated with Halloween. However, Mussorgsky was not envisioning an October evening. His original title was "St. John's Night on the Bald Mountain," referring to a Russian legend about Satan gathering his forces on that particular night; St. John's Night is June 24.

- Rimsky- Korsakov: *Scheherazade, op. 35*

Another younger son of a family with military interests, Nicolai Rimsky-Korsakov (1844-1908) first followed tradition, enlisting in the Russian navy and serving a tour that took him much of the way around the world. Yet music had been an early love, and in odd moments even aboard ship, he dabbled at composition. In the 1860s, when the young naval cadet had not yet settled firmly on a career either military or musical, he produced three symphonies. These were well enough received that upon his return to Russia, he gave up his ship and accepted a position as Inspector of Navy Bands, which allowed him to remain ashore and gave him more time for composition. More symphonic works followed, along with operas, chamber music, songs, and choral pieces, many achieving critical and popular success, but his greatest triumphs came in the summers of 1887 and '88, when he produced three dramatic orchestral pieces: not strictly structured symphonies, but rather freely-flowing flights of fancy, pictorial images painted in orchestral color. The works in question are among the most beloved in the orchestral repertoire: *Capriccio Espagnol*, *Russian Easter Overture* and *Scheherazade*.

Scheherazade, the most ambitious and most familiar of the three, is a symphonic suite of exotic inspiration, deriving its themes from the evocative tales of *A Thousand and One Nights*. Ancient Arabic stories from the oral tradition, the adventures of Sindbad, Ali Baba, and friends became widely known in Europe during the 1800s, thanks in part to the popular translations of Sir Richard Burton. Rimsky-Korsakov, famed as a virtuoso of orchestral coloration, recognized in these Near Eastern tales a perfect realm in which to give free rein to his abilities. "A kaleidoscope of fairy-tale images," he called it and, in an introductory note to his composition, he set the scene this way: "The Sultan Schahriar, persuaded of the falseness and faithlessness of women, has sworn to put to death each one of his wives after the first night. But the Sultana Scheherazade saved her life by interesting him in tales she told him during one thousand and one nights."

The suite is structured in four movements, each with its own subtitle: "The Sea and Sindbad's Ship," "The Story of the Kalandar Prince," "The Young Prince and the Young Princess," and "Festival at Baghdad; the Sea; The Ship Goes to Pieces on a Rock Surmounted by a Bronze Warrior." The subtitles derive from the original stories, but Rimsky-Korsakov always insisted that his music was not intended as an exact portrayal of those stories. Other than a sinuous violin solo that is meant as the shadow of Scheherazade herself, there are no character motifs. There is no "Sindbad" theme, no "Kalandar Prince" theme, no musical moment in which the listener glimpses, through the mists of a storm at sea, a magnificent Bronze Warrior. Moreover, there are many young royals in the collection, and Rimsky-Korsakov does not specify which ones he may have in mind, let alone quite exactly what they may be doing.

As far as the composer was concerned, this is not music to which one might read the stories aloud in perfect synchronization. The goal, instead, was that of a general mood. "In composing *Scheherazade*," Rimsky-Korsakov wrote in his memoirs, "I meant these hints to direct but slightly the hearer's fancy on the path which my own fancy had traveled, and to leave more minute and particular conceptions to the will and mood of each."

- Elgar: *Enigma Variations*, op. 36

Sir Edward Elgar (1857-1934) grew up with music. His father served as piano tuner and church organist in the English cathedral town of Worcester, where he raised seven children, Edward emerging in the exact center of the line. During Edward's childhood, his father also ran a music store. The family lived over the shop, so the musically inclined boy had early exposure to the field that would absorb him throughout his life. Young Elgar began studying the violin as a child, and at the age of ten wrote music for a family play, but his family discouraged him from seeking a musical career. Instead, the fifteen-year-old was sent to study law in a solicitor's office, but after a year or so, it was clear that music was his destiny. Eventually, Elgar found musical work in London, but it wasn't until the 1890s, when he had passed the age of forty, that Elgar's music attracted the attention it had long deserved.

His first acknowledged masterpiece was his opus 36, the *Variations on an Original Theme*, dating from 1899, a work that has since become known as the *Enigma Variations*. The work's origins were described by Elgar himself in a letter to his friend August Jaeger, an editor at the music publishing firm Novello and Company. "I have sketched a set of variations on an original theme," the composer wrote. "The variations have amused me because I've labeled them with the nicknames of my particular friends — you [meaning Jaeger himself] are Nimrod. That is to say I've written the variations each one to represent the mood of the 'party' . . . it's a quaint idea and the result is amusing to those behind the scenes, and won't affect the hearer who knows nothing."

Elgar is correct in believing that familiarity with the person's portrayed is not vital for enjoyment of the music. Nonetheless, a few clues about these people add a measure of humor that the casual listener might miss. So, for example, the lovely first variation belongs to the composer's wife Alice. The penultimate variation, devoted to a friend who was at the time on route to Australia, quotes Mendelssohn's overture *Calm Sea and Prosperous Voyage*. Variation number ten is named for the organist Dr. George Sinclair; however, Elgar admitted that he was thinking less of Dr. Sinclair than of the organist's bulldog Dan who made a great scene while fetching sticks thrown into the river. Most famous of all the variations is number nine, which bears the name "Nimrod." It is a Biblical allusion; Nimrod was a great hunter, and "hunter" in German is "Jaeger." This lyrical movement portrays a walk in the country with his friend Jaeger, a gentleman who, by Elgar's own account, offered valuable artistic guidance throughout a long partnership. The final variation is reserved for the composer himself, an appropriate placing, since it was his wife's variation that began the work. Yet in the midst of Elgar's own hearty variation, he brings back Alice's music from the beginning and Jaeger's theme of the Nimrod variation. Thus, he concludes the work not only with himself, but also his wife and his closest friend, bringing together the composer and the two strongest influences upon the composer.

Since the persons portrayed are only indicated by initials in the original score, one might imagine that their identities are the "Enigma" of the title, but in fact, Elgar was thoroughly forthcoming about this issue, so much so that he actually assembled and published a booklet naming each person, stating what he hoped to portray about them (thus, the thought above about Dr. Sinclair's bulldog), and including their photographs. So the enigma certainly does not lie in this aspect of the work; rather, the true mystery is the theme itself. Elgar always claimed that it was a counterpoint to some well-known tune, a theme which, in the composer's words, "goes through and over the whole set, but is not played." That is, although we never hear the theme itself, it would fit in with the harmonies; we could sing it to the accompaniment of his variations, if only we knew what it was. This theme has been variously guessed to be "Rule Britannia," "God Save the Queen," the "Dies Irae," "Auld Lang Syne," or even "Pop Goes the Weasel." Elgar, however, would never identify it, and this musical puzzle still challenges scholars today.

The composition premiered June 19, 1899, in St. James Hall, London, and was an immediate success. However, Elgar decided to undertake some revisions, mostly at the suggestion of Jaeger, who thought the finale would benefit from some expansion. This later version of the work, the one still performed today, had its first performance later that same year at the Three Choirs Festival in Worcester. It must have been a sweet pleasure for Elgar to return in triumph to the town where he had grown up, where he had first discovered the wondrous world of music.

- Richard Strauss: *Don Juan*, op. 20

Munich-born Richard Strauss (1864-1949) did not invent the symphonic poem. Franz Liszt is usually credited with that achievement. Yet Strauss remains the acknowledged master of the genre, for in his hands, these programmatic compositions — orchestral works with dramatic content — reached their most ambitious level of creative and imaginative power. Beginning with *Aus Italien* in 1886, Strauss went on to create symphonic poems on subjects ranging from the adventures of Don Juan to Strauss' personal adventures in *Ein Heldenleben* (*A Hero's Life*) and *Symphonia domestica* (*Domestic Symphony*). He even found the confidence to set the intricacies of Nietzsche to music in *Also sprach Zarathustra* (*Thus Spake Zarathustra*) Strauss became so devoted to program music that he once reportedly remarked that he did not really like to compose without a program, an admission that some observers might have viewed as damning. Yet Strauss' mastery of the genre proved that symphonic poems can be as musically creative as proper symphonies, with the added advantage of having a tale to tell, a tale that can aid audiences in understanding the composer's intent.

One of the first of Strauss' tone poems, *Don Juan* premiered in Weimar November 11, 1888. The composer recalled that "the horns certainly blew as though they weren't afraid of death . . . Afterward, a horn player who was sitting there sweating and quite out of breath gasped, 'Oh, God, what have we done wrong that you have sent us this stick to beat us! We won't get rid of him in a hurry!" The horn player may have been clairvoyant. *Don Juan* was an immediate success, its composer's first great hit. He would conduct it in dozens of concerts throughout his career, and included it in his very first recordings made in 1917. However, critics still found room for invective. Eduard Hanslick, dean of the Viennese critics, proclaimed, "This is no tone painting, but rather a torrent of brilliant splashes . . . half bacchanal, half witches' sabbath." Later, perhaps in the face of the work's persistent popularity, Hanslick recanted, admitting that the work possessed an "irresistible insolence." It may be no coincidence that those words would apply equally accurately to the character of the legendary Don Juan himself.

As the work opens, Strauss offers a theme that is forthright and virile. Yet this inconstant lover is also of inconstant moods, for this bold theme is soon followed by one of romance, carried by a solo violin. A tranquil oboe theme suggests an evening liaison. Then, the tender mood is split asunder by four strident horns who, having summoned up their strength, present a bold and confident theme: music for a hero's hero. These various themes are tossed about, always buoyed by Strauss' magnificent orchestration, charging along undaunted until a sudden alteration of mood. The music becomes soft and mournful, for Don Juan's life is coming to an end. Here, Strauss, and his inspiration, the poet Lenau, opt not for a dramatic passing. Instead, the protagonist, having tired of the unending chase, allows his life to be taken in a duel. In that light, the tone poem's final wistful phrases seem to speak of a dying breath.

- Sibelius: *Finlandia*

The best known of the patriotic works by Jean Sibelius (1865-1957), *Finlandia* has its origins in a political demonstration. Ostensibly a charitable fundraiser, the Finnish Press Pension Celebration of 1899 was in fact a thinly veiled rally in support of freedom of the press, which by this time was under restrictions not from the previous rule of Sweden, but under the new dictates of Tsarist Russia. Sibelius' contribution to the three-day pageant was a set of nationalistic musical tableaux. Several of these pieces he later recycled into the suite *Historic Scenes no. 1*, but the grand finale, originally called "Finland Awakes," became what we now know as *Finlandia*. Its first performances under that title were given by the Helsinki Philharmonic at the Paris World Exhibition of 1900.

Many people are under the impression that *Finlandia* is the Finnish national anthem, but that is true only in the informal sense. The true Finnish anthem, the one performed while waving flags for national heroes, is "Our Land," written by Fredrik Pacius in 1848 and first performed two years later. Having yet to be born, Sibelius had no role in it. Yet few Finns would not stand proudly to Sibelius' magnificent melody, though it is of belated appearance when heard in its original form. For the famed theme, referenced in some hymnbooks as "Be Still My Soul," does not arrive until the middle of the work. Sibelius begins with brass and timpani in tense and ominous mood, gradually joined by strings and woodwinds for a dark if regal atmosphere. A brisk, driving passage of martial energy storms forward, leading gradually to a bright and festive mood, then the serene familiar melody in broad, expansive phrases. The bright, festive music returns with much brass and percussion to charge into the final pages, though the lyrical familiar theme will earn one more statement in the coda just before the close.

- Debussy: *Prelude to the Afternoon of a Faun*

Wispy water lilies framed by a gracefully arced bridge. Airy ballerinas poised as the curtain rises. Stylish couples gathered at the Moulin Rouge. Such is the subtle aura of Impressionism, the most popular artistic style of the last two centuries. The term was used to describe Monet, Degas, and Renoir as early as the 1870s, but it played its role in music as well, particularly with Claude Debussy (1862-1918). Composer of *La Mer* and *Prelude to the Afternoon of a Faun*, the great Frenchman was considered the aural equivalent of his artistic contemporaries, a reputation based upon the gently colored orchestrations and softly shaped melodies that seemed to be his province. It is, however, one of the great ironies of music history that, regardless of how others regarded his works, Debussy himself loathed the label of "Impressionist" and disliked Impressionist art in general; his own tastes ran more strongly toward James Whistler. Yet whether or not he would have admitted it, there were commonalities between Debussy and the artists, if not in style, then in intellectual outlook. For the artists were consciously rejecting pre-established conventions, and so did Debussy. "I am more and more convinced," he remarked to his publisher, "that music is not, in essence, a thing that can be cast into a traditional and fixed form. It is made up of colors and rhythms. The rest is a lot of humbug."

Of all Debussy's works — indeed, of all those works by any Impressionist composer — one piece stands out as the most admired today and the most controversial in its own time. *Prelude to the Afternoon of a Faun*, dating from 1894, is a musical evocation of the Stéphane Mallarmé poem of the same name, a poem in which a faun — the half-man, half-beast of ancient Grecian legends — awakes to revel in sensuous memories of forest nymphs. "These nymphs," he muses, "I would perpetuate. So light their gossamer embodiment, floating on the air inert with heavy slumber. Was it a dream I loved? . . . Let us reflect . . . or suppose those women that you idolize were but imaginings of your fantastic lust!"

Debussy's ethereal score, with its sinuous flute melody so evocative of a graceful female form, seems the perfect musical vision of such fantasies, though some observers were less convinced. "Pretty sonority," observed Camille Saint-Saëns (1835-1921), "but one does not find in it the least musical idea; properly speaking; it resembles a piece of music as the palette used by an artist in his work resembles a picture. Debussy did not create a style; he cultivated an absence of style, logic, and common sense." But Saint-Saëns, a gifted composer in his eighth decade at the time of that lament, was utterly unprepared for the new realms of expression that Debussy was exploring, just as ballet audiences were unprepared for the work's choreographic incarnation that appeared belatedly in 1912, when Russian dancer and choreographer Vaclav Nijinsky offered a balletic interpretation of *Faun* so suggestive that even the famously open-minded Parisians were shocked. Despite its gentle tones, Debussy's masterpiece still held the power of controversy.

- Vaughan Williams: *The Lark Ascending*

The family name was "Vaughan Williams," not "Williams," and no hyphen. Although music lovers think only of Ralph Vaughan Williams (1872-1958), the family was a whole was prominent, including many respected English barristers. On his mother's side, he was related to the Wedgwood family of pottery fame and to Charles Darwin. Ralph's own father was a minister; during the boy's youth, they were living near London. He learned the piano and the violin, amongst other instruments, but was deterred from pursuing a performing career, as such would not quite meet the family's professional standards. Instead, when he enrolled at the Royal College of Music, it was composition that young Vaughan Williams chose as his focus. Through those studies, he met his slightly younger colleague Gustav Holst (1874-1934), with whom he would maintain a life-long friendship and an enduring interest in English folk song. Of Holst, more shortly.

Vaughan Williams also took composition training in Paris with Maurice Ravel (1875-1937) and in Berlin with Max Bruch (1838-1920), and admitted to a lasting admiration for the works of Finnish master Jean Sibelius (1865-1957), so his influences were diverse. By 1910, he had earned a strong reputation as composer, conductor, writer, lecturer, editor, and folklorist. After World War I, during which he had served as army musical director along with other less musical assignments — driving ambulances — Vaughan Williams joined the staff of the Royal College of Music. He remained busy as a composer to the end of his days, which would be both prosperous and lengthy; at the time of his death in 1958, he had outlived by some forty years the lyrical late Romantic style that he personally preferred and which he never himself abandoned.

The Lark Ascending, a one-movement tone poem for orchestra with solo violin, is a gentle, introspective work composed in a far from gentle time. It dates from 1914 in the early days of World War One, when a pastoral scene of a bird singing on the wing seemed far removed from reality. In fact, the war so occupied public attention that the work's premiere was delayed seven years, until June 14, 1921, when violinist Marie Hall, for whom the piece had been written, gave its first performance in London. The composition's title is sufficiently evocative to bring its images to the minds of most listeners, but Vaughan Williams also provided an additional inspiration, by prefacing the score with lines from the George Meredith poem of the same name:

He rises and begins to round,
He drops the silver chain of sound,
Of many links without a break,
In chirrup, whistle, slur and shake.

For singing till his heaven fills,
'Tis love of earth that he instills,
And ever winging up and up,
Our valley is his golden cup,
And he the wine which overflows
To lift us with him as he goes.

Till lost on his aerial rings
In light, and then the fancy sings.

Some observers criticized Vaughan Williams for having produced a work so little reflective of recent world turmoil. Others felt the piece was not out of touch with the times at all, that rather than focusing upon war and death, it chose instead to recall one exquisite image of life, the same life that they were fighting to preserve. For a man who had spent much of his war service in France, it must have been reassuring to look again at the sweet side of life.

- Holst: *The Planets*, op. 32

When Gustav Holst (1874-1934) decided to make music his profession, fame and fortune were the farthest things from his imagination. The near-sighted Englishman, latest generation of minor musical dynasty, was perfectly content teaching music at a London girls' school, studying Sanskrit and Hindu philosophy, and living quietly with his wife and daughter. It was a low-profile life, but one suited to Holst's own simple tastes. He might have spent his entire life in pleasant obscurity, were it not for the tactical error of writing one astoundingly popular work, his seven-movement orchestral suite, *The Planets*.

This collection of planetary portraits took three years to complete, for in this period from 1914 to 1916, his duties as director of music at St. Paul's Girl's School kept him away from composition for days at a time. Only on weekends and school holidays could he truly devote himself to the work. Progress was further slowed by an arthritic condition so severe that, when it came time to orchestrate the piece, Holst had to recruit two of his St. Paul's colleagues to do the physical labor according to his directions. At last, the epic work was finished and given its private premiere in 1918.

The first public performance followed in 1920, at which point the unthinkable happened: the public, enamored of the music, clamored for the composer. Holst was horrified. He dreaded the attentions of admirers, loathed the parties given in his honor, and resented the new-found pressure to write popular tunes. Certainly, the extra income generated by such popularity was appreciated, but Holst set greater store by his solitude, which vanished with the appearance of *The Planets*. When his popularity at last waned a decade later, due in large part to the composer's active avoidance of attention, Holst was greatly relieved to regain his private life.

Holst's grand composition portrays the seven non-earthly planets then known to exist (Pluto having yet to be either discovered or demoted). His inspiration came not from astronomy, nor even from mythology. Rather, astrology, as in horoscopes, drove Holst's imagination, and the composer was always quite clear that Greek and Roman gods should be nowhere in sight. "These pieces," he wrote, "were suggested by the astrological significance of the planets. There is no program music in them, neither have they any connection with the deities of classical mythology bearing the same names. If any guide to the music is required, the subtitle to each piece will be found sufficient, especially if it is used in a broad sense. For instance, Jupiter brings jollity in the ordinary sense, and also the more ceremonial kind of rejoicing associated with religious or national festivities. Saturn brings not only physical decay, but also a vision of fulfillment. Mercury is the symbol of the mind." So here are those subtitles which the composer suggests should answer all questions of meaning:

- Mars, the Bringer of War (grim and brassy; viewed by many as evocative of the war-stricken period in which Holst was living)

- Venus, the Bringer of Peace (gentle flutes and strings; a sweetly romantic mood)

- Mercury, the Winged Messenger (lively and spirited; the shortest of the seven scenes)

- Jupiter, the Bringer of Jollity (jovial in the truest sense; surging themes for strings and brass and changing meters to keep performers on their toes)

- Saturn, the Bringer of Old Age (ominous in mood; the most ponderous of the seven scenes)

- Uranus, the Magician (buoyantly reminiscent of Dukas' *The Sorcerer's Apprentice*)

- Neptune, the Mystic (haunting and ethereal, with a wordless women's chorus fading away in the final bars)

- Ives: *Orchestral Set no. 1 — Three Places in New England*

A native of Danbury, Connecticut, Charles Ives (1874-1954) came by his avant garde interests through his father, a former Civil War army bandsman. The elder Ives liked to gather the family around the piano and have them sing in so-called 'quarter-tones:' pitches between the actual keys. Also fond of polytonality, he would ask them sing simultaneously, though in several different keys. In leading the town band for summer concerts, the elder Ives occasionally divided his band in two, sent them to different locations in the town park, and then had them play different music, so that one might — by locating one's self between their positions — hear two different musical ideas at once. All these unusual approaches come to play in the son's music, and often those simultaneous themes would be readily recognizable all-American tunes.

The younger Ives were so progressive that he was the despair of his music professors at Yale; the college baseball coach, for whom Ives served as pitcher, was almost the only staff member to appreciate young Ives' efforts. Reasoning that the musical public would likely react to his compositions as his professors had, Ives saw that he would need to choose between two alternatives: either adapt to expectation and write music as the rules dictated, or find another means of fiscal support, so that he could compose as he wished without worrying about earning much money from it. He took the later approach, becoming a very successful insurance agent, a field that attracted him due to his own health insurance needs from a heart condition.

Ives composed mostly in his spare time and in publishing his music at his own cost, asked his publishers to make it available for free, so that it would more readily find audiences. Few other composers in history have been in a place to make such an offer, as few others had an independent career separate from music. That Ives was so placed allowed him to write works that were decades ahead of their time. His Symphony no. 3, completed in 1905, would not have its premiere until 1946, and then won the Pulitzer Prize for Music the following year. Piqued at such belated recognition, Ives gave the Prize back, though his name still stands on the list of those honored.

For insight into Ives' quirky musical vision, consider his *Orchestral Set no. 1 — Three Places in New England.* Completed in 1914, it takes the listener on a journey through historic and natural locations in Massachusetts and Connecticut, all the while drawing upon the composer's fondness for juxtaposing sharply contrasting, sometimes dissonant, melodic ideas. Ives' wife's name was Harmony, but one doesn't find much conventional harmony in his music.

In the first movement, "The St. Gaudens in Boston Common," offers a vision of "Col. Shaw and his Colored Regiment," the Civil War leader and his forces that are portrayed in a bas relief sculpture in Boston Common. A poetic preface printed in the musical score describes the scene: of a ghostly procession of soldiers steadily passing over a hill, their pace changing as the pitch of the hill varies, the Civil War setting brought home by fragments of Civil War tunes, which Ives would have learned from his father.

The second movement, "Putnam's Camp, Redding, Connecticut," imagines an Independence Day celebration at which a young boy wanders away from the crowd to drowse in the fields with dreams of the Revolutionary War winter camp that had been there. Melodies sampled in this movement include *British Grenadiers* and *Columbia, the Gem of the Ocean*. With a startling, clamorous crash, the boy awakes and rejoins the present day.

For the final movement, Ives has had enough of war reminiscence and instead sets out to evoke "The Housatonic at Stockbridge," remembering a time when he and Harmony were walking by the banks of that river, hearing church hymns from a worship service on the opposite bank. In his youth, Ives had been a church organist and easily called forth hymn tunes to flavor this final movement, closing the set of pieces more quietly than one might have expected from earlier outbursts. Only the brass-laden chords just before the final bars recall the tumultuous moods of the earlier movements. If one wished to find a quick, quarter-hour introduction to the essence of Charles Ives, *Three Places in New England* would be a fine choice.

- Respighi: *The Pines of Rome*

In a nation of composers devoted to opera and the church, Ottorino Respighi (1879-1936) was a markedly atypical Italian. He produced exactly one sacred work and completed only eight thoroughly insignificant operas, including one intended for a marionette theater. The two fields that absorbed so much of his countrymen's attention simply did not interest Respighi, whose divergent focus resulted from his training. Although Respighi had begun music studies in his native Bologna at the age of twelve, his strongest inspiration came in Russia, where he studied for three years while in his early twenties. Immersing himself in the Russian symphonic school that had originated with Peter Tchaikovsky (1840-1893), he came to appreciate the expressive potential of the symphonic genre. Orchestration studies followed, under the guidance of the acknowledged master of the field, Nicolai Rimsky-Korsakov (1844-1908), who encouraged his student's growing interest in colorful, vibrant scoring. In the process, the young Italian developed a musical language more typical of Russia, though still flavored with Italian sun.

Respighi's masterworks are his orchestral pieces, notably the so-called Roman trilogy: *The Fountains of Rome, The Pines of Rome*, and *Roman Festivals. Fountains* was the first of the three, premiering in 1917; *Pines* followed seven years later. In his own notes to the piece, the composer wrote, "While in *The Fountains of Rome*, the composer sought to reproduce by means of tones an impression of nature, in *The Pines of Rome*, he uses nature as a point of departure, to recall memories and visions. The century-old trees which dominate so characteristically the Roman landscape become testimony for the principal events in Roman life." *The Pines of Rome* premiered in 1924 in the city whose name it bears. It was a spectacular success, and within two years, Arturo Toscanini conducted the work with the New York Philharmonic in Carnegie Hall.

The Pines of Rome is structured in four movements, each of which has its own subtitle, though they are played without pause, so that the music flows uninterrupted from beginning to end. In the first, "The Pines of Villa Borghese," children are at play in the pine groves, with music that implies rambunctious action all around. For contrast, the second section "The Pines near a Catacomb," sets mournful hymn-like phrases against a dark tapestry of mostly string tones. A lighter mood returns for the third section "The Pines of the Janiculum," in which Respighi attested that he was imagining a moonlit scene with nightingales singing. Originally, he asked that a record of an actual nightingale be played, though more often, the melody is given to the flute. For the conclusion of the work, he takes his listeners to "The Pines of the Appian Way" with visions of the ancient past and the Roman army — trumpets blazing — marching in toward the capital city. It makes for a truly grand finale.

- Villa-Lobos: *Bachianas Brasileiras no. 2*

Brazilian-born Heitor Villa-Lobos (1887-1959) grew up with a fascination for the folk music of his native land. He heard it performed on the streets of Rio, and before long this young cellist and guitarist was participating in such performances, learning intimately the intricate constructions and melodic variations inherent in these works. Once he began to pursue more formal musical studies, Villa-Lobos became aware that some features of his nation's folk music had their counterparts in the music of Johann Sebastian Bach (1685-1750: much more about him in future chapters). For example, the Brazilian "conversa," in which musicians echo and answer each other's melodies, is not unlike a Bach fugue, and the lyrical "modinha" is reminiscent of Bach's graceful ariosi. These similarities inspired Villa-Lobos to compose nine instrumental suites that he called *Bachianas Brasileiras*, which could mean "Bach in the style of Brazil," or "Brazil in the style of Bach." In either case, Villa-Lobos chose to emphasize the parallel by giving two names to each movement, one drawn from Brazilian music, the other from the forms of Bach.

The various *Bachianas Brasileiras* suites have sharply varying sets of performers, ranging from small-scale chamber music to grand orchestral works. The second suite, dating originally from 1933, leans more toward the latter, though in its original form, it was for cello and piano, then for solo piano; only later did the full orchestra version arrive on the scene. Structured in four movements, the work is programmatic in nature, with each movement offering a different, rather specific view into Brazilian life.

The languid mood of the opening movement speaks of a casual fellow who ambles through his days. By contrast, the second movement, though little faster in tempo, yet offers a stronger energy, first with a broad, flowing, anthem-like melody, and then a slinky theme in which both saxophone and trombone have prominent roles; the anthem-like theme returns to close the movement. In the third movement, there are similar structures, with the opening melody being repeated to close the movement, while a contrasting theme, here a folk-flavored dance, occupies the middle. For the final movement, Villa Lobos offers what he described as an impression of a little country train carrying villagers and farm workers. The movement opens with steam and acceleration effects. Its flowing main theme evokes the little train's progress through the countryside until, with the gradual slowing of tempo and more gushes of steam, it glides into the next station.

- Revueltas: *Sensemayá*

A near contemporary of his better-known countryman Carlos Chávez (see Chapter Two), Silvestre Revueltas (1899-1940) was born in the northern Mexican state of Durango. His musical studies began with the violin at age eight and expanded to composition studies both in Mexico City and in Austin, Texas. Advanced studies would follow in Chicago. In his mid-twenties, Revueltas earned a living as a violinist and conductor in the southern United States. By the age of thirty, he had returned home at Chávez's request to lead the Mexico Symphony Orchestra in Mexico City. He also taught at the city's music conservatory and composed a series of lively, colorful orchestral works for his ensemble. In the late 1930s, Revueltas toured Spain where he became fascinated with the Republican cause. He died all too young back in Mexico City of the effects of alcoholism.

Revueltas' catalog includes operas, orchestral pieces, chamber works (amongst them two string quartets), solo piano pieces, songs, and even film scores. Perhaps in part due to their vivid tone colors, his orchestral pieces have earned the most attention. *Sensemayá* (Revueltas insisted that the title has no meaning, and is only a sound picture of its own) premiered December 18, 1938, with the Orquesta Sinfónica de México and came to the US in 1945 thanks to conductor Leopold Stokowski. Inspired by a poem by Afro-Cuban writer Nicolás Guillen, the piece concerns a formidable serpent, coiled and awaiting its next victim. The score's rhythmic complexity may be seen as conveying the serpent's motions; its unusual, sometimes dissonant, harmonies evoke a strong sense of impending doom. Along with the standard orchestral instruments, Revueltas called for an array of diverse percussion, including timpani, piano, xylophone, claves, maracas, bass drum, tom toms, cymbals, gong, glockenspiel, celesta, gourds, and raspador. Although not all are of Latin origin, even those with European roots serve to evoke a steamy Latin mood. The effect is less in the instrument itself than in how it is used, and Revueltas knew well the sounds of Mexican folk idioms.

- Britten: *Young Person's Guide to the Orchestra*, op. 34

Benjamin Britten (1913-1976) is widely considered to be the finest English composer since the death of Henry Purcell back in 1695. It was not that English audiences spent two centuries disinterested in great music; rather, they seemed to prefer their music imported, particularly from Germany as the British success of such German-born stars as Handel and Mendelssohn proved. English composers tended to attract little attention and have little impact. Perhaps the fact that Britten's birthday was November 22 — special day of St. Cecelia, patron saint of music — allowed him to rise from that obscurity.

Some observers would quarrel with placing Britten next on the pedestal, particularly those devoted to Edward Elgar, Ralph Vaughan Williams, or Gustav Holst, all of whom were born decades before Britten. Yet each of those men, though greatly gifted and much admired, failed to attract attention as quickly as Britten did, and none of those three masters proved as firmly as did Britten that the English language can find a powerful home on the operatic stage. We'll have more about his work in opera in Chapter Eight. Moreover, none of them founded an international music festival that over half a century later is still drawing audiences for the significance of its music old and new, as Britten's Aldeburgh Festival is. Here is a man who decades after his death is still influencing classical music in his native England and around the world.

Shortly after the close of World War II, Britten set to work on his most enduring composition: the *Young Person's Guide to the Orchestra*, op. 34, also known as the *Variations and Fugue on a Theme of Purcell*. Written at the request of the British Ministry of Education for use in the educational film *Instruments of the Orchestra*, the piece was intended to introduce new listeners to the varying voices within the orchestra. Such a mission could have been accomplished with a very simple work, but such was not Britten's plan. Instead, he chose a stately dance theme from Henry Purcell's 1695 stage music for *Abdelazer, or The Moor's Revenge* (see Chapter Nine), and began his own work by having different sections of the orchestra state the theme in turn. Next, he offered variant forms of the theme for each featured instrument, not neglecting to spotlight the percussion, and lastly combined all the sections of the orchestra in an intricate fugue on a new theme derived from the original, with each part stating the new melody in turn as overlapping layers of music gradually emerge. Thus, the piece not only allows listeners to hear the contrasting voices of the instruments but also offers a peek into musical techniques of earlier centuries, showing how a melody can bounce from one instrument to another in sequence while other melodic ideas occupy the background. The title may refer to "young persons", but it is a work that can be enjoyed by all, even those who are musically knowledgeable, as there is interest in following the melodies in their motion.

- Ligeti: *Atmosphères*

Born in the Hungarian town of Dicsőszentmárton (today Tîrnăveni), György Ligeti (1923-2006) was of exactly an age that World War II disrupted his education. He studied some music during the war in Klausenberg and then after the conflict at the Liszt Academy in Budapest. Very early in his compositional development, he became interested in the effects of combining various melodies simultaneously and of using very small intervals between one pitch and the next, intervals that a standard piano cannot easily achieve but string instruments and the human voice can. So both polyphony and quarter-tones find their way into his works.

With the Hungarian Revolution in 1956 and the rise of the Communists who opposed modern music, Ligeti left his homeland in favor of West Germany where he would ultimately obtain a post as professor of composition. Yet he never allowed academia to distract him from composition, continuing to compose prolifically and to promote his music on the international scene. His music achieved perhaps its widest audience when his work *Atmosphères* was included in the closing scenes of *2001: A Space Odyssey*. Ligeti later recalled that Kubrick had not asked his permission to use the music but apparently was a fan of the composer, though the two had never met. Ligeti was open-minded enough not to be angered by the filmmaker's action; audience, it seems, is a good thing even if one is not expecting it.

Atmosphères was commissioned by Southwest German Radio and premiered in Donaueschingen, West Germany, October 22, 1961. Of the work, the composer observed, "The sonorous texture is so dense that the individual interwoven instrumental voices are absorbed into the general texture, and completely lose their individuality." He allows sound combinations to become more important than structural rules or expansion and development of themes. Here, in place of those old Brahmsian ideals, subtle shifts of tone color are the continuing focus, resulting in an ever-varying tapestry of sound. The resulting score, in which each individual string player has a distinct part, rather than some duplicating others, is haunting and vaguely dissonant. Long sustained chords build through gradual alteration of pitch, with an increasing sense of building tension. Here, Ligeti declares, "Tone color, usually a vehicle of musical form, is liberated from form to become an independent entity."

- Adams: *Short Ride in a Fast Machine*

Massachusetts native John Adams (b. 1947) grew up at a lakeside resort in New Hampshire: far from the capitals of music, but not far from music itself, for both of his parents were musical and his grandfather ran a lakeside dance hall where Duke Ellington once played. Young John learned clarinet as a boy and played in the school marching band. He also composed for and sometimes conducted the community orchestra. Scholarship studies in Boston followed. However, the young composer felt out of time, for at Harvard only the most modern techniques were popular. A similar situation arose after graduation, when Adams accepted a teaching post at San Francisco Conservatory of Music. "I'd go to avant garde events," he later recalled, "and then drive home to end the evening deep in a Beethoven quartet." Therein one finds Adams' style in a nutshell: modern on the surface, yet retaining respect for the masters. That combination of inspirations has helped him to become this nation's most universally respected living composer, a Pulitzer Prize winner whose works attract both performances and admiration around the world.

Adams' *Short Ride in a Fast Machine* was one of his early triumphs. Written in 1986 for the Pittsburgh Symphony, the piece is essentially a fanfare. It is also a masterpiece of what has been termed lyrical minimalism: taking the repetitive rhythms made famous by Philip Glass (b. 1937) and twining them into a web of intricate musical texture. Note how the flute motif with which the piece opens is not that of the woodblock that joins moments later, and neither is related to that of the brass that come next in line. Yet the three patterns together create a scene of energy and excitement with an infectious musical drive that propels the listener into the heart of the composition. Repetitive without being redundant, *Short Ride* brings melodic flow back into a realm from which it has often been absent. In the hands of John Adams, modern music still sings.

- Daughtery: *Route 66*

Iowa native Michael Daughtery (b. 1954) has a reputation for dramatic and colorful orchestral scores often inspired by quintessential elements of the American experience. Amongst his titles are *Dead Elvis*, *Jackie O*, and *Brooklyn Bridge*. Few images evoke a wider swath of Americana than the old highway Route 66, which in the pre-Interstate years was the most travelled connection between Chicago and Los Angeles. Of his work on that theme, the composer says it is "a musical reflection on America, as seen through my rear view window."

Whether one takes that mirror literally, as an automotive attachment, or figuratively, as gazing back over the decades, either vision suits this orchestral piece. There is rhythmic drive, lyrical flow, and ever-changing impressions, made particularly vivid by Daughtery's orchestration. With instruments ranging from piccolo to contrabassoon and a percussion section that, along with the usual suspects, includes cowbells, bongo, and three different types of cymbals, there is nothing seen or felt along old Route 66 that could not be evoked by a composer of Daughtery's creative gifts. Listeners' imaginations can call forth their own specifics. In the composer's words, bring your own "emotions and associations into the musical experience."

- Higdon: *blue cathedral*

A native of Brooklyn, Jennifer Higdon (b. 1962) was raised in Atlanta and began her musical education with the flute. Composition only took the lead for her master's and doctoral degrees from the University of Pennsylvania, when experiences as a performer led her to realize that she had her own compositional ideas to express. Her early works were mostly chamber music, for when one is little known, it is easier and more affordable to assemble a small group of performers than a large one. However, as her reputation grew, she has become well-known for her vibrant orchestral scores, which have been performed by most major orchestras and have attracted favorable attention even in such popular media as *USA Today*. Speaking with this writer, Higdon described the joy of writing for full orchestra rather than for the smaller forces of a chamber ensemble as comparable to being a child with the giant box of Crayolas rather than the little box: all those varied colors at one's disposal. "There's a huge color palette in that orchestra," she says. "Use it!"

Higdon's *blue cathedral* (she told this writer that she chose the lower case letters for poetic effect) was written in 1999 at the request of pianist Gary Graffman for the Curtis Institute, where Higdon had earned her bachelor's degree. The color in the title is borrowed from the middle name of her brother, who had recently passed away. Higdon observes, "I just got to thinking about how many people cross your life, cross your path. All the events that occur in a lifetime. So that's the solo passages in the middle of the work, representing the people you meet." As for the cathedral reference, she says that came to mind from the Curtis Institute connection, "that Curtis — like a cathedral in the old times — represented a body of knowledge." Monet's Rouen Cathedral paintings, though generally blue in tone, are unrelated to the score, as Higdon attests she first saw those images after completing her work. Yet she admits there is a "similar mood:" serene, reserved, and floating with gentle and subtle changes of atmosphere.

Further Recommendations:

Here is a selection of other interesting orchestral pieces for which there was not room in the main body of the chapter:

- Georg Philipp Telemann (1681-1767): Friend and colleague of JS Bach — and godfather to one of Bach's sons — Telemann wrote much music to entertain in the royal courts as well as for civic festivities. His *Tafelmusik* suites (literally "table music") were intended originally for the former, as entertainment for aristocratic dinners.

- Felix Mendelssohn (1809-1847): *Calm Sea and Prosperous Voyage* Overture — deriving from two Goethe poems, in which sailors first despair over being becalmed at sea, and then rejoice when the wind brings them safely home again. Being apparently an optimist, Mendelssohn finishes with the despair fairly promptly, thus spending more time with the joy.

- Camille Saint-Saëns (1835-1921): *Carnival of the Animals* — a witty zoological fantasy; the composer was so worried that its high spirits would undermine his serious reputation that he refused to allow it to be performed or published during his lifetime. Its most famous movement is the big cello solo for "The Swan."

- Antonín Dvořák (1841-1904): *Carnival* Overture, op. 92 — the Czech master's effervescent vision of a lively gathering of townspeople, with the vivid coloration of folk dancing in the streets.

- Nicolai Rimsky-Korsakov (1844-1908): *Capriccio espagnole* — Rimsky-Korsakov was thoroughly Russian, but here offers a fantasy rich with the liveliness of Spanish folk rhythms. So challenging is it to play that he dedicated it to every individual member of the orchestra (naming each by name) that gave its premiere.

- Frederick Delius (1862-1934): *North Country Sketches* — The "north country" this Englishman had in mind was Yorkshire, with its moors and changeable weather, evoked with a British twist on the styles of Impressionism.

- Paul Dukas (1865-1935): The Frenchman wrote a fair quantity of music, but is now remembered mostly for his colorfully evocative *Sorcerer's Apprentice*, which brings to most minds visions of Mickey Mouse and rebellious brooms.

- Ralph Vaughan Williams (1872-1958): *Fantasia of a Theme by Thomas Tallis* — a lush string work of hymn-like rapture drawing upon a melody by his Elizabethan predecessor (more about Tallis in Chapter Eleven).

- Arthur Honegger (1892-1955): Of Swiss parentage, Honegger studied at the Paris Conservatoire and was one of the first film composers. In the orchestral realm, his tone poem *Pacific 231* is a musical evocation of a powerful locomotive. Consider also his gentle *Pastorale d'été* (*Summer Pastorale*).

- Ferde Grofé (1892-1972): Most influential in the world of great music through having assisted George Gershwin in preparing the music for the premiere of *Rhapsody in Blue* (see Chapter Four), Grofé was also a composer himself, especially known for his *Grand Canyon Suite*.

- George Gershwin (1898-1937): Gershwin's *An American in Paris* is a spirited musical recollection of the American's visit to the French capital, familiar to some from the Gene Kelly movie of the same name (the film made after Gershwin's death).

- Dmitri Shostakovich (1906-1975): His two *Jazz Suites* don't sound like what Gershwin would call "jazz," but they are a more cheerful side to this sometimes dark composer. Anyone who had to pursue his career under the shadow of Stalin had an excuse for being occasionally dark, but here he briefly sets it aside.

- Karl Jenkins (b. 1944): The Welsh composer is more often heard in the UK than in the US. However, his orchestral suite *Palladio* became widely familiar when its first movement was borrowed by the DeBeers diamond company for a television ad.

- Michael Torke (b. 1961): The American has made a name for his short, colorful orchestral pieces. Notable amongst them are the vibrant *Javelin* (written for the 1996 Olympics in Atlanta) and the more reflective *December* (recalling the composer's childhood in Milwaukee)

Chapter Four

Concertos

It's the opening of Felix Mendelssohn's Violin Concerto in e minor: a work so famed that German audiences, tongues firmly in cheek, have given it words. To Mendelssohn's notes, they croon, "Schon wieder, schon wieder, das Mendelssohn Konzert" — "Yet again, yet again, that Mendelssohn Concerto." Indeed, it is a regular feature of concerts, as are many of the other works detailed in this chapter, but works become favorites by being exceptionally well crafted. The Mendelssohn and the other works here are notably fine examples of what one can do with a concerto. So what is a concerto?

Take an orchestra. Add one or more featured soloists to stand up front in the spotlight and play the most attention-grabbing music, and the result is a concerto. The term comes from an Italian word meaning to contest or contend, and the idea is that the soloist and the orchestra are contesting with one another for dominance. Ideally, the contest should be amicably resolved to a point of satisfactory balance amongst the forces.

Concertos — the fancy Italianate plural is "concerti," but we can speak English here — originated late in the Baroque Era when technological improvements to instruments (especially strings) made it desirable to give them focused attention, whereas previously the human voice had been the star. Most concertos have three movements (the first with a fast tempo, the second slow, and the last fast). Overall length will vary, from ten minutes or so in the Baroque to three-quarters of an hour or more by the mid 1800s. Often, concertos include sections called 'cadenzas:' totally solo portions in which the orchestra waits while the soloist plays on, possibly improvising.

The instruments most frequently favored in the solo position are piano and violin. However, concertos have been composed to feature virtual any imaginable instrument, especially in recent years. This chapter includes not only concertos for piano or for violin, but also those for viola, cello, clarinet, oboe, trumpet, French horn, and guitar, as well as one recent work that shines the spotlight on the double bass, banjo, and tabla: all three together. Sometimes, the featured solo instrument is one at which the composer himself is a virtuoso; at other times, he intended the work as a showpiece for a friend or colleague. A composer may also write on "commission," that is, that someone has paid for this specific work to be composed.

- Vivaldi: *The Four Seasons* (Violin Concertos, op. 8, no. 1- 4)

They called him the "Red Priest." He was Antonio Vivaldi (1685-1741): violinist, composer, teacher, charismatic personification of the Italian Baroque. Here was a man who, in addition to his priestly duties and his responsibilities as director of a girl's school in Venice, found time to write dozens of operas and over four hundred concertos, while continuing to tour actively as a violin soloist. Eventually, the religious and academic careers took a back seat to musical pursuits. By 1737, the red-haired padre was under official censure for conduct unbecoming a priest. His clerical career ended in disgrace, even as his musical reputation was beginning to wane. Despite the notoriety that had accompanied his adult life, Vivaldi ended his earthly days in obscurity. Yet it may be that he had the last laugh, for now Vivaldi's reputation stands higher than ever, and any personal shortcomings are long since forgotten.

Of his many hundreds of compositions, Vivaldi's best known are the *Four Seasons* concertos, published in 1725, nearly a century before compositions with plot content — later generations would call it "program music" — became popular. In Vivaldi's time, composers were expected to master rules and structures, not express feelings and paint musical landscapes. That he managed to do both simultaneously may be why his *Four Seasons* concertos have been popular for nearly three hundred years. These four violin concertos are part of a set of twelve known collectively as *The Contest between Harmony and Invention*, that is, between structure and creativity. The other eight concertos, numbers five through twelve of the set, have nothing to do with seasons. It is only the first four that are so beloved in music.

So as to be certain that his listeners, and indeed, his performers, knew exactly what he envisioned in each season, Vivaldi provided for each concerto a sonnet describing the scenes at hand, even copying the lines of the sonnets into the musical score so as to draw unmistakable parallels between specific words and specific sounds. Historians are uncertain as to whether or not the composer himself originally penned the poetry, yet the music lies astonishingly close to the words. Listen, in "Spring," as three violins entwine in birdsong until a thunderstorm interrupts their song, as violas stand in for a barking dog who awakes his master, as drawn-out undertones evoke the drone of a bagpipe for a village dance. Marvel, in "Summer," as the turtledove (in Italian, "tortorella") sings to the rhythm of her name, as the rumbles of low strings provide the buzzing of flies, as the strident themes of a summer hailstorm flatten the farmer's fields. Observe, in "Autumn," the unsteady footsteps of a drunken reveler at a harvest celebration, then the revelers sleeping off their celebration, until later, they awake to prancing themes of bold hunters and their steeds in pursuit of their crafty prey, which will ultimately fall to their shots. Shiver with Vivaldi through a frosty "Winter" as bitter winds blow; then a weary traveler warms his feet by the fire while others, less fortunate, slip and fall on the ice. Of all the musical landscapes painted over the centuries, no other goes to such extremes to evoke tiny details of man's interactions with nature.

- JS Bach: Brandenburg Concertos, BWV 1046 - 1051

No composer even came of more determined musical lineage than Johann Sebastian Bach (1685-1750). For three hundred years, the Bach family was influential in music in central Germany, as composers, performers and teachers. JS Bach appeared approximately in the middle of that family tradition and is handily the most familiar and most respected of the many Bachs. His textbooks on how to play the keyboard and how to write a fugue are still studied today. He was one of the most admired organists of his day, and his music was known to scholars throughout the continent, although he himself was no traveler. Throughout his life, Bach never travelled more than about one hundred miles from his birthplace in Eisenach. Early in his life, he composed mostly for the small German royal courts, which were highly numerous, as the nation was far from united. His last three decades were spent with the church in Leipzig. Thus, in his earlier years, he composed mostly instrumental music for royal entertainment and in his later years, sacred works. In both worlds, he set the standard for intricate perfection.

Late in 1718, Bach traveled to Berlin to order a new harpsichord. While there, he performed for the Margrave Christian Ludwig of Brandenburg, younger brother of the Prussian ruler. No information remains as to specifically what works Bach played, but it must have been an impressive concert, for the Margrave soon commissioned several compositions. Such royal requests could be quite lucrative for a composer; however, this project was less than profitable. Two years passed before Bach delivered a set of six concertos scored for diverse soloists. Even once the pieces arrived, the Margrave never paid for them. Perhaps he knew then what historians have learned since: that these so-called "Brandenburg Concertos" were not new and were not specifically composed for the Margrave himself. Instead, they were revisions of earlier works, essentially gleaned from Bach's composition files. The composer was passing off old as new, but in one respect, the Margrave was well served. Thanks to Bach's efforts, the Brandenburg name is recalled fondly throughout the musical world.

Technically, the Brandenburg Concertos — of which there are six individual works — are concertos grosso, a popular Baroque genre in which multiple soloists are contrasted with a small orchestra. In the case of the Brandenburg Concerto no. 1, those soloists are so numerous that the work is virtually symphonic. At various points in the work, Bach crafted solo roles for one violin, three oboes, one bassoon, and two horns, nearly as many musicians as might make up the entire small orchestra. The Brandenburg no. 2 has trumpet (written perilously high), recorder (or flute), oboe, and violin. The Third features three each of violins, violas, and cellos, the Fourth two flutes and a violin, and the Fifth flute, violin, and harpsichord. The Sixth, the only one to have no violins whatsoever, spotlights the lower strings, supplemented, as always, by the harpsichord. Although a superior court orchestra would have had no difficulty in fielding such a large and diverse number of virtuoso players, the Margrave's orchestra was less skilled. As a younger son, he lacked the resources to support such a talented ensemble. Musicologists believe this piece was never played at the Brandenburg court.

- Hummel: Trumpet Concerto in E- flat major

He was Haydn's successor at Esterhazy, and Liszt's predecessor at Weimar, a student of Mozart and Haydn, a teacher of Mendelssohn, and a friend of Goethe and Beethoven. His piano teaching method became so popular that it is still in use today. He was Johann Nepomuk Hummel (1778-1837), praised in his time as having unsurpassed improvisation skills and even today considered one of the most important pianist-composers.

Hummel was born in Pressburg, which later became Bratislava; by the time he was eight, his family had moved to Vienna so as to better foster the boy's musical talents. In that cultural atmosphere, Johann was inevitably compared to Mozart, about twenty years his senior. Happily, this musical prodigy enjoyed a longer life and a more steadily successful career. Hummel first earned his living as a court musician and composer, a teacher and touring pianist. His keen business sense led him to work successfully for the systematization of international publishing and copyright laws. Widely admired for his musical talents, Hummel nevertheless remained unto his death an unassuming person, one who far preferred the quiet delights of gardening to the intricacies of court politics. His death in 1837 was marked in Vienna by a performance of Mozart's *Requiem*.

Trumpeters like to call it "the Hummel," as if there were no other works by the man. In fact, Hummel's Trumpet Concerto is only one of many hundreds of pieces, notably solo piano pieces and chamber music, a half dozen piano concertos, nearly twenty operas, and a variety of short orchestral works. Of all those, the Trumpet Concerto stands out, if for no other reason, than for its rarity. Very few trumpet showcases predate it, because of the challenges of playing the instrument's early versions, which lacked valves. Without them, finding a particular pitch required deft manipulation of lip position and pressure, with somewhat unpredictable results. Even Hummel's immediate predecessor, Haydn, had only an interim instrument at his disposal for his Trumpet Concerto in 1796. When Hummel composed his concerto in 1803, valves were a very new and long overdue conception, allowing composers at last to write more challenging solo parts for the instrument and remain confident that the music would come out as imagined. Look for much spirited interchange between the soloist and the orchestra, with the trumpet featured both in strictly solo passages, often very lyrical, and occasionally soaring above the orchestral texture.

- Mozart: Piano Concerto no. 21 in C major, K. 467

If one wished to learn everything there is to know about Mozart, but could only study a single type of composition, the best choice would be the piano concerto. In this one area, Mozart produced roughly thirty compositions, more piano concertos than any other important composer. Additionally, the concertos span his entire career. The first was written when he was only eleven; the last appeared less than a year before his death. Considering the entire range of these works shows how Mozart's style developed, and it shows how the Classical style as a whole came into being, for his earliest piano concertos are close adaptations of Baroque sonatas, whereas his final few works in the genre hint at the passion and power that would become popular at the turn of the century. As Mozart and his concertos matured, so did music history reach a new stage of development.

It was in March of 1785 that Mozart composed his Concerto no. 21, completing it merely one month after his previous concerto. He would write four more in the next twenty months. Each of those concertos was written for Mozart himself to perform in concert in Vienna. Since he intended to act as soloist, he did not bother to write out the solo cadenzas, deciding instead to improvise them on the spot. Such a practice brought great verve and spontaneity to a performance, but unfortunately it has left us without the composer's own cadenzas. Since Mozart's time, pianists have had to compose their own cadenzas, or use those created by others. For any modern pianist to match the master's seemingly effortless style is always challenging, but it is particularly so in this case, for this concerto is among the most technically demanding of all Mozart's concerti. The composer's own father, Leopold Mozart, described the Concerto no. 21 as "astonishingly difficult." Today, it is less frequently remembered for its difficulty than for its lyrical second movement, which was prominently featured in the 1967 Swedish film, "Elvira Madigan."

- Mozart: Clarinet Concerto in A major, K. 622

The majority of Mozart's concertos feature the piano; however he did not completely overlook other instruments. There are five violin concertos and concertos for clarinet, oboe, bassoon, French horn, flute, flute-and-harp, violin-and-viola, and one further for four wind soloists. Nearly all of those concertos over were written for a particular soloist to perform. The piano works were generally for Mozart himself, and he was up to the violin ones, too, but the other concertos were for his friends and colleagues: musicians with whom he worked on a regular basis, and the solo parts were adapted to their specific skills. Today, these works still carry the echo of a two-century old musical partnership, as we hear the composer's faith in a friend's talents.

Mozart's only clarinet concerto was completed just two months before his death. The work was intended for Vienna's greatest clarinetist, Anton Stadler (1753-1812). With his brother Johann, who was also a clarinetist, Anton Stadler served on the staff of the Russian ambassador to Vienna before taking positions in the imperial court wind band and imperial orchestra. He was also a composer in a small way and a popular teacher who counted members of the aristocratic Esterhazy family (for whom Haydn worked for so many years) amongst his students. Even before the completion of this concerto, Anton Stadler was well familiar with Mozart's music, for he had joined in many concert performances of his friend's symphonies and operas. On a more personal level, he received from Mozart a lovely clarinet quintet, and the prominent clarinet parts in the opera *La Clemenza di Tito* were composed specifically for Stadler, whom Mozart brought to Prague for the opera's premiere. Perhaps he knew that Stadler's skill exceeded that of Czech clarinetists, or he may have wanted to give his friend and lodge brother the opportunity to shine in a new venue. Certainly, that opportunity lies also in the pages of the Clarinet Concerto, which blends gently lyric passages with those of demanding virtuosity to create a true masterpiece of the repertoire.

Mozart adapted his melodies specifically to Stadler's own instrument, which had a more extended low range than standard clarinets. This approach allowed Stadler to showcase the famed purity of his tone even at the extremes of the clarinet's range, but it also meant that, in its original form, the concerto could never be played by any other clarinetist. When the concerto was finally published a decade after Mozart's death, some enterprising editor, dreaming of increased marketability, altered the problematic low notes so that they could be played on a standard clarinet. It may have been good business, but, in the process, Mozart's own score vanished, and, without a manuscript to refer to, the original notes can never be restored. Thus, for over two hundred years, audiences have had to settle for the concerto's modified version without ever hearing the work exactly as Mozart imagined it. Even this revised version is worthy of discovery, as it is not only melodic and graceful, but also gives attention to an instrument that does not often take center stage. Besides, the melodies and other big ideas are genuine Mozart; all the changes were to small details.

- Beethoven: Piano Concerto no. 5 in E-flat major, op. 73, "Emperor"

Scan the list of persons to whom Beethoven dedicated his compositions, and more than any other name, one finds that of Rudolf Johann Joseph Rainer von Hapsburg, better known as the Archduke Rudolf. Compositions dedicated to the Archduke include the Triple Concerto, the *Grosse Fugue*, the *Missa Solemnis*, two piano concertos, two piano sonatas, one violin sonata, and the eponymous "*Archduke*" Trio. About the last of these: more in Chapter Five. In some hands, such tributes might have carried mercenary undertones, with the hope of earning a healthy fee in return for a dedication. Yet here there is clear evidence that Beethoven was not merely placating a wealthy supporter, for the Archduke was friend as well as student, a musically talented young nobleman who accepted Beethoven and his compositions despite the eccentricities of both. That Beethoven remained close to Rudolf even after his own reputation became well-established stands as proof that the composer was not merely using the young man for his own gains. He was, apparently, grateful for the Archduke's attention and friendship.

Prominent amongst the works dedicated to the Archduke is the last of Beethoven's five piano concertos. He began the work in 1808, around the time that the Fifth and Sixth Symphonies and the Fourth Concerto were completed. Despite the grand scale of the piece, Beethoven finished it promptly, at least by his own usually arduous standards, and the new concerto was ready for its premiere in Leipzig in 1811. One might have expected that, on that occasion, Beethoven himself would have performed the solo part, as he had for the premieres of each previous piano concerto. By this time, however, his ever-problematic hearing had declined to the point of profound deafness, and public performance was no longer an option. The honor of the premiere went to a twenty-five year old church organist, Friedrich Schneider. Three months later, in February 1812, the concerto was given its Vienna premiere. The pianist on that occasion was Beethoven's student, Carl Czerny, a man still renowned in keyboard circles today for his own piano pieces. Thanks to its bold melodies and heroic spirit, the new concerto quickly won for itself a place in the piano repertoire, and even became a great favorite of Franz Liszt.

The Fifth Concerto's sobriquet, *"Emperor,"* dates from Beethoven's time, but not from Beethoven himself, for he very rarely gave nicknames to his works. Besides, since the composer had little regard for emperors, he would be unlikely to name one of his own works for a class of people he generally disliked, and his friend the Archduke Rudolf, to whom he dedicated the score, was a much younger son and not at all likely to ever become emperor. So where did the name originate? Evidence is unclear, but it seems that the "Emperor" title was the idea of Johann Baptist Cramer, a German-born, London-based pianist and publisher. Beethoven and Cramer were life-long friends, and Beethoven reportedly regarded his lesser-known colleague as the greatest pianist of their day. If Cramer did indeed crown the "Emperor" with its regal title, then it seems proof of Beethoven's friendship that he permitted the choice, for he rarely let anyone meddle with his music.

- Paganini: Violin Concerto no. 1 in D major, op. 6

In recent years, audiences become accustomed to the media hype surrounding certain well-known entertainers, but today's publicity cannot approach the notoriety of Nicolò Paganini (1782-1840), born in Genoa and possibly the most charismatic performer who ever lived. Contemporary accounts describe his audiences screaming with delight. Ladies brought him gifts, and pictures of the violinist were hawked on the streets of Vienna. His artistry drew praises from Schumann and Chopin. The great opera composer Rossini once said, "I wept the first time I heard Paganini play."

Some people claimed that his astounding virtuosity resulted from a pact with the devil. More likely, it was due to an intense regimen from an early age, combined with unusually long fingers and a specially adapted violin. He was known to work his fingers obsessively even when not holding a violin, so as to keep them supple. Even today, Paganini is remembered as a marvelous musical magician, and, like many magicians, jealously guarded his secrets. Few of his compositions were published during his lifetime. Fortunately, the manuscripts survived amongst his personal things and at his death they and his eleven Stradivari instruments passed on to his son Achille (whose mother Paganini had never married) and to selected museum collections.

Most numerous amongst Paganini's works are one-movement solo violin showpieces called *Caprices* and various pieces of chamber music. However, there are also six full concertos for violin and orchestra, the first of which dates from around 1817, when Paganini was in his mid thirties. It did not appear in print until 1851, about a decade after the composer's death. Although originally composed in the key of E-flat major, it was transposed to D major early on so as to allow the notes to lie more sympathetically beneath the performer's fingers, or at least, any performer other than Paganini himself. After a long vibrant introduction, featuring sustained chords and full-bodied wind parts, the violinist enters with a confident, elaborate theme typical of Paganini. The second movement contrasts the first with a lovely, courtly adagio, which reminded Schubert who heard the composer play it in person, of the singing of angels. The piece builds through its third movement to conclude in an astonishing burst of energy and intensity.

- Berlioz: *Harold in Italy*, op. 16

Harold in Italy is the product of a musical partnership between two of the most startling personalities of the nineteenth century, or indeed, of almost any century: Hector Berlioz, a young and radical composer who had scandalized Paris with his opium-inspired *Symphonie fantastique*, and Nicolo Paganini, an astoundingly talented violinist whose career took flight on rumors that he had sold his soul to the devil. Neither artist cared much for propriety;

both viewed music as an avenue for deep emotional expression. In *Harold in Italy*, those shared concerns are perpetuated.

In 1833, after hearing a performance of *Symphonie fantastique* (see Chapter Two), Paganini asked Berlioz to compose a viola concerto. The great violinist had recently acquired a Stradivarius viola, and wanted a new work to perform on the instrument. Although Paganini was himself also a composer, he believed that Berlioz, the composer of that bizarre and dynamic symphony, was the better man for this particular job. So Berlioz set to work. Years later, in his memoirs, Berlioz described his approach to the piece: "My idea was to write a series of scenes for the orchestra in which the solo viola would be involved as a more or less active character, always retaining its own individuality. By placing the viola in the midst of poetic recollections of my wanderings in the [Italian] Abruzzi, I wished to make of it a sort of melancholy dreamer after the manner of Byron's *Childe Harold*. Thus the title: *Harold in Italy*."

The composition that resulted had less to do with Byron than with Berlioz himself, and very little to do with Paganini, who apparently had envisioned a showpiece for his virtuosity. *Harold in Italy* he dismissed as having "too many rests" for the soloist. He paid for it, but never did perform the work he had commissioned, though he confessed to bearing it admiration. After hearing another violist perform it, he offered his sincere appreciation to Berlioz.

Harold in Italy is structured in four long movements. The first, subtitled "Harold in the Mountains," carries the subtitle "scenes of sadness, happiness and joy." It is an introspective introduction to our protagonist whose subtle theme, first played by the solo viola, echoes throughout the work. The second movement, "The March of the Pilgrims Singing Their Evening Prayer," contrasts Harold's lush romantic perspective with the pilgrim's gentle religious fervor. The "Serenade" of the third movement depicts a mountaineer of the rugged Abruzzi region singing to his beloved. Here, Berlioz lets the English horn (deeper voiced cousin of the oboe) serve as the voice of the singer, yet Harold is there as well, in the solo viola, observing the intimate scene. For the final movement, Berlioz turns to a more animated episode, "The Orgy of the Brigands," but even amidst the tumultuous action, he recalls the earlier scenes, with musical echoes of the pilgrim's march, the serenade, and Harold's theme.

- Mendelssohn: Violin Concerto in e minor, op. 64

Felix Mendelssohn was only twenty-six when he took over leadership of the Leipzig Gewandhaus Orchestra. Despite his youth, he had already earned an international reputation as composer and pianist. Soon, his conducting skills were also deemed praise-worthy. Under Mendelssohn's direction, the Gewandhaus Orchestra became known for its fine performances of Bach and of contemporary pieces by such composers as Schubert and Schumann (about whom more shortly). Mendelssohn's own works also appeared on the programs, and the greatest soloists of the century traveled to Leipzig to perform with Mendelssohn and his orchestra. It was a perfect pairing: a devoted conductor who was one of the great artists of the age, and a fine orchestra that equaled his talents.

One of Mendelssohn's great assets in Leipzig was his concertmaster, the violinist Ferdinand David. The men had been good friends since they were teenagers; as adults, they labored together to produce fine music. David even became the de facto assistant conductor, leading rehearsals when Mendelssohn was unavailable. In 1838, Mendelssohn decided to express his appreciation to David by composing a violin concerto. He mentioned the project in a letter to David, noting, "I want to write a violin concerto next winter. One in e minor is running in my head, and the beginning never gives me a moment's peace." David responded with genuine enthusiasm and an extravagant pledge: "I promise that I will practice it so well, that the angels in heaven will rejoice." Although Mendelssohn hinted at great urgency, he was a busy man who traveled frequently on conducting assignments. The concerto was not completed until 1844. It premiered March 13, 1845, with David as soloist with the Gewandhaus Orchestra. Mendelssohn was ill that day, and unable to conduct. The orchestra was instead led by Niels Gade, the Danish conductor and composer. Mendelssohn had to content himself with the second performance given later that year.

As he was at work on the piece, Mendelssohn frequently consulted with David about the solo part. It is perhaps for that reason that the work is beautifully suited to the violin, and is more lyrical and flowing than many other concertos. Although Mendelssohn uses the standard old classical structures for the concerto, he made changes of his own to better suit both his tastes and changing times. In the first movement, the solo cadenza — which in an earlier generation would have been improvised and placed just before the close of the movement — is fully written out and moved to more of a central location, just before the opening melodies are restated. There is logic in the change, as the section that immediately precedes this placement (called the 'development') offers new interpretations on previously stated melodic material, which is just what the cadenza does as well. Moreover, rather than bringing this movement to a defined close, with several seconds of silence before the start of the following movement, Mendelssohn has the bassoon carry the music over with a sustained tone that bridges into the restful mood of what follows. Mendelssohn's letters reveal that as a conductor, he found mid-composition applause to be distracting, and that he liked to connect movements so as to minimize the problem. It also allows the energy that he has built to move ahead uninterrupted.

- Robert Schumann: Piano Concerto in a minor, op. 54

After years of opposition from her father, composer/music journalist Robert Schumann (1810-1856) and his beloved, pianist Clara Wieck (1819-1896) married September 12, 1840, one day before Clara's twenty-first birthday. By the time of their marriage, Robert had already started work on a piano concerto for her. An early version of the piece, a one-movement fantasy, premiered during a rehearsal of the Leipzig Gewandhaus Orchestra on August 13, 1841, with Clara as soloist and their friend, Felix Mendelssohn, conducting the ensemble. The lack of an audience was not due to the work's brevity, but rather to the fact that Clara was two weeks short of the birth of their first child. Four years later, Robert expanded the piece to a full-fledged three-movement concerto, which would also premiere in Leipzig. Clara was thrilled with Robert's creation. Noting in her diary that she was "happy as a king at the thought of playing it," she described it as a "bravura composition." Others were more skeptical. One critic dismissed the piece as a "curious rhapsody," and the great pianist Franz Liszt, friend and colleague of the Schumanns, refused to play it. Not until years later, and largely through Clara's own promotional efforts, did the concerto earn wide acceptance with the public. Even after Robert's death — and she survived her husband by forty years — she continued to champion his music, winning thousands of fans for the artistic creations of the man she had loved.

The concerto encompasses the standard three movements. In the expansive first movement, based closely upon the initial piano fantasy, a fiercely powerful opening theme is contrasted with a lyrical piano and clarinet duet, providing elegant contrast between the two divergent moods. The second movement, a sweet and song-like intermezzo, could almost be imagined as a scene of quiet domestic bliss. If it is, then the vibrant finale may represent a shift to a waltz ball, with Robert and Clara swirling about to the rhythms of his flowing and forthright melodies.

- Brahms: Violin Concerto in D major, op. 77

Some of the finest compositions in the classical repertoire were written especially for friends of the composers. Mozart and Mendelssohn both produced works intended for close friends and colleagues, showcasing their particular strengths. Johannes Brahms, too, composed with friends in mind, particularly when it came to the violin. His Violin Concerto, his Double Concerto for violin and cello, and three violin sonatas were all created for the same man: Joseph Joachim, Brahms' frequent recital partner, musical advisor, and friend throughout their adult lives.

In the summer of 1878, while vacationing in the Austrian village of Pörtschach, Brahms began a violin concerto for Joachim. The two men had performed together for decades, and Brahms knew well the impressive extent of his colleague's talent. Not being a violinist himself, though, he was concerned about the practicality of what he was creating. With an eye toward solving problems before it was too late, he sent the first movement solo part to Joachim. "You should correct it," he wrote, "not sparing the quality of the composition . . . I shall be satisfied if you will mark those parts that are difficult, awkward, or impossible to play." The violinist, who was also something of a composer, eagerly complied, starting a three-month correspondence concerning the concerto.

The discussion continued until the concerto's premiere in Leipzig on New Year's Day, 1879, with Joachim as soloist and Brahms conducting. Some listeners were skeptical of the new piece, which seemed to be virtually beyond the abilities of merely mortal violinists. One observer, conductor/pianist Hans von Bülow, actually called it a concerto "against the violin," and Brahms and Joachim continued revisions on the work until its publication six months later. Even then, not all observers were satisfied. The noted Spanish violinist Pablo de Sarasate (1844-1908) flatly refused to play it, though not on questions of difficulty. "Do you think," he queried rhetorically, "that I would stand there with my violin in my hand and listen while the oboe plays the only melody in the entire piece?" Indeed, the oboe's second movement solo is exquisite, but the violinist, too, has lovely music in abundance, and audiences have always delighted in the concerto's lyrical melodies and rich orchestration. The first movement is of Beethovenian breadth (Joachim had fervently championed that master's violin concerto), the second a song-like cantabile, and the last a boisterous evocation of folk dance spirits from Joachim's Hungarian roots.

All too often, manuscripts for masterpieces vanish into history, yet this one is in safe hands. The virtuoso violinist Fritz Kreisler acquired it and in 1948 presented it to the US Library of Congress where it remains today.

- Bruch: Violin Concerto no. 1 in g minor, op. 26

Born in Cologne, Germany, Max Bruch (1838-1920) first studied music with his mother, an acclaimed soprano. By the age of eleven, he had begun writing chamber music and was only fourteen when he penned a quartet that won the Frankfurt Mozart Foundation Prize. Scholarship money facilitated advanced musical studies. Soon, the young man was an established composer and music teacher in his own right, a man whose cantatas and oratorios had won him a devoted audience even before he produced the violin concerto on which his reputation stands today. A succession of conducting posts followed, each more prestigious than the last until, in 1880, he was invited to serve as director of the Liverpool Philharmonic, where he would remain for about three seasons. In 1883, Bruch traveled to Boston, Massachusetts, to supervise performances of his music, then returned to Europe to take on positions first in Breslau, and later in the imperial capital of Berlin, where he spent his last years.

By the time of Bruch's death, musical styles had moved on the angular rhythms of Stravinsky, but Bruch never yielded, standing firm in the rich Romanticism of his youth. Although he lived to be eighty-two years old, in musical terms, he was always about thirty-five, persisting with the rich, mostly orderly styles of the mid nineteenth century. Like his French contemporary Saint-Saëns, Bruch supported established styles, utterly refusing to board the train of progress crewed by such radical spirits as Liszt and Wagner, men with whose music Bruch chose not to associate. He knew what he liked, and he continued to like it, no matter what trends dictated. Bruch's works were flowing and graceful even as his colleagues indulged in angst-ridden fantasies. Bruch didn't hold with angst.

Bruch's Violin Concerto no. 1 dates from 1866 when the composer was 28. In the half a century that remained to him, he would compose more violin pieces, along with symphonies, symphonic dances, and various other worthy works, but, throughout his life, and even to this day, the Bruch composition that seized the spotlight was that one concerto. Bruch's son told of his father, upon being invited to yet another performance of the piece, responding, "The g-minor Concerto again! I couldn't bear to hear it even once more! My friends, play the Second Concerto, or the *Scottish Fantasia* for once!" So tired had Bruch grown of the piece that he once published a tongue-in-cheek letter titled "Prohibition by order of the Police concerning Max Bruch's First Concerto," a document sternly banning any further performances of the concerto on the grounds that violins were beginning to play it "of their own accord." Bruch's frustration is easily understood. Who would wish to see one child soar while others languish? Yet the success of that one composition earned him a fine living, and perhaps it brought a few listeners to his other, equally deserving works. The concerto premiered in Bremen January 7, 1868, with the great virtuoso Joseph Joachim as soloist.

- Tchaikovsky: Piano Concerto no. 1 in b- flat minor, op. 23

Peter Tchaikovsky (1840-1893) was the first to admit that his piano skills were only adequate for personal amusement, not for virtuoso display. That fact did not prevent him from wishing to write for the instrument, but it did leave him uncertain that what he had written was practical from a player's point of view. Thus, when late in 1874 he finished his Piano Concerto no. 1, he decided that someone more skilled at the keyboard should be asked for commentary. With caution, he selected Nikolai Rubinstein, virtuoso pianist and director of the Moscow Conservatory, where Tchaikovsky served on the faculty. Later, the composer described the experience in a letter to his patron Madame von Meck, relating that Rubinstein, upon hearing the work run through at the keyboard, proceeded to tear it to shreds. Tchaikovsky described it this way: "My concerto, he said, was absolutely worthless, impossible to play; technical passages were trite, clumsy, and so awkward that they could not be fixed. Musically, too, my concerto was poor, banal, and furthermore borrowed from this or that work by someone else . . . . A stranger happening to step in by chance would think that I am some sort of maniac, an incompetent and uneducated scribbler who annoys a famous musician with his trashy productions."

Infuriated, Tchaikovsky marched out of the room in silence. When Rubinstein followed him and began to list the specific places in which the concerto needed to be revised — and exactly how it should be revised — the composer let the elder man talk. But when Rubinstein added that, if Tchaikovsky followed those instructions to the letter and completed the new version by a specific date, then Rubinstein would be content to premiere it, at last the composer found the nerve to speak up. As he explained to Madame von Meck, "To this I replied: 'I will not change a single note and will have the work published as it stands now.' And this is exactly what I did."

Lacking Rubinstein, Tchaikovsky needed another pianist for the premiere. His choice settled on the German virtuoso Hans von Bülow, who proved to be far more supportive of the new work than Rubinstein had been. "Original, noble, and powerful," was Bülow's verdict. He premiered the concerto in Boston on October 25, 1875 while on an American tour. It was a thorough success, and soon Europe was equally enamored of the piece. In the face of the new concerto's undeniable popularity, Rubinstein retracted his former remarks. Not only did he admit the work's value, but he also performed it frequently and he conducted its Moscow premiere, a fact which Tchaikovsky must have regarded as a moral victory. It is worth noting that, despite their disagreement in this case, Tchaikovsky and Rubinstein remained fast friends, and Rubinstein conducted the premieres of sixteen Tchaikovsky compositions.

- Dvořák: Cello Concerto in b minor, op. 104

In the 1890s, Czech composer Antonín Dvořák (1841-1904) spent about four years in the United States as director of the National Conservatory of Music in New York City. While there, he had a strong influence upon the next generation of American composers, encouraging them to seek an American spirit for their works. America had an influence upon him, as well, particularly in the colleagues with whom he became acquainted during his time in New York. One of these was the Irish-born cellist/ composer Victor Herbert (1859-1924). Herbert is now known mostly for his operettas, especially *Babes in Toyland*, but had also written two impressive cello concertos, and Dvořák managed to be in town for the New York premiere of the second one. So impressed was he that he soon set to work on his own Cello Concerto. Before long, Dvořák produced a piece that, although written in America, abounds with the passionate flavors of his native Bohemia, and the work was not completed until after his return to Europe in 1895.

Dvořák's Cello Concerto premiered in London March 19, 1896. Although Dvořák was in attendance, he had threatened to boycott the performance, for he objected to the choice of soloist. His complaint was not due to a perceived lack of talent of the part of the musician in question, one Leo Stern. Rather, the composer had dedicated the piece to Hanus Wihan, a cellist with whom he enjoyed an enduring friendship. They had performed together in a chamber ensemble that toured Europe before Dvořák's American sojourn, and the composer had promised Wihan the premiere of the new concerto. His wish would remain unfulfilled. Despite an angry letter sent by Dvořák to the London Philharmonic Society, the piece was premiered by Stern, not by Wihan. The incident proves that, although composers are creators, still they do not always have total control over their own creations.

- Elgar: Cello Concerto in e minor, op. 85

A late work in his career, the Cello Concerto of Sir Edward Elgar (1857-1934) is a sort of anomaly amongst his output. Instead of being hearty and self-assured, this work is introspective and restrained, especially in comparison with the composer's well-known *Pomp and Circumstance* marches (see Chapter Ten). Generally speaking, it lacks the optimism which England seemed eager to project. The piece is, however, a product of its times. When the concerto was completed in the summer of 1919, England and Europe were just emerging from the throes of a vicious war. Elgar, like many other composers, felt bound to express his feelings in music. Indeed, he said the concerto depicted "a man's attitude to life," and, despite its darkness, he called it "good and alive."

The public did not entirely agree. The premiere, which the composer himself conducted at Queen's Hall in London in October of 1919, was a failure, apparently due in part to a lack of orchestra rehearsal time. To blame the soloist, Felix Salmond, would seem unkind, as he had worked over the piece even while Elgar was writing it and consulted on details of the solo part. Perhaps the fact that the concerto was more serious and less virtuosic than normal expectation affected its reception. The concerto did not become a repertoire standard (that is, standard for those who can manage its interpretative challenges, which is by no means the majority of cellists) until Spanish cellist Pablo Casals popularized it several decades later. It gained further popularity when championed by the great English cellist Jacqueline du Pre in the 1960s, indeed becoming one of her calling cards. Her passionate playing style suited the concerto's varied moods and allowed it a fuller expression than it might have had in other hands.

- R. Strauss: Horn Concerto no. 1 in E- flat major, op. 11

According to his mother, Richard Strauss (1864-1949) evidenced a susceptibility to music at an early age. Frau Strauss did not claim that the future composer was pounding on the piano while still in diapers, but she did assert that the sound of a French horn always made the infant smile. Was young Richard's reaction due to an innate musicality? Or did he just recognize in the horn's mellow tones the sound of his father at work? For the elder Strauss spent forty-nine years as principal French horn of the Munich Court Orchestra, and there was surely plenty of practicing going on around the house. From a childhood that resonated with the horn, young Richard grew into a composer's career no less sensitive to the instrument. Many of his most notable compositions, including the tone poem *Don Juan* and the opera *Der Rosenkavalier* (for the former, see Chapter Three; for the latter, see Chapter Eight) grant the French horn a place of prominence.

In addition to working the French horn into his sumptuous orchestrations, the younger Strauss also composed a pair of concertos for the instrument. The two works date from opposite ends of his career: the first from 1883, the second from 1942. At the time of the first concerto's creation, Franz Strauss was still an active performer, and Richard wrote this concerto with the specific intent of having his father give the premiere. However, the work proved to be fiendishly difficult. The composer's sister would later recall that Franz practiced it for a short time but, deeming the numerous high notes as too risky to undertake in public, allowed the honor of the premiere to be passed on to one of his students, Bruno Hoyer. The Horn Concerto no. 1 first came before the public in Strauss' hometown of Munich in 1888. The composer was, at the time, all of twenty-four years old, and had many grand successes in his future.

- R. Strauss: Oboe Concerto in D major

It was April 30, 1945. Hitler had just committed suicide, but the war continued in his absence, with Allied armies sweeping across Germany. In far southern Bavaria in the shadow of the Alps, the American Army moved into the resort town of Garmisch-Partenkirchen and soldiers were sent door-to-door to commandeer homes for the Allies' use. Residents were given fifteen minutes to pack and leave. But at one address, Zöppritzstraße 42, the soldiers came upon an obstacle: a teenaged boy who declared that his family would not stir a step unless Grandfather approved. That elderly gentleman, stout and gray, joined the group at the door and, upon being informed of the problem, responded simply, "I am Richard Strauss, composer of *Der Rosenkavalier*." The officer in charge, fortunately a music lover, knew the name and immediately rescinded the evacuation order. Some poor neighbor was evicted instead.

Thus, in the midst of an occupation, the Strauss family was left in relative peace, other than the continuing stream of music-loving Allied soldiers who came in search of autographs. They admired the bust of Beethoven that stood in Strauss' study. They went home to America with stories of having met one of the grand old men of music. However, one soldier went home with somewhat more. John de Lancie, before his military service oboist in the Philadelphia Orchestra and a long-time admirer of Strauss' works, met with the composer and chatted in French about music. "I asked him," de Lancie later recalled, "if, in view of the numerous beautiful lyric solos for oboe in almost all of his works, he had ever considered writing a concerto for oboe." Strauss admitted that he had not, but apparently it seemed to him to be a good idea, for soon he was at work on just such a piece.

The difficulties of these post-war months slowed Strauss' progress on the concerto, which was not completed until October of 1946. The piece premiered in Zurich where the composer was staying at the time, but he expressed the wish that its American premiere should be given by "that Chicago oboist," meaning de Lancie. Once the geographic confusion was sorted out, a further problem arose. de Lancie, it was learned, was only the assistant principal oboist at Philadelphia, and his superior had no intention of granting the honor of a major premiere to the man who sat second chair, regardless of whether or not he had inspired the piece. Thus, the American premiere of Strauss' Oboe Concerto was given not by John de Lancie, but rather by his section leader, Mitch Miller. The occasion was a CBS broadcast concert. Miller would go on to fame in other areas, but in the long run of music history, it is yet de Lancie's name that is associated with this charming and graceful composition.

Incidentally, some readers may recognize the oboist's name as currently belonging to a popular television actor. Indeed, John de Lancie the actor is son of John de Lancie the oboist.

- Rachmaninoff: *Rhapsody on a Theme of Paganini*, op. 43

Sergei Rachmaninoff (1873-1943) was fully two decades into his career as composer, conductor, and pianist when the Russian Revolution occurred in 1917. The powerful new regime was strongly opposed to Western-style music, exactly Rachmaninoff's own style. Refused permission to emigrate after the revolution, he took advantage of an already-scheduled Stockholm concert, bringing his wife Natalya and their two young daughters along. The family never returned to Russia. They were free, yet had lost everything but the clothes on their backs. The next year, seriously in need of funds, the composer accepted an offer to come to the United States for a series of concerts and recordings. Not long afterward, the Rachmaninoffs purchased a home in New York. Once their finances had improved, they also acquired a villa on Lake Lucerne in Switzerland.

By the 1930s, Rachmaninoff had come to be regarded as one of the greatest living composer/pianists. His music might be banned in the Soviet Union — as was sometimes the case — but elsewhere, he had reached the top of his profession. In 1934, having already completed four piano concertos, Rachmaninoff began work on a new concerto-like piece inspired by a well-known theme by Paganini, the great violinist of the early 1800s. The idea caught his affections so firmly that he cut short a concert tour so as to spend the summer composing at his Swiss villa. The task was formidable, for the theme Rachmaninoff had chosen, the twenty-fourth solo violin Caprice, had been used by many other earlier composers, notably Liszt and Brahms, so any new work on the same theme would face inevitable comparisons. Fortunately, Rachmaninoff proved equal to the challenge. Perhaps it came down to the issue of virtuosity, for since Rachmaninoff was as much the master of his own instrument as Paganini had been of his, the later man may have been able to see somewhat into the mind of the earlier man, thus divining within the theme exciting new ways in which it could be expressed.

The *Rhapsody on a Theme of Paganini*, premiered by its composer in 1934 in Philadelphia, is a set of twenty-four variations upon Paganini's theme, with a brief introduction to set the stage. It is not a concerto in the conventional sense, in that it has only one movement, rather than the usual three, but observant listeners will note that this single movement still follows the usual tempo pattern, beginning and ending briskly, with a contrasting center section at a slower pace. This middle portion builds toward the *Rhapsody*'s most famous variation, the lyrical eighteenth that uses a free inversion of the theme, that is, where the pitch formerly rose, it now falls, and where it fell, it now rises. Although the Paganini caprice serves as the *Rhapsody*'s foundation, a subsidiary melody is also featured at times, the plainchant *Dies Irae* from the Requiem Mass. This most familiar of all religious themes, conveying its whiff of fire and brimstone, has been used frequently by composers in various devilish contexts. Its appearance here may be a recollection of the old legend concerning Paganini's fiendish skill deriving from a pact with the devil, or perhaps it is only due to the composer's awareness that this theme and the caprice are similar in shape. Whatever his reason, Rachmaninoff's use of these contrasting melodies brings an additional richness to the now much-beloved *Rhapsody*.

- Prokofiev: Piano Concerto no. 1 in D- flat major, op. 10

The only child of affluent parents, Russian composer Sergei Prokofiev (1891-1953) grew up surrounded by music, for his mother was a talented pianist who loved to play Beethoven and Chopin. The boy was both playing and composing by the age of five and within four years was tackling Beethoven sonatas. Before he reached his teens, his parents had hired him his own composition tutor and each winter, his mother brought him from their rural retreat in the Ukraine into Moscow to enjoy live performances. By late in 1904, young Prokofiev was enrolled at the St. Petersburg Conservatory where he would rock the boat for a decade, producing compositions that boasted unusual key changes and diabolically intricate rhythms. Together with his composition studies, he found time for parallel studies of piano and he would graduate with degrees in both fields.

However, controversy continued to follow the young man. In 1914, late in his piano studies, he chose to compete for the Rubinstein Prize, which required contestants to play a concerto with orchestra. Most of the competitors opted for Beethoven or one of the other established masters in the field. Prokofiev found the confidence to offer up his own Piano Concerto no. 1, which he had completed and premiered two years earlier. Many of the judges, apparently irked by such bravado, voted against him, but others insisted that he had indeed deserved the first prize, and their voices won the day. On the weight of that performance of this concerto, Prokofiev went home with a grand piano.

Some of the judges may have been irritated as much by the concerto's rule-bending as by the young man's self confidence. Here, Prokofiev takes the expected patterns of what developments should occur in what order, and turns them on their heads, juggling musical fragments to suit his own pleasure.

Though the concerto does begin and end with fast tempos, after a middle movement of quieter moods, as even Vivaldi would have done, the resemblance is only superficial. This is, moreover, an intense and dramatic work, in comparison to which even Beethoven sounds almost sedate. Prokofiev was more interested in rhythm than melody, and in his hands, the piano becomes, as often as not, almost a percussion instrument. The concerto would figure prominently in his first American tour four years later, bringing his music to a new continent, where audiences were again knocked back in their seats by the intensity of Prokofiev's musical vision.

- Hindemith: *Der Schwanendreher* (Viola Concerto)

For centuries, string instruments have dominated the musical world, serving both as frequent soloists and as the heart and soul of any orchestra. Violins stand particularly firmly in the spotlight, but cellos are also beloved for their rich, romantic tone, and even string basses are valued, especially when composers seek a grim or ponderous mood. Pity, then, the poor viola, often lost in the shadow of its more obvious cousins. The viola does add valued depth to harmony, but its contribution is a subtle one, like the blues and purples of an otherwise golden sunset. Without the other tones, the gold loses much of its impact, yet it is the gold that catches the eye, just as violins catch the ear, at the expense of their more mellow neighbors. Violas, so invaluable for enhancing harmonic blends, have rarely been welcomed on center stage, and their solo repertoire is sorely limited. Mozart wrote one concerto using a solo viola, though even he paired the instrument with the ever-present violin. Berlioz wrote his *Harold in Italy* for viola soloist, yet other than those two contributions to the repertoire, the viola was left largely alone until the twentieth century.

German composer Paul Hindemith (1895-1963) was the savior of the viola. At the age of eleven, he began supporting himself as a professional violinist, but soon turned to the viola and never looked back. Even after building a reputation as a composer, Hindemith continued to perform as a violist. When the instrument's slender repertoire began to wear thin, he corrected the situation by composing his own viola works, including two solo sonatas, two sonatas with piano, one work for viola with string orchestra, and three viola concertos. Single-handedly, Hindemith created more viola masterworks than had been produced by all the master composers who preceded him. Perhaps all the viola repertoire had needed in all those years was someone who, like Hindemith, understood and appreciated the instrument. Whatever the reason, violists ever since have been continually grateful for his efforts.

The last of Hindemith's three viola concertos, written in 1935, was based on German folksongs. According to the composer, the piece is intended to portray a medieval minstrel who, on returning from his journeys, plays for his friends the melodies that he learned during the course of his travels. The various songs are first heard in a relatively straight-forward manner, but gradually become more varied and embellished, as the mythical musician supposedly improvises upon his themes for the amusement of his listeners. As the three-movement composition progresses, four German songs are heard. The slow first movement is based upon "Zwischen Berg und tiefem Tal" (Between Mountain and Deep Valley). The second movement intertwines two melodies, "Nun laube, Lindlein, laube," in which a melancholy lover wishes that the linden tree would shed its leaves to better suit his mood, and a children's song about a cuckoo. The last movement, liveliest of the three, is a set of variations on a song about an organ-grinder, or, in German, "Der Schwanendreher." From this song, the composition takes its title. Although some of Hindemith's contemporaries were busily promoting dark, sometimes angry sounding dissonance, Hindemith himself still found room in his music for a good tune.

- Gershwin: *Rhapsody in Blue*

George Gershwin (1898-1937) lived the American dream. The son of Russian immigrants, he grew up playing in the streets of a poor Jewish section of Brooklyn. He dropped out of school at fifteen and took a job playing piano for a Tin Pan Alley publishing house, but had no intention of spending his life in such a menial position. Young Gershwin was convinced that he could write far better songs than those by established composers; at the age of nineteen, he validated that confidence with *Swanee*. When he was twenty-one, his first Broadway show, *La La Lucille*, ran for one hundred performances.

As his career progressed, Gershwin became the most successful composer on Broadway, with a list of hit shows that even Andrew Lloyd Webber would envy. After all, for all the popularity of *Phantom of the Opera*, it has yet to win a Pulitzer Prize, as did Gershwin's *Of Thee I Sing* in 1932. Gershwin's music proved central to the careers of such legendary performers as Fred Astaire, Ginger Rogers, and Ethel Merman. He came to define how a jazz song should sound, and in so doing, defined the very nature of American music. Gershwin once wrote, "When jazz is played in another nation, it is called American." Had he written his own name in the place of the word "jazz," he would have been no less correct, for though jazz may be the heart of America, *I Got Rhythm* is the heart of jazz.

One would think that a commission for a concerto would be a significant event, an event that the composer in question would take trouble to remember. Perhaps commissions were nothing new for Gershwin, or possibly he had produced so many works that the need to write one more slipped his mind. Whatever the reason, the impending premiere of one of his most important works came to him as almost a complete surprise. On January 3, 1924, George's brother Ira read in the newspaper that the band leader Paul Whiteman would soon lead his musicians in a concert of works by Victor Herbert, Irving Berlin, and George Gershwin, the Gershwin piece to be a jazz concerto. Ira asked his brother about the new piece. George's response was astonishment. He remembered talking with Whiteman about a concerto, but he had not understood Whiteman's timing. Now Gershwin had only five weeks left before the premiere.

As Gershwin had to begin the new concerto immediately, but also needed to be in Boston for the opening of his newest musical, the main theme of *Rhapsody in Blue* came to be written on the train from New York. The composer later claimed, "It was on the train, with its steely rhythms . . . that I suddenly heard — even saw on paper — the complete construction of the Rhapsody from beginning to end. . . . By the time I reached Boston, I had the definite plot of the piece." Gershwin worked quickly, sketching out the ensemble parts of the piece at the piano, and then handing over the score to Ferdé Grofé (1892-1972), Whiteman's arranger, who orchestrated it. Thanks to their team effort, the band's parts were ready in time, but the solo piano part was not yet on paper. It existed only in the composer's memory, and at the first performance he played from memory, for he had not yet found the time to write it down. But no matter: the concert, given February 12, 1924, at Aeolian Hall in New York, was a triumph. Gershwin had proven that jazz rhythms did have a place in a classical concerto.

- Rodrigo: *Concierto de Aranjuez*

Musically, the spirit of Spain seems best captured by the shimmering sounds of the guitar, and few compositions are more evocative of that character than the guitar concertos of Joaquin Rodrigo (1901-1999). This Spanish native was born in Sagunto on November 22, the day of St. Cecelia, patron saint of music. Although illness took his vision when he was only three, Rodrigo's parents encouraged him to reach out to the world, hiring an assistant to help him with reading at school. As an adult, Rodrigo refused to be limited by blindness. He found great success in musical studies, first in his native Valencia, later in Paris, which in the 1920s personified the bright lights/big city of artistic circles. He traveled frequently throughout the world, collected numerous honors, and wrote works for some of the most influential artists of the twentieth century, including the master guitarist Andras Segovia. In Rodrigo's music, the ambiance of Spain finds a home in a graceful, neo-classical framework

Rodrigo's most familiar and successful work is the *Concierto de Aranjuez*, which premiered November 9, 1940, in Barcelona. The name "Aranjuez" pays tribute to an ancient palace situated between Madrid and Toledo. A favorite residence of Spanish kings and site of many festive royal celebrations, Aranjuez was a royal center for many centuries. Rodrigo might have sought to portray numerous eras, but he always insisted that the concerto was inspired by one particular era: around the year 1800, during the reigns of Charles the Fourth and Ferdinand the Seventh. It's a time preserved today in the vivid canvasses of Goya, a time of beauty, passion and flamboyance. In this concerto, Rodrigo sought to capture that spirit of fire and grace.

Several technical points of the work are worth noting, for the extent to which they show Rodrigo's knowledge of his Spanish musical heritage. Firstly, he requires two particular guitar techniques: 'rasgueado', or strummed notes, and 'punteado', or plucked notes. Both techniques are highly typical of Spanish guitar music, so typical that even composers writing for other instruments, such as the piano, will attempt to evoke these sounds whenever they seek a Spanish flavor. Furthermore, he also calls for certain flamenco styles of playing, particularly in the second movement, in which the soloist must execute rapid turns and trills and insistent repetitive notes. Such techniques are so very idiomatic of Spanish music, as opposed to guitar music from any other nation, that the piece might by better termed a Spanish concerto rather than one merely for the guitar. Throughout his long life, Rodrigo was admired in his homeland for that intrinsic understanding of the Spanish spirit. So greatly did his native land revere him that, when the composer died in 1999, his body lay in state in Aranjuez itself.

- Glass: Second Violin Concerto "American Four Seasons"

For the general public, the hypnotic flowing lines of Philip Glass (b. 1937) are most familiar through his film music: *Koyaanisqatsi, Mishima, The Thin Blue Line,* and *The Hours.* However, his music takes many forms, including symphonies, songs, stage works, and especially operas, several of which have come to the stage at New York's Metropolitan Opera. He is not often imagined as a composer of concertos, and yet such works are numerous in his catalog. Glass has written concertos for such varied solo instruments as piano, cello, harpsichord, saxophone quartet, timpani, and violin.

The first of his two violin concertos dates from the winter of 1986/87 and premiered that April at Carnegie Hall. American violinist Robert McDuffie did not premiere it, but did record it, and performed it so frequently that he developed the idea of asking Glass to write a second one specifically for him. He suggested that the new work might make a companion to Vivaldi's famed *Four Seasons* cycle, a set of four concertos each portraying the moods and sights of a particular season. Glass agreed, and the new work premiered December 9, 2009, with the Toronto Symphony Orchestra and McDuffie. Other organizations joining with Toronto in the commissioning of the work include the Aspen Music Festival and School, the London Philharmonic Orchestra, the Krannert Center for the Performing Arts at University of Illinois at Champaign-Urbana, and the Carlsen Center at Johnson County Community College in Overland Park, Kansas. The length and variety of that list of sponsors proves the wide appeal of Glass' music. The concerto was given its American premiere at the Aspen Music Festival July 22, 2010, again with McDuffie.

Although the initial concept was of a concerto that would fit with the Vivaldi set, there are substantial differences. First of all, Vivaldi included a harpsichord in the string ensemble, and Glass uses instead a synthesizer. Additionally, Vivaldi's concertos have accompanying poems that specify what about those seasons is being portrayed; Glass' concerto has no text. Moreover, Glass does not title the four movements as to which season is which. The work might begin in spring, or might not, and it does not necessarily proceed in calendar order. In fact, he and McDuffie found they differed as to which movement made them imagine which season; thus, audience members might have utterly different ideas that vary from both the composer and the soloist. It all depends on how one envisions any given season, and that will vary with one's own particular memories. One further difference is that Glass prefaced each movement with a solo cadenza, imagining that the cadenzas might be extracted to make up a solo suite without orchestra.

One feature of Glass' new concerto that does draw upon old traditions is the fact that the first movement is intense and demanding, as if to seize the attention of listeners and performers alike by starting with a bang. The second is slow and lyrical for the sake of contrast. Then, the concerto speeds up again, with increasing verve through the third and fourth movements. Even a Haydn symphony would do much the same thing, though with perhaps more orderly rhythms and harmonies as it progressed. However, Glass has little use for harsh dissonances and throughout, the music is driven by beautiful sounds distributed over several movements of different tempos, just as Mozart or Beethoven would have done. Indeed, one finds Glass' trademark of rising and falling arpeggios, but one also finds richer textures and more varied tone colors than would be usual for this composer. New ideas and old traditions come together in a single work.

- Edgar Meyer: Triple Concerto for double bass, banjo, and tabla, "The Melody of Rhythm"

Many a composer has also been a gifted performer, most often on piano or perhaps violin. The double bass is a far less frequent choice. Perhaps something about standing at the back of the orchestra providing the foundation of the music doesn't well suit the composer's view of life. Yet double bassists, too, can compose — if they are the right bassists. Of past generations, the most respected such figure was Giovanni Bottesini (1821-1889), who in addition to much music for his own instrument also composed operas. Today, the bassist with success in the composer's spotlight is Edgar Meyer (b. 1960).

Americans have delighted in Meyer's artistry at Lincoln Center, the Aspen Festival, the Marlboro Festival, and numerous other prestigious venues, both as a performer and as a composer. Additionally, he indulges in bluegrass, jazz, and country music. The varied rhythms and harmonies of those divergent musical voices flavor his own compositions, which blend the scope and ambition of classical music with the vibrant spirit of other musical realms in which the bass is also welcome. Meyer's compositional success is such that such unsurpassed masters as Joshua Bell, Yo-Yo Ma, and Seiji Ozawa have been involved in the premieres of his works.

Meyer's Triple Concerto, like the more famous one by Beethoven, sets three soloists against an orchestra, sharing the spotlight evenly amongst all. Yet for Beethoven, the solo instruments were piano, violin, and cello. Meyer looks further afield, choosing double bass, banjo, and tabla — a type of Asian Indian hand drum. In drafting the work, Meyer accepted input from the two artists with whom he intended to share the premiere: Bela Fleck, banjo, and Zakir Hussain, tabla. The three men gathered together with their instruments and demonstrated ideas that they thought would work in the piece; Meyer was so impressed by their input that he asked for all three names to be listed on the published music as co-composers. He was by no means the first composer to take suggestions from others when at work on a work with solo parts. To cite just one prominent example, Brahms' Violin Concerto had significant input from his friend, violinist Joseph Joachim, for whom it was intended. For the premiere of Meyer's concerto, he and his two colleagues joined forces with conductor Leonard Slatkin and the Nashville Symphony September 6, 2006.

When one of the solo instruments belongs to the percussion family, one might expect the concerto to be more rhythmic than melodic in focus. Indeed, the other two soloists — double bass and banjo — often play rhythms as well as melodies, so Meyer could have taken the concerto in that direction. However, the Indian tabla is more than just a simple drum. It is a pair of hand drums sufficiently different in size as to give them different pitches. Moreover, a particularly skilled player can manipulate the fingers and heel of the hand so as to draw varied pitches from its halves, and Meyer calls upon this technique in the concerto. The dual capacity of all the solo instruments comes to the fore in the concerto's subtitle: "The Melody of Rhythm." Meyer also remembers to make use of his entire set of instrument forces — a full orchestra of woodwinds, brass, strings, and percussion — so that the orchestra is not just providing supportive harmonies. Textural colors and rhythmic effects exist for all the players, not merely the three soloists at center stage, and one finds significant tempo changes between the three movements. The performing forces may not look like those for a Vivaldi or a Mozart concerto, but the idea of a concerto as a work that sets soloists in contrast to a larger ensemble is still in use, even here in the twenty-first century.

- Golijov: *Azul* (Cello Concerto)

Few composers can claim both Argentine tangos and Jewish klezmer music amongst their inspirations, but Osvaldo Golijov (b. 1960) is one, and can additionally say that his music sounds like no one else's. Born in Argentina to parents of Eastern

European Jewish heritage, his diverse musical inspirations arose early in life. Studies in his homeland were followed by further training in Israel and then the US, in which lands even more divergent musical ideas came to his attention. By the age of thirty, he was hearing his compositions performed by respected soloists and ensembles around the world. Principal amongst those championing Golijov's sound are the Boston Symphony, the Kronos Quartet, and soprano Dawn Upshaw, for whom he has written a song cycle and the opera *Ainadamar*.

Golijov's unique lyrical sense, drawn from his divergent inspirations, leads to music of determined melodic flow and unusual harmonies, music that is by turns melancholic or energetic. He is a composer who cannot be pigeonholed. Later generations will likely labor in vain to find a label for his style, but current audiences have learned that in his music, there is always something interesting waiting around the corner. Stylistically, his work blends melodic flow with strong rhythms and emotional energy, drawing listeners into a colorful tapestry of sound. Every measure destroys any notion that modern classical music must be elitist and difficult. It does not recall Mozart and Beethoven, nor should one expect it to, but the sounds it does encompass are entrancing to the open mind.

Not for Golijov simple defining titles that say only what sort of piece a new work is with reference to its key and catalog number. Rather, when offered a commission for a cello concerto for the Boston Symphony's 125th anniversary in 2006, he chose instead to call the resulting piece *Azul*, Spanish for "blue." Knowing that the first soloist would be Yo-Yo Ma and feeling that such an artist hardly needed another standard concerto to showcase his virtuosity, Golijov chose instead to write an expressive and lyrical work, often borrowing the rhythms of the Spanish language. Just before the premiere, he observed, "I'm very curious to know if I discovered a new kind of beauty or if I was under a great delusion." Observers at that first performance at the Tanglewood Festival August 4, 2006 voted in favor of the former, and in its brief existence, this twenty-first century score has already earned performances by the Chicago Symphony, the Cleveland Orchestra, and the Aspen Music Festival, in addition to the Boston Symphony itself.

That the premiere was given at Tanglewood also influenced the work's musical character. As Frank Lloyd Wright would not design a building without first knowing its intended setting, so Golijov feels that where a composition will be heard colors how its music should be flavored. Tanglewood is an open-air summer festival with lawn seating and a view of the night sky. That sense of contemplative stillness inhabits the score with its open airy flow. Certainly one can hear *Azul* indoors as well, but if one allows oneself to be immersed in the music, it can inspire a journey of imagination. Even the scoring, with the usual orchestral instruments supplemented by multiple piccolos, English horn, basset horn (a cousin of the clarinet), bass trombone, hyper-accordion, and myriad percussion, encourages that journey.

In the score, Golijov draws upon some long-standing concepts in music, notably of a continuo group to provide a steady, somewhat repetitive foundation upon which the melodies will stand. Here, the continuo group is largely composed of percussion, but as many of them (such as marimba and vibraphone) can play pitch as well as rhythm, there is still much variety to the tone color. He also arranges his instruments unusually, with the soloist in the center where he belongs but other players grouped near or far, so that at times, their contributions seem to come from a great distance. It adds an otherworldly effect, drawing the listener out of mundane experience, which after all, the best music should try to do.

Further Recommendations:

Here is a selection of other interesting concertos for which there was not room in the main body of the chapter:

- Joseph Haydn (1732-1809): His Trumpet Concerto preceded even Hummel's concerto discussed above. There are also two charming cello concertos and several Haydn piano concertos, especially no. 11 in D major with its Hungarian flavored rhythms. Haydn wasn't Hungarian, but did grow up just across the border.

- Wolfgang Amadeus Mozart (1756-1791): The great majority of his concertos are for piano, but there are also various others, including a jaunty one for bassoon. Mozart was one of very few great composers to give the spotlight to this often neglected instrument.

- Frederic Chopin (1810-1849): This master of the piano – profiled in depth in Chapter Six – composed two masterful piano concertos, completing both before reaching the age of twenty.

- Henryk Wieniawski (1835-1880): A virtuoso violinist who composed for his own performances; his Violin Concerto no. 2 is so technically difficult that it terrified even the best of his colleagues. When the great violinist Joseph Joachim had to fill in for Wieniawski at the last minute on a concert, he declared that he would need to play Bach instead.

- Max Bruch (1838-1920): Since Bruch wants us to think about his other concertos – beyond the ever-famed Concerto no. 1 detailed above – let's mention at least one of them. Especially delightful is the so-called *Scottish Fantasy*, borrowing Highland themes that the composer came to know during his years of conducting in the north of England.

- Peter Tchaikovsky (1840-1893): His Violin Concerto was first derided as unplayable, but for over a century now, the greatest players (and their audiences) have delighted in its challenges.

- Edvard Grieg (1843-1907): His most frequently performed non-stage-related work is his only Piano Concerto; dramatic and virtuosic, it was almost too much so for the composer's own physical strength. His stage music for *Peer Gynt* appears in Chapter Nine.

- Victor Herbert (1859-1924): As Herbert's Cello Concerto no. 2 inspired Dvořák to compose his own Cello Concerto (detailed above), it would be worth the effort to explore the richly melodic Herbert work that launched his Bohemian colleague on that path.

- Alexander Glazunov (1865-1936): A Russian born colleague of Rimsky-Korsakov, Glazunov ended his career in Paris, where exposure to jazz clubs inspired him to write a striking Saxophone Concerto.

- Maurice Ravel (1875-1937): The Frenchman's Piano Concerto for the Left Hand was written for an Austrian pianist who had lost an arm in combat in World War I. Ravel manages impressive variety of mood and color in the work, despite the fact that the piano's range is restricted by the player's limitations.

- Béla Bartók (1881-1945): Dating from his years of wartime exile in the US, this Hungarian composer's Concerto for Orchestra treats virtually every instrument as soloist in turn. It was composed largely in hospital beds, as Bartók was dying of leukemia, but has little of the darkness that one might expect of a man in such a situation. Perhaps he sensed that he would live on through his music.

- Astor Piazzolla (1921-1992): The accordion-like instrument in the soloist role for this composer's Bandoneon Concerto is one central to Argentine tango. It was a dance-style that Piazzolla, who played bandoneon himself, knew exceptionally well. His musical vision came to be called "nuevo tango."

- Einojuhani Rautavaara (b. 1928): This Finnish composer's Violin Concerto seems to evoke the vast forests of his nation's countryside with its broad, flowing melodies. His great countryman, Jean Sibelius (1865-1957), had championed Rautavaara's work, and there is much influence from Sibelius in the more recent composer's style.

Chapter Five
Chamber Music

Even those with little experience in classical music, upon hearing the music above played for them, would likely agree that they had heard this melody. It's the opening theme from the so-called "Little Night Music" by Mozart. This chapter will explore not only that specific work, but also other prominent and interesting examples of chamber music, as well as the idea of what exactly "chamber music" is supposed to be

Chamber music is composed for a small group of performers, with each person playing what is called "one to a part." That means that each individual has a unique contribution to the composition, and no one is exactly duplicating anyone; even if there happen to be two violins, each has different music. Long ago, chamber music was often composed to entertain members of the aristocracy, who often had musicians and composers serving on their personal staffs. By the eighteenth century, though, it had also become popular with members of the middle class, who had come to feel that learning to play an instrument was integral to a cultured person's education. These every-day amateurs were playing for fun, not for fame and fortune, and required music that was somewhat simpler as they were not trained professionals. However, the trained professionals also got in on the act, playing chamber music in public concerts and in gatherings of their own friends. Nearly all the composers in this chapter played chamber music themselves at least from time to time. The music included in this chapter was intended for professional players, but amateur listeners were always welcome. One needn't be able to play all these many notes to enjoy hearing them played well by others.

Having said that chamber music uses a "small group of performers," one might ask how small is small. A piece of chamber music might be for just one or two players, or perhaps a few more. The word "sonata" generally referred to having just one or two, including at least one piano. Also popular was the string quartet, composed of two violins, one viola (a lower pitched cousin to the violin), and one cello (lower yet, and big enough that it stands on the floor resting between the player's knees). A "piano trio" was not three pianos together, as one rarely finds three pianos in one place. Rather, a piano trio was played by one pianist, one violinist, and one cellist, so that a range of different sounds and pitches were available to the composer. Similarly, a "piano quartet" was not four pianos, but a piano trio with the addition of a viola. One might also write chamber music for somewhat larger ensembles. Usually (not quite always), the title of a chamber composition hints how many performers of which types would be needed. When listening to (or, better yet, watching) chamber music, it's entertaining to observe how the players interact with one another, so that each gets the opportunity to shine. The best composers made sure that everyone had a share of the fun.

Sometimes, a composer may first imagine a new work in chamber form, requiring only a small number of players, and then decide to give it new life. Although Barber's "Adagio for Strings" was first a movement of a string quartet, it is now rarely played by only four musicians, as the composer re-imagined his music on a larger scale. That which was written as chamber music can evolve into a full-scale orchestral work, either with the composer's approval, or even long after his death. So Mozart's "A Little Night Music" was first conceived for eight players, yet may be performed by an entire orchestra. Schoenberg's *Transfigured Night* was first a sextet, but may be given with extra players. In honor of their composers' original intentions, these specific works are all included in this chapter, though one may well hear them with larger ensembles.

- Pachelbel: Canon in D major

Someday, someone will take a musical poll to determine which compositions are most immediately recognizable to those who have not studied music. The survey in question would not concern the titles of pieces; no one would need to name the compositions heard, or to say anything specifically technical about them. Rather, the person being surveyed would hear part of a composition, and then be asked if it sounded at all familiar, if he or she had ever heard that piece before in any context. In such a survey, the beginning of Beethoven's *Symphony no. 5* would certainly finish high, whereas its second movement might not register at all. Rossini's Overture to *William Tell* (think of the Lone Ranger) would be another winner, as would Gershwin's *Rhapsody in Blue* (thanks to about twenty years of United Airlines commercials). Another composition boasting a high recognition factor would be Pachelbel's *Canon*, the perfect example of a famous piece by an otherwise obscure composer.

Despite the neglected state of most of his music today, Johann Pachelbel (1653-1706) was famed during his lifetime, known as one of the leading progressives of the day. Born in Nuremberg, Germany, Pachelbel spent his career at various courts and churches in Central Europe, as composer and teacher. He was also a fine organist, and many of his compositions were written for that instrument with which he was so very familiar.

As a friend of the Bach family, Pachelbel served as godfather to one of Johann Sebastian Bach's sisters and taught music to one of the elder brothers, the same brother who later taught JS himself. Musicologists attest that Pachelbel's influence resounds throughout the early compositions of Bach. Pachelbel also proved indirectly important to music of the United States. His second son, Charles Theodore, immigrated to the American colonies in the 1730s, thus becoming one of the first European trained composers to settle in the New World.

A canon is a pattern for composition that became popular as far back as the Renaissance. It is not dissimilar from the round, such as *Frére Jacques*, though canons are more complicated in design. In a canon, the composer begins with one melody which subsequently is repeated in ever different layers of the music while other melodies join in, usually in the higher lines. In an intricate canon such as Pachelbel's, the basic melody gradually grows and evolves, becoming more and more elaborate each time it returns. Fugues, too, share some characteristics with canons, though fugues involve more detailed rules about how the various melodies are supposed to relate to one another. Although Pachelbel's *Canon* is simply scored for string ensemble with harpsichord, he makes the most of his forces by manipulating the melody on which the piece is based.

- JS Bach: Cello Suites, BWV 1007- 1012

As a performer, Johann Sebastian Bach (1685-1750) is most strongly identified with the harpsichord and the organ. Stories of his prowess at those two instruments abound, and his keyboard works are frequently acclaimed as the greatest such compositions ever produced. We'll give them detailed attention in Chapter Six. Yet that love of keyboards did not lead to a neglect of strings, for in Bach's day, composers and performers were required to be versatile. Thus this master of the keyboard also learned the bow, and learned it well enough that one of his younger sons, CPE Bach, declared that his father "understood the capabilities of the string instruments perfectly," an opinion borne out by later generations of performers. His solo works are challenging, yet still ideally suited to displaying the most endearing features of those instruments. Only a master composer with an intimate knowledge of strings could have produced such striking compositions.

That Bach knew what to make of a string instrument is best proven by his solo Partitas and Sonatas for violin and his unaccompanied Suites for cello. Of the latter works for the lower pitched instrument, they were long considered as practice etudes for honing a performer's skills, not as works appropriate for the concert stage. That changed when the superb Spanish cellist Pablo Casals (1876-1973) happened upon a published set of the suites in a used book store. At the time, he was still a teenaged artist of little reputation. That people would be willing to watch and listen as this one cellist occupied a stage by himself and played Bach's intricate suites would have seemed unimaginable to more observers. However, as his skills matured, Casals brought great passion and drama to the works, likely far more than Bach himself would have expected. At last, the Cello Suites gained a profile higher than they had ever had since Bach had written them in the 1720s. For a quick lesson in how much can be made out of a single instrument — one that, unlike a guitar, let alone a piano, cannot play full chords — seek out a copy of Casals' vintage recording of the Cello Suites. Many more recent artists also do fine work; one can hardly quarrel with Yo-Yo Ma's artistry. Yet it was Casals who first brought the suites back to public attention.

- Haydn: String Quartet in C major, op. 76, no. 3, "Emperor"

He was known as Papa Haydn, yet Franz Joseph Haydn (1732-1809), the Austrian master composer, fathered no children, that is, none of the human variety. In the musical realm, however, his children are legion. Over one-hundred published symphonies, roughly six dozen string quartets, as well as sonatas, trios, concertos, operas, masses, and songs: it is a body of work almost unimaginable both in variety and extent. Not only did he compose prolifically, Haydn was also an innovator who fathered new genres of music, new types of compositions that composers had not used before but which soon became so popular that one cannot imagine music without them. Classical music without symphonies and string quartets? Thank Joseph Haydn for the fact that we need not exist in such a world.

Haydn's last complete set of quartets was the six quartets that make up his opus 76. Written at the request of Count Joseph Erdödy in 1796, the pieces incorporate new ideas that Haydn had developed during his recent London tours, when he discovered for the first time the benefits of catering to a larger audience. Moreover, the composer, firmly settled into his sixties, brought to the works an unequalled wealth of experience. The English music writer Charles Burney — who lived in Haydn's own time and whose published commentaries show him to be a knowledgeable observer — wrote of these masterworks, "they are full of invention, fire, good taste, and new effects, and seem the production, not of a sublime genius who has written so much and so well already, but of one of highly-cultivated talents, who had expended none of his fire before." Burney added that he had never received more pleasure from an instrumental work.

The third of these six quartets earned its nickname for its second movement. Many a listener today will hear it and muse that he or she hadn't known that Haydn composed the German national anthem, which appears here prominently in a set of variations. The best response to that thought is that Haydn didn't know it either. The melody in question is one he composed after a concert tour to London, where he was favorably impressed by the stately sounds of the English anthem "God Save the King" and decided that the emperor of Austria, Haydn's own native land, deserved something equally impressive. So the composer quickly crafted a hymn to the words "Gott erhalte Franz den Kaiser" (God Support Emperor Franz). It served as an Austrian anthem for decades. Then, in the late nineteenth century, the German poet Heinrich Hoffman von Fallersleben drafted a text on the subject of German unity which happened to fit exactly the rhythms of

Haydn's melody. By 1922, it had become the German anthem, and the Austrians were left searching for a new one, for which they adopted a melody by Haydn's countryman Mozart. When this quartet was new, however, the theme was still specifically Austrian, not German.

- Mozart: Serenade no. 13 in G major, K. 525, "A Little Night Music"

The work "serenade" means "night music," and was used to describe a chamber work intended for light entertainment on a social occasion. Serenades have enjoyed great popularity, particularly in classical Vienna during Mozart's time. At the end of the eighteenth century, it was customary for wind bands to perform in Vienna's parks and gardens. Sometimes, an enterprising young lover might hire such a band to play in front of his sweetheart's home, and at least once, someone sent an ensemble to Mozart's house for a surprise performance of his own compositions. It was strictly social music, not an intellectual endeavor, and its prevalence is indicative of how deeply involved the Viennese people were with music, that they wished to hear it everywhere at any time. Soon, the creation of serenades was a good source of income for composers.

Mozart took to this trend with delight, producing over a dozen serenades, some for special occasions, such as family birthdays or friends' weddings. The last and best-known of his serenades is the Serenade no. 13, best known by its nickname, *Eine kleine Nachtmusik*, (*A Little Night Music*). According to the composer's dating of the manuscript, the piece was completed August 10, 1787. At this time, Mozart was also engaged in composing Act Two of his often somber opera *Don Giovanni* (*Don Juan*). In that context, he may have written this radiant serenade for his own respite, to clear his mind of Don Juan's dark adventures, but the specific occasion for which the work was composed has never been determined. Although the piece was not published in its creator's lifetime, it has become one of his most beloved works,

and has served to introduce many a novice to the effortless grace
and joy of Mozart at his best.

- Beethoven: Piano Trio no. 7 in B-flat major, op. 97, "Archduke"

Here is another Beethoven score that, like his Piano Concerto
no. 5 of 1811 (see Chapter Four), was dedicated to the Archduke
Rudolf, younger brother of Austria's Emperor Franz. Beethoven
began the *Archduke Trio* in 1810. It is a piano trio, scored for piano,
violin, and cello. Atypically for Beethoven, he worked quickly,
completing the piece early the next year, but its premiere was
delayed until April, 1814. The composer himself was the pianist
in the premiere, given as part of a charity concert in Vienna.

It was to be one of Beethoven's final concert appearances
as a performer, for increasing deafness made it virtually
impossible for him to play in public. Even at this performance,
some observers commented on a lack of clarity and precision in
his technique, yet the composition itself was roundly praised.
The trio survived even without its composer himself actively
playing it for audiences; other performers eagerly took it into
their repertoires. Most of a decade later, in 1823, the *Allgemeine
Musikalische Zeitung* (*General Musical Journal*) exuberantly lauded
the trio as "one of the brightest leaves in the laurel crown which
[Beethoven] has long since earned." It has continued to be one of
his most beloved compositions, generally bright and upbeat in
defiance of the poor hand that fate had dealt to Beethoven. Here,
music serves to overcome dark moods.

- Schubert: Piano Quintet in A major, D. 667, "Trout"

In the summer of 1819, Franz Schubert visited the Austrian
town of Steyr, about halfway between Vienna and Salzburg. He
had come with Michael Vogl, a baritone of the Vienna court opera
and tireless promoter of his young colleague's works. A native

of Steyr, Vogl introduced it to his friend, who in a letter home described the region as "unimaginably lovely." Music parties were often the order of the evening, with Schubert's songs and piano works enjoying great popularity amongst Vogl's social set. One favorite house was that of Sylvester Paumgartner, a wealthy mining manager and music lover, who allowed Schubert free use of his music room and staged midday concerts in his salon. Paumgartner also commissioned from Schubert a new work, requesting a quintet for piano, violin, viola, cello and double-bass. This instrumentation was quite unusual; most piano quintets were for piano and string quartet, with two violins, but no string bass. Yet a few years earlier, Jan Nepomuk Hummel (1778-1837: see Chapter Four) had written a work for these five instruments. Paumgartner so liked it that he requested from Schubert something similar that the same group of friends could play for their own pleasure.

Certainly, there is much pleasure in this sunny composition, atypically written in five movements, rather than the usual four. The first movement features a rippling triplet figure evocative of flowing water, beginning in the piano, but then moving to other instruments. By contrast, the second movement is more tranquil lake than bubbling brook. This gentle Andante is as indolent as a summer afternoon, but the calm is broken by a brisk third movement Scherzo reminiscent of folk dances. In most chamber music, one would now proceed to the finale, but Schubert inserts one additional movement, from which the quintet takes its nickname. It is based upon one of Schubert's own songs, "Die Forelle" (The Trout), a particular favorite of Paumgartner's, thus accounting for its appearance here. Schubert provides a set of variations on the song, ranging throughout each of the five instruments, so that even the bass has its moment with the melody. At last, the final movement is reached and a lively allegro, complete with those rippling triplets from the opening, brings the work to a charming conclusion.

- Mendelssohn: Octet in E- flat major, op. 20

Felix Mendelssohn's Octet for strings dates from 1825 when the precocious young man was all of sixteen years old. The work is remarkable not only for the facility of its melodies and the gracious balance of its various parts, but also because here Mendelssohn proved himself a pioneer in producing a masterful work for the combination of two string quartets. Haydn never wrote such a work, nor did Mozart or Beethoven or Schubert. Composer Louis Spohr (1784-1859) did, but his so-called "double quartets," written in his mature years, show less mastery of form and instruments than this one early effort of a teenaged genius. Despite his youth, Mendelssohn had a true gift.

Mendelssohn dedicated the work to his friend, the violinist Eduard Rietz, on the occasion of Rietz' twenty-third birthday. Historians presume that the Octet premiered at one of the Mendelssohn family home concerts, perhaps with Rietz and Mendelssohn amongst the performers. Alternately symphonic and intimate, the piece begins with a graceful allegro that soars with the first violin, and then proceeds to a gently thoughtful second movement. The third movement scherzo is all tip-toes and mystery suggestive of the *Midsummer Night's Dream* scherzo that Mendelssohn would compose in later years. The composer's sister Fanny maintained that her brother had in mind a particular ghostly vision from the pages of Goethe's *Faust*. The final movement begins with a bustling fugue, a technique learned from the young composer's extensive studies of Bach, and concludes in a mood of utter exuberance.

The Octet has remained a favorite of audiences and string players alike. Even the composer himself regarded it highly. Late in his tragically abbreviated life (he died at thirty-eight), Mendelssohn described the Octet as "my favorite of all my compositions," and he added, "I had a most wonderful time in the writing of it!"

- Schumann: Piano Quartet in E- flat major, op. 47

Robert Schumann (1810-1856) was a composer with a one-track mind, tending to devote himself to a single genre at a time, so that if he wrote one piano sonata, he would then write several more, just as one song would pave the way for a dozen more lieder. Thus, Schumann's biographers divide his life into chapters, including the lieder year and the symphonic year. There was also the chamber music year of 1842, the second year of his marriage to the great pianist, Clara Wieck. With only one infant daughter in their home, Robert and Clara devoted leisure evenings to studying musical scores together. In 1842, it was the trios and quartets of Mozart and Beethoven. In those exemplary models, Schumann seems to have found inspiration, for that one summer, he produced the only three string quartets he would ever write, along with a piano quintet, a piano quartet, and a piano trio. Although in later years, he occasionally wrote chamber music, never again did he show such a concentrated devotion to the field.

Prominent among the works from this "chamber music year" is the Piano Quartet in E-flat, completed soon after the Piano Quintet. In his diary, Schumann admitted that the piece cost him some sleepless nights, though whether that was from worry or from a frenzied obsession with the glories of music is uncertain. What is clear is that, from start to finish, he required only five weeks to create a masterpiece. Scored for piano and strings, the work is dedicated to Count Matthieu Wielhorsky, a Schumann patron who was also an amateur cellist. Perhaps Schumann had Wielhorsky in mind as he wrote the quartet, for the piece boasts several lyrical cello solos. Yet as he so often would, Schumann reserved the spotlight for the piano, in fact, for his beloved Clara, who served as pianist at the work's premiere. This quartet is thus one of many examples of the man's response to the woman's artistry. It is a composition that remained in her repertoire long after Robert's death. Clara outlived him by fully forty years.

- Franck: Violin Sonata in A major

Permit no one to tell you that Cesar Franck (1822-1890) was French. Indeed, he did spend much of his career in Paris, but in his youth was refused admission to the Paris Conservatoire because he was a foreigner, a Belgian born in Liège. It was in Belgium that Franck received most of his education. His early recitals were also in his native land, and his impressive keyboard technique was inspired by a Belgian organist. Franck's style and character were firmly established long before he settled abroad, and music-loving Belgians take pride in their native son. Such pride is easily justified, for in his chosen fields, Franck had few equals. His organ compositions stand at the heart of the repertoire, and his performing ability was compared favorably to that of Bach by the great keyboard artist Franz Liszt. Cesar Franck was a man whom any nation would proudly claim.

Although Franck produced very little chamber music, his Violin Sonata has earned a place as a concert favorite, thanks to a proliferation of song-like melodies that prove endearing to performers and listeners alike. The piece was written in 1886 as a wedding present for the great Belgian violinist Eugene Ysaÿe (1858-1931), who also gave the sonata's premiere later that year. The premiere itself was an extraordinary occasion. Ysaÿe arranged for the performance to be given on a winter afternoon in a Brussels art museum. In fear of damaging the paintings, authorities forbade the use of artificial light, and due to the late hour, all natural light faded with the setting sun. Before the sonata was half over, the room was in darkness. Ysaÿe and his pianist continued playing from memory, invisible to their listeners, who were themselves concealed in shadows. To hear melodies of such exquisite lyricism in an utterly darkened room must have been an unforgettable experience.

- Brahms: Serenade no. 1 in D major, op. 11

For most of the nineteenth century, a shadow hung over German music, a shadow from which up-and-coming composers struggled to emerge. The shadow was that of Beethoven, whose dominance in virtually every genre of music was so complete that no composer could escape comparison to the departed master. In whatever field one wished to work — symphony, sonata, concerto, quartet — Beethoven had set the mark against which all others would be measured. To be willing to undergo such a trial, knowing that one could hardly best Beethoven at his own game, one had to be immensely confident. Unfortunately, confidence was not a strong characteristic of the young Johannes Brahms (1833-1897). Yet he still managed to thwart the specter by putting off symphonies and quartets until later in his career, by which time he had honed his skills through work in other genres not linked to Beethoven's name. These compositions, spared from the shadow, were able to stand on their own merits, and through them, Brahms developed the confidence he would need to write a symphony.

One seemingly approachable genre was the serenade, a multi-movement composition often intended more for the purpose of casual entertainment than for insertion in a serious concert program. Serenades were less strictly structured than symphonies. Whereas a symphony would have specified forms that were expected to appear in particular movements, a serenade had no such restrictions. Furthermore, serenades often draw their rhythms from the dance, giving them a lighter, more carefree character than one would find in a proper symphony. Mozart composed thirteen serenades, included the famed *Eine kleine Nachtmusik*, yet Beethoven almost never bothered with them. Thus, Brahms regarded the serenade as a safe field for experimentation. It seems he feared Mozart less than he feared Beethoven.

Brahms' Serenade no. 1 was sketched in Detmold, Germany, in 1857 and '58, where the composer was spending the winter as part-time music master for Prince Paul Friedrich Emil Leopold. Perhaps it was that aristocratic setting that led Brahms to adopt a Mozartian genre, as Mozart, too, composed for aristocrats, yet Brahms did not set aside his own Romantic sensibilities. The piece seemed too grand for its modest orchestration comprising nine wind and string players. The composer's friends, notably pianist Clara Schumann and violinist Joseph Joachim, encouraged him to rework the piece for a larger ensemble. The new version, which included brass, timpani, and a larger contingent of woodwinds, premiered in Hanover March 3, 1860, with Joachim conducting. A few months later, Madame Schumann would ensure the Serenade's Viennese premiere by making its presence on the program a condition of her own concert appearance with the Vienna Philharmonic. The work would be published by Breitkopf and Härtel during this same year, making it Brahms' first orchestral work to appear in print. It was, however, still a fairly small orchestra for the times. It is a work of sunny optimism, perfect for the musical expression of a young composer just launching his international career.

- Dvořák: String Quartet no 12 in F major, op. 96

From the inside out, Antonín Dvořák (1841-1904) knew much about string quartets. Before the Bohemian composer achieved international fame for his music, he supported himself by teaching music, playing in theater orchestras, and joining in string quartet concerts, in which he most often played viola. His personal viola is currently resident in a museum, though the composer's great-grandson, violinist Josef Suk, recently succeeded in borrowing it for a recording on his ancestor's music. Even once Dvořák had made his reputation, he continued to play chamber music for his own enjoyment, and when he was invited to become director of a New York City music academy in 1892, he spent his last spring in Europe on tour with an ensemble of friends. Thus, it comes as no surprise that the homesick composer — who never adjusted well to his urban New World residence — sometimes assuaged his spirit by composing chamber music. Amongst his works of American origin is the String Quartet in F.

The quartet was written largely in Spillville, Iowa, where Dvořák would spend his American summers amidst a vibrant community of Bohemian immigrants, speaking his native language and feeling as much at home as he could on this continent. Dvořák began it in early June of 1893, only three days after his arrival in Iowa, and the work was finished before the month was out. Although the quartet uses no actual American songs, it does borrow the spirit of folk music, exuding the hearty character of life in the outdoors. In Dvořák's words, "The influence of America must be felt by everyone who has any 'nose' at all." Later, summing up all his works from these "American" years, the composer said, "I should never have written these works 'just so' if I hadn't seen America."

Of the quartet's genesis, Dvořák's younger son Otakar recalled a day in Spillville in his memoir of his father: "Once we visited a place called Riverside Park to the southeast of the village. Father, my friend Frank Kapler, and I went there. Frank and I got the idea to take simple fishing poles and try some fishing. We presumed Father would get some inspiration and that we would have a lot of time to fish. But it did not turn out that way. Father's command was clear: 'Well, boys, stop your fishing. We have to go back home.' I was surprised that our walk in his favorite place was discontinued so quickly. When I protested, I received a short answer: 'My cuff is already full of notes. I must hurry home to copy them down.' That was the day my father started his String Quartet in F major, op. 96. Father started to write it on June 12, and on June 16, the work was finished. I remember this so well because it is my favorite chamber work by Father."

Incidentally, Dvořák and his wife Anna had seven children who survived to adulthood and there are many descendants. However, as the great majority of their children were girls, the family name would have fallen by the wayside, except for Otakar. From his branch of the family alone does one still find Dvořáks who are descendants from the great composer. The name itself is not uncommon, but Dvořáks of the own composer's family line are.

- Schoenberg: *Verklärte Nacht (Transfigured Night)*

When a young man is born and raised in Vienna, he may have no choice but to give in to musical pursuits. Yet Arnold Schoenberg (1874-1951) came to music along a tortuous path, and would remain largely immune to the heritage of Mozart, Beethoven, Schubert, and Brahms. Together with several colleagues, Schoenberg would become one of the most influential members of the so-called Second Viennese School: reinventing music in ways never imagined by their famous predecessors.

Young Arnold began violin lessons at age eight and soon was dabbling in composition for his own amusement. However, the family was poor, and even as a teenager, the boy had to set aside schooling for work as a bank clerk, limiting his musical pursuits to free evenings. Before long, he and a group of friends began playing chamber music and formed an ensemble that entertained at cafes. Soon, he attracted the attention of Alexander von Zemlinsky (1871-1942), another young composer, though one with the benefit of an education at the Vienna Conservatory. Under Zemlinsky's guidance, Schoenberg began adding more structure to his early works and dreamed of a career in composition, though that career was slow to appear, as his compositions were so progressive that audiences literally did not know what to make of them.

Schoenberg compositions have a reputation for being austere and intellectually demanding, somehow beyond the reach of the general public. That is true enough of some of his works, but other compositions, especially early ones, are a different story, for Schoenberg began in the Wagnerian mold. His youthful works are lush and lyrical, a bit progressive, indeed, but still clearly derived from the spirit of Romanticism. Of all these early pieces, the most famed, and justly so, is *Transfigured Night*, written in 1899 when Schoenberg was twenty-five. Now, it is often described as his most beautiful work.

Transfigured Night is a tone poem, a dramatic composition in the tradition of Liszt's *Les Préludes* and Strauss' *Don Juan*. Although descended from their works, this piece differs from its models in two ways. First, it is a chamber piece, not an orchestral work. In addition, whereas most tone poems portray events, Schoenberg instead gives his attention to emotion, to a psychological portrayal derived from Richard Dehmel's poem, "Weib und Welt" (Women and the World). The essence of the story is this: a couple is walking in the night. They are in love, but the woman is already married to another man, and she is pregnant with her husband's child. She fears that her lover will condemn her and abandon her, yet the beauty of the evening and the intensity of their love overcomes their difficulties. "Oh look," the man exclaims, "how the universe glitters!", and their lives are transfigured by the night. It is that inner growth, that acceptance and understanding, which Schoenberg sought to portray in music.

- Bartók: String Quartet no. 4

Hungarian Béla Bartók (1881-1945) was destined for a musical career. His father, though professionally speaking director of an agricultural school, was a talented amateur pianist and cellist; his mother, a teacher, played the piano. The boy's first music lessons came from his mother, but life took a harsh turn with the death of Béla's father when the boy was only seven. Forced to support the family, mother Paula moved the family to a larger community where the teaching of piano lessons might be more profitable. Yet she did not neglect her son's ability. The best music teachers she could afford were procured for the boy, both for piano studies and for composition. Soon, young Béla, barely a teenager, was acknowledged as the finest pianist in town, and "town" was Budapest, so there was plenty of competition.

When the time came to consider college, Bartók faced a difficult choice. Until this time, all ambitious young musicians in the Austrian Empire pursued studies in Vienna, and in fact, the Vienna conservatory had offered him a scholarship. Yet in Vienna, what one learns is the Viennese approach to music, and Bartók had already grown so fond (and so knowledgeable) of his own culture that he feared losing touch with Hungarian traditions. At some financial risk, he rejected the tempting scholarship, choosing instead to complete his education in Budapest, and though Wagner and Richard Strauss played a role in the young man's evolving style, so did the Hungarian Liszt and, particularly, the rhythms and harmonies of Hungarian dances.

As Bartók's interest in folk music increased, he began to let folk music affect his concert works. He rarely used pre-existing folk melodies. Rather, he preferred to call forth the Hungarian style by evoking elements of folk music, perhaps bringing a dance rhythm into a piano piece or an unusual harmony into a string quartet. Always, the Hungarian element was blended with the true classicism of Mozart and Beethoven, for Bartók was too well trained to discard the Classical traditions that had stood for centuries. What he sought instead was a new tradition, one based on Mozart and friends, but with a distinct Hungarian accent. He wanted his concert music to sound as if it had been written by a Hungarian, not by a German or a Russian or an Austrian.

According to Bartók himself — in his time, the greatest expert in the field of Eastern European ethnomusicology — certain musical elements characterize true Hungarian music. The melodies draw upon two-bar melodic fragments that are repeated in varied forms. Rhythms frequently echo the rhythms of speech, specifically Hungarian speech rhythms, thus, rhythms quite foreign to most other cultures. Also prevalent is the ostinato: a repetitive pattern that does not change pitch level; that is, it neither goes up nor down, but rather straight across. Hungarian music is further distinguished by its unusual chords and scales, elements more closely related to Oriental music and medieval music than to most current Western European music. It is this feature that makes Hungarian-inspired music sound rather off-key to some listeners, an aura of dissonance arising from chords unfamiliar to Western ears. These features and others give Hungarian music — and Bartók's music — its distinct sound.

Bartók's catalog includes six completed string quartets, though there were also a few early attempts in his school years that he did not allow to survive. The survivors range from no. 1 of 1908 through no. 6 of 1939. The fourth of these dates from 1928, around the same time as the Piano Concerto no. 1 and the *Miraculous Mandarin* ballet. Structured in five movements, rather than the usual four, the work was conceived as an arch with the third movement as its keystone. The other movements were imagined as complementary pairs, with the first and fifth sharing themes and moods, as do the second and fourth. Thus, the entire quartet builds first towards and then away from that central movement, which Bartók imagined as a nocturnal scene. Throughout the work's progress, Hungarian-style dissonance becomes increasingly prevalent, as do formidable demands upon the performer's technique, with fearsome use of pizzicato and strumming, ideas borrowed from the folk music of the composer's homeland. The effect is thoroughly modern. Yet the careful structures of Bartók's classical core never vanish. Here was a man who succeeded in fusing the old and the new into something uniquely his own.

- Clarke: Sonata for Viola and Piano

Born in England to an American father and a German mother, Rebecca Clarke (1886-1979) learned music at an early age and enrolled in the Royal Academy of Music at age sixteen. Later studies at the Royal College of Music brought her under the influence of the respected English composer and pedagogue

Charles Stanford (1852-1924). Yet when she was twenty-four, a bitter quarrel with her father forced her from the family home and left her in sore need of an income. For many young Edwardian English women, that would mean governess work or clerking in a shop. Ms. Clarke found another option: her viola, becoming, in 1912, one of the first six women engaged to play in the Queen's Hall Orchestra.

Though her position in the orchestra first brought Ms. Clarke to public attention as a "lady musician," it was in chamber music that she would build her strongest reputation, particularly in the United States, where she toured successfully in the late Teens and early Twenties. American audiences might have been accustomed to seeing pretty young ladies at the piano, but the viola is a passionately physical instrument, and Ms. Clarke played hers with finesse, tackling challenging repertoire with both artistry and devotion.

Early attention for Clarke as a composer — not merely a woman with a viola — came in part thanks to the American arts patron Elizabeth Sprague Coolidge, whose Berkshire Festival of Chamber Music (launched in 1918) featured annual composition competitions. The theme for the festival's second year was the viola, with all submitted scores to focus upon that instrument. It was a perfect arena for Ms. Clarke, who entered her new Sonata for Viola and Piano. Judges perused the entries without knowing their composers' names. Thus, when Ms. Clarke's Sonata ultimately took second prize, no one was more surprised by the entrant's gender than those judges who had voted for the piece. The same would happen two years later with her Piano Trio, which also earned second prize. That work, and the previous Sonata for Viola and Piano, would be the two grandest creations of her career.

Sonatas for pairs of instruments — one of them a piano — are legion in the world of classical music. However, the viola so rarely rises to the top of that pile as to make Clarke's Viola Sonata a true stand-out. That it is well-crafted becomes the icing on the cake. She well exploits the instrument's various potential moods, allowing it to be song-like or strongly expressive in turn, far from the background color that it often is made to supply in orchestras. If one ever questioned what the viola adds to music, here is a work with an eloquent reply.

- Carter: String Quartet no. 2

Born in New York City December 11, 1908, Elliott Carter studied at Harvard, earning first a Bachelor's degree in English, and then returning for a Master's in music. The 1930s found him, like many of his countrymen, in Paris studying with the great music pedagogue Nadia Boulanger, who had also numbered Copland amongst her students. But Copland-style Americana would never be Carter's realm. Even his earliest compositions were flavored with experimentalism, his interests ranging from Stravinsky to Schoenberg. Also, he remained ever able to view music from new perspectives, seeing it as an ideal bridge between mathematics and the studies of literature and languages. Through his work on the faculties of Peabody, Columbia, Queen's College, and in Salzburg, Austria, he has passed his adventurous ideas on to a new generation.

Carter's music is rarely pretty in any conventional sense, but is usually intriguing in how he finds new things to say and new ways in which to say them. His catalog comprises roughly one-hundred works in virtually all genres, though particularly abundant in chamber music. It is in chamber music that Carter has made the greatest mark and received the greatest attention, with Pulitzer Prizes for both the String Quartet no. 2 (1959) and the String Quartet no. 3 (1971). So far, he has composed five string quartets, using widely varied techniques, as one would expect of works that span nearly fifty years of his expansive career. Considered as a whole, they show how a composer's style can evolve over time.

Of the Quartet no. 2, Carter attests "there is little dependence on thematic recurrence, which is replaced by an ever-changing series of motives and figures having certain internal relationships with each others." So whereas Beethoven or Brahms would unify a score by allowing its central melodies to reappear, perhaps evolved but recognizably from the same root, Carter is more interested in fragments of melodies and what can be built from them. Moreover, rather than building a texture of melody supported by harmony, he keeps the four instruments "quite distinct," imagining a "four-way conversation" in which there is perhaps more talking happening than listening. The layers are meant to contrast with one another, not to blend. Such an innovative approach not only won this quartet a Pulitzer but also the New York Critic's Circle Award, both in 1960.

In a field so populated with tragically short-lived composers — Mozart, Schubert, Mendelssohn, and Chopin all died before the age of forty — Carter is a reassuring figure. At the time of his 100th birthday in 2008, he was still actively composing and travelling to take a bow at concert premieres of his new works. As this book is prepared for publication in the summer of 2011, there is yet hope that he may make his 103rd birthday this December.

- Messiaen: *Quatuor pour la fin du temp* (*Quartet for the End of Time*)

Born in Avignon, France, to parents of literary interests (his father was a translator of Shakespeare, his mother a poet), Olivier Messiaen (1908-1992) began dabbling with composition at age seven. Three years later, his parents found him a private teacher for the subject, and then enrolled him at the Paris Conservatoire. Along with composition, the lad also began serious study of organ and improvisation, fields which would remain central to his adult career. Immediately after graduation, Paris' La Trinité church hired him as organist, a position he would hold until his death sixty years later. Starting in 1936, he taught music at several Parisian institutions, though academics were cut short by military service during World War II.

In the fall of Verdun June 15, 1940, Messiaen was captured by the Germans and spent a year in a prisoner-of-war camp in Silesia, in what is now Poland. Upon his release in 1942, he returned to La Trinité and also accepted a teaching post at the Conservatoire. Both there and in his own compositions, Messiaen fostered interest in far-ranging musical styles, from Hindu music to birdsong, which he collected in the field not with a tape recorder but by listening and writing it down. These diverse frames of reference color his very personal scores, which sound like no one else's. Even his solo organ pieces draw upon intricate rhythms, which are developed and combined with one another. His harmonies are similarly adventurous, creating original chord sequences reminiscent of those influences (not solely human) that he so admired.

One can scarcely imagine a less promising venue for a major premiere than that of Messiaen's *Quatuor pour la fin du temp* (*Quartet for the End of Time*), first performed at Stalag 8A in Silesia January 15, 1941. Messiaen had been putting his spare time into sketching out the piece, and when his activity came to the attention of a musically inclined guard, that man managed to provide music staff paper and sharpened pencils for the task. The camp commander then allowed the composer and a few friends access to instruments (specifically clarinet, violin, cello, and piano) and the work was heard by Messiaen's fellow prisoners and their captors. The hand-written score then managed to survive through the composer's next year of confinement and come home with him to Paris, where it belatedly made it into print.

The quartet was dedicated to neither side in the war; rather, Messiaen wrote upon the first page a dedication "in homage to the Angel of the Apocalypse, who raises his hand towards Heaven saying 'There shall be no more time'." The movement titles, too, come from the Book of Revelations. With such inspirations, one might suppose it to be a dark and grim score, but instead

Messiaen crafted a piece that has much lyric beauty, if one remains open to the composer's quirky rhythms. Continually, he ignores the usual Western tendency for regular rhythms and meters and instead offers ever changing, often unpredictable patterns, frequently based upon prime numbers, especially five, seven, eleven, and thirteen. Clarinet and violin phrases tend to be reminiscent of bird songs, and motifs recur from one movement to another. Although there are four instruments in the work, they rarely all play together; only about half of the piece (the first, sixth, and seventh movements, as well as parts of the second) contains four instruments playing simultaneously. More often, he draws upon those instruments which best convey the imagery he has in mind at that moment.

Curiously, Messiaen and Elliott Carter (see the previous item in this chapter) were born within twenty-four hours of one another, though an ocean apart. It seems that mid-December of 1908 was an auspicious time for modern music.

- Barber: *Adagio for Strings*

Born in West Chester, Pennsylvania, Samuel Barber (1910-1981) was a musical child, taking up the piano at age six and composition at seven; as a young man, he also turned to singing. The young man's principal inspiration in these musical endeavors came from his maternal aunt, Louise Homer, a noted contralto at the Metropolitan Opera, and her husband Sidney, a respected composer of songs. Under their influence, young Sam developed a lasting fondness for the beauty of the human voice. At age fourteen, Barber enrolled in the first class of the soon-to-be-prominent Curtis Institute of Music in Philadelphia. In addition to composition studies, he began to sing seriously, cultivating his naturally rich baritone voice. So successful was he in this area, that he gave vocal recitals both at Curtis and for NBC radio, and later recorded some of his own songs. A career as a singer seemed likely, but his compositions were also attracting positive notice. Even very early works, such as his 1933 song *Dover Beach* (see Chapter Seven), earned critical acclaim.

Samuel Barber composed works ranging from full operas and symphonies to songs and keyboard works. However, his reputation rests largely upon a single example of chamber music: the *Adagio for Strings*. That work owes its existence to the success of an earlier Barber composition. In July 1937, his first Symphony became the first American work to be performed at the prestigious Salzburg Festival. On the podium was conductor Artur Rodzinski, who had led the work's premiere in Cleveland earlier that year, but in the audience was Arturo Toscanini. The great Italian maestro found Barber's music so intriguing that he asked the young composer for something that his NBC Symphony might perform, and Barber soon provided the scores for two short works: his *Essay for Orchestra* (eventually to become the *Essay no. 1*) and the *Adagio for Strings*, adapted from the slow movement of his First String Quartet. A few months later, Toscanini returned the scores to Barber without comment, and the young composer assumed the worst: the maestro had rejected his music. Yet such pessimism was unwarranted, for as Barber soon learned, the music had so pleased Toscanini that he had memorized the scores and had already scheduled their premieres for the fall.

Both works were performed by Toscanini and the NBC Symphony November 5, 1938, a concert experienced not only by those in the hall in New York City, but also those in the radio audience. It was an unsurpassed triumph. The stunning impression left by the *Adagio* at the time of its premiere was no success of the moment; rather, the work remained in the repertoire. Some three years later, it would become the first American composition recorded by Toscanini, and long before its appearance in the soundtrack for *Platoon*, it won a place in American memory for the contribution that its elegiac mood would make to the funerals of two American presidents (FDR and JFK). More recently, the work became a last minute addition to numerous concert programs in the wake of the September 11 attacks. Barber's *Adagio for Strings* would come to represent an essential element of American culture. It has been called the saddest music ever written, yet it is also the most beautiful of all possible candidates for that honor.

- Pärt: *Spiegel im Spiegel (Mirror in the Mirror)*

Born in Estonia, Arvo Pärt (b. 1935) grew up under Soviet rule yet never produced the strictly political music that was being demanded of most composers under that regime. Instead, he felt driven to express his spiritual side, bringing his own Catholic interests into music that was often hauntingly minimalist in character. His early works, frequently choral, though also delving into instrumental realms, tended to gain their effect through the repetition of short rhythmic patterns, sometimes combined with the droning element of western European Medieval plainchant. This juxtaposition of contrasting material gives his music a complexity that is yet soothing to the ear, for dissonance has never been one of Pärt's interests. His music reaches listeners through a layering of ideas, not through the introduction of clashing sounds that would otherwise conflict with his usually serene mood.

Pärt's *Spiegel im Spiegel* is a fine introduction to his music. It reveals a style that has come to be called "tintinnabulation," in which simple fragments of sound recur, like the ringing of bells. In Pärt, these fragments float upward and downward, sometimes moving only slightly before beginning a new motion in a different direction. Subtle shifts of key and harmony add to the mood. It is an approach ideally suited to the work's title, for it might perfectly convey a room of mirrors, positioned so as to reflect each other in a kaleidoscopic array of visions. The result is deeply meditative and serenely floating. If one had ever come to think that late twentieth century music was caustic, here is the perfect antidote.

The work was composed in 1978 and premiered in that year by violinist Vladimir Spivakov, to whom it is dedicated. Although initially scored for violin and piano, *Spiegel im Spiegel* has been transcribed by its composer for various other combinations, including viola and piano, clarinet and piano, horn and piano, and even saxophone and piano. In almost any setting, it is a haunting score well worth discovery.

- John Williams: *Air and Simple Gifts*

It is for his film music that one most frequently encounters John Williams (b. 1932). When one has composed for *Jaws*, *ET*, all the *Star Wars* films, all the *Indiana Jones* films, most of the *Harry Potter* films, and a great deal else (see Chapter Nine), it can be hard to avoid typecasting. However, this American composer has also attracted attention outside of Hollywood. He studied at the Juilliard School, conducted the Boston Pops Orchestra for over a decade, and has recorded works as central to the mainstream of classical music as Holst's *The Planets* (see Chapter Three). His own catalog of works, in addition to over one-hundred film scores, includes orchestral works, numerous concertos, brilliant fanfares, and even some small scale works, such as his *Air and Simple Gifts*.

No composition was ever heard by more persons at its premiere performance than Williams' *Air and Simple Gifts*. Composed especially for President Obama's inauguration, its first performance by Itzhak Perlman, Yo-Yo Ma, Anthony McGill, and Gabriela Montero was given on the steps of the US Capitol January 20, 2009, before a live audience of tens of thousands with many millions more watching on television.

Controversy arose later when it was learned that what was heard was a recording that played while the musicians (all of unquestioned reputation) synchronized their motions, playing actually very softly. Some observers were infuriated by what they viewed as a deception. Others pointed out that the weather for this outdoor performance, though clear and sunny, had temperatures barely above freezing: not ideal for Stradivariuses, or, for that matter, for clarinets and pianos. The players themselves were willing to face the chill, but their instruments wouldn't have fared well, which would have done justice neither to the music nor to the stately occasion.

Williams' score — for violin, cello, clarinet, and piano — uses the old American hymn tune that appears so prominently in Copland's *Appalachian Spring* (see Chapter Ten). After a brief lyrical introduction largely for the strings, the theme itself takes center stage for a sequence of variations shared amongst all four players, though appearing first on the clarinet, which happens to be exactly how Copland introduced it in his ballet. From there, however, Williams goes his own way. The music makes the most of the contrasting voices of the instruments while exploring the potential of the theme at hand, making even more of it than Copland had done over sixty years earlier. Williams proves how much a gifted artist can make of even small scale musical forces.

- Tower: *Island Prelude*

American composer Joan Tower (b. 1928) was born in New Rochelle, New York, but grew up in Bolivia, where her father was working as a mining engineer. Her childhood memories include evenings when her Latin American nanny would take the young girl along to dance clubs, where she gained a fond and lasting affection for intricate rhythms. Tower later attended Bennington College, and holds a doctorate in composition from Columbia University, though she considers herself mostly self-taught, maintaining, "Everything I learned about writing music that was meaningful came from writing and hearing it." One might also add "playing it," as she is a skilled pianist who has been active as a chamber musician. Her works have been performed by such prestigious ensembles as the New York Philharmonic, the San Francisco Symphony, and the Aspen Festival Orchestra.

Tower's catalog of works includes symphonic scores and solo piano pieces, but most numerous are chamber works for small varied ensembles. In these, she often calls upon woodwinds, a feature that is especially prevalent in her *Island Prelude*, which premiered in 1989. Tower describes the work as being inspired by a vision of a tropical bird soaring and gliding above a white beach beside the jungle. The diversity of colors of that scene comes to life in the varied voices of the selected instruments. *Island Prelude* exists in several different versions: the oboe and string quartet setting (most frequently heard), another for oboe with string orchestra, and also a wind quintet version.

Further Recommendations:

Here is a selection of other interesting chamber music for which there was not room in the main body of the chapter:

- Arcangelo Corelli (1653-1713): Italy's greatest violinist/ composer before the arrival of Vivaldi a quarter century later, Corelli composed much fine music to spotlight his own instrument. His so-called Trio Sonatas actually use four musicians — two with solo lines and two with the accompanying "continuo" part. His works were favorites of Thomas Jefferson, who was a good amateur violinist.

- Luigi Boccherini (1743-1805): This Italian born cellist/ composer spent many years based in Spain, where he re-worked some of his string quintets so that one of the five parts was now delegated to the guitar. One, the quintet no. 4, nicknamed "Fandango," becomes especially Iberian in mood.

- Wolfgang Amadeus Mozart (1756-1791): Mozart composed violin sonatas, piano trios, string quartets, and string quintets in large number. However, he only wrote one Clarinet Quintet, scored for clarinet and string quartet.

It received its widest audience — and well deserved — in the final episode of the television series *MASH*.

-   Franz Danzi (1763-1826): Despite his Italianate name, Danzi was German and associated with the exceptionally fine orchestra in Mannheim, one that even Mozart admired. His quintets for winds (flute, oboe, clarinet, bassoon, and horn) are among the first such works for that combination of instruments.

-   Giuseppe Verdi (1813-1901): Particularly known as a composer of opera (much more about him in Chapter Eight), Verdi also composed exactly one String Quartet. As many of his operas include quartets for four voices, working here with four instruments was well within his abilities.

-   Pablo de Sarasate (1844-1908): This Spanish virtuoso violinist was so renowned that he appears in the Sherlock Holmes story "The Red-Headed League" — neither as a victim nor a culprit, but as an evening's diversion for the great detective. Sarasate wrote many short works for violin and piano, most of which are virtuosic in their demands.

-   Eugene Ysaÿe (1858-1931): The Belgian violinist was also a composer, producing various chamber works, but most prominently six solo violin sonatas — utterly solo, without even a pianist to share the effort. Success is all in the violinist's hands.

-   Maurice Ravel (1875-1937): Impressed by the sights and sounds he experienced at the Paris World Exhibition of 1889, Ravel infused his only String Quartet with stylistic elements borrowed from Javanese percussion music.

-   Ernest Bloch (1880-1959): Not to be confused with his near contemporary, philosopher Ernst Bloch, composer Ernest

Bloch was Swiss born but spent many years based in the US. His chamber music features quartets and sonatas, but especially a series of works inspired by his Jewish heritage. These include *From Jewish Life* and *Méditation hébraïque*, both for cello and piano, and *Ba'al Shem* for violin and piano.

- Paul Hindemith (1895-1963): Himself an avid performer of chamber music (he played viola), Hindemith composed sonatas pairing almost any imaginable instrument with piano. Even trombone and tuba are given their own sonatas, as well as more frequently spotlighted instruments.

- Jean Françaix (1912-1997): Born in Le Mans, France, Françaix composed in a Neo-Classical style, using generally Mozartian structures but somewhat more modern harmonies. As Haydn would have used strings, Françaix uses saxophones in his high-spirited Little Quartet for Saxophones.

- Leo Brouwer (b. 1939): His *Cuban Landscape with Rain* — Brouwer himself is Cuban — is an atmospheric quartet for guitars; the rain that comes is no gentle shower but a tropical downpour.

Chapter Six

Keyboard Music

Beethoven likely didn't imagine that this gentle little theme would become one of his most frequently heard piano melodies. Then again, he couldn't have imagined the existence of radio, let alone the long-running program "Adventures in Good Music" with Karl Haas, who chose the middle movement of Beethoven' Pathetique Sonata for his theme music. That movement serves as an elegant and understated example of what one can coax from a piano; the movements that precede and follow it offer contrary, far more extroverted cases. Indeed, of the varied keyboard works in this chapter, that's what one consistently finds: two hands on a keyboard can bring forth an impressive variety of musical effects, even within a single work.

Of instruments still in use today, the first keyboard instruments were harpsichords and organs. The organ, in the grand form of the pipe organ, is familiar to anyone who has set foot in a church. The harpsichord was a predecessor of the piano, though with a more delicate mechanism, giving it a lighter, rather plucky sound. Either instrument has keys laid out like a modern piano, though both harpsichords and organs might have more than one keyboard, one above the other, allowing for complicated combinations of sound.

As for the familiar piano, it came to life in Italy in 1709, but at first was just one man's unusual invention. It did not become truly popular until the 1770s and even then, wasn't the formidable instrument that one thinks of today as a concert grand piano. The large size and power of the piano dates only from the early 1800s, when manufacturers began giving the instrument a metal frame and sturdier strings. Of the important composers, Beethoven would have been the first to use one. Ironically, by the time this more modern instrument came to be, Beethoven was deaf, so though he appreciated its heft, he never really heard it.

As for electronic synthesizers and samplers, some modern composers use them, and since the keyboards are laid out in the same way as on a piano, one could play even Bach electronically. However, it isn't generally done. The usual idea is that it is best to use the sort of instrument that the composer had in his ears when he wrote the composition, so that the result bears more resemblance to what the composer would have expected.

Each of the composers featured in this chapter was a master of the keyboard instrument for which the featured piece was intended. Several of them principally earned their livings at the keyboard, playing their own music and works of other composers. All knew well what a piano (or harpsichord or organ) could do, and excelled at bringing out its finest points in their music. Like a golf course designed by a great master player, or a ski run designed by a World Cup competitor, a keyboard composition composed by a great master performer seeks to create an ultimate experience, bringing more from it than one would gain from another person with less personal perspective.

- JS Bach: Toccata and Fugue in d minor, BWV 565

The fugue was a popular pattern of composition during the Baroque Era and afterward, requiring composers to combine several sufficiently contrasting melodies that nonetheless could be played simultaneously without causing musical disaster. Each melody starts in one layer of the music, and then proceeds to another layer while other subsidiary melodies gradually appear to accompany it. Bach had not invented the idea personally, but made much use of it in diverse compositions, most famously in his solo organ pieces but also in instrumental works and choral cantata movements. Moreover, he spent the last decades of his life at work on what would become the principal text on the subject, a collection known as *The Art of the Fugue*, still studied now two and a half centuries after his passing. Bach knew more than anyone how to make all the parts fit together harmoniously while still keeping the music from becoming overly repetitive.

The word "toccata" derives from the Italian "toccare," meaning to touch, as in how one plays a keyboard instrument. Toccatas tended to have a great many fast runs and arpeggios pouring up and down the keyboard, but otherwise were generally free-form, giving the composer much latitude for personal expression. Toccatas often served as introductions to the greater complexity of fugues, setting the stage for the intricacy that would follow.

The most famous of all Bach's organ pieces — indeed, thanks to the first *Fantasia* film, which opens with conductor Leopold Stokowski's orchestration of the work, the most famous organ piece by any composer in all of history — is Bach's Toccata and Fugue in d minor, BWV 565. Given the notoriety of the piece, it is surprising to find that, in fact, there is some mystery surrounding this masterpiece, notably suggestions by some scholars that the work is not by Bach at all. These allegations are based on the fact that the piece deviates in subtle ways from Bach's usual style; supposedly, therefore, Bach could <u>not</u> have written it. Yet it does seem plausible that in this one work, Bach might have intentionally experimented with new techniques. Other scholars attribute these differences to youthfulness, theorizing instead that Bach wrote it as a young man, before developing a firmly established style. In fact, its date of composition is uncertain. Whatever the reason for the deviations, one point seems clear: it is one of the most effective and familiar organ compositions ever written.

- Bach: *The Well- Tempered Clavier*, BWV 846-893

Bach never composed even one work for the piano; the opportunity simply never presented itself. In the 1730s, when Bach composed most of his keyboard works, the piano was a brand-new invention, actually still a prototype in the Italian city of Florence. As Bach lived half a continent away in central Germany, he knew nothing of the new instrument, and never wrote for it. Lacking a piano, he composed instead for the harpsichord, the clavichord, and the organ. Contemporary pianists, in approaching the music of Bach, must adapt these works to their own, more modern instrument. Although they have more power and range at their disposal, they lack a certain amount of Baroque delicacy, and only the finest pianists can find a happy medium between those two extremes.

Bach's largest scale keyboard composition is the set of preludes and fugues known as *The Well Tempered Clavier*. "Clavier" was the generic term for a keyboard instrument, including harpsichords, clavichords, and organs. Indeed, although the instruments sound different from each other and have different mechanisms, any reasonably competent player can move from one to another without serious difficulty, so Bach seems to have felt no need to specify which should be used. Thus, transferring the music to a modern piano is not out of line. As to the "tempered" part of the title, it does not refer to the instrument's demeanor or that of the player. Rather, tempering was a system of tuning a keyboard instrument so that the various pitches would all be correct intervals from each other. So the title simply states that it comprises a group of pieces to be played on a well-adjusted keyboard instrument of whatever variety.

The collection is divided into two books, each with twenty-four preludes paired with another twenty-four fugues. The first book Bach completed while employed at the royal court in Cöthen in the 1720s, the second almost two decades later in Leipzig where church music had become his primary focus. Taken together, the pieces span all the major and minor keys. Apparently, they were intended to serve as instruction pieces, giving players experience in working with the chords, scales, and arpeggios in each key, as well as exploring the multi-layered techniques of fugue writing, which would require a player to keep all the intricate layers of music in alignment with each other. As such, the collection allows modern listeners to review in close order the ideas that Bach and his colleagues were expected to master. Even a century after Bach's death, pianists and composers were still studying the pieces as explorations of keyboard technique. When Chopin sat down to write a set of preludes himself, he felt driven to specifically deny that he would write as many as Bach had: such was the music world's familiarity with the Bach set that there might otherwise have been expectation of following his predecessor's example.

Long before the letters WTC came to signify World Trade Center, for classical aficionados they meant *Well-Tempered Clavier*. Although one cannot know to what degree Bach meant the pieces to be played all together in concert, one can admit that they make for an exciting and dynamic evening of exploration in the theories of the late Baroque.

- Scarlatti: keyboard sonatas

If a keyboard player of your acquaintance alleges to be working on a Scarlatti sonata, ask for clarification. Three generations of Scarlattis, most spending their careers in southern Italy, were successful composers in the late seventeenth and early eighteenth centuries. The most prominent member of the family was Domenico (1685-1757), but even in his case, further clarification is needed, as he composed well over five hundred solo sonatas, few of which came to press in an orderly fashion. In the time since Scarlatti's passing, several music historians have sought to bring order to this mass of music, each using different criteria for organization, thus resulting in varied numbering. The most frequently used system is that established in the 1950s by Ralph Kirkpatrick, so that Scarlatti works often bear K numbers (not to be confused with K for Köchel, the great Mozart scholar).

Whatever the numbering system, Scarlatti's sonatas show a mastery of keyboard technique equal to that of his great contemporary JS Bach, with elaborately decorated phrases and writing that sometimes requires the player to cross one hand over the other. Scarlatti may use less strictly layered counterpoint than Bach, but he had a different audience. Bach composed often for his own use, and always in central Germany; Scarlatti, though born in Naples, spent nearly forty years with the royal courts in the Iberian Peninsula, first with the Portuguese royal family, then in Spain when Portuguese princess Maria Barbara married the Spanish crown prince Fernando. Although Scarlatti would play for royal entertainment, he also taught members of the royal families to play, and needed some less virtuosic material at his disposal. However, it seems unlikely that many amateur players could comfortably play some of the sonatas; even those of slower tempos still require nimble finger work and informed interpretation. Scarlatti's name may be less familiar to the public than that of Bach, yet he was still a master in his field.

- Mozart: Variations on "Ah, vous dirai-je, Maman," K. 265

On first encountering this work, many listeners find themselves wondering why they hadn't known that Mozart wrote "Twinkle, Twinkle, Little Star." The answer is that he didn't, though that extremely familiar melody is the heart of this keyboard work. Mozart didn't know the tune as "Twinkle,

Twinkle," nor as "Baa, Baa, Black Sheep," nor as the Alphabet Song, all of which use the same old folk melody that Mozart knew in French as "Ah, vous dirai-je, Maman" (Ah, Mother, if I could tell you). But whatever words one imagines for it, the tune is the same, and it is that tune which lives at the heart of this set of variations.

Evidence suggests that he wrote it in the early 1780s, not long after leaving his native Salzburg for the imperial capital of Vienna. Variations upon familiar melodies were popular in concerts, but also for playing at home, as the middle classes were discovering the delights of domestic music making that had long been only the province of the aristocracy. This work would have served either need, though domestic pianists entertaining their families would have needed impressive skills, as some of the intricacies of the score would have sorely challenged less gifted players.

In structure, the work proceeds as expectations dictated: begin by stating the basic theme, and then offer various different interpretations of that theme, altering here the rhythm, there the harmony, elsewhere the way different layers of music interact with one another. Not only does the set show that Mozart understood the rules thoroughly enough to have high-spirited fun with them, there is also the fact that he manages to make over ten minutes of music out of what one now thinks of as "Twinkle, Twinkle, Little Star." In fact, the simpler the original theme, the more the composer can do with it, for there is that much more room for variation. The familiarity of the original melody makes this set an ideal introduction into how one would write variations, for despite the sequence of musical disguises, one can still hear the star twinkling off in the distance. For his last variation, he brings forth the biggest and most exciting music of all, so as to end with the proverbial "bang."

- Beethoven: Piano Sonata no. 8 in c minor, op. 13, "Pathetique"

Early in Beethoven's career, stimulated by the fertile musical environment in his new home of Vienna, he began an epic series of piano sonatas, which would ultimately number nearly three dozen. Twelve sonatas, including the beloved *Pathetique*, were completed before 1800, and another eleven, including the *Moonlight*, the *Pastoral*, the *Waldstein*, and the *Appassionata*, in the six years following the turn of the century. Nine more would follow from his years of deafness. No one could have been better suited to undertake such a formidable musical journey, for it was with the piano that Beethoven had first made an impact in Vienna and he knew better than anyone what drama could be called forth from it.

The eighth of his thirty-two piano sonatas was completed in 1799, and published that same year with a dedication to the composer's generous supporter, Prince Karl Lichnowsky, to whom he would soon also dedicate his Symphony no. 2 and Piano Sonata no. 12 and had already dedicated a set of piano trios, his opus no. 1. At this point in his life, not quite thirty years old, Beethoven's future deafness had not yet made itself obvious, and he had no handicaps to prevent his performing in public, an activity which proved not only enjoyable but also profitable. The sonata's dynamic energy soon attracted such attention that one young pianist, Ignaz Moscheles, hand-copied it at the library so as to be able to play it himself without having to spend the cost of purchase. Given the abundance of notes, it must have been a lengthy task.

Few of the sonatas with nicknames obtained them from Beethoven himself. Usually, the names were granted by publishers or enthusiastic admirers. However, it was Beethoven who named his Sonata no. 8 "Pathetique." The word is French and, in its original context, bears little of the disparaging context of the current English usage of "pathetic." Rather, it conveys a sense of heartfelt sympathy with a tinge of sorrow. As such, it seems better suited for the gentle middle movement (well familiar to fans of the Karl Haas radio program "Adventures in Good Music") than for the stormy passages of the first and third movements. Taken as a whole, the work serves as a dynamic example of how the best piano sonatas were written: with an abundance of contrasting themes allowing built in variety yet recurring often enough to give the piece cohesion. Mozart, too, offered contrasting melodies, yet in Beethoven, the contrasts come more abruptly and more dramatically. Though his great predecessor had been gone less than a decade, the younger man was dragging the piano determinedly into a brave new world of musical expression.

- Beethoven: *Diabelli Variations*, op. 120

In addition to composing many piano sonatas, Beethoven also produced other solo piano scores with humbler titles, though the music itself may be just as imposing. Such is the case with the *Diabelli Variations*, his last expansive solo piano score. In 1821, the music publisher Anton Diabelli mailed to Beethoven a little waltz theme that he had composed and asked the great master to write a variation on it. His plan, as he informed the master, was to collect variations on the theme by various composers and publish them together. It was an imaginative idea; however, he did not take into consideration Beethoven's own lofty impression of himself, for no man was less likely to participate in a group endeavor. Rather, he left the little waltz sitting on his desk for over a year. Then, rather than writing a single variation, he produced thirty-three, packaged them up together, and in 1823 sent them off to Diabelli, with the instruction that this was its own composition, not to be mixed with the others. Diabelli published it as Beethoven's opus 120. As for the other variations that he had collected (from fifty composers, including Schubert and Liszt, the latter of whom was then not yet in his teens), he afterward published a separate collection.

Diabelli's theme itself is nothing special, but such is the advantage, for the simpler the original material, the further the composer can then range in varying it. Range is the operative word here, for Beethoven runs far afield, not only in the quantity of variations, but also in musical style, drawing ideas from such diverse models as Bach and Mozart, amongst others. Having completed the score, he asked that it be published with a dedication to Antonia Brentano, an aristocratic woman much younger than the composer, yet object of his sincere affection. Letters revealed than he adored Antonia, and, however improbably, also got along well with her husband Franz, whom he sometimes consulted on business matters. Evidence strongly suggests that Antonia may have been the "immortal beloved" of the composer's famed passionate though never mailed love letter. If so, this dedication is proof of the durability of his affections, for the Brentanos had moved from Vienna to Frankfurt a decade before Beethoven finished this set of variations, and though he still kept in touch with them, he saw them rarely.

- Chopin: master of the piano

More than any other composer, Frederic Chopin (1810-1849) was a specialist. In his entire career, he never wrote anything that didn't include a piano in it, and the vast majority of his works are for solo piano. He found means of expression for two hands on eighty-eight keys that no one had previously imagined, ideas that have influenced composers and performers for two-hundred years. As such, it would have been possible to devote this entire chapter utterly to the works of Chopin, but to do so would have been unfair to other composers who also had something to say with the piano. So let us allow one extended article to sum up Chopin's pivotal place in the piano world.

He was the Polish pianist who conquered Paris: putting all the P words in one sentence sums up his career in a very small nutshell. Son of a Polish mother and a French father, he was born in his mother's homeland where his father had come to teach. By the age of eighteen, Chopin was already performing in public to ecstatic reviews, playing not only piano masterworks of the past, but also his own new compositions, which made the most of his strengths: not dominating the piano with muscle and flamboyance, but coaxing lyrical moods from it with poetry and finesse. His talent seemed too big for Warsaw. However, a visit to Imperial Vienna left him feeling out of place, so instead Chopin went to his father's homeland. He arrived in Paris at the age of twenty, and in the remaining half of his life, never again set foot in Poland.

Chopin quickly established himself amongst the social elite of Paris as the preferred entertainer in their elegant salons. He also taught piano to their daughters and published his solo piano pieces, some so intricate as to challenge the virtuosos; other, less formidable, approachable by talented amateurs. Yet even those simpler works benefited from refined and subtle playing, like that of Chopin himself. However, the chance to hear him in performance was rare, for his friends attest that he abhorred the hullabaloo that surrounded public concerts. If one were not so well-placed as to frequent those elegant salons of the elite, one might have known Chopin only by reputation.

His catalog of solo piano works includes three full sonatas, one of which (the second) contains as its slow movement the famed Funeral March, which was, in fact, played at the composer's own funeral. More numerous, however, are the shorter works: single movement pieces of various types that allowed him to examine some aspect of piano playing, as a poem might explore a particular image. Take different views of it, and one can find much to say, even in just a few minutes.

The largest single collection of solo piano pieces in his catalog is the Preludes, op. 28: two dozen expressive pieces in various keys, examining how those keys sound different from each other. Each of the preludes focuses upon a particular corner of playing technique and only the most gifted players — Chopin was one

— can play all of them with equal facility. They were inspired by the Preludes of JS Bach, who composed twice as many, but also lived significantly longer.

One might also investigate Chopin's nocturnes, roughly twenty in number and published a few at a time under various opus numbers. Their night-time moods — hence the "nocturne" label — are sometimes lullaby-like, but at others, seem to speak of some approaching storm. Chopin did not invent the ideas of nocturnes for piano; that honor actually goes to Irishman John Field (1782-1837). Yet Chopin's have earned a more loyal following, thanks in part to their more varied expressive moods.

The Chopin catalog additionally includes solo piano works of dance-like inspiration. They may not have been intended specifically to bring listeners to their feet for spontaneous dancing, but even if not, they made clear use of the rhythms of those dances. There are dozens of Chopin waltzes, some rather brief, others more expansive. Of the so-called "Minute Waltz" (opus 64, no. 1), it cannot be played in a minute, unless one simply leaves out about half of it. Even closer to his heart were the dances of Polish inspiration: the mazurkas (over three dozen of these) and polonaises (over one dozen of these). So popular did these become that composers who were not themselves Polish took to writing them, taking advantage of a visible demand. Without Chopin, that demand would have been less marked.

In his own performances of his own music, Chopin experimented with a technique that came to be called "rubato." It involved a rather flexible approach to tempo, speeding up or slowing down — just fractionally — for expressive effect. Skeptics of the time, Chopin's contemporary Mendelssohn amongst them, joked that he was making a virtue of necessity: that not being able to maintain a consistent tempo, he'd decided to make the most of the small variations that happened to appear. Others have suggested that rubato in music resembles the way in which a gifted actor approaches a soliloquy; rather than rattling off the words at a steady pace, he will vary it for the sake of expression.

From either point of view, rubato is part of Chopin. It is, in fact, the part that less gifted players find the most difficult to master, for it is the subtlety that sets Chopin apart from most of his pianistically inclined colleagues.

- Liszt: Hungarian master of the piano

Fine pianists come and go, but as a showman, Franz Liszt (1811-1886) may remain ever unequalled. Anecdotes abound of the electrifying effect his presence and his playing had upon otherwise well-behaved nineteenth century ladies, who fell under his charismatic spell, tossing personal mementos onto the stage. Men, too, were moved. The composer Robert Schumann had heard virtually all of the great pianists of the day, and his wife Clara was one of the greatest, yet of Liszt he observed, "It is unlikely that any other artist, excepting only Paganini, has the power to lift, carry and deposit an audience in such high degree... In a matter of seconds, we have been exposed to tenderness, daring, fragrance, and madness... It simply has to be heard and seen." The comparison to Paganini (see Chapter Four) would have pleased Liszt, who — in his youth having seen the great violinist perform live — set out intentionally to bring that level of magnetism to his own playing at the piano.

That Liszt ultimately succeeded was proven not only by the fainting ladies in his audiences, but also by favorable words from some colleagues. "I am thoroughly impressed," Felix Mendelssohn remarked once to a friend, "both by his playing and his striking personality." Yet when Mendelssohn invited Liszt to join him in concert with the Leipzig Gewandhaus Orchestra on the occasion of Liszt's birthday, he declined to allow Liszt to play his own music, and insisted instead that they should play Bach. Liszt's own piano music was flashy and flamboyant, far beyond Mendelssohn's personal tastes. Conservative critics often expressed the opinion that Liszt lacked musical substance, yet his works have stood the test of time, at least for those pianists who possess both the strength and the determination to approach it.

When it comes to playing Liszt, one cannot quite say "conquer" it, for even the most gifted players find the music just manageable. The great Chinese pianist Lang Lang has remarked in interviews with *Gramophone Magazine* that, to play Liszt, he wishes he had a few extra fingers.

Liszt's solo piano music comes in many flavors. Most frequently heard are the various *Hungarian Rhapsodies*, nearly twenty in all, borrowing the vibrant rhythms of the composer's ethnic heritage. Then there are the so-called *Transcendental Etudes*, which live up to their name by handily "transcending" what any other composer of the time thought was possible to achieve on a single piano. The three *Years of Pilgrimage* suites recall Liszt's musical impressions of his travels, mostly in Italy but also in Switzerland. Frequently featured on his personal concerts were the numerous "paraphrases" on popular opera themes: arias and scenes reworked for solo piano performance. When the pianist is the caliber of Liszt, one hardly misses the singers. The truly ambitious pianist might also brave the heights of Liszt's transcriptions of Beethoven symphonies, which attempt to capture at the keyboard the entire scope of an orchestral score. Not only need the player cover all those many notes, but also attempt to make a trumpet line sound trumpet-like in its intensity, or a violin line sound violin-like, and so on. Chopin would never have taken on such a task, but Liszt was a big thinker when it came to his music.

These two master pianists were well-acquainted with one another. Only a year and a half apart in age, both had left their Eastern European roots by the age of twenty in favor of the bright lights of Paris. They moved in the same social circles, but remained distinct in personality and style. Chopin was known for the finesse of his playing, Liszt for flash and fervor. Chopin disliked giving public concerts, preferring instead to play in private salons; Liszt thrived in the spotlight and personally popularized the idea of attending a solo piano recital for an invigorating experience. Liszt was also the ladies' man of the two, being not only charismatic but also tall and handsome. He possessed a sequence of lovers, generally of aristocratic birth, and with one of them, fathered multiple children, including the girl who would become second wife of Richard Wagner (1813-1883). Celebrity exploits that fill the covers of magazines nowadays have nothing on Liszt, but his music has survived without falling out of favor, so he was clearly more than a matinee idol. His music preserves for us today the excitement of an evening in his presence.

One significant difference between Liszt and Chopin is that Liszt was no specialist. Chopin put all his musical energies into the piano; by contrast, Liszt composed also for orchestra and wrote a large quantity of sacred choral music. Additionally, he was an influential conductor, working especially in Weimar, Germany. For more on Liszt, and particularly his orchestral music, see Chapter Three.

- Clara Schumann: Four Fugitive Pieces, op. 15

Throughout her long career, Clara Wieck Schumann (1819-1896) had an international reputation as a pianist. A Leipzig-born child prodigy whose father had her performing Beethoven sonatas in Vienna before she was ten, she was widely famed as one of the era's foremost Beethoven interpreters, and her restrained and elegant style of playing drew praises from all those who found Liszt a bit too flamboyant for their tastes. Composition was not a major facet of her career, for performance and family (ultimately, seven children) demanded most of her time. Yet in her day, all great soloists studied theory and harmony, and were expected to perform their own compositions occasionally.

Clara was no exception. Her first works were published in 1831, when she was not yet twelve years old, and she completed a piano concerto in her early teens. After her marriage, Clara concentrated on performance instead of composition. Statements in her diary show that she felt one composer in the family was enough, and that composer was her husband Robert, whom she married the day before her twenty-first birthday. Yet she did not completely abandon composition. In fact, some of her best compositions date from the years of her marriage.

The *Four Fugitive Pieces* were written in the first five years after the wedding. Wistfully understated in mood, they show a Romantic fondness for introspection and are suffused with the same gentleness that characterizes the nocturnes of Chopin. Those works may be better known, but these are no less consoling. By "fugitive," Clara cannot have meant to imply evading legal pursuit. Rather, the focus was upon the unrestrained nature of the music, freer in its flow than that of earlier eras.

- Brahms: *Variations on a Theme by Haydn, op. 56a*

From the modern perspective, Johannes Brahms (1833-1897) is often viewed as the ultimate Romantic composer, whose lush and lyrical works came to characterize an age. Yet when he was alive, the story was quite different. Other composers of his day, themselves devout Romantics, thought Brahms hopelessly old-fashioned. To Wagner and Liszt, he seemed out of step with the day, and to some extent, they were correct. Brahms' compositions consciously recalled earlier times and styles at a time when other composers were looking strictly toward the future. However anachronistic he may have seemed to his contemporaries, it is still fortunate that Brahms had these interests, for he was able to preserve long-beloved musical concepts which might have otherwise been lost. Even Liszt admitted, "One sees what can still be done with the old forms, in the hands of one who knows how to deal with them."

A fine example of Brahms' interest in earlier styles is the well-known *Variations on a Theme of Haydn*. By the time the piece was written in 1873, Haydn's name and music were largely neglected. In the six decades since Haydn's passing, many of his manuscripts had been lost, and even the now-popular symphonies were rarely performed. One of the few scholars to show an interest in the earlier master's music was Karl Ferdinand

Pohl, librarian of the Vienna Philharmonic and a good friend of Brahms. Through Pohl's influence, Brahms learned about the music of Haydn. He studied many scores, and, in a set of wind partitas, found a setting of a melody known as the St. Anthony Chorale. This stately theme became the heart of the *Haydn Variations*. The fact that scholars today are certain that the partita in question was not, in fact, the work of Haydn at all, but had only been mistakenly credited to his name, does nothing to diminish the magnificent imagination that Brahms brought to this simple and gracious theme.

The *Haydn Variations* was first heard at a private gathering in Bonn in August 1873, as Brahms and his dear friend Clara Schumann (by this time, Robert's widow) played a two-piano version of the piece. Brahms also prepared an orchestration of the work, which premiered a few months later with the composer himself conducting the Vienna Philharmonic. Whether speaking of the original keyboard edition or the later orchestral setting, the *Haydn Variations* stand today amongst his best-loved works, and the work was also one of the composer's personal favorites. Late in life, Brahms wrote, "I have always had a weakness for that piece and I think of it with more satisfaction than any other."

- Mussorgsky: *Pictures at an Exhibition*

The greatest talents of Russian Romanticism all began their careers outside the musical realm. Peter Tchaikovsky (1840-1893) scribbled away part of his twenties as a government law clerk. Nicolai Rimsky-Korsakov (1844-1908) toured the world as a naval officer. For Modest Mussorgsky (1839-1881), son of a wealthy landowner, the profession of choice was also military, but in his case, without the oceanic element. In his late teens, the cultured and educated Mussorgsky left cadet school and joined the Preobrazhensky Guards, an elite unit far more concerned with handsome uniforms and bright ceremony at the Tsar's court than with the perils of combat duty. Yet even that was not where Mussorgsky's heart lay; before the age of twenty, he had resigned his commission and taken up a composer's career.

Pictures at an Exhibition was written in 1874 as a memorial to the composer's late friend, the artist Victor Hartmann. Mussorgsky had been devastated by Hartmann's death. "What a terrible blow!" he lamented. "There can and must be no consolation — it is a rotten mortality!" Others, it seems, were also moved by the loss, for soon a retrospective exhibit of Hartmann's sketches, stage designs, and architectural studies was presented. After visiting the exhibition, Mussorgsky was possessed by the need to capture his experience in music. By early summer, he had completed the work, a lengthy and fiendishly difficult suite for solo piano, but from there, it went no further. At the time of Mussorgsky's premature death in 1881 from alcoholism, the score was still unpublished. It fell to his friend and colleague Rimsky-Korsakov to tidy up the manuscript and bring it to print in 1886. Although better known now in Maurice Ravel's orchestration from 1922, *Pictures* began life as a solo piano score, and it is only that version that has any chance of giving us Mussorgsky's personal vision.

The suite portrays ten Hartmann pictures, interspersed with stately promenades recalling a visitor — in this case, the composer — strolling through the gallery. The powerful nature of this "Promenade" theme, first heard in the work's opening bars, may recall the fact that Mussorgsky himself was a large man. The first four pictures, in order of appearance, are: "the Gnome," conveyed through irregular rhythms and forceful outbursts; "the Old Castle," a solemn and lyrical depiction of a medieval troubadour; "Tuiliries," a sprightly portrayal of children at play in the gardens of Paris; and the ponderous "Bydlo," an appropriately ponderous illustration of a Polish ox-cart. Next is the scampering of "the Ballet of the Chicks in their Shells," a costume design by Hartmann for a children's ballet. The sixth picture is "Two Jews: One Rich, One Poor," in which overbearing moods contrast with nervous fragments of melodies. "The Market at Limoges" is folksy and cheerful. "Catacombs," by contrast, casts an eerie shadow with ominous chords and variations on the promenade theme.

The last two scenes are the most renowned. "The Hut on Fowl's Legs" is a nightmare portrayal of a cackling witch on the prowl, determinedly hunting her prey. The hunt charges unabated directly into the tenth and last picture, "The Great Gate of Kiev," bringing the suite to a triumphant conclusion as Mussorgsky captures Hartmann's sketch of a proposed city gate topped by cupolas in which carillons ring.

- Grieg: *Wedding Day at Troldhaugen* (Lyric Piece, op. 65, no. 6)

Edvard Grieg (1843-1907) was born in the Norwegian coastal city of Bergen. His mother was an amateur pianist of local fame; his father, the British consul at Bergen, was also an amateur musician. Although some of their ancestors derived from Scotland, just across the North Sea from Bergen, the family had been established in Norway for a century at the time of Edvard's birth. The fourth of five children, Edvard began studying piano at age six, and throughout his life maintained a facility for that instrument.

By 1858, his talent had so matured that his parents sent him to Leipzig to study. In that musical city, former home of Bach and Mendelssohn, Grieg developed a lasting affection for the works of another Leipziger, Robert Schumann, recently deceased, though not yet forgotten. Grieg even had the opportunity to hear Schumann's Piano Concerto (see Chapter Four) performed by the composer's widow, the renowned Clara Schumann. Yet it seems the German master's works were the only fact of Leipzig life that Grieg found palatable, for Grieg's letters otherwise describe his experience there as repellant. Left to personal choice, Grieg would have departed briskly, but for the sake of his parents, he remained through graduation in the spring of 1862. Free at last, he returned at first to Norway, but soon relocated to Copenhagen, the most prominent cultural city in Scandinavia. Ultimately, he would make his way back to his native Bergen where today, his mountainside home with a view of the fjord is a popular tourist site.

In the popular imagination, Grieg is most often remembered as an orchestral composer, specifically as the composer of music for the play *Peer Gynt* (see Chapter Nine). Indeed, that most Norwegian of all works is generally viewed as his masterpiece, and is the only Grieg that is widely familiar, but he also composed many other pieces, relatively few of which were orchestral. He produced only one symphony, which he later suppressed. That work, along with one piano concerto and a few occasional pieces and sets of incidental music, are his entire orchestral output. Grieg was far more prolific, and some would suggest more creative, in the realms of chamber music. His numerous songs (his wife Nina was a singer) and solo pieces for piano (his own instrument) show an intimate side of his musical voice, poetic and melodic.

Edvard and Nina Grieg moved to their Bergen home, named Troldhaugen, in 1885, and remained there the rest of their lives. Twelve years after moving in, he published a set of six so-called "Lyric Pieces" for solo piano in which one piece was named for the home. Last of the set, *Wedding Day at Troldhaugen* is a sweetly reflective mood piece, having more to do with sunny skies and flowers than with grand wedding marches. The composer, himself of variable health and lacking not the skill but only the power to dominate the piano, had discovered that one need not always depend upon thunder for dramatic effect.

- Albeniz: *Asturias*

Isaac Albeniz (1860-1909) was born in provincial Spain. He learned the piano so quickly that, at the age of four, he gave a public concert. In the years that followed, he supported his parents by concertizing throughout Spain, ever on the road, yet scarcely seeing the money he was earning, as his father pocketed it. By the age of eight, the boy had had enough. Twice he ran away, supporting himself by giving concerts; both times, he was fetched home. Finally, age twelve, he decided to run further away: to South America, stowing away on a steamship to Buenos Aires. Aboard ship, the boy attracted the attention of a fellow Spaniard who took him on a concert tour of the Americas that would reach as far as San Francisco. By the time he returned to Spain in 1875, still only fifteen, Albeniz was an international star.

Albeniz continued to appear as a concert pianist, but turned more and more to composition. In 1890, he moved to London, then to Paris. For most of the rest of his short life (he died of a kidney condition two weeks before his forty-ninth birthday), Albeniz lived outside of his native land. Still, his compositions are filled from start to finish with the spirit of Spain, and though most of his works are for his own instrument, the piano, other instrumentalists, from orchestras to string quartets to solo guitarists, have taken his music into their hearts as transcriptions, unable to resist the lively rhythms and rich coloration.

Albeniz' most frequently performed work is *Asturias*, dating from 1887. Its name comes from a principality on the northern coast of Spain, abutting the Atlantic. Ethnomusicologists have pointed out that the rhythms Albeniz uses are not, in fact, those of the Asturias region and that the piece should be called something else. However, to do so would only confuse generations of music lovers, particularly those of solo guitar, for guitarists have adopted it determinedly. It was not composed for them. Albeniz wrote it for piano, yet its rolled chords work so well as strummed ones for guitarists that the piece fits their instrument at least as well as it fits the piano.

There are two main melodies in *Asturias*. First is a determined, driving, strongly accented theme that ever builds in energy. Eventually, this theme gives way to a more melancholy middle section. Here, Albeniz seems to have in mind his own subtitle for the piece: "leyendas," referring to a kind of folk tale; the music here can be heard as evoking a sort of 'once upon a time' mood. After the shadows of the middle section, the driving opening melody returns to charge toward the conclusion. Whether played on piano or guitar, as long as the steady pulse of the opening and closing is maintained, *Asturias* is a strongly evocative work.

- Debussy: *Suite bergamasque* (including *Clair de lune*)

It is on his ethereal orchestral score *Prelude to the Afternoon of a Faun* (see Chapter Three) that the reputation of Claude Debussy (1862-1918) mostly rests. In that work and its siblings, notably *La mer* and the *Nocturnes for Orchestra*, the essence of Debussy and of Impressionism in general rests. Yet he was also a devotee of the piano and, in fact, it was as a piano student that the eleven-year-old was admitted to the Paris Conservatoire in 1873. Composition studies followed and soon took precedence, but he never ceased to play, and always continued to write for piano, producing dozens of solo pieces. Contemporary descriptions of his playing style hint at how one must approach these works, for he was known for the lightness of his touch. There is subtlety in Debussy's piano music, as in earlier generations there was in that of Chopin. It was a role model worth attention.

Of all Debussy's many solo piano pieces, none is played more frequently, by professionals and amateurs alike, than *Clair de lune* (*Moonlight*). Yet it is often forgotten that the lyrical miniature originated as part of a four-movement suite, the *Suite bergamasque*, composed in 1889 (even before *Prelude to the Afternoon of a Faun*) and published in 1903. The suite's title derives from Bergamo, a community in the foothills of the Italian Alps, though in Debussy's time, the adjective had come to have less to do with the town itself than with its conversational implication of a comic rustic. Yet these rustics seem astonishingly elegant, as what the composer has crafted is in part a suite of French courtly dances, the first and third open and flowing with much use of legato tones, the second and fourth quick and light-footed, more staccato in mood. Heard in its original context, the third movement *Clair de lune* is not just an elegant wisp but rather serves as an important transition between contrasting scenes.

- Satie: *Trois Gymnopedies*

If one's image of an artiste tends toward an eccentrically dressed denizen of a Montmartre café, one needs look no further than Eric Satie (1866-1925). The Frenchman attended the Paris Conservatoire mostly to stay out of military service. His friends attested that he owned twelve identical suits. He collaborated on ballets with those masters of the avant garde Cocteau and Picasso. He gave his piano pieces outré titles such as *Desiccated Embryos (Embryons desséchés), Three Pieces in the Shape of a Pear (Trois morceaux en forme de poire), Three Flabby Preludes — for a Dog (Trois preludes flasques — pour un chien)*, and even *Three Genuine Flabby Preludes — for a Dog (Trois veritable preludes flasques — pour un chien)*. Had he lived most of a century later, he might have fit right into Berkeley's counter-culture. As it is, Satie would have been the perfect Bohemian to populate Puccini's *La Bohéme* (see Chapter Eight).

Satie is principally remembered for his solo piano music, and not just for the colorful titles of those works. His piano scores offer open, airy harmonies flavored with the south-east Asian techniques to which Satie had been exposed at the Paris Exhibition of 1889. Structures are often abstract, though he could also write a fugue when he wished. Yet focused direction was never his strong suit, and were it not for friends and colleagues sorting out his papers when Satie died of sclerosis of the liver, little of his music would have survived. He was, however, influential in his time, and even Debussy let Satie's ideas affect his own piano scores.

Most familiar of Satie's works are the *Trois Gymnopedies* for solo piano. "Trois" simply means "three;" as for "gymnopedies," it is a reference to athletic dance of ancient Greece, memorably evoked on pottery and friezes. The mood is stately and serene, almost drifting from one moment to the next. Here is a vision of the piano far more abstract than Brahms ever imagined, though the *Gymnopedies* date from 1888, and Brahms still had nearly a decade left to him. Satie was imagining a new frontier of music, one that anticipated the trance-like moods of some music in the late 1960s.

- Vierne: Organ Symphonies

Nearly blind from birth, apparently due to congenital cataracts, Louis Vierne (1870-1937) yet managed a successful music career. He learned the piano by ear, then the organ, and began composing by writing the notes large enough that he could see them. Although the bulk of his compositions are for organ, his preference for that instrument did not prevent him from writing other works; chamber music, songs and choral music, and one orchestral symphony are also to be found in his catalog. However, the organ was closest to his heart, in part from having heard the great composer/organist Cesar Franck (1822-1890) play at the church of Ste. Clothilde in Paris. Vierne himself would become organist at the church of St. Sulpice, and then later held the grandest organ post in all of Paris: that at Notre Dame. It was at the keyboard of the Notre Dame organ that he died, having wanted to hear that impressive instrument one last time at his command.

Amongst Vierne's organ works are six he labeled Organ Symphonies, the first written in 1899 and the last in 1930. One may be accustomed to seeing the word "symphony" applied to a multi-movement composition for a full orchestra to play, with the various instruments set against one another to exploit the contrasts between their voices. However, an organ can do those things, too, especially when it is in the care of a master performer such as Vierne. His organ symphonies are part Bach in inspiration (in their deft exploitation of the instrument's features) and part Beethoven (in their development and juxtaposition of melodic material), and, as with either of those models, the various movements of each symphony offer different musical visions for the sake of variety of expression.

Given the harmonic resources of the organ, one can get as much out of it as out of a full symphony orchestra, and Vierne's Organ Symphonies prove this fact. One need not be Bach to make the most of an organ, and even in the early twentieth century, there were still new musical statements to come from this impressive piece of musical architecture.

- Scriabin: Six Etudes

Alexander Scriabin (1872-1915) was Russia's answer to Richard Wagner: a composer who, in his own outlandish way, sought to revolutionize music, thereby dividing his listeners into devoted supporters and confused detractors. An only child, Scriabin was raised by his aunt and grandmother after his mother died young and his father vanished into consular service abroad. The women doted upon their charge and spoiled him immeasurably, producing a fussy young man determined to follow his every whim. In 1888, the sixteen year old entered the Moscow Conservatory for piano and composition studies. He excelled at the work, ultimately graduating with the school's second highest honor, his classmate Sergei Rachmaninoff (1873-1943) having made off with the top prize.

In the solo career that followed, Scriabin's repertoire leaned toward the early Romantics: Chopin, Mendelssohn, Schumann, and Liszt. Before long, however, his own works would be gaining an audience, as would his reputation for theosophy: musing on the nature of God. By his mid-thirties, Scriabin had come to regard himself as a musical messiah who was sure his mystical works communicated the essence of God and of existence. His musical philosophy became similarly unusual; had he not died in 1915 at age forty-three, he might have successfully promoted his unusual harmonic approaches even before the progressive Viennese such as Arnold Schoenberg (1874-1951) finally brought those ideas to the public ear.

Whatever one makes of Scriabin's philosophy, the fact remains that his music holds a lasting allure. One might debate the colors that he envisioned in different chords (specific shades for specific tonal combinations), but that it remains colorful in the broader sense is beyond denial. The gently shifting harmonic tones of his finest works rival Debussy for their subtlety; set against the rhythmic intensity of his younger colleagues, such as Igor Stravinsky (1882-1971), Scriabin's languorous moods are appealingly sensuous. His etudes, like Chopin's before him, convey atmosphere even as they hone technique. These are not just pedagogical pieces with which a pianist fine-tunes his fingering; rather, they are worthy concert works in their own right in which a wealth of mood and expression awaits discovery.

- Cage: Sonatas and Interludes for Prepared Piano

John Cage (1912-1992) stood on the most cutting edge of the avant garde. As such, his music is not often heard either on classical music radio or in concert halls. Yet his ideas were at least intellectually interesting and, in the 1940s and '50s, influential amongst progressives, so he deserves attention. The existence of John Cage says much about American music in the post-war years, and often brings to mind the popular bumper sticker, "I'm not lost — I'm exploring."

Born in Los Angeles, Cage studied composition with the Austrian Arnold Schoenberg, who in the 1930s was driven by politics to forsake Europe in favor of the US. Schoenberg had been a leading figure in the strongly progressive Second Viennese School, a fact that one might imagine influenced Cage. However, Schoenberg expected his students first to have a strong foundation in the old ideas of Bach, Beethoven, and the like before moving on to modernist rule-bending, and like Schoenberg, Cage knew the "rules" perfectly well. However, he chose to look beyond them. Moreover, Cage's father was professionally an inventor, and the son, too, was accustomed to thinking outside the box. His music, it seems, never saw the inside of a box.

Cage's various Sonatas and Interludes for Prepared Piano date from the '40s and '50s, and to make sense of them at all, one must grasp the concept of a "prepared piano." Surely all pianos are "prepared," at least by the piano tuner? Here is something different. The "preparation" is a specific set of instructions to follow as to exactly how one must insert between the piano strings various nuts and bolts and other pieces of hardware. These inclusions vary the timbre (voice) of the instrument, giving it at times a gong-like or bell-like sound. It is as if the piano's keyboard were mystically controlling an Asian percussion ensemble, giving an entirely new voice to what would otherwise be a thoroughly familiar instrument.

This search for new ideas was central to Cage's world view. This writer interviewed him in 1987 in Telluride, Colorado, to which he had been tempted by the fortuitous (and by no means coincidental) juxtaposition of two summer events: a festival of new music and another of mushroom hunting. Cage was known to be a devoted mycologist, and festival organizers thought this was the best way to assure his attendance. When asked what parallels he saw between the two fields, he responded by first pointing out that they appear on the same page of the dictionary: first "mushroom," then "music." Then he added that, in either field, change is inevitable and "you never quite know what you'll find." When it comes to Cage's music, that spirit of uncertain adventure is ever-present.

Ginastera: Piano Sonata no. 1, op. 22

Argentina draws its musical accent from diverse influences. Portuguese and Spanish settlers brought with them a passion for the guitar and a preference for rhythmically intricate compositions. Those interests, mixed with the percussive energy of indigenous traditional music, led to an eclectic style that is uniquely Argentine and well demonstrated in the music of Alberto Ginastera (1916-1983). Ginastera began composition studies in his native country in 1930. Later, he worked with Aaron Copland at Tanglewood in the US before returning to his homeland. He filled many prestigious positions in the Argentine musical community, notably professor of composition and conservatory director, but the politics of the Peron regime adversely affected his career in the '40s and '50s. By the end of the 1960s, Ginastera had been forced out of Argentina. Eventually, he settled in Geneva, Switzerland, where he remained until his death.

The Piano Sonata no. 1 dates from 1952, when Ginastera was dividing his time between composition, academics, and international travel to stay in touch with the greater musical community and conduct his compositions. That his reputation stood high on the international scene is clear when one notes that of his two string quartets, his opus numbers 20 and 26 (one before, the other after this sonata), premiered on different continents: the earlier quartet in Buenos Aires and the later in Washington D.C. Audiences and colleagues were noticing Ginastera, and he was proving himself worthy of such notice. Here, he takes the idea of a solo piano sonata in several carefully structured and contrasting movements, as it has stood since Haydn's day, and offers his own interpretation of what such a work could be, flavoring it with the lively rhythms of his native land.

It is not a sonata such as Haydn would have written two centuries earlier, but like those of Ginastera's predecessors, it takes the styles of the day and incorporates them into an accepted overall blueprint, making the sonata simultaneously old and new in substance. The first movement is essentially a sonata form, with two contrasting main themes that grow and evolve as the music progresses. The second is energetically scherzo-like with a strong beat; the third is a lyrical, song-like movement with a first theme that returns after a contrasting middle section. The last is a driving toccata filled with busy rhythms.

The sonata was commissioned by the Carnegie Institute and the Pennsylvania College for Women for the Pittsburgh Contemporary Music Festival, where it premiered November 29, 1952. The performance was given by pianist Johana Harris, wife of American composer Roy Harris (1898-1979), and the work was dedicated to both Harrises. Of the work, Ginastera observed that his intention was to reflect an Argentine accent while crafting his own melodies, intending them to sound folk-like though not quoting pre-existing songs. So, although there are no Argentine folk melodies per se, the spirit is intended to be of his homeland.

- Gabriela Montero: the art of improvisation

It isn't the title of a specific work, rather a practice that Gabriela Montero (b. 1970 in Caracas) brings to her live performances. By including a sequence of improvisation in her concerts and recordings, Ms. Montero recalls a long tradition of keyboard performance. Back in the days of Mozart and Beethoven, it was considered crucial for any soloist, though particularly for a pianist, to be able to improvise deftly, crafting music off the cuff that nonetheless held together as a cohesive musical experience by drawing upon expectations of chord structures and progressions. Contemporary accounts of their concert appearances are filled with praise for their improvisational abilities. Beethoven specifically once won a keyboard contest with a professional colleague based on his superior improvisational abilities; even the loser of that contest admitted that Beethoven had simply out-improvised him. In the next generation, Liszt would be so fond of improvising that he rarely bothered to play anything as written, preferring instead his own new interpretations. Each of these great masters would be impressed to know that two centuries later, Ms. Montero is not tentative to show her own hand. To play written notes perfectly is an impressive skill; to imagine equally interesting ones spontaneously before a live audience is a rarer one.

Incidentally, many millions of persons have heard Ms. Montero perform, even though she was not improvising at the time and they may not have caught her name. She was the pianist for the premiere performance at President Obama's inauguration of John Williams' *Air and Simple Gifts*. On that occasion, the notes were by Mr. Williams, not Ms. Montero, but had her artistry not been of the highest order, she would not have been invited. For further details about that Williams' composition, please see Chapter Five.

Further Recommendations:

Here is a selection of other interesting keyboard music for which there was not room in the main body of the chapter:

- Johann Sebastian Bach (1685-1750): One ought not overlook Bach's *Goldberg Variations*, an expansive solo piece supposedly composed as late night entertainment to a nobleman who was prone to insomnia.

- John Field (1782-1837): Irish born, this international superstar of the piano ended his days in Moscow; his many Nocturnes for solo piano had a strong influence on Chopin, younger by nearly thirty years.

- Franz Schubert (1797-1828): Mostly identified with songs (see Chapter Seven), Schubert also devoted much energy to the piano; his Sonatas are some of the grandest solo piano works composed at his time; the Impromptus offer a more concise musical vision.

- Felix Mendelssohn (1809-1847): He composed about four dozen so-called *Songs without Words* — solo piano pieces of abstract musical character. Though Lucy van Pelt of *Peanuts* fame once mused of the titles "Couldn't he think of any [words]?" Mendelssohn himself declared in a letter that if he knew of any words for them, he wouldn't admit to them, as he preferred that the music stand on its own merits.

- Robert Schumann (1810-1856): His wife Clara was one of the greatest piano virtuosos of the day, and Schumann often composed for her. His *Carneval* offers musical portraits of friends and family, including his colleague Chopin and Clara herself.

- Louis Moreau Gottschalk (1829-1869): Born in New Orleans, he built an international reputation as a virtuoso pianist, especially playing his own dance-flavored works that are sometimes evocative of Latin American styles.

- Cecile Chaminade (1857-1944): A gifted French pianist and composer of hundreds of solo piano pieces, her music was marketed with her attractive face reproduced on the cover — a tactic not generally used by her male colleagues.

- Enrique Granados (1867-1916): This Spanish master crafted music in many genres, but most famously his solo piano suite *Goyescas*, inspired by the paintings of Goya. Granados was returning from a concert tour of the US (and an appearance at the White House) when his ship was torpedoed in the English Channel.

- Edward MacDowell (1860-1908): Not much caring for it, the American composer had thrown out his *To a Wild Rose*, but his wife Marian rescued it from the wastebasket. It was published as part of his *Woodland Sketches* and has gone on to great popularity for its guileless atmosphere.

- Sergei Rachmaninoff (1873-1943): Pianists need only attempt the Russian's numerous virtuosic solo piano works if they, like he, happen to be tall and lanky. He composed for his own hands, and any player less than six feet tall is unlikely to be able to manage the scope of the music. Listeners have no such problems: we can just marvel at the intricacy and power of his Preludes.

- Ariel Ramirez (1921-2010): The Argentine composer is most remembered for his folk-flavored *Misa Criolla*; however, he also crafted much attractive solo piano music equally influenced by his national roots.

- Philip Glass (b. 1937): Best known for his film music, operas (some composed specifically for the Metropolitan Opera), and orchestra works, Glass has also written and recorded a continuing set of piano Etudes. Of them, Glass himself observes that he wrote them in part to "challenge his playing," a fact which shows him to be mindful of tradition, as that is exactly what Chopin had in mind with his etudes.

Chapter Seven
Art Songs and Lieder

As the opening vocal line of Schubert's song *Der Erlkönig*, this melodic fragment should have made him a star. It leads into four minutes of drama that seems unimaginable to be coming from only two performers. Yet the best art songs — and Schubert's stand high on that list — often manage the impossible, and can sometimes prove that, in a work no longer than a modern pop song, a composer yet can move the world.

The fancy word, borrowed from German (because many of the greatest composers in this field had German as their native language), is "lieder," pronounced "LEE-der." However, it's fine to think of them as art songs: short works for a singer and a pianist, largely a matter of setting a poem to music, so that the singer has a melody to go with the poem's words and the pianist provides the accompaniment. The "art" part is important, so as to distinguish them from drinking songs, nursery songs, work songs, or folk songs. Some art songs were written in the eighteenth century, even by Bach and Mozart, but it was in the nineteenth century that the field gained its first immense popularity.

The reason seems to be that in the early 1800s, composers delighted in giving musical expression to literature, and if one is going to draw upon a poem, one might as well let it be sung. Moreover, those talented amateur musicians of the middle classes liked to have music that they could perform at home for fun, and something for one pianist and one singer tended to work in most middle class living rooms. Art songs might be written with them in mind, but sometimes also for professional performance in concerts. Although few important composers were themselves talented singers (Samuel Barber being the notable exception), most had friends or family members who sang well, and those connections gave them insights into what worked well in a song, as well as what kinds of poems had potential for becoming good songs.

So what poems make good songs? Often, those that are simplest in construction, thus giving the composer more space to make of the music what he/she will. It also helps if phrases are short enough to give singers a chance to breathe when they need to do so. Moreover, poems with words that have a great many hard consonants (such as k or q, or for that matter, s, which can regrettably snake-like) are very hard to sing beautifully; most singing is done on the vowels, not the consonants.

Most art songs are written for one singer and one pianist. However, sometimes the composer expands the accompaniment, looking further than a simple keyboard. A string quartet might be the medium of choice (as in the Samuel Barber song discussed in this chapter), or a piano quartet (as in the Ned Rorem song), or even a full orchestra (as in several particularly expansive offerings). The choice of accompaniment colors the background against which the vocal line is heard, thus strongly affecting how we as listeners perceive the music.

- Schubert: *Der Erlkönig*, D. 328, op. 1

Inspired in part by friends who were talented singers and also by the regrettable fact that most of his music was heard only by groups of friends at private musical gatherings rather than in public concerts, Franz Schubert (1797-1828) consistently turned out art songs, beginning in his teens and continuing until the last months of his all-too-brief life. Ultimately, he would compose over six-hundred songs. Their continuing appeal nearly two centuries later proves the man's mastery of the field. For particularly superior examples of his songs, consider *Heidenröslein* (a sweet tempered ballad of a boy picking a wild rose), *Du bist die Ruh* (one of the most exquisite love songs ever written in any century), and especially *Der Erlkönig* (a darkly supernatural tale).

Many authorities have cited *Der Erlkönig* as perhaps the greatest art song ever composed. The dramatic effect of these four minutes of music has never been exceeded by any similarly scaled work by any composer, though Schubert was all of eighteen when he wrote it. By all rights, it should have made his fame and fortune, but even in the arts, the world is rarely fair. Schubert did find a publisher for it — in 1821, six years after he had written it, it became his opus 1 — but he still remained little known and little appreciated outside his circle of friends. Only after his highly premature death at the age of thirty-one would Schubert's genius finally get the appreciation it had long merited.

Der Erlkönig sets a poem by Goethe (1749-1832) telling of a mystical spirit of death seeking to make off with a small child sheltered in his father's arms while riding at breakneck speed through the woods. Schubert's music perfectly conveys the contrasting voices of those three (father, child, Erlkönig*)*, as well as a narrator's voice and, in the piano, the pounding hoof-beats. For a composer so young to manage so much with only two performers was an astonishing achievement. The song was even performed for Goethe himself — a dedicated music lover — who was at first unimpressed. A later performance by a singer of apparently greater skill made a more favorable impression, and Goethe had to admit that the quality of the interpretation made a difference. Given top-flight artists — not just the singer, but the pianist, too — this little song packs as much power as many a grand opera.

- Schubert: *Ave Maria*, D. 839, op. 52, no. 6

It is the most frequently performed of all Schubert's thousand compositions. Even in his own brief lifetime, it counted as a hit, for his *Ave Maria* actually found a publisher before his death, which was true of barely ten percent of his compositions. Technically, it was called "Ellen's Song III," and indeed, there are two other songs for Ellen. Ellen was not a lady of the composer's acquaintance. Rather, she was a character in Sir Walter Scott's novel *The Lady of the Lake*, and Schubert, having come upon a German translation of the work, thought it would lend itself to music. He composed it for one singer and one pianist in 1825 and happily saw it published the following year. Any orchestral or choral settings one may hear are not entirely his own creations.

His *Ave Maria* — there are many by other composers, but Schubert's is the most familiar — acquired its widest hearing with the first *Fantasia* film, in which the Schubert is tagged onto the very end, after the chaotic turmoil of Mussorgsky's *Night on Bald Mountain* (see Chapter Three). Perhaps Disney and Company thought audiences might benefit from a clearing of the palate. Schubert's serene song was perfect for that purpose, and its wide familiarity is well deserved.

- Schumann: *Dichterliebe*, op. 48 (*Poet's Love*)

Robert Schumann (1810-1856) was a composer with a one-track mind. Throughout his career, he tended to devote himself to a single type of music at a time. Thus, Schumann's biographers divide his life into chapters, including the chamber music year and the symphonic year. The year of songs was 1840, in which the soon-to-be-wed composer poured his happiness into art songs, producing over one-hundred-thirty musical settings of poetry in that single year. Most of these songs appeared in sets or "song cycles," in which the various songs were usually settings of texts by the same poet.

One of the most expansive of these song cycles was the opus 48 collection known as *Dichterliebe*, or *Poet's Love*. All sixteen of its songs are settings of poems by Heinrich Heine (1797-1856), one of the most widely read of all German poets and a perennial favorite of Schumann. Heine's lyrics are ideally suited for the composer in their range of expression, covering a gamut from touching love songs to simple folk-like texts to epic ballads. As such, they allow Schumann to delve into divergent styles of expression, exploring both the bright and the dark sides of love. It is worth noting that the singer is not the only key to musical expression; the pianist, too, is given responsibility for conveying the changeable moods of Heine's texts. Schumann's *Dichterliebe* songs are a showcase for two, not just for the singer.

- Brahms: *Liebeslieder Walzer (Love Song Waltzes)*

The *Liebeslieder Walzer*, or "Love Song Waltzes," capitalize upon two musical trends of the 1800s. One such trend was for dances to be played by piano four-hands, that is, one piano, but two pianists. The other trend was for vocal solo and choral pieces, especially those concerning love, whether mutual or unrequited. In both cases, the pieces were to be light and unpretentious, suitable for diversion at casual social gatherings, and not requiring too much virtuosity. Such works were designed for the enjoyment of talented amateurs, not only for the display of concert artists.

One might imagine that a great master such as Johannes Brahms (1833-1897) would have little interest in these unambitious works, but in fact, he himself enjoyed relaxing with such music. Moreover, as the conductor of amateur choirs, he understood both the appeal of such compositions and the limitations within which a composer would have to work so as to suit his audience. Brahms wrote hundreds of short pieces for these amateur singers and pianists. The *Liebeslieder Walzer* combine those forces of keyboard and voice into two sets of songs that, in their gentle way, are sweetly appealing and continuously popular.

There are two sets of *Liebeslieder Walzer*. The original op. 52 collection, published in Berlin in 1869, was so popular that Brahms produced a second set, op. 65, in 1874. Throughout these years, Brahms himself was suffering pangs of unrequited love, first for the fine pianist, Clara Schumann (see Chapter Six), fourteen years his senior, then for Clara's daughter Julie, twelve years his junior. Although both women were friendly with the composer, neither sought romance. It seems possible that the darker of the *Love Song Waltzes* were colored by this discouraging experience, though perhaps the brighter ones came in moments of hope. As it is, Brahms himself never married: neither the Schumann ladies nor any other lady.

- Dvořák: *Moravian Duets*, op. 32

Were it not for the support of Brahms, Antonín Dvořák (1841-1904) might never have come to the attention of the public, and it was this set of vocal duets that made it happen. As a man widely listed amongst the greatest living composers of the late 1800s, Brahms was a natural to serve on the judging panel for an Austrian state sponsored competition for young composers. Year after year, he kept seeing the music of Dvořák and kept voting for it. In the mid-1870s, Dvořák won that competition three out of four years. Finally, Brahms was so convinced that in 1876, he urged his own publisher, Simrock, to issue an edition of fourteen Moravian songs that Dvořák had composed: folk poems set to original music in the traditional style.

Simrock complied, more to please his best client than from any altruistic wish of his own. The opus number was intended to reassure possible purchasers who might be discouraged to see an opus number 1; moreover, Dvořák had published a few works prior to these duets, though only with small publishing houses and limited financial success. Simrock was a large international firm with the resources to properly promote the young Bohemian's music. The *Moravian Duets* sold so well that the publisher decided to ask Dvořák for something new, which would prove to be the first set of *Slavonic Dances* (see Chapter Ten), and a dozen more compositions would come to press with Simrock in the following twelve months alone. Their partnership would continue for most of Dvořák's career.

Here, one finds the first music by Dvořák that the general public would have encountered. Though admittedly less majestic than his more famous Symphony no. 9, "From the New World" (see Chapter Two), it is equally well-crafted and proves that Brahms was wise to take the young unknown under his wing. If Brahms was impressed by it, we can be, too.

- Tchaikovsky: *None but the Lonely Heart*, op. 6, no. 6

In English, it's known as "None but the Lonely Heart." Peter Tchaikovsky (1840-1893) himself, being Russian, called it "Nyet, tolko tot, kto znal." Those even passingly familiar with European languages may observe that the two titles have not quite the same meaning; after all, one needn't know much Russian to have gathered that "nyet" means "no," a word not in the English title at all. In fact, neither title is a literal translation of the original poem here set to music.

This best-known of Tchaikovsky's songs (he wrote dozens) derives from a poem by the great German writer Goethe (1749-1832), in whose novel *Wilhelm Meisters Lehrjahre* (*Wilhelm Meister's Apprentice Years*) it appears as "Nur wer die Sehnsucht kennt" (Only One Who Knows the Longing). Goethe imagined it as a song text — he tells his readers that here Mignon sings — and innumerable composers both great and small took him at his word. Schubert and Schumann both set it, as did Hugo Wolf (yet to come in this chapter). Tchaikovsky followed suit, though not using the German words. Rather, he relied upon a loose translation by the Russian poet/dramatist Lev Mey.

Phrasing and vocabulary vary from the Goethe original, but the basic idea remains the same: only one who has been disappointed in love can understand how it feels. Tchaikovsky chose to evoke that concept with moods ranging from wistful yearning to strong passion, most frequently revolving upon various ways of articulating in music the concept of "alas." Throughout, one finds flowing phrases that test both a singer's lungs and his/her vocal expression. In whatever language it is sung — or even if one encounters one of the many instrumental transcriptions — the song shows Tchaikovsky's gift for managing a melodic line. At the time (late in 1869), he was still earning his daily bread as a college professor of music. He may have hoped, but could not have guessed, that international fame would soon be his, but the song hints that the skill was already there awaiting discovery.

- Chausson: *Poème de l'amour et de la mer*, op. 19 (Poem of Love and the Sea)

Frenchman Ernest Chausson (1855-1899) began his adult life in the legal profession in 1877. In that same year, however, he wrote his first composition, and soon exchanged the legal profession for a music career. Despite his late start, he immediately earned admiring attention, and was nominated for the prestigious Prix de Rome only one year after beginning his studies. Unlike many of his countrymen, he had a long-lasting fascination for the works of the determinedly German Wagner, devotion so strong that he spent his honeymoon at Bayreuth, where he (and presumably his bride) attended a performance of Wagner's epic opera *Parsifal*. From those varying influences,

Chausson developed a deep love of rich melodies and lofty emotions, expressed in a lyrical style that was uniquely his own. He might have become the leader of a new generation of French composers, but tragically his life was cut short when he died in a bicycling accident. He was not yet forty-five.

Although Chausson had too few years to compose a quantity of masterpieces, he did produce several works deserving of lasting admiration. His published catalog, comprising not quite forty works, includes mostly songs with piano, and voice with orchestra works, as well as a single symphony, some chamber music, and a half-dozen stage works. The *Poème de l'amour et de la mer* (*Poem of Love and the Sea*) for solo voice (either male or female) with orchestra, busied him intermittently from 1882 through 1893. For text, he turned to Maurice Boucher, a fellow law school graduate who also had given up the law in favor of the arts. Set in two broad movements with an orchestral transition, the work's first half "La Fleur des eaux" (The Flower of the Waters) is an evocative love song telling of a beautiful woman in a seaside setting and her lover mourning as they are parted. A brief orchestral interlude leads into the second half "La Mort de l'amour" (The Death of Love), in which the lover looks back at the time of their parting. Throughout, there is much imagery of sea and wind and flowers, but the beauty is in vain: the lovers cannot reunite. Despite the dark moods, it is music of incomparable beauty, leaving one to regret that Chausson did not have much time remaining to him.

- Mahler: *Des Knaben Wunderhorn* (*The Youth's Magic Horn*)

The Brothers Grimm were not the only folklorists at work in Germany in the early 1800s. Several years before those fairy-tale aficionados began publishing the stories they had collected, another equally ambitious effort appeared. Titled *Des Knaben Wunderhorn*, or "The Youth's Magic Horn," this three-volume compilation of folk songs, poems, and aphorisms was the work of two young writers: Clemens Brentano and Achim von Arnim.

Brentano and Arnim viewed their collection as a tribute to German culture; Arnim, in his introduction to *Wunderhorn*, went so far as to describe the material as "the wisdom confided to the keeping of centuries, wisdom which should be proclaimed to all in song, fable and story." The book's editors were not alone in their high regard for *Wunderhorn*. Goethe believed that all intelligent people should possess a copy, and Heine observed that it was essential to one's understanding of the German people. Indeed, numerous German authors studied the collection, but composers remained largely unmoved until late in the century when Gustav Mahler (1860-1911) began to draw upon *Wunderhorn* for melodic inspiration.

Of all the songs that Mahler composed in course of his career, over half are settings of lyrics from *Wunderhorn*. Mahler also used melodies from the collection in orchestral compositions, notably his first four symphonies. Yet the most concentrated usage of this folk source in Mahler's music is in a set of twelve solo songs with orchestral accompaniment, a cycle named for the original folk collection. In these songs, Mahler covered a vast range of subjects and emotions. Wistful romances are juxtaposed with tragic tales of starving children. St. Anthony preaches valiantly to inattentive schools of fish, while in another song, an avian vocal contest judged by the donkey conceals a satirical parable of musical tastes. Martial imagery abounds in this ambitious cycle. Each of the first three songs as well as the last of the twelve concerns the harsh lives and harsher deaths of soldiers.

Taken together, *Des Knaben Wunderhorn* is a microcosm of German cultural obsessions, yet the songs also symbolize Mahler himself, for from the many hundreds of items in the original collection, he selected these dozen texts as relating in some particularly significant way to his musical goals, as well as to his complex personality. In the *Wunderhorn* songs, Mahler melded the complexity of a modern artist with the deceptive simplicity found in German traditional art.

- Wolf: *Spanischliederbuch* (Spanish Song Book)

Often considered the greatest composer of German art song after Schubert, Hugo Wolf (1860-1903) was born in a German-speaking enclave of Slovenia. His father, though employed in the family leather business, delighted in music and took upon himself the pleasurable duty of instructing young Hugo, fourth of his six children, in piano and violin. Soon, the boy's skills earned him a place in the family chamber orchestra. In 1875, he made his way to the Vienna Conservatory, where the sociable lad formed a friendship with fellow student Gustav Mahler (1860-1911). Yet the greatest influence upon his emerging style would come from the German opera specialist Richard Wagner (1813-1883), whom Wolf idolized. Though the younger man would never master his mentor's flair for epic endeavors, he absorbed much of Wagner's progressive harmonic sense, and, like Wagner, learned to set German words to music with unsurpassed artistry. Wolf's art songs are noted for their wide-ranging moods and deft characterization, which draw the listener into the heart of the subject at hand. Essentially a miniaturist, Wolf managed to concentrate into a short vocal piece much of the majesty of the Wagnerian style.

In the course of a compositional career that spanned some thirty years, Wolf composed a small amount of instrumental music, but mostly art songs, which would eventually number nearly three hundred. One of the most expansive collections under his name is the *Spanischliederbuch* (Spanish Song Book). That an Austrian composer would write a song cycle called "Spanish Song Book" becomes less unexpected when one remembers that throughout the nineteenth century, composers often looked to other nations for inspiration. Nicolai Rimsky-Korsakov (1844-1908) was Russian, not Persian, though that fact did not prevent him from composing the Arabian-Nights-themed *Scheherazade* (see Chapter Three). Georges Bizet (1838-1875) was French, not Spanish, but few works more effectively capture the Spanish spirit than *Carmen* (see Chapter Eight). As for Wolf, he encountered a collection of Spanish poems translated into German by Heyse and Geibel. Many of the original texts were anonymous, though one was by Cervantes (of *Don Quixote* fame) and half of the others had known, though not particularly significant, authors. Wolf found the collection sufficiently entrancing to make it his professional focus for much of 1889, 1890, and 1891. By the end of the last of those years, he had completed the full cycle, which he divided into two books: the "Geistliche" (Spiritual) and the "Weltliche" (Worldly). Perhaps the original collection contained more worldly verses than spiritual ones, for the Geistliche book has ten songs and the Weltliche thirty-four.

The Worldly songs all deal with love, and few from an entirely optimistic view. More frequently, the tone is of unrequited love or a person parted from a lover. Yet such subject matter does not make for songs that are all slow and dark. Rather, Wolf concerns himself with turbulent emotions, which often surge out of control, demanding fiery music to match. Some abound with exuberant energy, others with intense dramatic power. One singer might be able to manage the full cycle in one evening, but having several is preferable, as some of the songs seem to offer a masculine point of view and others feminine. Moreover, with the quickly changing moods, giving a singer a few minutes to regroup before the next song he/she must sing is ideal.

As for the audience, listeners can just revel in the changing colors, and let it flow over one, like an afternoon storm preceding a sunset. The stronger the moods, the more complicated the key signatures and the more intricate the interaction between singer and pianist. Those challenges are more for the performers than the listeners, yet listeners can keep in mind that the moodier the music, the harder the performers are working.

- Richard Strauss: *Four Last Songs*

Most of Strauss' art songs were written between 1885 and 1906. Throughout that time, his wife Pauline, a highly regarded soprano, was busy on the opera and recital circuit. Many of the songs were written specifically for her use, and she often performed them to the accompaniment of her husband at the piano. For texts, Strauss chose from a wide variety of literature. In fact, he once admitted that generally the music came first, and only then would he go looking for a poem to fit the melody in question. Fortunately, Strauss was an avid reader. He especially liked Goethe, but he knew enough poetry from sufficiently diverse sources that he was rarely at a loss for text. Although some of the poems he set are now considered insignificant, with Strauss' music, the poems reach the heights of the most exquisite lieder.

Strauss' *Four Last Songs* are not literally his last works in the genre. One more song would follow. However, the title of this set of songs was chosen after the composer's death by his publisher, who did not yet know of the existence of the one remaining score. When Strauss began the songs, he was past eighty years old and living in exile in Switzerland, afraid to go home to his native Germany because, in these post-war years, questions had been raised as to his participation in Nazi government activities. All Strauss was suspected of doing was serving as president of the Reich Music Chamber, from which position he would be dismissed by Goebbels for collaborating with Jewish artists. Thus, even the Nazis didn't approve of him, but the fact that Strauss had held the job title for three years starting in 1933 was enough to attract suspicion. Certain that his health was not up to a stay in prison and unconvinced that he would be acquitted, the composer and his wife remained in Montreaux, their expenses covered by his publisher but all their personal assets in the care of the Allies. Not until June 11, 1948 — ironically, the composer's eighty-fourth birthday — was his name cleared, allowing his return to his beloved villa in Garmisch-Partenkirchen. He would live only another fifteen months.

It was a melancholy way for a man who had stood at the pinnacle of the musical world to spend his declining years, and some of that melancholy is perceivable in these lovely songs. The chosen texts, by the poet Hermann Hesse (whom Strauss had met in Switzerland) and the early nineteenth century poet Joseph

Eichendorff, reflect upon life's fading days and seem particularly poignant in light of the fact that Strauss never heard these songs performed. Although he had completed them in the summer of 1948, and had even chosen Kirsten Flagstad as the soprano to premiere them, the first performance was not given until a concert that his old colleague Wilhelm Furtwängler conducted in London May 22, 1950, eight months after Strauss' death, and nine days after the passing of his very favorite soprano: his dear wife Pauline.

- Rachmaninoff: *Vocalise*, op. 34, no. 14

Sergei Rachmaninoff (1873-1943) composed many dozens of songs, but curiously, the best known of them all is a song in which the singer is given no words to sing. Usually heard on its own, his *Vocalise* was originally part of a set of fourteen songs. Its title refers to the fact that in the original version, there was a vocal part, but no text. That's what a "vocalise" is: a wordless vocal line. The other songs in the set all had texts, but not this final offering.

He had written *Vocalise* for soprano Antonína Nezhdanova, completing it September 21, 1915, according to the date he wrote on the manuscript. The original version was for voice and piano, but the composer himself saw further potential in the music and made two different transcriptions: one for voice with orchestra in 1916 and another for orchestra alone in 1919. As even the original had no words, the melodic line was easily transferred to instruments. In the last of these versions, most frequently performed of all, that which was originally the vocal line is shared by violins and clarinet, allowing a nice contrast of musical character. All the arrangements, whether by the composer himself or by acquisitive soloists on sundry instruments who long to make the music their own, showcase one of Rachmaninoff's finest skills: imagining a memorable melody with long, gracefully flowing lines.

- Vaughan Williams: *Songs of Travel*

Englishman Ralph Vaughan Williams (1872-1958) was an avid composer of songs, particularly early in his career, since a young man of little reputation could more easily persuade one singer and one pianist to take on his works in concert than convince an entire orchestra and its conductor to oblige him. His song cycle *Songs of Travel*, settings of poems by Robert Louis Stevenson from a collection of the same name, premiered in London in 1904. Originally, there were only eight songs, but when the composer passed away over half a century later, one more was found in his personal papers and added to the earlier set.

When he began the songs, Vaughan Williams was barely in his thirties, but had already mastered the art of crafting diverse musical moods, even from limited resources. He calls upon his two performers to offer moods that may be bold and forthright, as in 'The Vagabond,' or quietly reflective, as in 'Youth and Love,' or regretful musings upon loss, as in 'I have trod the upward and the downward slope.' Throughout the cycle, Vaughan Williams balances the meanings of the words against the atmosphere of the music so well that even a listener unfamiliar with English as a language would yet grasp the sense of the individual songs. It is proof that this young composer with so much time ahead of him had the skills required for a successful career in music.

- Schoenberg: *Gurrelieder*

More than a symphony, yet still not quite an opera, *Gurrelieder* by Arnold Schoenberg (1874-1951) is one of the most imposing musical creations this side of the dramatic stage. Roughly two hours in length, it requires an orchestra of over one hundred players — including ten horns and seven varied clarinets — and four wholly different choirs. One of those choirs goes further still: rather than being divided into the customary four parts (soprano, alto, tenor, bass), it has eight. Moreover, the score additionally calls for five vocal soloists (two of them tenors), and one speaker.

Performing *Gurrelieder* is no humble task, and the situation is further complicated by the composer's reputation. So much is made of the dissonant, expressionistic works of Schoenberg's mid to late periods that one can overlook the fact that *Gurrelieder* is an early score, rich with the lush beauties of post-Wagnerian Romanticism. It takes courage to perform *Gurrelieder*, but for the listener, the work is a rewarding tapestry of musical moods.

The title translates as "Songs of Gurre." Gurre was a castle, its tales evoked by the Danish writer Jens Peter Jacobsen (1847-1885). Jacobsen began with actual medieval Danish events, overlaid them with mythological elements, and produced scenes of both dark beauty and dark anger. Schoenberg came to know it from a German translation published in 1899 and almost immediately began work on a musical setting. His three-part orchestral symphony of songs was begun in 1900, just after Schoenberg's lovely sextet *Transfigured Night* (see Chapter Five). Its basic structure was in place by the end of the following year. However, Schoenberg did not finish scoring the orchestral parts of the third segment until 1911, giving those portions of the work a rather different flavor. Later, he observed, "I had no intention of hiding this." In fact, even if he could have recaptured his earlier style, since the story told in the score has evolved, moving from sunshine to darkness and back to light, letting the music also evolve allows it to portray changing states of mind in the central character.

It is not just the story that evolves. Even in Schoenberg's life — he was not yet forty — music itself was evolving. Many composers, Schoenberg amongst them, were moving away from old ideas of tonality, in which a composition would have a central key as focal point, with temporary diversions to other keys serving as passing contrast. The new mindset rejected this plan as overly restrictive, choosing instead to craft new, previously untried harmonies, in which any one chord might bear little relationship to those around it. The result was not necessarily dissonant but certainly unpredictable, and to some extent unearthly, thus ideally suited to Jacobsen's tale of ill-fated love.

Gurrelieder tells of King Waldemar, who has fallen for a commoner, the girl Tovelille (Little Dove), much to the fury of his wife Queen Helwig. Part One opens with rapturous music for scenes of natural beauty and songs for the love of Waldemar and Tove. The music darkens as the queen plots her revenge and the girl is slain, with tolling bells to suggest her funeral. Part Two, much more concise, concerns Waldemar's despair. With Part Three, he has summoned a troop of spectral horsemen who ride forth on the wind. It is a diabolical scene, propelled by much determined brass. The various choirs contribute to the chaotic mood, often singing utterly different melodies from each other. At last, dawn breaks, dispelling the ghostly hoards and leading Schoenberg to recall his earlier music of the beauty of nature. "Behold the sun," the choruses declare, and the glorious, triumphant music that follows suggests that in the dawn, there is renewal. Tove is lost, but love survives.

Gurrelieder premiered in Vienna February 23, 1913. Few in the audience entirely understood what they had just witnessed; arguably even Schoenberg might not have been quite sure. Yet it was clear to all that they had been part of an event, the scope of which would have been overwhelming, even if compared to an imposing Mahler symphony. So grand are the performing forces required for *Gurrelieder* that, nearly a century later, it is still rarely performed. When the opportunity to witness *Gurrelieder* arises, one ought not let it pass.

- Canteloube: *Songs of the Auvergne*

Marie-Joseph Canteloube de Calaret (1879-1957) was one of few French composers to not much care for Paris. Canteloube was born in rural Annonay in the Auvergne region, south of Lyon in the Rhone River Valley on the lower western slopes of the Alps. In Canteloube's time, it was a land of farmers and shepherds, small towns and quiet roads. It had nothing to do with the Champs-Elysées, and as such was unlikely to produce a composer of cosmopolitan tastes. As a boy, Canteloube learned to play music from his mother, who was an accomplished pianist, but he learned to love music from his father, with whom he would take long walks in the countryside. Years later, Canteloube recalled the delights of these rural walks, in a time when the people of the countryside were still living simpler lives than those of the towns and cities, singing songs for pleasure, not for art's sake. He was impressed by the poetry of their surroundings and their music, and determined to collect their songs less for purposes of musicology than simply because he thought it was beautiful.

Canteloube spent his youth collecting melodies, then devoted much of the 1930s and '40s to editing and arranging them for publication. Some were published in choral versions, but the *Songs of the Auvergne* are for solo soprano (or mezzo-soprano: somewhat lower in pitch, and perhaps a richer voice as well) with orchestra. These are *the Songs of the Auvergne* that have won the hearts even of those listeners who allege to not much like vocal music. They are lusciously orchestrated, marvelously evocative, and strike a delicate balance between singer and orchestra.

Of the several dozen *Auvergne* songs, the most frequently heard are the several "B" songs: *Brezairola, Bailero,* and the *Trois Bourrées.* The *Brezairola* is a lullaby with long open lines to test the singer's breath support. The *Bailero* — in which one shepherd calls out tauntingly to another across the river — is gently playful in mood. For the *Bourrées,* Canteloube crafts a bright and flirtatious mood with much bright coloration for the woodwinds, even as the singer's lines seem to dance. Taken together, the song cycle is handily Canteloube's best-known work, but is of such charm and varied character that it can comfortably represent him to a new generation.

- Copland: *Old American Songs*

There are several good reasons to use American folk songs as a melodic source. One is that the music is harmonically familiar. It sounds American, and when we hear it, even if we do not know that particular song, we can recognize that an American atmosphere is being evoked. A second reason to use such melodies is rather more practical than evocative. As Aaron Copland put it, "They're free! Anyone can use them." Copland knew well what he was saying. He frequently used folk melodies in his compositions. His opera *The Tender Land* and the ballets *Billy the Kid*, *Rodeo*, and *Appalachian Spring* all contain echoes of popular tunes, and occasional outright quotations. Another example, even closer to its sources, is the *Old American Songs*. Copland chose ten nineteenth-century songs, two sets of five each, and arranged them for voice and piano. The first set of five premiered in 1950 in Aldeburgh, England, with tenor Peter Pears and pianist Benjamin Britten (also one of the finest English composers of all time), then afterward in New York with baritone William Warfield and Copland himself as pianist; the second set premiered in Massachusetts with Warfield and Copland. Later, he orchestrated both sets. The collection includes ballads and hymns, children's songs, minstrel songs, even a political campaign song. Together, they depict the great variety of American traditional music.

The first song, "The Boatman's Dance," is a banjo melody by Dan Emmett, who also composed "Dixie." The second song, "The Dodger," is a satirical campaign song from the 1880's. "Long Time Ago" is a traditional ballad; in "Simple Gifts," one finds a now-familiar Shaker tune which also appears in Copland's ballet *Appalachian Spring* (see Chapter Ten). "I Bought Me a Cat," the last song in the first set, is a light-hearted children's song full of barnyard noises. The second set of five begins with the lullaby, "The Little Horses." The next song, "Zion's Walls," is a stirring revivalist song. "The Golden Willow Tree" is an Anglo-American ballad. "At the River" is a hymn written in 1865 by the Reverend Robert Lowry. The last song of all is "Ching-a-ring Chaw," a minstrel song with visions of paradise.

- Barber: *Dover Beach*, op. 3

Many great composers have been pianists of impressive skill. Some excelled at the violin, but very few have been gifted singers, and of those, only Samuel Barber actually embarked on a career with his voice. A lyric baritone, he studied voice seriously at the Curtis Institute, even while also pursuing composition studies, then sought further training in Vienna. Back closer to home, he gave recitals on NBC Radio, made recordings, and sometimes performed his own songs. As a good singer must, he well understood how the voice flows and composed idiomatically for the voice, so that phrases and breathing work together for musical expression. By his own account, Barber felt that the music needed to emerge from the words, not simply be imposed over them.

Although many music lovers know Barber only for his *Adagio for Strings*, the fact is that songs are far more numerous than instrumental works in his catalog. One of his most remarkable songs is his opus 3 *Dover Beach*, setting a text by the English Victorian poet Matthew Arnold. The lines imagine two loves at a seaside retreat, seeking to lose themselves in each other so as to shut out the sorrows of the world. Barber's score, more expansive than most songs and unusually scored for baritone (or mezzo) with string quartet, rather than piano, imaginatively captures the surge of the waves and of the lovers' emotions. Much of the song is lyrical and melancholy, with the strongest statements reserved for the last verse, when the lovers turn to one another for reassurance: "Let us be true to one another! For the world . . . hath really neither joy, nor love, nor light." *Dover Beach* premiered in New York March 5, 1933. Barber was four days short of his twenty-third birthday. The composer himself later recorded *Dover Beach* and sang it on NBC Radio.

- Britten: Serenade for tenor, horn and strings, op. 31

Britten's Serenade for tenor, horn and orchestra was written in 1943 for Sir Peter Pears and Dennis Brain. Pears was possibly England's best-known tenor ever and Britten's companion for half his life. Brain was the most famed French horn soloist of his generation. With this *Serenade*, Britten combined their talents with his own harmonic flair and the verses of some of England's most introspective poets to produce a work of haunting originality that is both new and old in inspiration. Some of the harmonies, particularly in the seventh movement, feel quite modern, yet other techniques, such as the fugue that appears in the fifth movement, are borrowed from Baroque techniques. Britten clearly felt that the present and the past of classical music could co-exist, particularly in musical interpretations of poems that span the centuries.

The *Serenade*, which premiered October 15, 1943, in London's Wigmore Hall, has eight movements, including a Prologue and an Epilogue. Between those two instrumental segments are settings of six English poems. The first, "The day's grown old," by Charles Cotton, is a tender pastorale with images of sheep and the setting sun. The next poem, Tennyson's "The splendor falls on castle walls," is a fairytale of elves hunting in the night. Third is Blake's verse of wasted love, "O rose, thou art sick." Next is an anonymous fifteenth century dirge with its frightful portrayal of death and hell. The fifth poem, thus, the sixth movement, is Ben Jonson's "Queen and huntress, chaste and fair," a salute to the goddess of the hunt, and the sixth poem is Keat's sonnet, "To sleep," which begins, "O soft embalmer of the still midnight." In the concluding Epilogue, the horn solo is performed from offstage as a subtle echo of farewell. Many of the horn passages make use of harmonics — notes that lie between the usual fingerings and can be reached only by subtle adjustments of the lips against the mouthpiece — a fiendishly difficult process. Only a player approaching Brain's ability can feel entirely comfortable in the attempt, as only a singer with skills near to Pears' can attempt the vocal parts, in which Britten uses musical coloration to illustrate the meanings of individual words.

- Rorem: *Santa Fe Songs*

Were it not for his nationality and longevity, American composer Ned Rorem (b. 1923) might almost be the Franz Schubert of the twentieth and twenty-first centuries. Both men rank as perhaps the greatest and most prolific composers of art songs of their generation. Schubert's songs — over six hundred in number — long served as the mark by which all other songs were measured; Rorem's catalog is a few hundred short of that number, but he is still adding to the list and has outlived his Austrian predecessor by over half a century. Both men — the past master and the current one — have an uncanny sensibility of how best to convey the ideas and feelings behind a particular text in musical terms. With that ability comes the fortunate knack for choosing just the right poem to fit within the composer's preferred expressive style. In Rorem's case, this has often been the great names of poetry — especially Whitman, though also Tennyson, Frost, Yeats, and Gertrude Stein — as well as more recent names. He has tended to choose short texts telling of intimate scenes. Epic grandeur is not in his vision, but the crystalline focus of Rorem's songs is an integral part of their charm. Say what needs to be said in the most evocative terms possible and bring the image to a close: there is the essence of Rorem's art songs.

Although many of Rorem's songs are free-standing individual short pieces of music, some have been grouped into song cycles related to one another. One such collection is the *Santa Fe Songs*, composed in 1980 for the Santa Fe Chamber Music Festival, where Rorem was spending a summer as composer-in-residence. There are twelve of them, setting poems by the early twentieth century poet Witter Bynner, and scored for voice with accompaniment of a piano quartet (piano, violin, viola, and cello). In the various songs, one often finds open, spacious harmonies, as if Rorem — himself from Indiana — were thinking of the landscape of New Mexico. Long, flowing melodies are alternately rapt or poignant, with the instrumental parts sometimes taking the lead and at others, yielding to the vocalist. The words, though readily perceivable, are not always the point; rather, Rorem seems more interested in painting mood pictures with his five performers treated relatively equally.

- Lieberson: *Neruda Songs*

Some of the most touching tales in classical music concern composers writing works for their spouses. JS Bach compiled the so-called *Anna Magdalena Notebook* as a collection of little songs and keyboard pieces for the use of his second wife. Mozart composed his great Mass in c minor in thanks for his wife Constanze, a talented soprano, having recovered from a serious illness. Robert and Clara Schumann each composed songs and piano pieces for the other's enjoyment, and his Piano Concerto (see Chapter Four) was written particularly for her performance. More recently — and even more poignantly — there is American composer Peter Lieberson (1946-2011), whose *Neruda Songs* were inspired by his wife Lorraine Hunt, the great mezzo soprano. She performed them at their May 2005 premiere with the Los Angeles Philharmonic, then in a recording with the Boston Symphony before she was struck down by breast cancer barely a year after the songs were composed. They remain to us now as a tribute to his vision of her talent and her spirit.

Born in New York City, Lieberson was of impeccable musical roots. His mother was the ballerina Vera Zorina; his father Goddard was president of Columbia Records. Music studies at Columbia and Brandeis, varied by devoted study of Buddhism in Boulder, Colorado, led to a successful international career in music, with a catalog of works including orchestral pieces, chamber music, solo keyboard works, compositions for soloist with orchestra, and one opera, *Ashoka's Dream*. The opera was composed for the Santa Fe Opera and premiered there July 26, 1997. Lieberson had come to supervise the production and thus met Lorraine Hunt, cast in the role of Trirashka. Two years later, they married.

Of the *Neruda Songs*, the Liebersons recalled that in an airport bookstore the summer they met, they picked up a collection of love sonnets by the Nobel Prize winning Chilean poet Pablo Neruda (1904-1973), noticing it first for its vividly colored cover. The words themselves proved equally attractive, and the composer decided, "I must set some of these for Lorraine." He selected five of the sonnets (numbers 8, 24, 45, 31, and 92) and set them for solo mezzo with orchestra, the latter liberally provided with woodwinds and brass, as well as harp, piano, and marimba. Moods range from sultry and languid to bright and brilliant, depending upon the needs of the texts. Lieberson dedicated the score "to my beloved Lorraine."

Although his composition instruction came in part from instructors of radical leanings, Lieberson's own style is more melodic and flowing; perhaps it is a legacy of the Buddhist influence and its vision of the connected nature of life. A lighter mezzo voice would find it difficult to carry over the rich orchestration, but Lorraine's timbre was widely praised for the dusky richness it brought to repertoire ranging from Bach to modern works. The New York Times described her voice as "luminous." In her absence, a singer faces the challenge of finding similar qualities and working within the varied colors of Lieberson's orchestral writing. One could study Lorraine's recording, or let the character of the music develop itself with its own voice. After all, since one cannot be Chopin or Liszt, one must eventually allow another's musical spirit to speak through one's own gifts.

- Larsen: *Sonnets from the Portuguese*

Libby Larsen's *Sonnets from the Portuguese*, a song cycle using six of Elizabeth Barrett Browning's poems, was written for soprano Arleen Augér. Not only had Augér chosen Larsen (b. 1950 in Wilmington, Delaware) for the project; she had also specifically asked for the Barrett Browning sonnets, being struck by how they are love poems of an adult woman, not an innocent young girl. Composer and singer together chose several of the sonnets and agreed that they would be scored not for soprano and piano, but rather for soprano and chamber orchestra: string quintet, harp, woodwinds, horn, and percussion.

The cycle premiered at the Aspen Music Festival August 3, 1989. After that debut, Larsen — with Augér's input — undertook revisions, eliminating one song, adding one new one, and revising one of the original songs. This second version was completed late in 1991, though by then Augér was too ill with cancer to give the premiere; she died in 1993. The music survives as Larsen's tribute to Augér's artistry and to their mutual admiration of Barrett Browning's vision.

Further Recommendations:

Here is a selection of other interesting art songs — both with piano and with orchestral accompaniment — for which there was not room in the main body of the chapter:

- Ludwig van Beethoven (1770-1827): Rarely remembered is that the great master of symphonic and chamber works also composed many dozens of songs, both as individual, free-standing musical settings of poetry and collected into song cycles. Notable amongst the latter is *An die ferne Geliebte (To the Distant Beloved)*, showing a gentler side of Beethoven than one is accustomed to hearing.

- Franz Schubert (1797-1828): In addition to the individual Schubert songs named above, one should consider his song cycles *Winterreise (A Winter's Journey)*, *Schwanengesang (Swan Song)* and *Die schöne Müllerin (The Lovely Miller's Girl)*, each with thoughtful moods derived from poetry of the day. There is also *Der Hirt auf dem Felsen (The Shepherd on the Rock)*, for which Schubert expanded his performing forces, adding a clarinet to the usual singer and piano.

- Robert Schumann (1810-1856): His *Dichterliebe*, op. 48, cited above, can be on the moody side. For a more optimistic set of Schumann songs, consider his *Liederkreis (Song Cycle)*, op. 39. Here, Schumann sets texts by Eichendorff (rather than Heine), sending a wanderer out into the woods to reflect upon love and nature.

- Johannes Brahms (1833-1897): Of his hundreds of songs, the most famed is that known as the Brahms Lullaby. By all evidence, it was not original to him, but rather an old folk song that he liked well enough to work up and publish an orderly setting of it, giving a more defined nature to what might otherwise be an a cappella cradle song.

- Antonín Dvořák (1841-1904): Earlier in this chapter, we explored the songs that were Dvořák's first published works. However, his most familiar art song is the plaintive *Songs My Mother Taught Me*, from the collection called *Gypsy Songs*. One can find it both in the original version for voice and piano, and also in various transcriptions for instruments without singer. Recently, the composer's great-grandson, violinist Joseph Suk, released a recording of it and other Dvořák songs in instrumental arrangements, performing on the composer's own viola.

- Edvard Grieg (1843-1907): The Norwegian composer, most frequently identified with his stage music for *Peer Gynt* (see Chapter Nine), wrote far more art songs than orchestral music. That his wife Nina was a gifted singer was one strong influence; Grieg admitted in letters that he thought she was the perfect interpreter of his music, best sensing how he wanted it to sound.

- Arnold Schoenberg (1874-1951): *Pierrot lunaire* is far from easy listening, but strongly evocative of the dark Expressionist moods in the early twentieth century's Second Viennese School. Poor Pierrot is going slowly mad from too much exposure to moonlight, and the songs in this cycle explore the bizarre visions he experiences.

- Charles Ives (1874-1954): Usually, the American was a determined member of the edgy avant garde. However, amongst his art songs — many dozens in number — one finds a more conservative, more Americana-flavored side of his musical personality. Most are to English texts, though sometimes French and German pop up when something about the poem caught his attention

- George Butterworth (1885-1916): The English composer left little music, for he died all too young in combat at the Battle of the Somme. However, his surviving works include a lovely song cycle on Housman's poems of *A Shropshire Lad*. Butterworth recycled some of the melodies into an orchestral rhapsody of the same name.

- Samuel Barber (1910-1981): Most ambitious of his song settings is *Knoxville: Summer of 1915*, using a text by the American writer James Agee imagining gentle days of times gone by, like those of the composer's childhood. Here, Barber chose an orchestra to join the soprano, rather than simply piano.

Chapter Eight
Opera and Operetta

Even one who knew little of classical music would likely admit, upon hearing the above theme in performance, that it was familiar and could likely even put a name on it: "Ride of the Valkyries." That it originated in an opera by Richard Wagner might spring less instantly to mind. Yet themes from operas and operettas are more familiar than one might imagine had one not visited an opera house, and the fact is that these grand works can be far more accessible than modern stereotypes might suggest.

Opera was the original multi-media entertainment, like a concert, a play, and perhaps a ballet all rolled into one. Eyes and ears alike are diverted, and hopefully the mind and emotions, too, if the story was well chosen and well portrayed. Opera began in Italy around 1600, first as entertainment for the royalty, who were the only ones with the resources to hire singers, musicians, dancers, set builders, and costume makers all for one evening's diversion. By the 1700s, it had become popular in public theaters, too, and from the end of that century up until the early twentieth century, opera filled the niche currently filled by Broadway musicals: an entertainment that combined music and a story. Although musicals, and for that matter, movies, have given opera a run for its money over the last ninety years, opera still survives, both in continued performances of old masterworks as well as in performances of new works, which often reflect recent cultural developments. Mozart would be utterly puzzled by the plot line of John Adams' opera *Nixon in China*, but that it was an opera he would not question.

Like plays, opera are blocked out into broad acts, with shorter scenes within those acts. Often, an opera begins with an overture: an instrumental introduction used to hint at the nature of the story to follow. A serious opera will have a somber overture, a comic opera a more light-hearted one. One cannot do opera without singers, so it's worthwhile to know the vocabulary for types of singers. A high woman's voice is a soprano, a lower one a mezzo-soprano ("half-soprano"), a very low one (uncommon in opera) a contralto or alto. With men's voices, tenor is highest, baritone is a mid-range, and bass is the lowest. Although operas have plot, which few of the other compositions in this book have, other than the presence of an overall story in program music (see Chapter Three), it tends to resemble the popular styles of the time in which it is composed. So except that it has singers, Handel's *Julius Caesar* sounds much like Handel's *Water Music*. Knowing what stylistic ideas were popular in any period helps one to know what to expect from its operas, too.

Most of the works covered in this chapter are operas, that is, dramatic productions for singers with orchestra in which virtually every word is sung. Admittedly, in Verdi's *La traviata*, the character Violetta reads aloud in spoken words an excerpt from a letter that she has received from her absent lover, but that occupies only a few moments of the whole work, so it still qualifies as an opera. Give such a work a quantity of spoken dialog and it becomes an "operetta." Even Mozart wrote a few such works, notably *The Magic Flute*, though he called these works by the German term "Singspiel." Whether it's "operetta" or "Singspiel," it's a lighter opera with spoken dialog. A few particularly famous operettas by composers of Austrian, French, and English origin are included in this chapter.

By the time the early twentieth century arrived, American theater producers had set aside the term "operetta" as old-fashioned and were calling such pieces "musical theater," a term that gradually evolved into what one now tends to think of as "Broadway musicals." Musicals are modern-day descendants of what used to be called operetta. One of the most famed of all musicals is *West Side Story*, which would have fit in this chapter, but since it's most familiar in its film version, you'll find it instead in Chapter Nine with music for stage and screen.

Incidentally, until the early 1800s, Italian was imagined as the best language for opera, in part because Italians had invented opera, but also because the abundance of vowels and limited number of strong consonants in Italian make it favorable for singing. So even non-Italian composers tended to write their operas to an Italian text (the technical word for an opera text is "libretto," which would be written by a "librettist"). Yet by the early Romantic Era, approximately the 1820s, a new idea developed that opera could and should be sung in the composer's own language. So starting in that time frame, one finds more and more operas in other languages: French, German, Russian, Czech, Spanish, and even English. One could cite other examples, such as Hungarian, but those languages in the previous sentence are those most likely to be encountered in opera houses.

A few more opera terms might be of value. In the Baroque Era of the late 1600s and early 1700s, operas were usually of the type called "opera seria," with serious moods and plots derived from ancient history or mythology. In the late 1700s and very early 1800s, tastes shifted more to comic operas set in the present day; these were called "opera buffa," deriving from the word "buffoon" and referring to the high spirits of such a work. Opera buffa was still encountered into the early 1800s, but was soon displaced by a larger scale, more strongly dramatic

241

type of opera known as "grand opera." Grand operas often had very flamboyant singing styles and certainly existed as much to show off the singers as to tell a tale. By the mid to late 1800s, the German Richard Wagner (1813-1883) began to promote his own new creation, with greater use of the orchestra and a strongly German inspiration, which he called "music drama." It is still opera, just opera of his own style, and he wished to be very clear to audiences and performers alike that this would be a different type of operatic experience. In the late 1800s and early 1900s, a new idea came to the fore. The Italians called it "verismo," and sought with it to emphasize realism, with believable characters and believable emotions. Twentieth century has no convenient labels for operatic styles, though many seem to blend characteristics of grand opera with those of verismo. Certainly, greater realism has come to be valued, which arguably benefits audiences that like to be able to identify with the characters.

- Handel: *Julius Caesar*

George Frideric Handel (1685-1759) wrote about four dozen operas, the vast majority to Italian texts. Though he was German born and living and working largely in London, at that time in history, neither German nor English was considered an appropriate operatic language. *Julius Caesar*, Handel's sixteenth opera, like most of its predecessors, told a tale drawn from ancient Rome. The choice was dictated less by Handel's own interests than by expectations of "opera seria" at the time; mythology and ancient Rome were the strongly preferred settings for these staged musical dramas, which tended to be less about the story itself than about dramatic opportunities for vocal display. Like most operas of the day, Handel's score focuses more upon exciting and challenging arias, broken up by occasional choruses, than upon plausible plot development.

The opera's full name — *Giulio Cesare in Egitto* — clarifies which portion of the man's career was to be explored, and that one can expect appearances by non-Roman characters. Indeed, the tale deals as much with Cleopatra as with Caesar, as the Egyptian ruler sets out to win Caesar's support against her brother, Ptolemy, who aspires to the Egyptian throne himself. Unlike in Shakespeare, all ends happily for Cleopatra and Caesar in a love duet, Ptolemy having quietly faded from the action a few scenes earlier and an angry mob which had sought to assassinate Caesar having been quelled. Originally, the title role was written for a castrato, a male alto voice that enjoyed some popularity in Handel's time. In recent times, the role is often performed by a female alto in male clothing, although some countertenors (unusually high male voices) have the range for it as well.

Julius Caesar premiered at King's Theatre in London February 20, 1724. When the work reappeared the following season, it had been revised to include additional arias so as to more thoroughly showcase the singers. It would be a busy season. Handel would write two more operas in the later months of the 1723/24 season, and over two dozen more in the twenty-five years that remained to him. That with so many operas at his disposal, *Julius Caesar* yet enjoyed many revivals serves as proof of its popularity with audiences.

- Mozart: *The Marriage of Figaro*

"Randy husband with roving eye chases reluctant young woman while neglected wife schemes to regain husband's affections. Meanwhile, woman's fiancé struggles with issues of trust as young neighbor comes to terms with coming of age."

The latest sitcom? No, the central plot of an opera that dares to keep its sense of humor while tackling the timeless themes of love and forgiveness. Welcome to *The Marriage of Figaro*.

This first of three collaborations between composer Wolfgang Amadeus Mozart and librettist Lorenzo da Ponte almost perished at birth. The Beaumarchais play from which it drew inspiration had been banned in Paris for its volatile political content: finding dark humor in class power struggles was dangerous business in pre-Revolutionary France. Austria's Emperor Joseph II, elder brother to the embattled French queen, adopted the same prohibition in his own realm. One could possess a copy of the text (Mozart did), but it could not be staged. Thus, writing an operatic *Figaro* was optimism at its best. Yet Mozart would not be deterred. Having decided he liked the idea, he went to work. Ponte later recalled in his memoirs, "As fast as I wrote the words, Mozart set them to music. In six weeks everything was in order."

Of course, there was still the little problem of obtaining permission to perform it. However, Ponte, either through foresight or good fortune, had replaced Figaro's pointed political diatribes with misogynist complaints. No longer were monarchs immoral; now, only women were untrustworthy. The alteration proved acceptable to the emperor, who blessed the project. Rehearsals soon began under Mozart's watchful eye. Tenor Michael Kelly, cast in the smaller roles of Basilio and Curzio, later recalled the delight with which the performers responded to the music: "Viva, viva, grande Mozart! Those in the orchestra I thought would never have ceased applauding . . . The little man [Mozart] acknowledged, by repeated obeisances, his thanks for the distinguished mark of enthusiastic applause bestowed upon him."

Behind the scenes, though, all was not well. The composer's father Leopold Mozart wrote in letters of "cabals" against his son, and named "Salieri and his followers" as principals of the opposition. The conspirators' best-placed ally was Count Rosenberg, Director of the Court Opera. Much as was shown in the film "Amadeus," Rosenberg tore two pages of dance music from the score and burned them. Ponte's memoirs claim himself as the witness, and assert that when Mozart later heard of the confrontation, he was determined to resolve it with physical violence, that only Ponte himself could restrain his distraught colleague. The librettist may be claiming credit where none is due. Yet the fact remains that the conflict was settled as Hollywood saw it: with the emperor himself insisting that the music be reincorporated.

Figaro premiered at the Vienna Burgtheater May 1, 1786, and quickly attracted the acclaim it deserved. So insistent were the calls for encores that after the work's third performance, the emperor declared that only arias would be reprised; otherwise, performances would run too late into the evening. But perhaps Salieri and Company had not entirely conceded. Late in the summer, one local reviewer remarked upon "the unruly mob in the gallery" that was still determined to disrupt *Figaro* with boos and hisses. Yet, he added, "one would have to side with the cabal or tastelessness if one were to entertain a different opinion than that which admits the music of Herr Mozart to be a masterpiece of the art. It contains so many beauties, and such a richness of thought as can proceed only from the born genius."

Indeed, *Figaro* is magnificent music magically constructed. The technical mastery with which Mozart invested this, his first true operatic masterpiece, has never been surpassed. Still, it is not for the little black dots on the page that *Figaro* retains one's affections. Rather, one revels in the humanity displayed upon the stage. Characters who Beaumarchais sketched as ideologically shaded silhouettes gain through Mozart's music the hearts and souls of persons one might embrace: a youth trembling with new passions; a young man confident of his cleverness; a loving wife, forlorn, her husband estranged; couples that, like real couples, can both quarrel and forgive. Without characters for whom one can care, an opera is little more than so much music. Mozart understood, and used his music to draw listeners into their lives. *Figaro*'s text is impressive, its music even more so. The combination is an opera that entwines one's heart in the fates of these otherwise fictional persons.

- Weber: *Der Freischütz*

Carl Maria von Weber (1786-1826) always believed he was descended from nobility, because of the "von" in his name. They had no noble background, only noble aspirations, and his father had adopted the "von" with no particularly authority. However, the family's musical background was strong. Weber senior was a composer of small reputation, the mother was a singer and actress, and two of Carl's elder half-brothers had studied with Joseph Haydn (1732-1809). Yet it was with this younger son that the family's name would achieve eminence. Carl was only seventeen when he was named music master in Breslau, Germany. By 1813, not yet thirty, he was running the opera in Prague, and later in Dresden. He championed German opera, a style that would come to grow in a manner distinct from Italian opera as personified by Rossini (about whom more shortly). German opera was not only sung in German; it was also based in German legend and literature, and borrowed the rich emotional styles familiar from German symphonic works. Weber came to represent German art, adopting the role long before Wagner was out of diapers.

Opera would remain central to Weber's career, and would bring him much international success. Most acclaimed of his nine completed operas (thanks to a lung ailment, he did not quite make it to the age of forty) was *Der Freischütz* (*The Freeshooter*), a dark romantic tale of a young huntsman who finds himself, unknowingly, in league with the devil as he attempts to win a shooting contest. Good fortune saves both Max and his beloved Agathe. The opera premiered in Berlin June 18, 1821 to immediate acclaim, its supernatural elements being at the time much in vogue and its struggle between good and evil one that seized the emotions. International productions soon followed, and the work even achieved the notable tribute of being parodied by other composers, who must have bet that its popularity was such as to ensure that audiences would get the joke.

- Rossini: *The Barber of Seville*

Famed for *The Barber of Seville* and *William Tell*, Gioacchino Rossini (1792-1867) was destined for an operatic life. His father played horn in Italian opera orchestras. His mother was a singer of respectable ability. Gioacchino himself, who had spent his early years at his grandmother's home while his parents traveled to performances, was singing on stage by the time he had reached his teens. Yet it was as a composer that he would make his name. Rossini was only eighteen when his second opera, *La cambiale di matrimonio*, premiered in Milan in 1810. Within the next three years, eleven more Rossini operas would be presented to critical Italian audiences. Not all of these works were successful, for the young composer was still honing his skills. Yet there were enough hits that Rossini, not yet legally of age, quickly established himself as a leader of the operatic world.

Unfortunately, that rapid rise to prominence attracted jealous spite of some colleagues, who began to work against him. Early in 1816, their fury centered on Rossini's newest opera, *The Barber of Seville*, soon premiere in Rome. The story was derived from the first of French playwright Beaumarchais' Figaro plays (Mozart's *The Marriage of Figaro* sets the second), but also happened to be a tale previously set by one of Rossini's predecessors, Giovanni Paisiello. Paisiello had confirmed with Rossini that he didn't mind the younger artist taking on the same story, but Rossini's enemies disagreed. Determined that the young upstart would not have another hit on his hands, they turned out in force at the premiere — February 20, 1816 at Rome's Argentina Theatre — to ensure its failure.

Rossini himself conducted in a Spanish costume of such opulence that it attracted jeers. The tenor Manuel Garcia who sang the opening serenade had as yet no aria to sing (it was completed the next day), and so instead offered an authentic Spanish song to his own guitar accompaniment. The song did not satisfy the audience, which also objected to the accidental breaking of one of the guitar strings. Figaro's big aria was similarly met with scornful laughter, and when Basilio, tripping over a trapdoor, fell and smashed his nose, more hisses arose. That the poor baritone then bravely sang his aria through the filter of a bloody handkerchief did not earn for him the favor of the hostile crowd. Yet the greatest chaos was reserved for the Act One finale, when a prankster released a cat onto the crowded stage. The gentlemen of the cast attempted to capture the beast, chasing it back and forth until at last it sought refuge in the only available location: under the mezzo soprano's skirts. Laughter was so sustained that no one heard a note of the rest of the opera.

For the next night's performance, Rossini chose, perhaps prudently, to remain at home, but was awakened late by the ominous approach of a noisy, torch-bearing crowd. Convinced that his life was in danger, the composer hid in the stable and would not emerge until the tenor routed him out, saying, "Get a move on, you! Listen to those shouts of 'Bravo, bravissimo Figaro!' An unprecedented success!" And a success it has remained. No less an authority than Giuseppe Verdi (1813-1901) declared at the end of the century, "I cannot help believing that, for abundance of ideas, comic verve, and truth of declamation, *The Barber of Seville* is the most beautiful *opera buffa* in existence."

- Donizetti: *Lucia di Lammermoor*

It is a sad irony that the composer of the best-known scene of operatic insanity himself fell prey to madness, but such was the life of Gaetano Donizetti (1797-1848). Born in the same year as Schubert, Donizetti was the most prolific opera composer of his generation, producing sixty-two operas, some written in only two or three weeks. His catalog also includes sacred choral works, songs, chamber music, and orchestra pieces in large number. Most composers, in working so quickly, would have created little of note, yet amongst those numerous operas are many masterpieces, notably *Don Pasquale, The Elixir of Love, Lucia di Lammermoor,* and *The Daughter of the Regiment,* the last of which so impressed Felix Mendelssohn (1809-1847) that he said he wished he had written it himself. Of his contemporaries, only Rossini exceeded Donizetti's popularity.

The fifth of six children in a poor family, Gaetano grew up in Bergamo. By the time he was twenty, he was writing operas and seeing them on stage not only locally, but even in Rome, Milan, and Naples. His first work to earn performances beyond the borders of Italy was his thirty-first opera, the very serious *Anna Bolena (Anne Boleyn)* in 1830, which would reach the stage in both Paris and London. The comedy *The Elixir of Love* would follow in 1832, the tragic *Lucia di Lammermoor* in 1835, and then two more comedies: *Daughter of the Regiment* in 1840 and *Don Pasquale* in 1843. Only two more operas would follow *Pasquale,* for long unhappiness (triggered by the death from cholera of his young wife and of all three of their children in infancy) was escalating into full-scale mental incapacity.

Donizetti would spend the last year and a half of his life in an asylum, at first near Paris, though in his last months, he was moved home to Italy. He died early in 1848, before the premieres of four of his operas, which he had managed to complete before his decline became incapacitating. Yet within a dozen years of his death, virtually all of his operas would reach the stage, many at the most respected opera houses on the continent. Although his colleague and contemporary Rossini would enjoy a longer and happier life, it was Donizetti who could claim the greatest number of successes.

Lucia di Lammermoor is arguably Donizetti's greatest creation, at least on the serious side. His inspiration came from Sir Walter Scott's tragic novel of 1819 *The Bride of Lammermoor,* which was itself based on supposedly actual events. This story of a sensitive young woman, deceived and betrayed by her family, forced into a hateful marriage, and ultimately driven insane by the pressures of events is ideally suited to the operatic stage, for its emotions and passions find even stronger expression in music than in Scott's elaborate prose.

Although the title character becomes a murderess, one can come away feeling that her brother Enrico all but held her hand through the deed, pushing her over the edge, by forcing her into a marriage that he knows is repellant to her. It is an opera that requires a powerful dramatic soprano, but other characters are not slighted, for all major characters — including that hateful brother — have their own arias, and the duets and ensembles are among the finest ever written. Particularly memorable is Lucia's so-called "mad scene," in which she reappears amongst the wedding guests after having slain her new husband and proceeds to sing almost impossibly elaborate music meant to prove to the audience that, quite unaware of what she has done, she has lost her wits. More than any of his other numerous works, this opera proved Donizetti's prominence in his field. The opera premiered September 26, 1835, at the San Carlo Theatre in Naples, forty-second of the composer's sixty-eight operas.

- Verdi: *La Traviata*

When Giuseppe Verdi (1813-1901) first applied for admission to the Milan Conservatory of Music at age eighteen, he was rejected: not untalented, just too old, according to policies. Fortunately, he managed to arrange private lessons, and soon embarked on a life-long career in opera. His first opera came to the stage at Milan's La Scala Opera House in 1839, his second in 1840. That was nearly the end, for inside of two years, Verdi's infant daughter, his infant son, and then his young wife all died, leaving him heartbroken and, he was convinced, utterly unable to compose. Friends encouraged him to try once more, and that next opera — *Nabucco* — was such a success that he resolved to go on. Before long, he would be the king of Italian opera, so revered that when Italy finally united, he was elected to its Senate, despite the fact that his name was not formally on the ballot. When Verdi died at a great age, tens of thousands of persons turned out for his funeral, marching along after the hearse and singing together choruses from his operas.

Verdi was adored both in Italy and abroad. Yet even he had operas that were not instant successes. When his opera *La traviata* opened in Venice at the La Fenice opera house March 6, 1853, the audience mocked the tenor for being in poor voice and the baritone for being too young to be convincing in his "father" role. As for the soprano, she was so badly overweight that her character's protestations of weakness and ill health drew nothing but cruel laughter from the audience. No one was willing to believe that she was wasting away from tuberculosis, nor that she was a fabulously desirable courtesan. Verdi, then not quite forty years of age, called the night "a fiasco," yet he did not allow himself to be overly distressed. "I do not think that the last word on *La traviata* was uttered last night. They'll see it again," he wrote to a conductor friend, "and then we'll see." History has shown his optimism to be well-placed.

The audience's reaction was not due solely to the shortcomings of the cast. Verdi, too, came in for criticism due to his choice of story. The piece is adapted from *La Dame aux camélias*, the play and novel of Alexandre Dumas the younger, in which the writer recalls an actual "lady of pleasure" whom he has known and adored. Like Violetta in the opera, the historical Marie du Plessis conquered Parisian society with her wit, charm, and beauty. Even Franz Liszt fell under Marie's spell, but her reign was a brief one. She died of tuberculosis in 1847 at age twenty-three, and was soon memorialized in Dumas' exuberant prose. The tragic tale caught Verdi's attentions. He began work on the score even as the play was still on stage in Paris. Yet what is acceptable in drama may yet be controversial in opera, and operatic audiences were not prepared to accept a "fallen woman" as heroine. Whether or not she had a heart of gold, Violetta was still not seen as a lady to be admired, and since the opera house was as much a social diversion as an artistic experience, the mere suggestion of a Violetta conflicted with society's mores.

La traviata's setting was seen as a further affront. Verdi specified that, since the opera was based upon contemporary events, so its action should be set in the present day, with modern costumes and other accoutrements. However, his audience preferred to imagine that such scandalous happenings could only occur in the less moral past. Many early productions of *La traviata* dodged this issue by moving the action back into the early eighteenth century, despite the composer's specific directions to the contrary. Ironically, contemporary opera directors have been known to take the opposite view, placing the piece in modern high society so as to more clearly remind observers that Violetta's plight is not so remote from our own world. She has lived her life as well as she can, yet now finds herself held to account for earlier decisions. That those judging her are less caring than she is herself is simply one of the cruel realities of life, a point that Verdi brings vividly to life in his music. His score, even without the accompanying text, shows her to be a person more sympathetic than any of the other characters; whatever she has done, it seems to say, she is still a good person.

Despite its early hurdles, *La traviata* is now Verdi's most frequently performed score. *La traviata* may not have been exactly what some observers at its premiere were hoping, but that was in part because they had come into the theater with their own impressions of what they hoped Verdi might do. Once directors paid closer attention to casting and audiences became open to modern-day settings, the work was able to prove itself the equal of anything Verdi had ever composed.

- Wagner: *The Ring Cycle – Das Rheingold, Die Walküre, Siegfried, Götterdämmerung*

It was in 1848 that Richard Wagner (1813-1883), Germany's most determined operatic specialist, first decided to compose an opera based upon the German epic, *The Nibelungenlied*. At the beginning, he imagined a single work depicting the death of the poem's great hero, Siegfried. Wagner quickly set to work on this project, not only writing the music, but also adapting his own libretto from the original tale. Three years later, however, when the proposed score was already well underway, he realized that such a mythic subject required a broader field, that he could not tell of Siegfried's death without telling first of his birth, and of the legendary events which set the stage for his great adventures. Thus, the original opera was set aside, and three other operas were begun to tell those earlier portions of the story.

Wagner was an industrious worker, but the task he undertook was so monumental that twenty-five years would pass before the entire project was completed in 1876. The resulting four operas, known together as *The Ring Cycle*, are an unequalled exaltation of German heritage and mythology. In places, he tells the story less with the singers than with the orchestra, using so-called "leitmotifs:" fragments of melody that convey plot content to the audience as they recur in varying contexts. Only in Wagner can the orchestra tell listeners as much, indeed, more, than the singers can, for the orchestra can convey ideas that are hidden from the characters themselves. It was an idea that later generations of film composers would take to heart.

Although Wagner devotees are now legion, the composer himself faced a lack of supporters while he was still at work on the four-part tetralogy. The lengthy composition process left him in continual need of funding, and he realized that the staging of these operas would be extremely expensive. Faced with a double motivation, Wagner began conducting a series of concerts that featured orchestral excerpts from his forthcoming epic, most famously the "Ride of the Valkyries," which opens the last act of *Die Walküre*, second of the four operas. The concerts provided him with a steady income, and served as a nineteenth century equivalent of a Hollywood sneak preview, whetting the public appetite for the operas that would follow. Ever since that time, Wagner's spectacular orchestrations have had a happy home on symphonic programs and their melodies are familiar even to those who have never sat through a staging of a Wagner opera.

Excerpts from *Das Rheingold* — first of the four Ring operas — premiered as early as 1862 in Vienna at the Theater an der Wien, where in earlier years Beethoven works had first come before the public. The complete cycle of operas would not come to the public until August 1876, when it premiered at the Festspielhaus in Bayreuth, built to the composer's specifications at the command of Bavaria's King Ludwig (and even now, managed by Wagner's descendants). Too expansive to be performed all together on one day, the four premieres were spread over several days: August 13, 14, 16, and 17. The event had been so well publicized that many of the leading lights of music — including Liszt, Tchaikovsky, Saint-Saëns, and Bruckner — came to witness the occasion. Some were put off by Wagner's vocal writing, but most were honest enough to admit that no one could surpass him for grand orchestral effect. It was a new way to imagine opera, and Wagner made the strongest possible case for it.

Although most often identified with the mythological adventures one finds in *The Ring Cycle*, Wagner could also bring a lighter side to operas. *Die Meistersinger von Nürnberg* is his only comedy — a long one, but containing much grand music, not least its opening overture. Here, one finds neither dragons nor magic rings of power; everyone survives and the principal lovers are united. It is a kinder world vision than that of *The Ring*.

- Gounod: *Faust*

Few legends have enjoyed greater popularity over the centuries than the story of Faust. From Christopher Marlowe to Thomas Mann, great authors have been fascinated by this tale of a man who seeks love and wisdom at any cost. It is a theme that never becomes dated and knows no international borders. With its engrossing mixture of passion and evil, the Faust legend is ideally suited to the stage.

At the time that Charles Gounod (1818-1893) set out to write an operatic *Faust*, Goethe's dramatic poem on the subject was one of the most widely admired literary works on the Continent. Gounod himself, when barely twenty, had devoured the work in a French translation, and immediately began sketching musical settings of its scenes, but Goethe's poem is of epic scope. The young composer could not imagine how to confine it to the limits of the stage. Not until he saw Michael Carre's play, *Faust et Marguerite*, which confines its action to part one of the poem, did he renew his enthusiasm for the subject. It is a happy coincidence that, shortly after seeing that drama, Gounod met the librettist Jules Barbier, for Barbier had on his hands a *Faust* libretto that another composer had rejected. Gounod gladly tackled the project. When *Faust* premiered at Paris' Théatre-Lyrique March 19, 1859, it was an immediate success.

Fourth of a total of ten operas from this composer, *Faust* was Gounod's first great hit, the work that established his international reputation, but also earned him the lasting wrath of Germans, enraged by the strictures that the opera imposed on what they saw as their national masterpiece. Even today, Germans rarely call the work by its proper name. Instead, they give its title as *Margarethe*, to emphasize that it is not truly "Faust." Indeed, the opera focuses far more upon the leading lady and how she eventually overcomes both Faust and the devil to achieve salvation. It is she, not Faust, who in the opera's final scene is taken in by the angels. Indeed, Gounod's opera draws only upon Part One of the Goethe original, completely ignoring the more philosophical developments of Part Two, but philosophical discussions rarely make for good theater. As long as they are willing to stage such fine music, the fact that they change its title should not cause Gounod to roll over in his grave. If one wished to see faithful operatic treatment of a work of literature, one would need to wait a few more years until Gounod's *Romeo and Juliet* (1867), in which every sung word is very close to Shakespeare's original text.

Several versions of the opera *Faust* exist. In its first incarnation, Gounod's *Faust* included spoken dialog between the musical numbers. The following year, he reworked it with sung recitative, a kind of narrative singing related to the rhythms of everyday speech. Later yet, he composed lengthy scenes of ballet for the later acts, as that was the demand of the Paris Opéra which wished to revive the work in 1869. It only performed operas that gave the corps de ballet something to do, and Gounod preferred meeting their demands to turning down their request. In modern productions, the dance scenes are usually omitted, though they found a home in an orchestral suite. The usual focus in *Faust* is not upon dancing, but upon singing, especially the arias for the four leading characters and the famed Soldier's Chorus. Taken together, they prove the diversity of styles that Gounod could call forth, from playful to gently lyrical to sardonically mocking to determinedly forthright. He well understood that a diversity of moods makes for the best theater.

- Offenbach: *Orpheus in the Underworld*

Although he is remembered today as a French master of operetta, Jacques Offenbach (1819-1880) was German born, in Cologne. His father, a music teacher and cantor at the synagogue, saw to it that the boy, then known as Jacob, learned the violin and the cello. With a brother and sister, the boy soon formed a trio which earned extra money for the family by playing in local bars. He was only fourteen when his compositions first appeared in print in 1833. Later that year, the father took Jacob and his elder brother to Paris for studies at the Conservatoire.

Under his new French first name, Jacques soon found work in the orchestra of the Opéra-Comique. Social connections gave him access to Paris salons, where he, like Chopin before him, found both audiences for his music and music students for income, as well as commissions for new works. By the time he was in his mid-thirties, Offenbach was gaining a reputation for his light comic pieces with spoken dialog. These works, which fit the mold now remembered as operetta, blazed a trail for the later success of Johann Strauss Jr. as well as Sir Arthur Sullivan, for in both Vienna and in London, light French musical comedy soon earned a strong following. By the time of his death in Paris at age sixty-one, Offenbach had composed nearly one hundred mostly comic operas and operettas. His choice of plot material was wide ranging, from Jules Verne's *Voyage to the Moon* (*Le Voyage dans la lune*) to the far more classic myths of ancient Greece.

At first glance, the story of Orpheus wouldn't seem to lend itself to comedy. The familiar ancient Greek tale concerns a marvelous musician so distraught over his wife's death that he attempts unsuccessfully to rescue her from the Underworld, the place of the dead. Such a tragic tale concerning a character who sings seems custom-made for operatic presentation, and indeed, Claudio Monteverdi, Christoph Gluck, and Joseph Haydn all composed operas on Orpheus (in 1607, 1762, and 1791 respectively); Gluck's specifically was considered one of the greatest operas of the day. As for Offenbach, he gave the story a farcical twist. As he tells it, Orpheus and Eurydice are amicably separated, each blissfully occupied with new lovers. Rather than dying tragically, as she does in the original story, Eurydice willingly relocates to the Underworld, where her new lover rules, and Orpheus, much against his will, is forced by convention to make some rescue attempt, however trifling. No one could be more pleased than Orpheus when he fails, though Eurydice is also relieved, for her new life of love seems preferable to any marital relationship. Clearly, Offenbach played fast and loose with the original story. He was equally irreverent in terms of music, pairing courtly minuets with high-kicking can-cans, and quoting satirically from Gluck's earlier opera.

Orpheus in the Underworld premiered October 21, 1858, at the Théâtre des Bouffes-Parisiens, Offenbach's own personal theater, as he had quarreled with the managers of the more prominent Opéra-Comique. The media expressed shock at the work, both because it mocked Gluck's revered telling of the tale and because it dismissed the idea of the perfection of ancient Greece. However, when media despise something, audiences often decide to take the opposite view. They loved it, and within a few years, *Orpheus in the Underworld* had become an international success. From its original two-act form, Offenbach reworked a four-act version that would premiere in 1874. So marked was *Orpheus'* fame, and so lasting, that in 1886, Camille Saint-Saëns would himself satirize the satire by taking from its finale the famed can-can and awarding most lead-footedly to tortoises in his *Carnival of the Animals*.

- Johann Strauss Jr.: *Die Fledermaus*

"A potpourri of waltz and polka themes:" with these disparaging words, Vienna's most prominent music critic, Eduard Hanslick, brushed aside one of the most popular operettas ever to reach the stage. Perhaps he felt *Die Fledermaus* was too frivolous for its Easter Sunday premiere. Perhaps he judged it to be insufficiently lofty for its venue of the Theater an der Wien, which in an earlier decade had hosted the premieres of Beethoven's *Symphony no. 5* and his only opera *Fidelio*. Whatever the reason for his discontent, Hanslick has proven to be at odds with a century of music lovers, who have embraced *Die Fledermaus* for its wit, its charm, and its delightfully danceable themes.

Despite his obvious flair for the field, the Waltz King came reluctantly to operetta. Johann Strauss Jr. (1825-1899), eldest son of one of Vienna's greatest dance band conductors, had built his reputation with waltzes and polkas, and saw no reason to risk his good name in a notoriously fickle field. So opposed was he to the entire concept of writing an operetta that the impetus had to come from beyond Strauss himself. The composer's wife, Jetty Treffz, was an opera singer. Convinced that her husband's music was perfectly suited for the stage, she conspired with theatre director Max Steiner to prove the point. Treffz and Steiner had words set to some of Strauss' melodies to show the effectiveness of the combination. When these new songs were performed for their unsuspecting composer, he was at last persuaded. Strauss began a successful collaboration with Steiner's Theater an der Wien.

Die Fledermaus was Strauss' third operetta for Steiner. The piece is based on a popular French vaudeville comedy, *Le Reveillon*. In its original version, the play was very Parisian, offering some controversial morals and rather more infidelity than the Viennese could accept, at least in the judgment of Steiner, who ordered an extensive reworking. The chosen librettists for the new work, Haffner and Genee, actually never worked together, or even met. Haffner created a straight-forward German translation of the original play. Then Genee, working independently, thoroughly restructured the piece to better suit Viennese sensibilities. He reined in the French excesses, causing leading lady Rosalinda to reject her would-be lover's advances, and Eisenstein, husband of that leading lady, rather than dining with pretty young women, to unknowingly flirt with his own wife and her maid. Such moderation was apparently sufficient for public morality. *Die Fledermaus* premiered April 5, 1874, and regardless of certain critical observations, audiences were enchanted.

Die Fledermaus became the first Strauss operetta to reach the London stage. Its Paris premiere was more sharply delayed, due to the fact that the composer had neglected to obtain the blessing of the original playwrights, Meilhac and Halevy. Furious, they refused to allow the work to be staged in Paris, and a compromise was only reached when Strauss agreed to let his libretto be brought more in alignment with the original play. Presumably, he did not have to worry about offending the French, who, after all, had enjoyed *Le Reveillon* in all its scandalous splendor. The idea of reworking the text of *Die Fledermaus* while maintaining its music is one that has lasted to the present day. It is a rare director who does not bring into the dialog a few contemporary jokes and references, yet Strauss' masterpiece soars despite such changes. *Die Fledermaus*, one of the most timeless of all light opera scores, retains its charm even in a new century.

- Bizet: *Carmen*

Georges Bizet (1838-1875) had music in his blood. Born in Paris, he had a singing teacher for a father and a talented pianist for a mother. He grew up immersed in music, and was only nine with he entered the Conservatoire, first to study piano, then adding composition. By the age of twenty, he had already won numerous accolades, including the highly prestigious Prix de Rome. His adult career was devoted in part to composing a great quantity of widely popular solo piano music, though also to a series of operas. He showed a good sense for using music to propel the stage action, yet his operas were almost entirely unsuccessful, often due to inadequate librettos. Even the best music cannot overcome absurd dialog and characters. In the case of Bizet's most famous work, the libretto (by Henri Meilhac and Ludovic Halévy, after the novel by Prosper Merimée) was faultless, as was the music itself. The problem lay in public expectations.

Carmen's initial failure was at least partially due to its composer's ambitions. Bizet had been asked to write a new work for the Paris Opéra-Comique, which for a century had specialized in presenting rather light, moralistic pieces in which virtue is ultimately rewarded. It was largely a family theater where parents might bring their eligible daughters to display them to possible suitors. No doubt the director expected his new work to be in a vein appropriate to such a scene. However, Bizet chose instead to bring to light the shady world of gypsies, smugglers, deserters, factory girls, and other ne'er-do-wells (the bullfighter, at least, is a heroic soul) little suited to pristine upper class tastes of the day. Just as bad, the leading lady is made to die not of some genteel bout with tuberculosis but rather from being stabbed by her tenor. Reaching beyond both his audience and his contemporaries, Bizet rejected the conventions of Verdi in favor of the passions of Puccini, who at the time was but a child. Although Bizet began with a sufficiently ambitious plan to change the standards of the Opéra-Comique, he achieved far more than he expected, blazing a new operatic trail into realism. The verismo composers of Puccini's generation owed a debt to Bizet's pioneering effort.

If there is any justice in the musical afterlife, Bizet has somehow heard of the eventual success of *Carmen*. Certainly, he heard no such good news while he still lived. At its premiere March 3, 1875, the piece was roundly condemned as shocking and vulgar. "There is no plan, no unity in its style," alleged one appalled critic, who continued his remarks, declaring (however improbably), "it is neither dramatic nor scenic." Another critic caustically advised, "Mademoiselle Carmen should temper her passions." Bizet, only thirty-six years old, was devastated. At the time of his death exactly three months later of a heart condition, he remained convinced that *Carmen* was the greatest failure in the history of opera. He did not survive to experience the accuracy of Tchaikovsky's prediction: "Ten years hence *Carmen* will be the most popular opera in the world."

- Massenet: *Werther*

It was only a matter of time before Goethe's 1774 novel *The Sorrows of Young Werther* became an opera. The work was the world's first international best-seller, translated into numerous languages even during the author's lifetime. Napoleon — whom one might suppose had other things to do with his time — so admired it that he read it again and again, and, on passing through Goethe's Weimar during his attempts to conquer all of Europe, sought a personal meeting with the author. Young men of the time made a point of dressing as Werther was portrayed on the book's cover: in blue jackets and yellow vests. Others went entirely too far in imitating fiction by taking their own lives as does Werther. That last bit of mimicry so horrified the author that he began begging readers to remember that the novel was a piece of fiction, not a rule-book for behavior. Yet Goethe's work had captured the mood of the day, which German-speakers such as Goethe liked to call *Sturm und Drang* — storm and stress — an artistic movement advocating not necessarily suicide, but at least strong and dramatic emotions. Such is the mindset of poor Werther.

So revered was the novel that German composers wouldn't touch it, much as they wouldn't touch Goethe's even grander work *Faust*. It took a French composer — Charles Gounod — to make an opera of *Faust*; it took another Frenchman — Jules Massenet (1842-1912) — to make an opera of *Werther*. Having first learned piano from his mother, Massenet entered the Paris Conservatoire at age eleven, initially as a piano student, then adding composition studies. At the age of twenty-one, he won the Conservatoire's top prize for composers and from that time on remained in the spotlight. His catalog of works includes orchestral pieces, chamber music, a vast quantity of songs, but most prominently operas, numbering nearly three dozen in all. Of all the important opera composers, only Donizetti outdid Massenet in quantity. One cannot claim that all those many Massenet opera are masterpieces, yet there are enough fine ones to bring him well up any list of important composers in the field.

Werther stands about halfway through Massenet's list of works and premiered February 16, 1892, not in Paris as had most of his operas but rather at the Vienna Court Opera. Some in that German-speaking audience would have been startled by the pronunciation of the central character's name. In German, it's "VAIR-ter," with a clear accent on the first syllable and a short second syllable. In French, it's "vair-TARE," both accenting and prolonging the last syllable. Purists might have quarreled that Goethe would not have pronounced it in that way, but the opera sets a French version of the text, so it seems reasonable to pronounce the proper names as the other words are pronounced: in the French fashion.

Those familiar with the book — which would have included the great majority of the literate population of Europe — would have observed some small changes that the composer and his librettists (Edouard Blau, Paul Milliet, and Georges Hartmann) made to the tale, particularly to the female characters. In the novel, Werther's adored Charlotte is so devoted to her young siblings and her husband Albert that she scarcely notices his attentions, which ultimately drives Werther to suicide. In the opera, the suicide still occurs (in the final minutes of the opera), but Charlotte is written to be more responsive, regretful that she is not available. An opera director can make much of that shift in attitude. Another change concerns Charlotte's sister Sophie, who in the novel is only part of the background. In the opera, she serves as a recurring spot of vivacity considerably more light-hearted than the other characters; one can be left wishing that poor Werther would notice her and find his happiness there.

As for Werther himself, Massenet has attended to the fact that in the novel, the young man is not all gloom and doom. There are passages of vivid delight in the beauty of the world, and Werther's Act One aria is suffused with this spirit. His Act Three aria also relates to natural beauty, but by this time in the tale, he has come to see irony in beauties he can no longer enjoy. Thus, the character grows and changes as the opera progresses, and his music grows and changes as well. Similarly, in the duets that he and Charlotte are given, they have an increasing awareness of their dilemma. Although they never quite get a love duet per se, they certainly explore their feelings for each other. Despite the tragedy of the opera's final pages, there is much beauty here for a listener to explore.

- Dvořák: *Rusalka*

Rusalka was the earliest of twentieth century operas, premiering in Prague March 31, 1901. That it is not heard more frequently is due largely to language, for opera singers study the art of singing Italian, French, German, and maybe Russian, but rarely Czech, the language of the opera's composer, Antonín Dvořák (1841-1904). Yet the opera's beauties are well worth discovery, not only for singers, but for audiences as well, since in this work — as in the composer's better known Symphony no. 9 "From the New World" — one finds themes for love songs, laments, dance scenes, and strong drama. It has something of everything, and all of it finely crafted.

The tale bears some similarity to Hans Christian Andersen's familiar *Little Mermaid* tale, though various folk traditions, including Dvořák's Bohemian roots, have similar stories about female water spirits driven to transition into a life with humans. In the Andersen version, the mermaid has rescued a shipwrecked prince and falls in love with him, but as Dvořák tells it, the prince simply bathes in the lake that the water nymph inhabits. In either case, she is determined to have him, even at the price of her voice, and a not entirely well-intentioned witch, here named Ježibaba, makes it happen. The prince falls for the silent woman and a wedding is planned, but on the wedding day itself, he decides he prefers a more talkative princess, and Rusalka is drawn back into her watery realm by the angry Water Goblin. She is told that the only way to regain her original form is to slay the prince. Her chance arrives when he comes to the lake to beg her forgiveness. She refuses to take his life, but yields to his plea for a kiss, and with that kiss, the prince drowns blissfully. He is redeemed, but she is not, for now her last chance for recovery is gone. "Woe! Woe! Woe!" sings the Water Goblin, and Rusalka fades sadly away.

One might puzzle over why sopranos would delight in a role when the character must be silent for much of the middle of the score. The fact is that even silence has its challenges to perform convincingly, and as for the non-silent scenes, these are of incredible beauty. The first and last acts are largely her showpieces, and very early in the first act, she has one of the most glorious soprano arias in the entire repertoire, the Song to the Moon, its soaring, flowing lines compensating well for the scenes of silence. Even listeners who think they've not heard of *Rusalka* are likely to find that this aria is familiar, and the rest of the score is equally beautiful. One may hear Dvořák's New World Symphony more often, but here is an opera that proves he was a composer of varied gifts.

- Sullivan: *The Pirates of Penzance*

Born in London, the boy who would become Sir Arthur Sullivan (1842-1900) was of musical heritage, for his father was a bandmaster and professor of brass instruments at a military school. Yet young Sullivan would not become his nation's equivalent to John Philip Sousa. By age twelve, he was a chorister at the Chapel Royal, where he gained not only performing experience but also music instruction. Two years later, he won a scholarship to the Royal Academy of Music, where he would remain for two years. Studies followed at the Leipzig Conservatory, where he pursued not only composition but also conducting. By the time he returned to England in his early twenties, Sullivan had already earned international attention and was on his way to a major career. His legendary partnership with librettist William S. Gilbert began in 1871 and continued for over a dozen astonishingly popular operettas.

Thanks to lax international copyright laws in the late nineteenth century, Gilbert and Sullivan's *The Pirates of Penzance* premiered on two continents within twenty-four hours. Such was the only practical way to ensure their rights to their work. The English masters of operetta had tired of unscrupulous American theater producers staging productions of their works — first productions in the US — and never needing to pay the creators for the privilege. So when both Gilbert and Sullivan planned to come to New York City in the fall of 1879 to supervise a production of *HMS Pinafore*, one of those already pilfered works, they brought along the work-in-progress which would soon become *The Pirates of Penzance*. Sullivan finished *Pirates* in his New York hotel, all the while hiding news of its existence from the American press. After two quick rehearsals, it was thrust on-stage December 31, 1879, in the midst of the scheduled *Pinafore* run, using, in fact, many of the same costumes. In so doing, Gilbert and Sullivan secured their American copyright.

They had also made a copy of the score and sent it back to England, where a first performance was given in their absence the night before the New York premiere. Since then, *Pirates* has rarely been off the stage.

Despite having been written quickly, *Pirates* shows no signs of haste. This, after all, is the operetta in which one finds the famed Major General's Song, containing some of the wittiest rhymes ever crafted in the English language. The music, too, is deftly managed. Sullivan writes leading lady Mabel as an extreme coloratura, making her stand out from the many other women in the cast. He also uses some Bach-style counterpoint in which utterly different melodies are sung and played simultaneously. Sometimes, he has even given them different meters (for example, 3/4 set against 4/4), yet still manages to make everything fit. Along the way, Sullivan even spoofs operatic conventions, particularly that many serious operas of the time call for characters to sing on stage at the same time yet remain oblivious to each other's presence. The trick is especially humorous in Act Two, when the pirate-hunting policemen fail to notice those pirates who have just stalked on stage singing the very loud "With Cat-Like Tread," for which Sullivan specified a fortissimo dynamic. Another operatic insider's joke occurs in the entrance aria of leading lady Mabel, in which she and a solo flute engage in a highly ornamented coloratura duet which would have brought to many opera lovers' minds the similar interchange in the mad scene of Donizetti's *Lucia di Lammermoor*. That the creators of *Pirates* were having fun with their creation helps the cast to have fun, and that rubs off on the audience.

- Humperdinck: *Hansel and Gretel*

Son of an academic, Engelbert Humperdinck (1854-1921) dabbled in architecture before returning to a youthful passion for music. Studies at the Cologne Conservatory and Munich's Royal Music School gave him a thorough grounding in the classics. Yet it was in Italy that the direction of his musical future was established when, on March 9, 1880, he was introduced to Richard Wagner in Naples. Reigning monarch of Germany's radical nationalist composers, Wagner invited Humperdinck to join him in Bayreuth, where work was already underway for the 1882 premiere of Wagner's last opera, *Parsifal*. The twenty-five year old agreed, and spent much of the next two years with Wagner, serving principally as copyist, though also in various other capacities. This intimate contact with the nuts and bolts of Wagner's music would have its effect on the young apprentice, whose works would eventually show many of the tricks of modulation and orchestration made famous by Wagner himself.

The years after *Parsifal* would take Humperdinck to Cologne, Frankfurt, Paris, and Barcelona, working as conductor, composer, teacher, and journalist. In 1889, he was invited by the now-widowed Cosima Wagner (her husband Richard had died in 1883) to become private music tutor to her twenty-year-old son Siegfried. Soon afterward, Humperdinck began his masterwork, an operatic setting of the Brothers Grimm favorite, *Hansel and Gretel*. If the innocence of the topic seems an odd choice for a Wagner disciple, remember that the Grimm tales stand as close to the heart of German literature as does the *Nibelungenlied*, from which Wagner derived his epic *Ring Cycle*. Humperdinck was not diverging from his master's lead; he was extending it.

The libretto for *Hansel and Gretel* was penned by the composer's sister, Adelheid Wette, who originally intended it as a family entertainment. As such, she softened the story from original, arranging events so that the mother, rather than sending the children off in hopes that they will die, only orders them to pick strawberries lest they continue to break the crockery and spill the milk. It is, perhaps, the only known opera libretto to contain the timeless line, "Just wait till your father gets home!" Frau Wette further lightened the mood with folk-like rhymes, songs, and dances, both for the children and for their slightly tipsy father. The Sandman, the Dew Fairy, and the fourteen angels are other gentle additions, as are pious pronouncements concerning the value of prayer.

From the original set of songs that his sister requested, Humperdinck expanded the piece to an operetta-like Singspiel, then ultimately to a full opera. A premiere was arranged for Munich late in 1893. However, a singer's illness forced cancellation of that production, so the honor of the first performance fell to Richard Strauss, who, as the composer's friend, had already planned to conduct *Hansel and Gretel* in a Christmas-season run in Weimar. Strauss delighted in the honor of bringing so charming a work to the stage. Yet his production, too, nearly suffered cancellation when the soprano cast as Hansel injured her foot three days before the premiere. Only when another singer stepped in could the December 23 premiere take place as scheduled. The injured Hansel, Pauline de Ahna, did not rejoin the cast until January 7. The following September, she would become Strauss' wife.

With *Hansel and Gretel*, Humperdinck scored his first and only genuine triumph. The opera was presented at more than fifty German theaters in its first year alone, and by Christmas of 1894 — only twelve months after its premiere — had made its way to the Vienna Court Opera, where it was rapturously received. Eduard Hanslick, dean of the Viennese critics, credited the work's success to its abrupt diversion from the hot-blooded verismo style of Mascagni (*Cavalleria rusticana*): "On the one side, we have criminals, suicides, betrayed lovers and couples; on the other, a little brother and sister whose only pain is hunger and whose greatest pleasure is a candy bar — no passion, no love story, no intrigue. It is another world, and a better one.

Although Hanslick pointed out the innocence of the story, he also recognized what all too many observers miss. *Hansel and Gretel* is an opera about children, not specifically for them, and so its score is far from nursery music. "With his little children," the critic wrote perceptively, "[Humperdinck] wanted to get hold of the big children, and not at home but in the opera house . . . Thus:

a children's fairy tale with brilliant adornments, a large orchestra and the most modern music, preferably Wagnerian."

- Puccini: *La Bohéme*

Music flowed through the veins of the Puccini family, though that music was not always opera. More often, the Puccinis were busy with church music, and starting with an earlier Giacomo — great-great-grandfather of the famous one — had served as organist at the church of San Martino in Lucca, Italy. So fixed had the tradition become that when Michele Puccini died in 1864, the decision was made to hold the organ position open for Michele's son Giacomo (1858-1924), then only five years old. A maternal uncle filled in until the boy was old enough to take on the job at age fourteen. He would last only four years with the church, for in 1876, he attended a performance of Verdi's *Aida* in Pisa that moved him to give up the organ in favor of opera. He scored his first triumph in 1893 with his third opera, *Manon Lescaut*. That work would be followed three years later by *La Bohéme*.

This most human of operas had, like some humans, an arduous birth. Its composer was the most painstaking of artists, demanding constant revisions of the libretto-in-progress. Some of the alterations were dictated by time constraints, for the Murger novel upon which *La Bohéme* is based was far too lengthy to be staged complete. Yet Puccini's requests reached well beyond the general outline of the piece. Some lines he rejected as "superfluous chattering." At other times, he insisted upon having a few more phrases, even just a few more words, inserted into the text for the purposes of transition. The composer's tinkering so infuriated his librettists, Luigi Illica and Giuseppe Giacosa, that on several occasions the team nearly disintegrated. Puccini's publisher, Giulio Ricordi, needed all of his diplomatic abilities to preserve the troubled partnership. At long last, *La Bohéme* was completed and premiered in Turin February 1, 1896. The results so pleased all concerned that the men Ricordi jokingly dubbed "The Holy

Trinity" reunited to create two more equally beloved operas: *Tosca* in 1900 and *Madama Butterfly* in 1904.

Although the music of *La Bohéme* is undeniably beautiful, still it is the characters to which the opera owes much of its extraordinary popularity, for here is a world inhabited not by clichés, but by human beings. Which of us cannot believe in these vibrant young people, laughing in the face of poverty, as their passions draw them together and drive them apart? Mimi and Rodolfo embody the idealistic side of love. Theirs is a rose-tinted romance that can conquer all things but death. Musetta and Marcello, by contrast, personify a more sharp-edged desire, more mature, perhaps, in its admission that love is not all hearts and flowers. Although we may not live the lives of these four lovers, we all encounter them from time to time. For nearly a century, audiences have embraced this remarkable opera because its characters have within them the breath of life, finding new life — and entirely new music — in the Broadway musical *Rent*.

As in the majority of Puccini's operas, the leading lady Mimi does not survive to the end of *La Bohéme*. Finding great emotional power in tragedy, Puccini tended to kill off his leading ladies, and sometimes the leading men as well. However, of his twelve operas, there are two in which no one dies at all, both composed for New York's Metropolitan Opera, so perhaps the composer thought Americans preferred happy endings. These two brighter sides of Puccini are his three-act Wild West drama *La fanciulla del West* (1910), in which the soprano and the tenor literally ride off into the sunset, and the one act comedy *Gianni Schicchi* (1918). If one wishes to sample Puccini without tragedy, those are the available options.

- Richard Strauss: *Der Rosenkavalier*

Der Rosenkavalier (*Cavalier of the Rose*) often appears on lists of the greatest operas of the twentieth century, yet it is exactly the sort of opera that Mozart might have written, had he lived in a later age. In company with the Classical master's finest stage works, Richard Strauss' masterpiece boasts a score that is airy and elegant, a story humorous and poignant, and characters rich with human foibles by which they win our laughter and affections. Even the setting is appropriate for Mozart. Set in Vienna in the mid-eighteenth century, *Rosenkavalier* plays out against a background of both noble and bourgeois sentiments. Figaro himself might easily find a place in the pages of this richly varied work.

Credit for the concept must be granted to Strauss' librettist, Hugo von Hofmannsthal, who began the text after re-reading Beaumarchais' play *The Marriage of Figaro* and other works of the period. He proposed a comparable opera to Strauss, who delighted in the plan, in part because of its connection to Mozart, whom he held in the highest regard. The composer set to work at once, even before the libretto was complete, and, at Hofmannsthal's suggestion, worked many a waltz melody into the score. That the waltz was utterly unknown in eighteenth century Vienna, for the story predates the dance by half a century, bothered Strauss not at all. He knew an affecting melody when he heard it, and trusted that his audience would, too.

Some audience members might have been apprehensive after seeing the creators' names on the poster. The previous time that composer Strauss and librettist Hofmannsthal had collaborated had been two years earlier for the Greek inspired *Elektra*. The work had been dark and gritty in character from first bar to last, and some might have worried that here the two collaborators would play the same game. Any such worries would have been quickly dispelled, for there is no darkness to be found in *Rosenkavalier*; even its supposed villains are far more foolish than evil.

The opera's premiere in Dresden January 26, 1911, was greeted with almost unprecedented acclaim, earning fifty performances that season alone, and a further thirty-seven in Vienna. Its popularity was so pronounced that railroad companies added extra trains so as to meet the demand of out-of-town music lovers. By years' end, *Rosenkavalier* had reached the stages of Munich, Nuremberg, Cologne, Hamburg, Milan, and Prague. In 1913, productions would be staged both in London and at New York's Metropolitan Opera. Not all observers were pleased. At La Scala in Milan, purists booed the waltz tunes, incensed that they were being inflicted with dance music without any ballet. Critics, too, lampooned the anachronistic dances, but the cheers of audience members carried the day. Strauss made the most of his opportunity, arranging many of *Rosenkavalier*'s themes into concert suites, so that orchestras, too, might join in the fun. Other arrangements also came into being without the composer's direct participation, further tribute to the work's astonishing popularity. From café band medleys to full-scale operatic productions, *Rosenkavalier* and its marvelous melodies won the hearts of millions.

- Berg: *Wozzeck*

Like Franz Schubert, Alban Berg (1885-1935) was a native of Vienna, that most musical of cities. Yet the differences between the two are more striking than the coincidence of their birthplace. In Schubert's day — the early nineteenth century — the Austrian capital reigned supreme. Cultural, political, and economic heart of a massive empire, Vienna dictated policy not only at home but also throughout Central and Eastern Europe. One could no more compose a symphony than conclude a royal marriage without considering how it would be received within the Hapsburg realm. By Berg's time almost a century later, the world was a different place. Empires were breaking up; new philosophies challenged the status quo. Long complacent in its dominance, Vienna saw its influence waning and its confidence undergoing similar decline, even in musical terms. Whereas once Vienna had determined the rules by which great music was judged, now the old rules had fallen from favor. A new musical reality came to take its place, more reflective of the tenuous position in which Vienna now found itself.

Of a privileged upbringing, Berg was nearly twenty and had been dabbling in music for several years when he responded to a newspaper advertisement announcing that one Arnold Schoenberg (1874-1951) was accepting composition students. Schoenberg, also a Viennese native, was only a decade older than Berg, but was an adept instructor who insisted that his students first grasp the old "classical" ways as the roots from which their art had come. Only once the foundations were mastered had a composer any right to diverge from those foundations to explore new ideas of harmony and melodic form. And diverge they did: rejecting theories of melody and harmony that had stood for centuries, embracing increasing degrees of chaos and dissonance that would never have found a hearing in earlier years. This new approach to composition came to be called the Second Viennese School, and it bears little resemblance to the first, represented by Haydn, Mozart, Beethoven, and Schubert.

Were it not for those changes, reflecting as they do the changing times, the opera *Wozzeck* would not exist. A dark story of madness and murder, it derives from a play by Georg Büchner, who had died in 1837 at age twenty-three, generations before the play reached the stage in 1913. Berg saw the play's Vienna premiere the following year and was so moved by the power of its story that he immediately decided to make of it an opera. His progress was slow, as World War I intervened and Berg had military service before him, mostly passed in guard duty and office work. When idle minutes came, he worked on his opera, crafting both the libretto and the music. It would not be complete until 1922 and came to print the following year, even before a stage performance was arranged. However, Berg, like Wagner before him, realized that he could pique interest in his new opera by presenting orchestral excerpts from it in concert, which he managed in 1924. It would be December 14, 1925 before the opera itself came to the state at the Berlin Staatsoper.

Berg tells his tale with rhythmic and melodic fragments that carry dark, ominous moods from one scene to the next. His harmonic structures sometimes verge into atonality — leaving the listener with no clear sense of the direction in which the music might move next. It was an idea that Berg and Schoenberg and their colleagues were developing, and seems ideally suited for the story of Wozzeck, as he, too, proceeds through life in a generally disoriented fashion. It sounds nothing like Verdi, or even Puccini, who at the time of *Wozzeck*'s premiere had been in his grave barely a year. Yet it was not Berg's intention to sound like his predecessors. With *Wozzeck*, he was imagining not only a new way to think about opera, but also a new way to think about the world. After all, at this exact time in history, Sigmund Freud was alive and well and working in Vienna just up the street from where Berg and Schoenberg were reinventing music. Freud's ideas of ego are a useful tool for understanding the psyche of *Wozzeck*.

- Lehar: *The Merry Widow*

Viennese operetta owes much to Parisian theater. *Die Fledermaus*, perhaps the most adored of all operettas, originated as a French play, and *The Merry Widow*, the other top candidate in the contest of favorite operettas, arose from similar origins. Franz Lehar's high-spirited confection was based on the 1861 comedy *L'Attache d'ambassade* by Henri Meilhac (who would later collaborate with Bizet on *Carmen*). This tale of a wealthy widow being courted for her millions so as to avert the financial ruin of a small country was preserved almost intact by Lehar's librettists, Victor Léon and Leo Stein, whose only major alteration was to the identity of that pocket-sized principality. In fact, their version so closely resembled its inspiration that Meilhac's heirs sued for and were awarded a share of the French royalties. As it happened, there was much to share, not only from productions in France, but also from all the stages of the world. In the first five years following the premiere December 30, 1905 in Vienna, Hanna, Danilo, and their friends cavorted in ten languages through 18,000 performances from Vienna to Rhodesia to Broadway.

Son of a military bandmaster, Franz Lehar (1870-1948) was Hungarian-born at a time when Hungary was still a province of the Austrian Empire. At age twelve, he entered the Prague Conservatory to study violin and composition. A stint as violinist in a theater orchestra followed; then upon being drafted, Lehar joined a military band directed by his father. In 1890, at age twenty, he became a military bandmaster himself, but left the military in 1902 to pursue his fortune as a conductor and composer of waltzes and operettas in Vienna, a field made all the more attractive by the recent passing of Johann Strauss Jr. (1825-1899).

Lehar would soon prove a worthy successor with the 1905 triumph of *The Merry Widow*, the first of many successes. In the 1920s, seeing the future in new technology, Lehar began adapting his operettas for film, but by the mid Thirties, he had virtually set aside composition in favor of running his own publishing house, Glocken Verlag, a firm that is still in business now most of a century later. The composer's public image suffered during and after World War Two due to his reluctance to speak out against Nazi atrocities, and the additional fact that Hitler had expressed a liking for *The Merry Widow*. The latter situation was hardly unusual: most of Europe had been in love with the piece for decades. That Lehar's wife was Jewish may have contributed to his silence. His last years passed in relative seclusion until his death in 1948, yet *The Merry Widow* has outlived him and kept his artistry before the public.

- Gershwin: *Porgy and Bess*

Despite his phenomenal success in popular music, George Gershwin (1898-1937) did not overlook the realms of concert music. He viewed jazz styles as a means of enlivening the old classical genres, bringing to them a true American spirit. His first such crossover work, *Rhapsody in Blue* (see Chapter Four), was followed by the Piano Concerto in F and *An American in Paris*. The success of those pieces, and his own growing comfort with a classical orchestra, led Gershwin to return to an old dream: writing an American-style folk opera. In 1926, after *Rhapsody in Blue* and the Piano Concerto, but before *An American in Paris*, Gershwin wrote to author DuBose Heyward to suggest that they collaborate on an operatic version of Heyward's novel *Porgy*. Although Heyward was enthusiastic about the project, Gershwin's other obligations delayed work until 1934. In that year, Gershwin — with his brother Ira, who was serving as librettist — spent the summer working with Heyward on an off-shore island near Charleston, South Carolina, the setting for *Porgy*. There, the composer hoped not only to have the author at his ready disposal but also to internalize the story's Southern setting and its people. The ambience was inspirational; Gershwin finished the three-hour opera within a year.

Although the initial creative stages had proceeded smoothly, Gershwin ran into difficulties with casting, for *Porgy and Bess* is not merely a story of the South. It is, more specifically, a story of black culture in the South, and other than a few incidental characters, it requires a black cast. This was not a problem in the jazz world, for black jazz singers abounded, but Gershwin required singers of operatic power. Even once he assembled an appropriately skilled black cast, it was clear that the operatic world was not yet ready for a black opera, whereas the jazz world was not yet ready for opera at all. Most frustrating of all was when various Broadway theater producers, for whom Gershwin had made large fortunes, asked him to hire only white singers and put them in blackface. Only after much negotiating, and refusal to compromise on his black cast, did Gershwin finally arrange for an opening on Broadway, where he could be sure that his own reputation could carry the show; to reach even that agreement, he had to promise to cover all the costs from his own pocket.

Porgy and Bess opened in New York October 10, 1935. It was not an immediate financial success; jazz fans were apparently put off by the work's serious tone and opera fans by its jazzy voice. Nonetheless, Gershwin was pleased with his effort, convinced that he had created a work of art, the first true American opera. Not until after his death in 1937 did this most-beloved child earn wide-spread approval.

- Britten: *Billy Budd*

Billy Budd by Benjamin Britten (1913-1976) is the only important opera by a major composer to have an entirely male cast. With its action taking place in 1797 on a British naval vessel, there was simply no place for sopranos and mezzos, unless one wished them to represent a quantity of cabin boys. The story, from a Herman Melville tale, concerns a young merchant sailor (the title character) who is forced to transfer into service on a naval vessel, the HMS Indomitable. There he finds a well-meaning captain but an evil-hearted master-at-arms who is determined to destroy the handsome new recruit. Of the three, only the captain survives to the final curtain. Britten's operas as a whole reveal the composer's recurring fascination with misunderstood innocents; Billy is another of this type. That the ship on which Billy formerly served was called the Rights of Man, to which he must bid farewell, becomes symbolic.

Librettists for the opera were the novelist EM Forster and Eric Crozier, a young man of the theater who had worked with Britten before and was brought in when Forster expressed doubts about his ability to write for the stage. Of this three-man creative team, Crozier was the only one concerned about the lack of female characters, on the grounds of dramatic variety. However, Britten managed to convince him that it could work. So the librettists set about reworking Melville's tale, shifting emphasis, drafting powerful scenes, and creating singable lines, even traveling to the British harbor of Portsmouth to visit a sailing ship of the correct vintage. They spent most of 1949 on the task. Britten's time for composing came in 1950, though he admitted that he had been sketching out preliminary ideas while awaiting the text.

The premiere came at London's Covent Garden December 1, 1951, with Britten conducting. Of the leading roles, Peter Pears, Britten's partner throughout their adult lives, sang Captain Vere, Theodore Uppman was Billy, and Frederick Dalberg was the evil Claggart. Billy is the golden boy of the piece, but dramatic emphasis is more upon Vere, and how a good man deals with insoluble moral dilemmas. It is perhaps for this reason that Billy is a lyric baritone and Vere is the tenor of the two, to give the more dramatic role to Pears, and the part's music was specifically designed for Pears, known for his ability to evoke subtly different colors with his voice. Claggart is a bass, as villains so frequently are. Their three voice types, and those of the other, less prominent characters, are sufficiently varied as to prove that the lack of female voices need not be a problem.

- Floyd: *Susannah*

A folk-flavored parable set against a Bible Belt background, *Susannah* is the creation of a composer well familiar with the scenes he evoked. Son of a Methodist minister, Carlisle Floyd (b. 1926) was raised in the small towns of South Carolina. Throughout his youth, he remained in the South and, after obtaining a master's degree from Syracuse University in New York, Floyd returned to the region of his birth. He served on the music faculty of Florida State University from 1947 to 1976, and then relocated to the University of Houston.

Susannah, dating from the composer's Florida years, is not only his greatest success; it was also his first full-length opera, written with, in Floyd's words, "the reckless confidence of a twenty-eight year old with no reputation to lose." The opera premiered February 24, 1955, at Florida State University with Phyllis Curtin as Susannah and Mack Harrell (father of cellist Lynn Harrell) as Blitch. That Floyd obtained such high-profile artists for a college production was due to the fact that, in the previous summer at the Aspen Music Festival and School, he had asked Curtin and Harrell to sing through some of the scenes for him; upon doing so, they were so impressed that they asked to be included in the work's first performances. Although the premiere was successful, some critics felt the opera had little future, believing such a specifically Southern piece could only be of regional interest. Despite the skeptics, *Susannah* reached the stage of the New York City Opera only eighteen months later, and has since received nearly a thousand performances in the United States and Europe.

The two-act opera is loosely based on the Apocryphal biblical tale of Susanna and the Elders, in which the heroine is unjustly accused by a lustful theocracy. In the original, her innocence is proved and her accusers are punished, but Floyd, under the influence of turbulent times, envisioned a grimmer verdict, for as Floyd was at work on *Susannah*, Senator Joseph McCarthy was at work on much of America, attempting to purge imagined enemies of the nation. The campaign affected Floyd deeply. "Accusation," he observed, "was all that was needed as proof of guilt," and into that exact situation he placed his heroine. Yet though the political background enriches the tale, it is still a story with which anyone can identify, even those who did not experience McCarthy's time, for, in Floyd's view, "The triumph of one human being over the moral pressure of a community makes for powerful drama."

With *Susannah*, Floyd began a trend toward composing operas with rural settings. Others in his catalog include *Wuthering Heights* and *Of Mice and Men*. For these pastoral scenes, Floyd often turned to traditional music for inspiration, not quoting exact folk melodies, just their styles and rhythms, so as to more vividly evoke a specific scene. Floyd's folksy realism is heard in *Susannah*'s use of back-woods dialect; the text was written by the composer himself, who knew well how Southerners spoke. Musically, he set his scene with lively square dance melodies, heartfelt hymns, and folk-like ballads. Susannah's plaintive Act Two aria, "The trees on the mountains," almost begs for a dulcimer accompaniment, yet even with its folk-lament mood, it still draws upon classic operatic devices, maintaining the old within a New World setting. Although other soprano roles — for example, Mozart's Countess in *The Marriage of Figaro* — are given similar arias of loss, only Susannah's arises directly from the mountain air of Appalachia.

- Adams: *Nixon in China*

Political drama is nothing new to opera. Even as long ago as 1642, Claudio Monteverdi brought as much politics as ambition-driven romance into his *Coronation of Poppea*, and though the censorship office continually missed it, Giuseppe Verdi (1813-1901) regularly gave a political flavor to his operas. Yet when Monteverdi was at work, the ancient Roman politicians were more than a millennium in the past, and Verdi's operatic ties to dreams of freedom were usually populated by fictional characters. However, there is nothing fictional about Nixon, Kissinger, Mao, and Cho En Lai. Moreover, when *Nixon in China* premiered with the Houston Grand Opera in 1987, the Americans amongst the principal characters were still alive and fully capable of buying a ticket to see themselves portrayed on stage.

It might not have worked. However, the libretto by poet Alice Goodman was solid, and the original director, Peter Sellars (not to be confused with the actor of similar name) was inspired. It was Sellars who, after reading Kissinger's memoir, had first suggested the opera to composer John Adams. At that point, Adams had never composed an opera, and at first refused the project. He changed his mind eighteen months later when he realized that the work could be a human drama as much as a political one, and of that point of view, he later observed, in the context of a concert performance at the Aspen Music Festival, "I thought of it like a Shakespeare play or a historical novel. Those deal with human nature and so did this." So it is the human side of these familiar names to which he seeks to give musical voice, and succeeds in doing so without falling into parody.

The story is set during the historic visit that President and Mrs. Nixon, together with Secretary of State Henry Kissinger, made to Communist China in February 1972. As much as politics and human nature drive the tale, the opera also deals with how media attention affects one's world view. One of the opera's most visually striking scenes — taken straight from the front pages of virtually any respected newspaper — has Nixon and his wife exiting Air Force One, the president waving his familiar 'V for Victory' sign. Many of the ensuing scenes also derive from history, with Mao's secretaries repeating every word he says in strongly poetic terms, and with a regal banquet at which the main participants toast each other. As the opera shows, Pat Nixon was taken on a tour of the region, a tour focusing upon things of which the Chinese leaders were especially proud. Her words on the occasion might not have been as inspired as those in her ensuing aria, but one cannot speak what impressions might have been echoing quietly in her mind. So in her case and in those of the other characters, a bit of poetic license seems not out of place. If one cannot be sure that one or the other of the political couples never had an introspective scene together during those days, then one can allow Goodman's libretto to give them those scenes, the better to emphasize Adams' vision of a human drama.

- Catán: *Florencia en el Amazonas*

Born in Mexico City, composer Daniel Catán (1949-2011) never limited his musical influences to those derived from his homeland. His academic training was both diverse and international, with a degree in philosophy from England's University of Sussex, and music degrees from the University of Southampton and from Princeton in the US. Back in Mexico, he became music administrator of the capital city's Palace of Fine Arts. Those varied experiences flavored his compositions with an almost Post-Romantic flavor that still remembers regional influences; it is almost as if French composer Maurice Ravel and Brazilian Heitor Villa-Lobos had joined forces to produce richly atmospheric music for the stage. Modernist avant grade techniques had no apparent appeal for Catán, making his music deeply appealing to a wide range of listeners.

Florencia en el Amazonas (Florencia in the Amazon) was composed in 1996 for the Houston Grand Opera, one of the world's most eager homes for new opera. The opera's story — set on a riverboat in the Amazon and concerning the loves and losses of the various passengers, particularly the title character, who is an opera singer — derived from Columbian author Gabriel Garcia Márquez' novel *Love in the Time of Cholera*, adapted into an operatic libretto by Marcela Fuentes-Berain. The tale concerns what Catán described as "the journey to transcendent love . . . with all its intricacies, subtleties, wretchedness, and glorious happiness." That his tale is set in the Amazon rather than a salon in Paris does not deny *Florencia*'s kinship with the established masterpieces of the operatic canon. As for the magical interventions of the character Riolobo, such narrative techniques appear throughout Garcia Marquez' works, and indeed this so-called 'magical realism' is a favorite approach in much Latin American literature. Arguably these plot developments are not far different from certain scenes in Wagner's *Ring Cycle*, though Catán lets them build to more optimistic developments than does Wagner. In Catán's opera, there is no equivalent of the burning of Valhalla. Although the leading lady does not find her missing lover, Catán implies that her love will endure: a strongly positive vision. *Florencia* is an opera that one can genuinely hope will still have a following in generations to come.

- Heggie: *Three Decembers*

If one's impression of opera is that it must be grand in scale and long established in the repertoire, as one might observe of Wagner or Verdi operas, American composer Jake Heggie (b. 1961) may manage to change one's mind. An almost thoroughly twenty-first century composer (his first important work, *Dead Man Walking*, premiered barely ten weeks before the close of the twentieth century), he more often than not writes for just a few singers together with a small orchestra. Even more numerous in his catalog of works are songs for one singer and one pianist: about two hundred such works.

So Heggie is not a man for epic scenes. Rather, by his own account, he prefers to explore individual personalities and how they fit into and interact within families. Such tales do better with small casts, lest personalities become overwhelmed in the crowd. He also feels that smaller orchestras tend to better serve such ideas. Thus, the opera *Three Decembers* has all of three singers and a chamber orchestra of less than a dozen players (the woodwinds playing more than one instrument) and is beautifully suited to smaller opera houses.

Three Decembers arose from the success of the opera *Dead Man Walking*, which since its San Francisco premiere October 7, 2000, has been performed more than one hundred times. Librettist for that work was playwright Terrence McNally who happened to mention to Heggie that he had recently written a short play for an AIDS benefit. Upon reading the text, Heggie decided it would make a fine chamber opera, and invited Gene Scheer to rework the play as a libretto. Complete rewriting wasn't the issue; rather, one needed words that sing well, and those are not always words that speak well.

The new work was given a new title, rather than McNally's original *Some Christmas Letters (and a Couple of Phone Calls)*. Re-titling the piece shifted the emphasis from the holiday itself, for the piece is much more about family members attempting to connect with one other than it is about mangers or Christmas trees, and adds the thought that this is not a single December, but three of them, each a decade apart. So Heggie's opera explores the relationships of a mother and her two grown children, and how those relationships evolve with the passing of years. The music is by turns lyrical and rhythmic, often closely aligned to patterns of speech. As relationships are the focus, so is much of the musical structure, with ensembles for two or three of the performers, with only a few arias.

Three Decembers premiered February 29, 2008, at the Houston Grand Opera, with the great American mezzo-soprano Frederica von Stade in the mother's role, and soon after was staged in the grandeur of the San Francisco Opera. For a new opera to have productions at two different important opera companies within its first year of existence is almost unprecedented: even Puccini did not often do so well. Heggie's next operatic project was an operatic adaptation of *Moby Dick* which premiered at the Dallas Opera in 2010 to favorable critical reception. His record of successes even in just the last decade bodes well not only for his career but also for the future of opera itself.

Further Recommendations:

Granted that all the composers in this chapter made multiple contributions in this particular corner of the musical world, and granted that it would be impractical to list every interesting opera by each of the men in this chapter (even just the Italians would fill dozens of pages), here are some other operas to consider:

- Ludwig van Beethoven (1770-1827): Beethoven's only opera, *Fidelio*, is a politically-tinged drama for which he composed four different overtures (one called *Fidelio*, the others *Leonora*), deriving from the different versions of the work.

- Vincenzo Bellini (1801-1835): One of very few composers who could give Rossini and Donizetti a run for their money in Italian opera houses in the early 1800s, Bellini is especially remembered for two very different works: the epic and tragic *Norma* and the happy-ending love story *La sonnambula (The Sleepwalker)*.

- Friedrich von Flotow (1813-1883): His best-known opera is the bright comedy *Martha*, containing the famed tenor aria known as "M'appari" or "Ach, so fromm," depending on one's language: it isn't always performed in Flotow's native German.

- Bedrich Smetana (1824-1884): Of the Czech composer's many operas, *The Bartered Bride* is the only one to maintain an audience outside his native land. In addition to a sparkling overture, it contains bright folk-flavored dance scenes, lovely vocal music, and a plot in which one of the central characters literally runs off to join the circus, allowing the principal lovers to be united.

- Peter Tchaikovsky (1840-1893): Tchaikovsky wrote numerous operas, but most often performed is *Eugene Onegin*, borrowing the Alexander Pushkin tale of unrequited love, or at least "requited" too late. By the time the title character realizes he shouldn't have rejected Tatiana, she has found another man.

- Ruggiero Leoncavallo (1857-1919): The Italian's most famous opera is the darkly dramatic *Pagliacci*, borrowing elements of a true crime story — the composer's father had been the judge in the case — and containing the famed tenor aria "Vesti la giubba."

- Claude Debussy (1862-1918): Deriving from Maeterlinck's plaintive tale of a tragic love triangle, Debussy's *Pelléas et Melisande* is Impressionism on a broad canvas. Rarely for an opera, it is more concerned with moods than with vocal display.

- Pietro Mascagni (1863-1945): One is most likely to encounter the aggressively melodramatic *Cavalleria rusticana*, though Mascgni's lighter side is represented in the sweetly romantic *L'Amico Fritz* (*My Friend Fritz*), with its lovely Cherry Duet.

- Douglas Moore (1893-1969): His 1956 opera *The Ballad of Baby Doe* was championed by the great American soprano Beverly Sills, and offers music both lyrical and lively not only for the soprano, but also for the mezzo and the baritone; the chorus, too, has its moments. Its story is loosely derived from the history of the American West.

- Kurt Weill (1900-1950): Born in Dessau, Germany, Weill ended his days in New York, having fled Europe with the rise of Hitler. However, before leaving Berlin, he completed and staged the phenomenally popular *Three Penny Opera*, containing amongst many other numbers, the famed "Mack the Knife." The Nazis would try, unsuccessfully, to quell the opera's popularity.

- Gian-Carlo Menotti (1911-2007): *Amahl and the Night Visitors* is a Christmas-themed piece, most frequently performed of this Italian-born, American naturalized composer's many operas. Three men, a woman, a boy, all with strong voices, and effective visuals for that star in the sky: that's what one needs to present *Amahl*.

- Christopher Theofanides (b. 1967): A native of Dallas, Theofanides has found much success in his career, but no higher profile than the premiere September 10, 2011, of his opera *Heart of a Soldier* with the San Francisco Opera. Written to commemorate the tenth anniversary of the World Trade Center attacks, the work deals less with chaos and destruction than with how one comes to be a person who can do the right thing at the most difficult of times.

Chapter Nine
Stage and Screen

It may not look like it on the page, divorced here from its marching bassoons and building energy, but this theme is the essence of suspense. The Norwegian folk hero Peer Gynt is seeking to escape from the trolls, and they are hot on his heels. Such is music for stage and screen: a composer's attempt to reinforce what's happening in the dramatic story itself. Even without singers, there can be plenty of drama.

For centuries, composers have written music to accompany live theater, providing romantic pieces for love scenes, dramatic pieces for fight scenes, and much else for everything in between. These collections of short movements were called 'incidental music,' and include some of the most famous works from the realm of classical music. One may have never heard live music with a theatrical production, but one has certainly heard some of the music written for such purposes.

Once movies arrived on the scene in the very early twentieth century, it was natural that music should find its way in the door, for the presence of music intensifies those emotions on the screen just as it does emotion on the stage. Of the composers in this chapter, those who spent most of their lives in the twentieth century gave attention to movie music, though few worked only with film. One who has a gift for movie music may also dream of writing for the concert hall; the two worlds are not mutually exclusive.

The film music composers included here are those who have also written for the concert hall, and some have spent more time there than in the film studio. Moreover, one who starts with the concert hall may begin to find film music also of value. The American composer Aaron Copland once correctly observed that in film music, he could reach out to millions of potential listeners who might never have set foot in a concert hall, and perhaps now, exposed to good and exciting music, they would make an effort to come to a concert. Don't look down on film music or theatrical music: both are communicating with an audience just as a symphony does.

- Purcell: *Abdelazer, or the Moor's Revenge*

Henry Purcell (1659-1695) was the first important English composer and for nearly two centuries after his death, almost the only English composer any music aficionado would have been able to name. Indeed, there were other composers popular in England, but most were foreign born, and of the actual Englishmen, few made much of a mark. None had the impact of Purcell, who in his songs, choral works (often for royal celebrations), keyboard pieces, and an abundance of theatrical music proved that the English could match the Italians, Germans, and French note for note. After all, nearly three hundred years later, when Benjamin Britten was seeking a melody on which to base his *Young Person's Guide to the Orchestra* (see Chapter Three), it was a theme by Purcell that he chose.

Purcell was of a musical family, with a father and brother in the business; eventually, a son and grandson would follow suit. As a boy, he was a chorister in the Chapel Royal and began composing at the age of eight. When his changing voice cost him the chorister's post, he was named instead as organ tuner and copyist at Westminster Abbey. Much of Purcell's early music is for the church and would have been heard in that august venue where he would later be entombed next to the organ. However, he had wide-flung interests, and when barely twenty, was already composing for the stage. Songs, dances, and interludes were needed to accompany plays, and with the revival of English theater in the years after Cromwell's departure, there was much demand in the field. Purcell would compose music for over forty plays, and if the plays themselves are long since forgotten, his music has survived.

Most familiar of all Purcell's music is a single theme from the incidental music for Aphra Behn's 1695 play *Abdelazer, or the Moor's Revenge*. It stood late in Purcell's career; only a few more months remained to him, though these would be highly productive, for he kept busy to the end. The play would be of no particular interest without the music, and even the music must thank Benjamin Britten for its revival, for it was here that he found the grand processional theme that would become the heart of his *Young Person's Guide to the Orchestra* (see Chapter Three). It's a good tune, well worth revival, yet in hearing the original score, one can appreciate it even further by hearing it in the context of the other melodies amongst which it was originally heard. Purcell shows a deft hand for dance rhythms, and brings fine contrast into his creation by carefully altering moods and tempos from one movement to the next. Thanks to Britten, the most famous movement is the Rondeau, though in the original, it is more expansive than the shorter portion that the later Englishman borrowed. The other movements range from slow and gentle to light and lively with much nimble passagework for the string ensemble.

- Mendelssohn: *A Midsummer Night's Dream*

Most compositions relate specifically to one time in a composer's life. Pieces are classified as early, middle, or late, student works, mature pieces, or later creations, depending on when they were written. Such a spectrum allows observers to examine a composer's developing style, but the fact remains that in this situation, no single composition can reflect an entire career. Yet for Felix Mendelssohn (1809-1847), such a work does exist. His music for Shakespeare's *A Midsummer Night's Dream*, written both at the beginning and near the end of his career, shows to us both the youthful composer and the mature man at the peak of his talents.

The familiar *A Midsummer Night's Dream* overture is the earliest part of the collection, dating from 1827 when Mendelssohn was seventeen. Mendelssohn had achieved fame young and made the most of it, with international concert tours and an active conducting schedule, particularly with his own ensemble, the Leipzig Gewandhaus Orchestra. His return to the Shakespearean subject came at the request of the Prussian king, Frederick Wilhelm IV. The king had always loved the overture and, indeed, all of Mendelssohn's music. In 1842, he invited the famed composer to teach at a newly-founded music institute in Berlin, and, as part of the job, requested a set of incidental music for an upcoming production of *A Midsummer Night's Dream*. Mendelssohn responded with twelve short pieces based on themes from the earlier overture.

These new creations, ranging from a lullaby for a fairy queen (called the Song with Chorus — the only piece in the classical realm known to contain a reference to hedgehogs, which are told to keep away from the dozing monarch) to a Wedding March, perfectly recaptured the magical spirit of their predecessor. The suite as a whole premiered October 14, 1843, and since that time has been featured in many a theatrical production, as well as on the concert stage, for it is music that does not require the presence of actors to have an effect. As for that perhaps overly-familiar

Wedding March — this is the one heard at the close of a great many weddings — those give it an attentive ear may well find that there is more to it than they had remembered, for that movement actually has contrasting themes that appear in and amongst statements of the familiar melody.

- Bizet: *L'Arlesienne*

In 1872, three years before composing *Carmen*, Georges Bizet (1838-1875) was invited to write incidental music for a performance of Alphonse Daudet's drama, *L'Arlesienne (The Girl from Arles)*. Based on a supposedly true story, the play concerned a young man torn between two loves: the gentle girl-next-door and the more seductive charmer from Arles. When the Arlesienne (who in fact never appears on stage) is proven to be unfaithful, the man attempts to console himself by returning to his quieter sweetheart, but he is unable to forget his other passions. Ultimately, lost in love-sick despair, he takes his own life. The premiere of this tale of tragic obsession came October 1, 1872. Despite Bizet's exquisite score, it was not a success. The Parisian audience chortled at emotionally wrenching scenes, and the playwright himself gloomily admitted, "It was a resounding flop amidst the prettiest music in the world." After only twenty-one performances, the play closed, and is now remembered only for the music which accompanied it.

After the drama failed, Bizet decided to cut his losses by arranging selections from his score into a concert suite, thereby allowing the music to survive. He chose four movements from the incidental music for this purpose, and might have crafted another suite, had he not died of a heart condition only a few years later. Fortunately, a colleague, Ernest Guiraud, set about finishing the project, leaving us now two suites of music from *L'Arlesienne*. In both, one finds the familiar bold strains of what had first been a folk melody known as the Marcho dei Rei; many listeners will be able to hum along with it, even if they don't know the French words that make of it a Christmas carol: "Il est né" (He is born). The tune itself is not Bizet's, but he made fine use of a folk source.

- Grieg: *Peer Gynt*

Those who have heard the *Peer Gynt* music of Edvard Grieg (1843-1907) without having read the play for which it was written may have mistaken notions of the drama itself. The music is alternately sweet and charming (as in "Morning Mood"), or airy and delicate (as in "Anitra's Dance"), or folkishly boisterous (as in "The Hall of the Mountain King"). However, Henrik Ibsen's play shows few, if any, of those characteristics. It is, by contrast, sharply satirical, a psychological exploration of the dark side of Norwegian culture through the adventures of its incorrigibly amoral title character. Far from the Norway of colorful folk dances, this Norway is searching for its soul, the Norway of Edvard Munch's stark paintings. Indeed, Munch, whose painting "The Scream" is his best-known creation, crafted the posters for one *Peer Gynt* production. When Grieg was first asked to compose something to accompany the play, he nearly rejected the subject as being utterly unmusical. It is fortunate that he finally agreed, for the resulting score, once extracted from the drama, was a phenomenal success, its popularity far surpassing that of the play itself.

This unlikely alliance of a quiet composer with a contentious playwright began early in 1874, when Ibsen wrote to Grieg about the project. The play *Peer Gynt* had been written much earlier, in 1867, but had never been staged. At last, a much-edited and shortened version was due to be performed in Norway's capital, and Ibsen thought that it might benefit from music. As Norway's best-known composer, thanks to the popularity of his songs, solo piano pieces, and Piano Concerto, Grieg was the natural choice. The collection of songs, dances, interludes, and other short pieces that he produced far exceed in number the handful of movements that are known today.

The performance in 1876 was a great success, but the project did not end there. For subsequent productions, different versions of the play were used, requiring different music, or at least new arrangements and orchestrations of the original pieces. "It is absolutely disgraceful," Grieg wrote to a friend, no doubt wishing that this hateful beast could be laid to rest, so he could return to his other compositions. One can only hope that he found some solace in the large royalty checks that began to pour in as concert suites from *Peer Gynt* were performed throughout Europe.

A full performance of the music from *Peer Gynt* — even without the accompanying play — would take much of two hours, once one assembled all the songs, all the dances, and all the orchestral interludes. However, one most frequently encounters the music in orchestral suites extracted from the score: something of a Reader's Digest approach, but better than nothing at all. Of the selections in the two orchestral suites, the most familiar are:

- Morning Mood: Redolent of what seems to be bird song and gentle Norwegian forest breezes, this music actually accompanied a dawn in Arabia to which the protagonist has journeyed.

- In the Hall of the Mountain King: The play's unsuspecting title character has followed an attractive young woman to her home, which turns out to be the underground lair of the trolls. Now Peer flees, with the trolls close on his heels. Grieg wrote it with choral parts as the hunters seek their prey; these are very rarely heard now. This is the music that appears at the head of this chapter.

- Anitra's Dance: Another excerpt from Peer's Arabian excursion, here, he watches an attractive young lady dancing seductively for him.

- Solveig's Song: Solveig is the girl Peer left behind in Norway, and ever since she has been waiting in the cabin by the fireside with only her spinning wheel for company. Here, she muses upon her absent sweetheart and hopes that all is well with him, even as she admits that by now, he may be in heaven. Given his behavior since his departure, this option seems unlikely, but Solveig would not have waited so long by the hearth were she not an optimist.

- Prokofiev: *Alexander Nevsky*

Long before John Williams and his enduring *Star Wars* scores (about whom more shortly), serious composers turned their hands to composing for film. Frenchman Camille Saint-Saëns (1835-1921) was apparently the first, in 1908, but those of the next generation gave the field more frequent attention, particularly Russia's Sergei Prokofiev (1891-1953). Between 1933 and 1945, Prokofiev, better known now for his ballets, symphonies, and concertos, composed eight film scores including *Lt. Kije* (usually heard as a concert suite) and music for two Russian nationalistic epics: *Ivan the Terrible* and *Alexander Nevsky*. Both *Ivan* and *Nevsky* were films by Sergei Eisenstein, the master Russian filmmaker of the age.

Nevsky tells the tale of a historical figure, Prince Alexander Nevsky, who in 1242 led the Russian forces against the Teutonic knights, ultimately scoring victory in the famed Battle on the Ice. Such an epic tale allowed free rein for Eisenstein's directorial imagination, and also brought out the best of Prokofiev's abilities, inspiring him to produce music that is by turn grand and glorious, heroic and evocative, and strongly flavored with the mysterious harmonies of Russian liturgical music. The combination of these two masterful talents proved to be as triumphant as Nevsky himself had been. The film opened December 1, 1938, in Moscow to universal acclaim. Even Stalin liked it, a fortunate fact that would somewhat shelter both the composer and the filmmaker from later cultural purges. Prokofiev was so pleased with his own work that he made double use of the score, reworking much of it into a patriotic cantata that premiered the following spring. In this later form, *Alexander Nevsky* scored another victory.

Of the various movements crafted for the film, longest and most dramatic is that from the film's pivotal scene, the "Battle on the Ice," in which the mounted forces of both armies contend on a frozen lake which will prove the literal downfall of Nevsky's enemies. As the scene opens, the mood is of a storm on the horizon, which soon breaks over the armies' heads, the chorus comparing Nevsky's forces to the Crusaders. As the energy builds, Prokofiev often sets one section of the orchestra against another, with differing rhythmic ideas in opposition to one another, evoking visions of the contending forces. Unexpectedly, all ends quietly, as if even Nevsky's victorious forces are overcome with weariness.

The other movements include patriotic choruses, prayerful scenes, and at the end, a scene of triumph. It is "Alexander's Entry into Pskov," in which Nevsky and his forces stride into the city to the accompaniment of heroic brass and chorus punctuated by cymbals and chimes. The city's churches, it seems, are welcoming the soldiers home even as the chorus does so. Grand final chords wrap it up in a mood of patriotic glory.

- Prokofiev: *Peter and the Wolf*

A far lighter side of Prokofiev's vision of stage music arose from a day at the children's theater for a father and his sons. Born in Russia, the composer had spent many years living abroad in the wake of the Russian Revolution. He and his wife Lina had two sons: Svyatoslav and Oleg. The boys had grown up living in Paris when their father's music was very popular, but in the spring of 1936, the Prokofiev family decided to return to Moscow. At the time, the boys were twelve and eight years old. Soon after their arrival, Prokofiev took his sons to see a performance at the Moscow Children's Theatre. The boys enjoyed themselves immensely, and their father, seeing their delight, began to think he might like to compose a children's theater piece.

He discussed the idea with the theater's director, Natalia Satz, who was delighted at the idea of having a Prokofiev work to present. Together, they decided to tell the old Russian story of a boy capturing a wolf, and to have instruments represent each of the characters. The bird would be represented by a flute, the cat by a clarinet, the duck by an oboe, the grandfather by a bassoon, the wolf by French horns, and the hunters by percussion. It was the composer who decided that the hero Peter, being a boy of much personality, would require more than one instrument to represent him. Thus, Peter was given the entire string section, and a wonderfully light-hearted melody that is the very image of a boy striding through the forest in search of adventure. One further change that Prokofiev made in the original plan was that the director had provided him with a set of rhyming verses to set to music. However, the composer thought the verses distracted from the music. In their place, he wrote a simple narration to tell the story of Peter and his animal friends.

Peter and the Wolf premiered May 2, 1936. The first performance was not, in its composer's view, a great success, but its popularity quickly grew; soon it had been adapted into a ballet, and released on record. Yet its greatest fame was still ahead. Soon afterward, while on a concert tour in the US, Prokofiev saw the new animated Disney film *Snow White*. He was immediately struck by the appeal of blending music and animation. The next time he was in California, he made a point of seeking out Walt Disney himself and recommending that the great animator take on the tale of Peter. Disney agreed, and the animated version of *Peter and the Wolf* was made with the composer's full cooperation.

- Virgil Thomson: *The Plow that Broke the Plains*

Many of the most influential American composers grew up in New England, that long-standing center for American high culture. Not Virgil Thomson (1896-1989), for whom Kansas City, Missouri, was home. Admittedly, he attended Harvard and sang with the respected Harvard Glee Club, but as to "growing up in New England," one can only say that of Thomson in the sense that one's education plays a role in one's development. Thomson also studied in Paris with Nadia Boulanger, whose other pupils included Aaron Copland. Back in the States in the Thirties, Thomson stayed busy in opera, theater, and film, working with such noted figures as Gertrude Stein and Orson Welles. In the Forties and Fifties, he served as music critic for the New York Herald-Tribune, where his opinions came to shape the direction of fine music in the US. No aspiring composer would have willingly crossed Thomson, and even established ones regarded him with cautious respect.

As for his own works, Thomson wrote everything from art songs to orchestra pieces. His catalog also includes three operas, a great deal of incidental music for various Shakespeare plays, and, most famously, two film scores for the documentary director Pare Lorentz. In 1936, it was *The Plow that Broke the Plains*, the following year, *The River*. Both were projects of the United States Resettlement Administration and sought to inform the public as to more sustainable use of natural resources. In those years in the wake of the Dust Bowl, it was a topic on the minds of many.

After the release of the film *The Plow that Broke the Plains*, Thomson crafted from his score an orchestral suite to broaden the audience for his music. It is in this form that Thomson's work is most frequently heard today, though the complete Lorentz film is currently available in a format for home viewing. Even in the abbreviated orchestral suite, one finds the compositional tools

Thomson brought to this attempt to capture wide-open spaces in trouble. For example, in "Pastorale (Grass)," Thomson crafted a calm and peaceful scene of the untroubled grasslands before the arrival of the farmer. It is followed by "Cattle," given a distinctly Western feel by the inclusion in the orchestra of a guitar and the use of a pair of old cowboy songs: "I Rode an Old Paint" and "Streets of Laredo." Later, Thomson evoked "Drought" with spare melodic lines and despairing harmonies; one scarcely needs to see the film to feel the tension. For the final scene of "Devastation," a mood arises as if of Okies on the move, though a brighter horizon is hinted at in Thomson's incorporation of some old American hymn tunes, suggestive of hope. *The Plow That Broke the Plains* is a work in which, by the end, all is not quite lost.

Incidentally, this Thomson (Virgil) was a near contemporary of another American composer of similar name, Randall Thompson, who was neither a music critic nor a man for film. Thompson with a 'p' most often wrote choral music, and he can be found in Chapter Eleven.

- Korngold: *The Adventures of Robin Hood*

Erich Korngold (1897-1957) was born in Brunn, Moravia, now Brno in the Czech Republic. His father, an eminent Austrian music critic, trained his son well in music and soon found Erich to be a prodigy composer. At the age of ten, he played his cantata *Gold* for Gustav Mahler, who pronounced the boy a genius. Not long afterward, Puccini remarked, "That boy's talent is so great, he could easily give us half and still have enough left for himself," and Richard Strauss summed up his impressions of the young composer by saying, "It is really amazing."

Although many child prodigies fail to achieve adult success, Erich Korngold built a solid career, finding his greatest success in the theater. His opera, *Die tote Stadt*, written when he was twenty, was acclaimed around the world, and his operetta, *Waltzes from*

Vienna, was especially popular in the US. In the Twenties, Korngold became a professor of opera at the Vienna Staatsakademie, and might well have spent the rest of his career in Europe, had not politics taken an evil path. In 1934, the Jewish composer was badly beaten by a gang of Nazi thugs; it became clear that his future was in danger. When, later that year, the Viennese opera producer Max Reinhardt suggested that Hollywood might provide a lucrative working environment, Korngold jumped at the suggestion. He would spend the rest of his days in southern California.

In California, the young composer's operatic background revolutionized cinematic music, winning Academy Awards for his numerous scores, and drawing particular attention when setting to music the swashbuckling adventures of Errol Flynn, most famously *The Adventures of Robin Hood*, which in 1938 won an Oscar for its music. It is all too easy to regard film music lightly, but Korngold raised the genre to a high art, matching the rhythms of his melodies to the rhythms of spoken words, often using pitches close to those of the actor's voice. He also made frequent use of leitmotifs, devising musical themes for various characters and concepts. Wagner had popularized such techniques in opera; Korngold was the first to apply them to film. Although he continued to write music for the concert hall, sometimes bringing in themes from his film music (his Violin Concerto premiered in 1947 with Jascha Heifetz), these innovative film scores are now the basis of Korngold's reputation.

- Copland: *The Red Pony*

Early in 1948, Aaron Copland — already known for his ballet Appalachian Spring (see Chapter Ten) — was at work on his sixth film score, this one for director Lewis Milestone, with whom the composer had previously worked on *Of Mice and Men*. This time, it was *The Red Pony*, another John Steinbeck story, and would star Myrna Loy, Robert Mitchum, and a very young Beau Bridges. The tale was set in the ranchlands of central California which Steinbeck knew so well; a young boy receives the gift of a pony, and proceeds to have adventures great and small, some only in his imagination, as he interacts with those around him. Of his music for the piece, Copland observed, "Although some of the melodies in *The Red Pony* may sound rather folk-like, they are actually mine. There are no quotations of folklore anywhere in the work." Yet he had studied his models well, and masterfully produced a score deeply evocative of the scenes portrayed on screen. Were it not for the composer's assertion, one would be left frantically searching through folk music collections to identify the melodies.

After the film's premiere, the composer was asked by Efrem Kurtz, conductor of the Houston Symphony Orchestra, to prepare an orchestral suite from the film music that would be suitable for concert performance. Copland happily obliged. Even without the original film's visuals, the suite effectively evokes the spacious and spirited scenes of the tale. The movements sound like what their subtitles tell us they are meant to be, be it visiting a circus or walking to the bunkhouse; there's even one called "Happy Ending." The suite premiered in Houston October 30, 1948.

- Walton: *Henry V*

Second of four children of an English choirmaster and a singer, William Walton (1902-1983) might have seemed destined for a future in vocal music. Indeed, from the age of ten, he did serve as chorister at Christ Church Cathedral, Oxford. Yet it was as a composer, not as a performer, that he would make his career. From the time of his departure (without degree) from Oxford in 1920, he began composing prolifically, writing concert overtures and incidental pieces, as well as arranging dance band tunes to pay the daily bills. Later, Walton would turn to film music, a field in which he achieved great renown.

His reputation grew to the point that twice he was chosen to compose the official coronation march for a new British monarch, an honor never accorded to his younger countryman, Benjamin

Britten. Throughout his long career, Walton stood as one of the leaders of English twentieth century music, a man known for robust melodies woven into intricate combinations, who made use both of modern harmonies and of traditional forms. Only Walton would have taken themes composed to portray a soaring Spitfire of World War II and combined them into a fugue in the manner of Bach. For Walton, the new and the old were both equally valid.

Walton composed the music for about a dozen films, beginning with *Escape Me Never* in 1934. Most prominent in his film catalog are the three Shakespearean films he did for Laurence Olivier (1907-1989). These included *Henry V* (1944), *Hamlet* (1947), and *Richard III* (1955). The task of crafting music for such timeless dramas, and especially for such an unsurpassed acting talent might have intimidated lesser men, but for Walton, it was further inspiration. After all, in writing concertos for virtuoso friends, Mozart, Mendelssohn, and Brahms pulled out all the stops, knowing that the men who would be playing the music were equal to any challenge (see Chapter Four). For Walton, composing music to accompany the words of Shakespeare as delivered by Olivier brought out some of his very best work.

In *Henry V*, he drew upon some pre-existing material appropriate to the time of the play, using melodies from the Fitzwilliam Virginal Book (the virginal was not an innocent young lady, but rather a small keyboard instrument popular in Elizabethan days). For the French scenes, he borrowed a pair of old French battle songs and a few themes from Canteloube's *Songs of the Auvergne* (see Chapter Seven). These inclusions, together with Walton's own melodic ideas, made for a span of music that perfectly matched the intensity of Shakespeare's drama yet also spoke to the days in which the film was made and released: the heart of World War II. It was music to make the Allies' hearts sing — for after all, Henry proves victorious — and could not have been so well achieved by a lesser artist.

- Kabalevsky: *The Comedians*

Dmitri Kabalevsky (1904-1987) was born in St. Petersburg, Russia, not quite two years before his better known countryman, Dmitri Shostakovich (1906-1975), was born in that same city. As a teenager, Kabalevsky moved to Moscow, where, in 1925, he rejected his father's dream for the boy of a career in mathematics and enrolled instead at the Moscow Conservatory. At that institution, he developed a conservative style reminiscent of the nineteenth century Russian masters.

Although some of his contemporaries avoided involvement in official organizations, Kabalevsky did not. In addition to serving as professor of composition at the Moscow Conservatory; he also headed the music department of the Soviet Radio Committee and the Institute of Arts History at the Academy of Science. As a conservative, he succeeded in avoiding official Soviet sanctions that fell heavily on Shostakovich and many other colleagues. Kabalevsky was active in the Union of Soviet Composers and edited the magazine *Soviet Music*. His compositions included concertos, symphonic works, chamber pieces, choral pieces, songs, and stage works.

Kabalevsky produced a great quantity of music, but is known in the West for only two compositions, both dating from 1938. Kabalevsky had just completed the first version of his opera, *Colas Breugnon* — possessed of a famous overture — when he was asked to provide music for a comedy to be produced at the Central Children's Theater of Moscow. The play was called *The Inventor and the Comedians*, and concerned the adventures of a band of traveling entertainers. The usage of "comedians" might be better translated as "buffoons;" these performers were not stand-up comics. Whatever the intent of the title, Kabalevsky delighted in the commission. He quickly completed the music, and it was soon produced with the play. Two years later, the composer chose selections from his score, changed the order of the pieces and arranged them as an orchestral suite. It's fortunate he did so, for the play has long since vanished, yet the music survives.

The ten selections that made their way into the suite are Prologue, Galop, March, Waltz, Pantomime, Intermezzo, Little Lyrical Scene, Gavotte, Scherzo, and Epilogue. Most are characterized by Kabalevsky's inventive inclusion of percussion and his preference for lively rhythms. A wry sense of humor is also evident. The March is alternately somber and tipsy, and the Waltz comes complete with "oom-pah" brass. At times, echoes of Mendelssohn appear, particularly in the Intermezzo and Scherzo, which seem rather reminiscent of their counterparts in *A Midsummer Night's Dream*. The suite concludes with a giddy Epilogue that resurrects the theme of the first movement, bringing the suite full circle to a jovial conclusion.

- Shostakovich: *The Gadfly*, op. 97

For Russian composers in the 1930s and '40s, career decisions had to be filtered through the lens of what Stalin would permit music to do. Music that served no perceived "practical" purpose - notably symphonies and chamber music - was derided as bourgeois and more often than not banned from performance. However, music for stage and screen often passed muster, as it could be viewed as entertainment for all, not just for the imagined idle rich. Thus, Dmitri Shostakovich (1906 - 1975) made frequent contributions to these genres, composing about a dozen sets of incidental music to accompany stage plays and roughly three dozen film scores. These he was sure would reach the public, even though his symphonies might spend years on the shelf.

Some of this quantity of music Shostakovich wrote for stage and screen has remained unfamiliar in the West, as Russian plays and films rarely make it beyond that nation's borders. Even his scores for familiar Shakespearean tales - including *Hamlet* and *King Lear* - were given enough of a sardonic Russian twist that they don't often reach non-Russian audiences. Yet one of Shostakovich's film scores has managed to transcend the film for which it was created. That one is *The Gadfly*, dating from 1955. The tale, set in Italy in the 1840s, as it struggled for unity, it is a dashing adventure story the music for which draws inspiration both from Verdi operas and from Italian folk dance. Its most famous selections include a boisterous *Galop*, a high-spirited *Barrel Organ Waltz*, and a sweetly lyrical *Romance*. This last movement was long beloved by figure skaters and has been featured as the theme music for television programs on both sides of the Atlantic.

In *The Gadfly*, one finds the brighter, more optimistic side of Shostakovich, perhaps in part because the film for which the music was written came two years after the passing of Stalin. Hope may have seemed to be on the horizon.

- Miklós Rózsa: *Ben-Hur*

Although most Americans remember his name only in the realm of film music, Miklós Rózsa (1907-1995) was thoroughly trained in classical traditions. Younger countryman of Béla Bartók (1881-1945), Rózsa was born in Budapest, where his musical studies began with violin lessons at the tender age of five. By age seven, he had taken up composition and developed a fascination for the spirited folk music of his country. Although unlike Bartók, he did not pursue academic study of ethnomusicology, Rózsa would often evoke the lively spirit of Hungarian dances in his concert pieces. Advanced musical studies in Budapest and Leipzig allowed him to further develop his innate talents, and by 1929, his works were finding publishers and audiences. Into the 1930s, most of his focus was upon orchestral music and chamber compositions. Only in 1937 did he develop an interest in film music, thanks to an association with a London-based producer.

In 1940, Rózsa relocated to Hollywood, where his flair for lively and melodic compositions found expression in such highly regarded films as *Spellbound, Quo vadis* and *Ben-Hur*. Yet he did not set aside music for the concert hall. Even after his first Hollywood successes during the years of World War II, Rózsa was still at work on concertos and symphonic overtures, chamber music and band works, composing for the concert hall nearly until his death. Some of these draw upon themes from his film scores, thereby inviting audience members to come from the movie palace to the concert hall while still feeling at home.

Of the several dozen films on which Rózsa worked, none achieved a higher profile than *Ben-Hur* (1959). Then again, very few films of any description have done better than *Ben-Hur*, which earned eleven Academy Awards, one of them for Rózsa's music (his third Oscar). It is a tale of Biblical setting (and proportion), starring Charlton Heston in the title role of a wealthy Jerusalem merchant who, falling afoul of the Romans, is condemned to be a galley slave. An act of heroism on his part redeems him from this fate and makes of him a competitive charioteer. In the arena, he bests his closest competitor and returns to Jerusalem, in time not only to be reunited with his loved ones but also to meet Christ just before the Crucifixion. With such a tale at hand, film-maker William Wyler did not think small, nor could Rózsa. His music is grand when necessary, poignant when possible, and, especially in the intense chariot race, unsurpassed in its dramatic potential. Richly Romantic with lush, flowing themes like the best of Tchaikovsky, it is music that makes even more of the film-maker's epic vision.

- Nino Rota: *La Strada*

For centuries, Italian composers have generally chosen between two career alternatives: music for the church, or music for the opera house. Nino Rota (1911-1979) came along late enough to have an additional option, that of film music. Born in Milan — where one finds the revered La Scala Opera House — Rota learned piano and the rudiments of composition as a boy. Studies at the Milan Conservatory followed, then later at the Curtis Institute of Music in Philadelphia. By the time he reached his early twenties, he was already composing the expected sacred and stage works, but in his thirties, film music came to the fore. Ultimately, he would compose well over one-hundred film scores, some of which he would later re-work into forms for the concert hall and ballet theater. Rota had no intention of forgetting this other half of the music business, just because he was having such success in cinema.

Although some of the films on which he worked were intended for Italian audiences and thus were not widely distributed in English-speaking lands, other Rota scores accompanied films with an international following. He worked frequently with Federico Fellini, Franco Zefferelli, and Francis Ford Coppola. Amongst the best-known films in Rota's catalog are *La Strada* (1954), *8½.* (1963), *Romeo and Juliet* (1968), and the first two installments of the *Godfather* series. For the second of the *Godfather* films, Rota was awarded the Academy Award for Music in 1974.

Rota's score for Fellini's *La Strada* did not win an Oscar, in part because in 1954, foreign films were not being considered for such awards. Foreign born composers were winning Academy Awards for their music, but only if they were working out of Hollywood. *La Strada* itself won a foreign film Oscar, but the music received little notice at the time. However, Rota's score demonstrates his deft handling of music to portray quirky characters, differentiating between the different personalities and images on the screen. Especially crucial was the final scene of the film for which he had to craft a melody meant to remind the Anthony Quinn character of his lost wife; as Wagner or Puccini might have done in operas, with melodies related to specific ideas, Rota managed to do in film. A dozen years later, the music was still on some minds, as La Scala asked Rota for a ballet. The resulting balletic version of *La Strada* premiered in 1966 and neatly recaptures the mood of the original score.

- Herrmann: *Psycho*

Like many of the greatest names in American music of his generation, Bernard Herrmann (1911-1975) was a first generation American, son of Eastern European Jewish immigrants. He was born in New York City where his father, a medical doctor, regularly took the family to concerts and operas. Independent reading of Berlioz's respected *Treatise on Orchestration* led the boy to decide that composition was the career for him. In high school, he began more formal study of composition and ultimately ended up at New York University and Juilliard. He came under the influence of his elder colleague Copland who had set about inspiring young American composers to express their own ideas, rather than just mimicking the Europeans.

By 1934, young Herrmann was working for CBS radio as assistant to its music director, in which position he sought to broaden the spectrum of featured composers. Through his work with CBS, Herrmann came to be associated with the network's series "The Mercury Theater of the Air" and its director Orson Welles. When the powerful radio drama *War of the Worlds* aired in 1939, it was Herrmann who conducted the orchestra, though the score itself was compiled from pre-existing music.

In 1941, Welles was off to Hollywood for *Citizen Kane* and asked Herrmann to come along and compose an original score for the film. It would be the first of many cinematic milestones for Herrmann. In later years, he would often partner with Alfred Hitchcock, scoring such famed films as *Vertigo, North by Northwest*, and *Psycho*. With Hitchcock's sometimes surreal images at hand, Herrmann occasionally drew on the most avant garde music techniques, thereby exposing tens of millions of film-goers to edgy harmonies and dissonances, as well as electronic instruments, which might have worried more conservative orchestral conductors. In so doing, Herrmann did a service to progressive composers, in that their techniques came to seem somewhat less quarrelsome than they might otherwise have been. His last film was Martin Scorsese's *Taxi Driver*, released after the composer's passing, his film career having spanned four decades.

Most famed of Herrmann's film scores is that for Hitchcock's 1960 thriller *Psycho*; indeed, the minute-and-a-half of the murder scene contains some of the most famed music in any film score by any composer. It is music that makes the scene even more violent than it might otherwise have been. That Herrmann managed this with the simple string ensemble that he chose to use is especially impressive. Due to budget constraints, he had been forced to limit his orchestra, but arguably, the sparer textures of strings worked perfectly with the black-and-white cinematography. Hitchcock had decided against using color, and thus so did Herrmann. Yet strings can evoke color through playing technique, provided the composer is wise enough to call for it. Herrmann did so with such power that many listeners who have somehow never seen Hitchcock's film (setting entirely side the more recent remake) still hear Herrmann's music knowing it's for a scene of deathly violence.

Herrmann also composed a quantity of works for the classical concert hall, especially orchestral pieces and chamber music. His opera on Emily Brontë's novel *Wuthering Heights* was completed in 1951 but did not reach the stage until 1982. Since that time, the main aria for its leading lady — the character of Cathy — has been championed by soprano Renee Fleming and other artists who delight in its richly emotional lines.

- Bernstein: *West Side Story*

Before *West Side Story* opened at the Winter Garden Theatre in New York September 26, 1957, there were few clues the work would be a triumph. Its creative team was composed of men early in the careers who had yet to prove themselves in theater. Lyricist

Stephen Sondheim, playwright Arthur Laurents, choreographer Jerome Robbins, impresario Harold Prince, and composer Leonard Bernstein: their names are familiar now, but in 1957, they were yet unproven. Only Bernstein's name was widely known, thanks to his triumphant debut with the New York Philharmonic November 14, 1943 and other high profile activities since that time, but an orchestral conductor tackling Broadway did not seem to be a prescription for success. Yet the chemistry was magical, and the New York setting for a new Romeo and Juliet caught the affections of the audience. *West Side Story* ran for 729 performances. Although it did not win the Tony Award that season (the honor went to Meredith Willson's *The Music Man*), the film version four years later scored ten Oscars. From its vocal challenges to its choreographic intensity to its heart-wringing story, *West Side Story* has survived as one of the great masterpieces of the American stage.

That the piece is *West Side Story* at all was something of an accident. Bernstein had imagined a story derived from *Romeo and Juliet* but somewhat closer to his own family roots, set on the east side of New York City, where the immigrant population was largely Eastern European in origin. It was to be of a Catholic/Jewish divide, and with his personal roots in Eastern European Jewish culture, Bernstein felt this was a tale he could tell. However, one day, while driving into New York for a rehearsal, he literally got off at the wrong exit and found himself on the west side of town, populated by a large proportion of Latin American immigrants. Seeing the unusual signs and clothing and hearing the voices, Bernstein decided that this setting was more exotic than his original concept, and was intrigued by the idea of working Latin rhythms into the music. Thus we have instead Tony and Maria, the Jets and the Sharks, and even a highway bridge (under which the pivotal rumble takes place) representing that wrong exit: a timeless new telling of those star-crossed lovers.

For many music lovers, *West Side Story* is the definitive Bernstein composition, a situation that in later years would rather annoy its composer. At this point, he'd already written two symphonies, two operas, a ballet, chamber music, and a pair of concertos (neither of which actually has the word "concerto" in its title). More such works would follow, including a Mass for Jackie Kennedy, and yet it was *West Side Story* that got the attention. Still, his conducting appearances worldwide never lacked for headlines, and if *West Side Story* was almost too popular for its own good, at least it brought more people into the concert hall than otherwise might have attended. Getting music into the ears of an audience is a crucial goal on any terms. It might well have fit into Chapter Eight with operas and operettas, but as its widest exposure came through its Hollywood edition, the decision was made to place it here.

- Williams: *Star Wars*

The compositions of John Williams (b. 1932) are among the most familiar in America, even for those listeners who do not know the composer's name. Who could not recognize the ominous two-note theme of the shark in the movie *Jaws*, or the five-note pattern used to communicate with the aliens in *Close Encounters*, or the brisk and hearty marches heard with the opening titles of *Star Wars*, *Raiders of the Lost Ark* and *Superman*? Other notable Williams film scores include *ET* and *Schindler's List* (both of which won Academy Awards), *Home Alone*, *Jurassic Park*, and *Saving Private Ryan*. Williams has scored over one hundred films, and has been the dominant composer in Hollywood for the past three decades.

However, unlike most of his film music colleagues, Williams is also active in the realm of concert music. He succeeded Arthur Fiedler as conductor of the Boston Pops Orchestra. With that ensemble, he made numerous recordings of standard classical works, including Holst's *The Planets*. He has also produced notable concert pieces of his own, including a symphony, a tuba concerto, and a bassoon concerto titled *The Five Sacred Trees*. His various works, driven by the different venues in which they are heard, exhibit much diversity of style. Yet still there is a quintessential "Williams" sound that comes most easily to mind: that of bold and brassy marches brightened with silvery xylophones, and mellowed at times with gracious cello and woodwind themes.

Such are the sounds familiar from *Star Wars* of 1977, Williams' most enduring creation, a vision he has revisited with each subsequent film in the Lucas series. Like Wagner, he awards to his characters (and the scenarios they inhabit) identifying melodies that help listeners to stay in touch with the tale. Also like Wagner, he allows those melodies to grow and expand, gaining in complexity as the story progresses, often linking one character to another through the repetition of motifs. So the Luke Skywalker theme, so dark and shadowed when he stood gazing upon the smoking ruins of his boyhood home, turns bold and heroic as he triumphs in battle. Intervals from the Darth Vader theme echo in the themes for his two children, even before George Lucas has bothered to tell his audience — or even hint — that these two persons are indeed the offspring of the evil figure. The only hints were musical.

It was a big enough task for the original film; returning to the old ideas for the later films brought additional challenges. Williams himself has observed, "I wanted to try to develop material that would wed with the original and sound like part of an organic whole . . . I had to look back while at the same time begin again and extend." That he succeeded is proven by the legions of soundtrack purchasers who enjoy his work even without the visual imagery that inspired it. As filmmaker George Lucas declares, "Every fan of *Star Wars* — and of great music — is in his debt."

- Corigliano: *The Red Violin*

One of the most acclaimed of contemporary composers, John Corigliano (born in New York City in 1938) comes of strong musical lineage. His mother was a talented pianist, his father and namesake the long-time concertmaster of the New York Philharmonic under Leonard Bernstein. Composition studies at Columbia University and the Manhattan School of Music led to early professional work, including a post as Bernstein's assistant in scripting the famed Young People's Concerts in the late 1950s, but in the years since that time, he has stood firmly upon his own compositional feet. His honors include a Pulitzer Prize for his Symphony no. 2, an Academy Award for *The Red Violin*, and commissions from the Metropolitan Opera (*The Ghosts of Versailles*), the Chicago Symphony (Symphony no. 1), and flutist James Galway (*Pied Piper Fantasy*). He joined the faculty of the Juilliard School in 1991.

Corigliano has generally kept busy with music for the concert hall and the opera house. However, when the chance arose to work on the film *The Red Violin*, he leapt at the chance. Its story concerns how a single particular violin originating in the late 1600s tied together the lives of various persons as it gradually made its way through history to the late twentieth century; the film was released in 1999. As music plays a crucial role in the film, having a composer who understood that history was vital, and who better than the son of a professional concert violinist?

Beginning by crafting a theme to represent one of the early characters, Anna, who comes to be the soul of the violin, Corigliano then brought that theme back in the later scenes. He allowed it to evolve, thus reflecting the new time at hand, from Cremona of the Italian Baroque, to Vienna of Mozart's day, to Oxford of the Victorian years, to communist China, and finally to the present day. Corigliano did his task so well that in 2000, *The Red Violin* won the Academy Award for best original film score.

Before the film itself premiered, Corigliano crafted from his score a one-movement concert piece for violin and orchestra derived from some of the film's principal themes; the work is called *The Red Violin Chaconne*. A chaconne is a compositional form in which a repetitive bass line underlies an array of varying melodies, pointing out the relationships between those themes in that, though each sounds different from the others, all yet stand on the same foundation. The form was particularly identified with the Baroque Era around 1700 and thus is a graceful choice for a work the roots of which lie in a film partially set in the seventeenth and eighteenth centuries. The chaconne premiered late in 1997 with violinist Joshua Bell, who had played the solos in the film, and served to call attention to the forthcoming film. Wagner himself, who also used orchestral music to promote his forthcoming operas, would have been proud of Corigliano for seeing the wisdom of that marketing approach. Later, Corigliano expanded the score into a full, four-movement concerto, in which the earlier chaconne served as the first movement. In this form, it was first heard September 19, 2003, with Joshua Bell, the Baltimore Symphony, and conductor Marin Alsop.

- Shore: *The Lord of the Rings*

A native of Toronto, Canada, Howard Shore (b. 1946) first came to international musical attention when he was hired as the first musical director of *Saturday Night Live* in the mid 1970s. It wasn't serious music, but it was a serious opportunity for networking, an advantage that wise composers over the centuries have understood. Even before he left *SNL* in 1980, Shore was beginning to work in Hollywood, and since then has scored over five dozen films, with such important directors as Martin Scorsese, David Cronenberg. Tim Burton, and, most famously, Peter Jackson. For Jackson, Shore took on the epic challenge of the three *Lord of the Rings* films, ultimately winning Academy Awards for his work on the first and third films and a Grammy for the soundtrack recording of the second.

As Wagner had done before him in opera, Shore, too, seeks to let a film's music express unspoken ideas, drawing parallels between scenes so that viewers can sense connections. Similarly, and again, like Wagner, Shore set out to create an historical view of a mythical time. In Shore's case, this meant imagining music to evoke the character of a fictional culture. For example, his

313

hobbit music is generally Celtic flavored, the elves are distantly oriental in harmonic mood, and the evil orcs have percussive and violent music that might be the darkest side of Schoenberg-style Expressionism. Differentiating characters through musical color is something that Wagner brought to his operas with his leitmotifs. By bringing these techniques into the world of film, Shore proves his awareness of and facility with enduring compositional tools.

Once the *Lord of the Rings* films were finished and premiered, Shore found himself with some ten hours of music on hand that he felt deserved a wider audience. Thus, he set about crafting from the film music a grand symphony for orchestra, chorus, and vocal soloists. *The Lord of the Rings Symphony: Six Movements for Orchestra and Chorus* premiered November 29, 2003 in Wellington, New Zealand, the location chosen because Jackson's trilogy had been filmed in that nation, so as to take advantage of its dramatic landscapes. Since that premiere, the symphony has earned many dozens of performances world-wide, proving that the best film music is also worthy of standing on its own, even when the only visual element is the orchestra and the singers. Through his symphony, Shore takes listeners through the epic journey of Tolkien's tale in rather less time yet with equally vivid colors.

Incidentally, in addition to his *Lord of the Rings Symphony*, Shore has also returned to his work for David Cronenberg's 1986 film *The Fly*, crafting from it an opera that premiered in Paris in 2008. Music for the opera is largely distinct from that of the film score, as Shore took advantage of the opportunity to do things differently when not constrained by film requirements. In its review of the premiere, the respected British magazine *Gramophone* had many positive words for the music, and of the overall work, only questioned the stage value of the story, which, after all, was not exactly Shore's own, or even Cronenberg's, but predated both men. The admitted creepiness of the story is mostly George Langelaan's responsibility, for his short story was the immediate inspiration, though at least in part Kakfa's, who'd tried it first.

- Tan Dun: *Crouching Tiger, Hidden Dragon*

The public at large has heard more music of Chinese composer Tan Dun (b. 1957) than it might imagine, for amongst his works is the Academy Award and Grammy Award winning score for *Crouching Tiger, Hidden Dragon*. Even more recently, he composed his Internet Symphony no. 1 for the YouTube Orchestra and the opera *The First Emperor* for the Metropolitan Opera. Those high profile projects are the culmination (so far) of a career that got its start when the nineteen-year-old Hunan native first heard Beethoven's Symphony no. 5. He promptly set aside his work as arranger and fiddler with a Peking opera troupe for serious music studies, first at Beijing's Central Conservatory and then at Columbia in New York City.

Since that time, he has largely been based in the US, but his music has a strong international following. The greatest soloists and ensembles have eagerly commissioned and performed his works, and audiences react enthusiastically to his style, which blends some of the rhythms and harmonies of music of his native China with the broader structures and fuller orchestrations of Western music.

As for *Crouching Tiger*, the film by Ang Lee was released in 2000 and set in China's Qing Dynasty of the 1700s. Part love story and part adventure, the tale revolves around a struggle to possess a powerful sword, the Green Destiny. In that very small nutshell, the story seems related to Wagner's epic *Ring Cycle* of operas (see Chapter Eight), though the costuming for *Crouching Tiger* would have puzzled the German master. However, as with the Wagner, Tan Dun needed to craft music of various moods for the different scenes, and also wished to make use of both folk and orchestral instruments. Many passages have prominent solo lines for cello, for which the composer recruited the esteemed cellist Yo-Yo Ma (b. 1955). Born in Paris to Chinese parents, Ma has spent his career not only on mastering the great masterworks of the classical repertoire — including the Dvořák and Elgar cello concertos (see Chapter Four) — but also exploring international music of the old Silk Road. So he was the perfect choice of collaborator, even beyond the fact that his unsurpassed reputation lent gravitas to the project.

In return, Tan Dun took the time after *Crouching Tiger*'s release to rework themes from the film score into a concerto for Ma. The *Crouching Tiger* Concerto premiered in London with Ma as soloist September 30, 2000. A second version of the concerto then appeared, designed for the cello-like Chinese folk instrument called the erhu. This one came to the public about a year after the original. Both do a fine job of capturing the musical vision of the original film score, but had the original not possessed that vision, there would not have been enough content of interest to make the music worth reworking. Tan Dun had made the most of the original opportunity, thus making a musical reinvention practical and possible.

Further Recommendations:

Granted that all the composers in this chapter made many contributions in this particular corner of the musical world, here are some other options to consider, first from composers whose main focus was on other types of music (not for stage and screen), and then by film composers of recent years:

Stage Music:

-   Ludwig van Beethoven (1770-1827): *Egmont* — play by Goethe

-   Sir Arthur Sullivan (1842-1900): *The Tempest* — play by Shakespeare

- Richard Strauss (1864-1949): *Le bourgeois gentilhomme* — play by Moliere (though Strauss set a German version of it, as *Der Bürger als Edelmann*)

- Jean Sibelius (1865-1957): *Kuolema* — play by Arvid Järnefelt (contains the famed *Valse triste*)

- both Sibelius and Gabriel Fauré (1845-1924): *Pelléas et Melisande* — play by Maeterlinck (there's also a Debussy opera on this story: see Chapter Eight)

- Ralph Vaughan Williams (1872-1958): *The Wasps* — play by Aristophanes

- Igor Stravinsky (1882-1971): *The Soldier's Tale* — based on folk tales of a man outsmarting the devil. Sets and costumes were by René Auberjonois, patriarch of the family of the modern actor bearing the same name

Film Music:

- Max Steiner (1888-1971): *King Kong, Casablanca, Gone with the Wind,* inter alia

- Alfred Newman (1900-1970): *The Greatest Story Ever Told, How the West Was Won, The Song of Bernadette,* inter alia

- Maurice Jarre (1924-2009): *Lawrence of Arabia, Doctor Zhivago, Grand Prix,* inter alia

- Jerry Goldsmith (1929-2004): *Patton, Papillon, Planet of the Apes,* inter alia

- John Barry (1933-2011): *Born Free, Out of Africa, Dances with Wolves,* inter alia

- Philip Glass (b. 1937): *Koyaanisqatsi, Thin Blue Line, The Hours, Mishima,* inter alia

- Alan Silvestri (b. 1950): *Back to the Future, Contact, The Polar Express,* inter alia

- James Horner (b. 1953): *Braveheart, Titanic, Apollo 13, Avatar,* inter alia

- Hans Zimmer (b. 1957): *The Lion King* (in part — songs by Elton John), *Gladiator, The Da Vinci Code,* inter alia

Chapter Ten
Music for Motion
(Dancing and Marching)

Thanks to Stanley Kubrick — who was, after all, not a composer, but a film director of strong reputation — there is no more famous waltz than this one: *On the Beautiful Blue Danube* by Johann Strauss Jr. It was written nearly a century before the creation of the film *2001: a Space Odyssey*, but reaching out to many hundreds of millions of film fans proved advantageous to the work's reputation. Yet if Kubrick hadn't known it in the first place, it wouldn't have appeared in his film, and it happens that music for the dance is some of the most familiar music ever composed. March music, too, has a ready audience, and in either case, the subject is music conceived for physical motion.

All music requires motion. Even if there is only a single singer standing alone on stage, that singer's vocal chords are busily vibrating. A chamber concert or an orchestral concert provides an even more visible sense of motion. However, in most cases, neither the performers nor the audience members are getting up and moving around to the music, but music intended for motion

319

is the topic of this chapter. Most often, that is music for dancing, either at the ballet, at which the audience is stationary but there are dancers moving in time to the music, or in the ballroom, in which other than persons lacking dance partners, the assembled crowd is there for the specific purpose moving to music.

Of formal ballet with its theatrical component, many observers are accustomed to thinking of it as a Russian art form, thanks in part to the fact that Tchaikovsky, composer of *Swan Lake, Sleeping Beauty,* and *The Nutcracker,* was Russian, and also to the fact that some of the most famous dancers of all time — including Pavlova, Nijinsky, and Baryshnikov — were Russian. However, the Russians didn't invent the idea of grand music and dance telling a story. That honor goes to French composers, who back in the days of Louis XIV "The Sun King" (1638-1715), developed the art form in part because Louis himself liked it.

From its origins as diversion for royalty, ballet evolved to become entertainment for the general public, and the Russians copied it from the French. Tchaikovsky was the first important composer for the concert hall (symphonies, concertos, and the like) to also compose excellent ballets; the French ballet composers who preceded him and served as his models were theatrical specialists not troubling themselves with such things as symphonies.

Marching music also has a component of motion, whether it is a military march for soldiers or a general march, perhaps for patriotic expression. After all, a parade with no marching music would not be much of a parade, but a parade with dance music instead of marches would have band members waltzing down the street: a rather awkward image. Sousa may be the best known composer of marches — and he is here in this chapter — but he is far from the only example.

This chapter includes various types of music for motion, both the sit-and-listen-and-watch type as in a formal ballet and the get-up-and-get-involved type, as in a social dance or a march. Some of the selections here might have been included in Chapter Eight, as they are dances from operas; however, if the dance scene in question is better known than the opera as a whole, these selections seemed to fit better here.

It seems worth remembering that, with determination, one can dance to almost anything. Witnesses of the time recalled watching bemused as Richard Wagner danced to Beethoven's Symphony no. 7 as played on the piano by Franz Liszt, incidentally not merely a fine pianist and composer but also Wagner's father-in-law. Many great works of earlier years have been adapted for ballet performance by the addition of choreography; the great choreographer George Balanchine was especially fond of doing so. Thus, one may see Tchaikovsky's Serenade for Strings performed as a ballet, but he did not write it for that purpose.

Similarly, music to which one marches may or may not have originated as marching music. This writer knows of a high school marching band that, having spent one full football season with excerpts from Bizet's opera *Carmen*, then decided that Holst's *The Planets* should be its next challenge. That some of the selected movements have odd numbers of beats per measure (though the band members all had exactly two feet, not three or five) was not seen as a disadvantage, and they worked around that complication. Yet one cannot fairly say that either *The Planets* (see Chapter Three) or *Carmen* (see Chapter Eight) was composed for the purpose of marching.

Since one might endlessly prepare lists of everything to which one might dance or march, the focus of this chapter is upon music originally intended by its composer for dancing and marching. By and large, such works will have a beat that lends itself readily to one of those activities.

- Adam: *Giselle*

He was, perhaps, destined for a music career. Adolphe Adam (1803-1856) was born in Paris, son of a piano instructor at that city's famed Conservatoire. Young Adolphe, too, learned the piano, and then studied composition at the Conservatoire. By the age of twenty, he was working in the city's theaters, contributing songs to vaudeville shows. Soon, he was in strong enough demand to be composing entire entertainments himself, rather than needing to collaborate with more established composers. Theatrical music would become his central focus, writing both light operas and ballets. By the end of his career, Adam had composed about five dozen light operas, all of which reached the stage before his death. On the ballet side of the equation, there are about a dozen Adam scores, most from the last decade and a half of his life. Of the ballets, the most beloved is *Giselle*.

We can thank the Germans for *Giselle*. The composer was French and the premiere was in Paris, but the story was of German inspiration. Theophile Gautier, the French poet and novelist, was reading in Heinrich Heine about classic German legends. One particular story, concerning the ghostly spirits of girls who have died before their wedding day, caught his fancy. Gautier imagined a version in which a girl betrayed by her sweetheart dies of a broken heart, but then as a spirit intervenes to save him from retribution, thus giving something of an upbeat ending to the tale.

With superb timing, Gautier brought his idea to the creative forces at the Paris Opéra, home not only for opera but also ballet. The Opéra had just presented a new dancer, Carlotta Grisi, who had been so well received that the management wanted to feature her again as soon as possible, particularly in something exactly suited to her skills. This new tale, with its young heroine, seemed perfectly suited to Mademoiselle Grisi's talents, for she could both dance and act, and also look the part.

As he had worked with the Paris Opéra before — indeed, he had worked with most of the city's popular theaters — Adam was quickly recruited for this newest project. Work on the score and its choreography began at once. Within two months, *Giselle* moved from conception to realization. Its premiere June 28, 1841, was a triumph for composer and ballerina alike. The music, by turns sweetly romantic or swirling dramatically, has stood the test of time.

- Johann Strauss Jr.: *On the Beautiful Blue Danube, op. 314*

In the world of waltz music, the Strauss family functioned as a royal dynasty. The combined efforts of Johann Strauss Sr. and his sons, Johann Jr., Josef, and Eduard, led to the creation of roughly a thousand compositions, with waltzes and polkas most numerous on the list. Although all four men were prolific composers and active conductors, the younger Johann proved to be the most influential of the clan. Johann Jr. (1825-1899) took a dance form that was still intended mostly for the ballroom and deftly raised it to concert-hall status, producing compositions almost symphonic in scope, making great demands on both his orchestra and himself. In his hands, the waltz introduction, which had originally served as a mere call to the dance floor, became an extended evocation of the mood or scene he wished to convey, and the varied themes of each waltz are as intricately linked as they would have been in a symphony by the greatest of masters. Strauss' influence in the musical world was so pronounced that when the composer died in 1899, the Viennese critic Eduard Hanslick, who more frequently occupied himself by boosting Brahms symphonies and blasting Wagner operas, wrote a laudatory obituary praising Strauss as Vienna's "most original musical talent."

Strauss Jr.'s best-loved waltz, indeed, the most adored waltz of all time, is *On the Beautiful, Blue Danube*, op. 314, dating from 1867. Written for the Vienna Men's Singing Club, the work soon moved from vocal form to orchestral, in the composer's own orchestration two weeks after its initial premiere. The title comes from the grand, trans-continental river that flows through the heart of Vienna. Natural references were not common in titles to Strauss' compositions. More often, his titles refer to people, social occasions, and even machines, as he often composed and conducted for Vienna's annual engineer's ball. Yet this outdoor-flavored waltz has remained at the summit of his list of popular works, in part because of the superiority of the craftsmanship. Note the gentle, lyrical introduction that leads the way toward the waltz melodies proper, and how each subsequent waltz melody (five in all) brings new elements of expression into what might otherwise be too much of a good thing. In Strauss' hands, the waltz becomes a high art in its own right, not merely an excuse for dancing.

Of this work, Brahms, a good friend of the composer, once joked that it was "unfortunately not by Johannes Brahms." Whether he was admiring it for its popularity alone or also for its musical value is hard to say; Brahms was known for his dry sense of humor.

Incidentally, Johann Strauss and Richard Strauss (whose works were featured in earlier chapters) were not related. The waltzing Strausses were Austrians from Vienna; Richard's family was German, from Munich. They would have known of one another's work. Richard was nearly forty years younger than Johann, yet became renowned young enough for Johann to be aware of his achievements. However, their surname was common in German speaking lands, even outside of the world of music.

- Delibes: *Coppélia*

The best possible background for a composer of theatre music, such as operas and ballets, would be to work in a theatre, gaining practical experience in how a performance comes together backstage. From such a perspective, one could gain a strong understanding of the interactions of singers, dancers, and musicians, then draw upon that knowledge in the creation of one's own operatic or balletic works. Certainly, this approach worked for Leo Delibes (1836-1891). In the 1860s, the young Frenchman became chorus master at the Paris Theatre Lyrique, where he prepared singers for performances of Gounod's *Faust*, Bizet's *The Pearl Fishers*, and Berlioz's *The Trojans at Carthage*. His work exposed him to the finest efforts of France's most prominent composers. That Delibes dreamed of joining his countrymen in the creation of stage-works was surely expected by everyone, except perhaps his father, who apparently imagined a different career for his only child. The elder Delibes was a postal worker who hoped his son would follow him into civil service. However, he died when the boy was just eleven years old, and Madame Delibes — daughter of an opera singer — took her son to Paris for studies at the Conservatoire. From that day onward, music would be his life.

Two weeks before turning twenty, Delibes witnessed the premiere of his first light operetta, *Deux sous de charbon*. The piece was sufficiently successful that the ambitious young composer decided to continue creating such works, producing fourteen more over the next decade. Yet it was not until 1866, when Delibes was thirty, that he expanded that operatic interest into the equally dramatic realm of ballet, the field in which he would earn his greatest fame. In that year, Delibes contributed to a collaborative ballet titled *La Source*. Delibes' share of the piece was praised for its charm and lyricism, and astute observers noted that even finer things should follow. The next Delibes ballet, *Coppélia*, arrived in 1870. It quickly took its place amongst the most beloved ballets in the repertoire.

Coppélia was based upon ETA Hoffmann's story "Der Sandmann," a dark psychological fantasy concerning a man's destructive infatuation for a lifelike mechanical doll. The same tale would soon earn operatic treatment from Jacques Offenbach (1819-1880), in whose version (*The Tales of Hoffmann*) the story's surrealism was partially preserved, yet Delibes rejected such a literal approach. He too well understood French theatrical tastes to make such stern demands of an audience that was merely seeking amusement. Rather than clinging to the original tragic mood, Delibes transformed Hoffmann's brooding Romanticism into the gay glitter of the Parisian stage, creating a sweet-tempered comedy. The doll-maker has been outwitted, and Frantz has come to his senses in time to marry Swanhilde, who had rescued him from his fate.

The premiere, before an audience that included Napoleon III and Empress Eugenie, was an unalloyed triumph for all concerned, notably for the composer, the choreographer, and the prima ballerina. Tragically, two of those three did not live long enough to fully enjoy their laurels. The choreographer, Arthur Saint-Leon, died of a heart attack three months later, and the prima ballerina, Giuseppina Bozzacchi, fell prey to smallpox later in the year, perishing on her seventeenth birthday. Of the persons most responsible for *Coppélia*'s success, Delibes alone witnessed her ascent to the heights of balletic fame.

- Brahms: Hungarian Dances

Brahms' Hungarian Dances capitalize upon two musical trends of the nineteenth century. One such trend was for dance-style pieces written for piano four-hands, that is, one piano, but two pianists, one playing the right half of the keyboard, the other the left. The other trend was for compositions inspired by Europe's diverse blend of minority cultures, particularly the vibrant and colorful Gypsy culture. Both piano four-hands music and gypsy music made early entrances into Brahms' life. He had begun writing piano duets while still in his twenties, and had discovered the excitement of Hungarian gypsy music as a youth. Due to geography, the composer's native Hamburg became a favored jumping off point for Eastern Europeans exchanging political turmoil in their homelands for the optimism of the New World.

Thus, even in northern Germany, young Brahms had numerous opportunities to hear the intricate rhythms of Gypsy music.

One particular influence was the Hungarian violinist Eduard Hoffmann Remenyi, a concert of whose Brahms heard when he was only seventeen. In later years, he would have the opportunity to serve as the great violinist's accompanist at the piano, and learned in even greater detail exactly how Hungarian music should be played. His familiarity both with piano four-hands music and with authentic Gypsy dances led Brahms to try his hand at composing Hungarian-style pieces for which he knew there would be a ready-made audience. He would compose twenty-one such dances, published in two sets in 1869 and 1880. For a few of them, he would later prepare orchestrated versions; others are sometimes heard in orchestrations by his friends and colleagues. Yet all began life as duets for piano, with the melodies and accompaniments distributed over two pairs of hands. Thus, they could have been placed in one of several chapters in this book, but the title seemed to suit them for this chapter.

- Ponchielli: *Dance of the Hours*, from *La gioconda*

Thanks to animated crocodiles and comic songs about summer camp, vast numbers of persons can recognize *Dance of the Hours* who wouldn't be able to name it, let alone its composer. Yet the influence of Amilcare Ponchielli (1834-1886) is wider than that of most one-hit wonders. He composed everything from operas to band music to solo piano pieces. He taught composition at the Milan Conservatory, and numbered Puccini amongst his students. He was the most admired Italian composer of opera in the generation between Verdi and Puccini, and if his operas (numbering about a dozen) are little performed today, that is more the fault of their poorly structured librettos than of the well-crafted music. Even the best music cannot save an incomprehensible story. Fortunately, orchestral excerpts, such as *Dance of the Hours*, escape that trap.

La gioconda, the opera from which *Dance of the Hours* derives, premiered at Milan's La Scala April 8, 1876. Reworked from Victor Hugo's 'Angelo, tyran de Padoue,' its story was developed into a functional libretto by Arrigo Boito. Widely considered one of the best librettists of the day, Boito (himself also a composer) provided Ponchielli with a better libretto than the composer usually received. The opera would become the composer's biggest success, even before twentieth century audiences found comedy in its famous dance. The scene comes from the second of the opera's four acts, in which the vengeful and murderously minded Duke Alvise is hosting a dinner party. As the entertainment — consisting of the *Dance of the Hours* — is meant to divert the guests from his dark plans then in progress, it carries no hint of his hidden fury in its alternately lyrical and prancing moods.

- Saint-Saëns: *Samson et Dalila* — *Bacchanale*

Although best remembered today for his orchestral works and concertos, Camille Saint-Saëns (1835-1921) was also a busy opera composer, completing thirteen works in the field, each of which premiered soon after its completion. The most frequently performed of these today is his third opera, *Samson et Dalila (Samson and Delilah)*, which premiered not in France but in Weimar, Germany, December 2, 1877; its Biblical setting had discouraged opera houses in the composer's homeland from tackling a topic they felt would have been better told through a sacred oratorio. Indeed, Saint-Saëns had begun it as an oratorio, but was persuaded of the story's dramatic potential.

Telling of the life of the legendary strongman and the woman who brings him low, the opera builds to a perversely optimistic conclusion, in that Samson is destroyed but so are his foes when he pulls down the temple around them and is himself crushed in the chaos that he brings upon them. Opera directors delight in the challenge of staging the temple's fall; orchestral fans prefer to focus their attention on the opening of that last act, in which a wild and sensuous bacchanale is danced to taunt Samson. Deleting the dancers and singers, it yet remains a dramatic tour de force for orchestra, and it is in this form that the *Bacchanale* is most frequently heard.

- Waldteufel: *The Skater's Waltz*

Despite his Germanic family name, Emil Waldteufel (1837-1915) was thoroughly French, born in Strasbourg, in that border region over which the two nations have so frequently quarreled. His father, professor of music at that city's conservatory, recognized the boy's interests and gave him early encouragement, even moving the whole family to Paris when Emil was eleven so as to begin studies at the more prestigious Paris Conservatoire.

Due to financial difficulties, young Waldteufel would leave before graduation, but had progressed far enough in his training to launch a career as piano teacher and accompanist, and to find work testing new pianos at the factory. It was thus his skill at the keyboard that earned him attention sooner than his compositions, particularly when he gained a post as Empress Eugenie's court pianist. Yet favor for his compositions would follow, particularly in the ballroom, for which he composed about 250 works, largely though not exclusively waltzes. He would be Paris' answer to Vienna's Johann Strauss Jr.

Best known of Waldteufel's many waltzes is *Le Patineurs* (*Skater's Waltz*), the graceful flow of which would be equally suited to a ballroom or an ice rink. As his rival Strauss would have done, Waldteufel offers not a single waltz melody, which might outstay its welcome, but rather a sequence of contrasting waltz themes, some serene, others exuberant. Also as the Viennese master popularized, the music does not waltz from its very first notes but rather opens with a kind of call to the dance floor, music that returns near the close of the work. As for the wintry image implied by the title, listen for jingle bells to appear in the percussion midway through the score. A bold coda concludes the whole with the flair of dancers who bow and curtsey at the close of the dance.

- Tchaikovsky: *The Nutcracker*, op. 71

The history of ballet is lengthy, but discontinuous. Its earliest prominence was in the seventeenth century, when French courtiers delighted in this dramatic mix of music and dance, and the greatest composers, notably François Couperin and Jean-Philippe Rameau, turned their talents to the field. That interest in ballet continued well into the eighteenth century, but by the nineteenth century, ballet's popularity had waned. Few important Romantic composers produced ballets, other than as scenes in their operas. Not until late in the century did a person of prominence, one of the most admired and respected composers of the day, chose to compose ballets, in large part because it was a field admired and supported by his nation's ruler. By bringing his reputation to a neglected field, Peter Tchaikovsky (1840-1893) restored ballet to its former prominence, and it has remained in the spotlight ever since.

Tchaikovsky composed three ballets: *Swan Lake*, *Sleeping Beauty*, and *The Nutcracker*. The last of these is loosely based on the ETA Hoffmann story "The Nutcracker and the Mouse King." Hoffmann's original is far from a children's tale. In his version, sugar-plums are far outnumbered by warriors, and images of mice attacking an infant in her cradle would preclude any use as a bedtime story. Yet in passing through the hands of Russian Imperial Ballet choreographer Marius Petipa en route to Tchaikovsky, the tale was changed from a dark fantasy to a sparkling fairy tale, and it is in that form that it has come to world-wide appreciation.

The composer began work in February, 1891, continuing his efforts while on an American tour later that year for the opening of Carnegie Hall. It was a painful time for the composer, for he had recently lost the support of his long-time patron Nadezhda von Meck, and, though he no longer needed her financial backing, he sorely missed her correspondence. This loss, combined with homesickness, and depression resulting from the death of his sister, left Tchaikovsky barely able to compose. Not until his return from the States was he able to make any real progress on the work.

Fortuitously, the homeward journey took Tchaikovsky through Paris, where he found a wondrous new instrument: the celesta, whose clear, bell-like tone was perfectly fitted to *The Nutcracker's* fairy-tale ambience. In the celesta's ethereal notes, Tchaikovsky recognized the "voice" of his Sugar Plum Fairy, and he immediately wrote to his publisher, asking that the instrument be acquired for the performance. Yet secrecy was vital. Tchaikovsky wanted to surprise the audience, so he cautioned his publisher, "I don't want you to show it to anybody, for I am afraid that Rimsky-Korsakov or Glazunov will smell it out and take advantage of its unusual effects before me." A celesta might have been just the thing for *Scheherazade,* but Tchaikovsky kept his secret. Russia first heard the instrument through his composition.

Selections from *The Nutcracker* were first performed as an orchestral suite in March of 1892. The ballet proper waited until December 18 of that year (December 6 on the Russian-style calendar). It was presented at St. Petersburg's Mariinsky Theater on a double-bill with Tchaikovsky's one-act opera, *Iolanthe*. In a letter to a friend, the composer himself remarked, "Apparently the opera gave pleasure, but the ballet not really; and, as a matter of fact, in spite of all the sumptuousness it did turn out to be rather boring." Tchaikovsky thought little of it, describing it as "infinitely worse than *Sleeping Beauty*."

Yet responsibility for the failure was not, apparently, wholly the composer's. Petipa had fallen ill, and the choreography was instead devised by his less-inspired assistant. Additionally, the scenery and costumes were panned as tasteless, and the ballerina who danced the role of the Sugar Plum Fairy apparently lacked the charm and grace required for the part. Tchaikovsky's brother Modest said she was downright ugly, a sin for which apparently a Russian ballerina cannot be forgiven. The newspapers reviled Tchaikovsky, and he did not live to see the piece succeed. Time, however, has proven Tchaikovsky's pessimism to be incorrect. Regardless of his opinion, *The Nutcracker* is now seen as a universal delight, one as popular in the concert hall as in the ballet theater.

- Tchaikovsky: *Marche Slav*, op. 31

Tchaikovsky's *Marche Slav* was composed in October of 1876, just after his Symphony no. 3, and premiered in Moscow that fall. At the time, he had yet to gain much of an international following, though he was on the verge of acquiring the patron, Madame Nadezhda von Meck, who would allow him to make that transition to fame. His first ballet, *Swan Lake*, had been composed the previous spring, though had not yet had its premiere. Like much of musical Europe, Tchaikovsky had spent part of that summer in Bavaria at Bayreuth for the premiere of *The Ring Cycle* by Wagner, whom he declared to be a misdirected genius who ought to be writing symphonies. Although many composers of the day were finding inspiration in Wagner's orchestral flourishes, Tchaikovsky stayed closer to himself, particularly in *Marche Slav*, which is almost wholly Russian in flavor.

At the time, Russian composers were declaring their independence from Western European musical ideas and setting out to express their own national pride in their music. From this movement comes Mussorgsky's epic opera *Boris Godunov* (which premiered in 1874), and various other works by composers determined to prove that Russian music could stand on its own two feet with pride. Tchaikovsky had sometimes been criticized by his colleagues for not following their lead and for allowing too much Western style to influence his works. Here, he seems to prove his patriotism with a "Slavic march" of determined energy and drive.

It was composed specifically for a benefit concert on the subject of Russians joining with their fellow Slavs in a battle against the Turks, hence the fact that it is not declared to be a "Russian" march but rather one for all the Slavs. As the march progresses, its intensity increases, and even woodwinds and strings come into play together with the more obvious choices of brass and percussion, adding varied coloration to the score. Bright, festive moods contrast with ominous ones, producing together a work that, though relatively brief, yet proves the breadth of Tchaikovsky's musical imagination.

Marche Slav was not Tchaikovsky's only memorable march. Marches appear, at least briefly, in his ballets. Portions of the *1812 Overture* contain marching themes. Even the otherwise somber Symphony no. 6 in b minor, op. 74, "Pathetique," offers a jaunty march in its third movement. That one is sufficiently buoyant that it has occasionally tempted listeners into premature applause, thinking it must be a final movement. In fact, another movement follows for a deeply sorrowful and utterly un-march-like finale.

- Dvořák: *Slavonic Dances*, op 46 and op. 72

Here is a work — actually, two sets comprising eight pieces each — that could have fit in one of several chapters of this book. Antonín Dvořák's *Slavonic Dances* were first composed as piano duets, then revised and reworked by their composer for orchestral performance. However, since at their heart, they draw upon the spirit of Bohemian folk dance, let them appear here in the company of other dance-flavored works.

These dances were amongst Dvořák's first published works. Having won an Austrian state-sponsored competition for young composers, he had attracted the favorable attention of one of the panel judges: the great German composer Johannes Brahms. So impressed was Brahms by Dvořák's music that he asked his own publisher, Simrock, to print some of the young Bohemian's music. Simrock complied, and the songs sold so well that he asked Dvořák for more. He requested a set of dances for piano duet, and since ethnic-flavored works were then quite in vogue, he specified that they should be Slavonic dances, based upon the folk music of the composer's Bohemian homeland. Dvořák complied with a set of original works, some lively, some gentle, not quoting any specific traditional dances, but evoking their spirit through his own vision.

The resulting set of eight contrasting dances appeared in print in 1878 both in the original piano duet version and in orchestral settings by the composer himself; both bore the same opus number of 46. Eight years later, Dvořák would produce a second set of eight dances, which would be given the opus number 72. By that time, the composer had already achieved both commercial and artistic success. The initial set of *Slavonic Dances* had been a stepping-stone to international fame.

- Sousa: *The Stars and Stripes Forever*

In the field of marching music, no name stands more prominently than that of John Philip Sousa (1854-1932), who during his lifetime was amongst the world's best-known musical artists. He composed nearly one-hundred-fifty marches, so many marches and such fine ones that his preferred march form of three contrasting melodies preceded by a short introduction became the standard followed by innumerable other composers.

Yet marches were but a fraction of his prodigious output. Sousa also composed fifteen operettas, seventy songs, twenty band fantasies, and over three-hundred arrangements and transcriptions. He was both a novelist and a newspaper writer, and in his prime was the most famed conductor in America, drawing audiences that the great conductor Leopold Stokowski would have envied. As if those numerous activities were not enough for any one human being, Sousa also was a leader in the founding of the American Society of Composers, Authors, and Publishers (ASCAP), an organization which even today seeks to protect the financial rights of composers. When his entire career is considered, Sousa is undoubtedly one of the most influential American composers who ever lived.

Of all his many marches, the single best-known one — indeed, perhaps the best known march by any composer — must be *The Stars and Stripes Forever*, published in 1897. From that year until the end of his career, Sousa and his band performed it at nearly every concert appearance, yet always managed to find new intricacies deep down inside it. For example, there is the formidable piccolo solo, not only difficult in its complexities, but also in making that tiny instrument heard over the massed band. Having multiple piccolo players may not be the answer, as then one must make all those myriad notes occur exactly together between the various players. Also, any conductor must balance the musical forces so that no section of instruments overwhelms the others, as would be easy for the trombones to do. And how fast should it be played? Those who knew Sousa personally attest that his answer to that question was always "it depends on how soon the train is leaving. Substitute your favorite current transportation for the train, and choose your own tempo.

- Elgar: *Pomp and Circumstance* March in D major, op. 39, no. 1

Sir Edward Elgar's first acknowledged masterpiece was his *Variations on an Original Theme*, op. 36, dating from 1899, a work that has since become known as the *Enigma Variations* (see Chapter Three). However, his most frequently performed composition is the first of the five *Pomp and Circumstance* Marches, which were written gradually in the decade following *Enigma*. The central melody of this march — that is, not the very first one, but that in the center of the work — also appearing in Elgar's *Coronation Ode* for Edward VII, has served as support music for uncounted American graduation ceremonies, though few of those graduates are aware that in Elgar's time, this stately theme acquired a text and came to be known in England as "Land of Hope and Glory." The melody conveys a regal mood perfect for solemn ceremonies, a mood also found at the heart of the other four, less famous *Pomp and Circumstance* Marches. An English march, it seems, need not bear the boisterous spirit that one so often finds in American marches such as those by Sousa. Elgar himself once observed, "There are a lot of people who like to celebrate events with music. To those people, I have given tunes."

- Ravel: *Bolero*

Maurice Ravel (1875-1937) was born in the foothills of the Pyrenees. His mother's family was from that region, but after Maurice was born, the family moved to Paris; there, he was exposed to many cultures, some of which ultimately influenced his music. He drew inspiration from ancient Greece and eternal Java, as well as other, rather more predictable sites, such as the palace of Versailles. Ravel was also moved by the rich orchestrations of Nicolai Rimsky-Korsakov and the grotesque tales of Edgar Allen Poe, demonstrating an adventurous intellect.

Of Ravel's most famous work, one can quote a famous remark: "Unfortunately, it contains no music." The carping of a disgruntled critic? Far from it. With those words, Ravel himself damned his own *Bolero*. It has been called a fifteen-minute crescendo; a concerto for snare drum; a theme without variations; a minimalist triumph fifty years before Philip Glass. Yet for all the arrows launched in its direction, *Bolero* still retains a magic fascination, its inexorable beat enthralling one's attentions and even affections.

Ravel conceived of the piece as ballet. In 1928, the dancer Ida Rubinstein requested of him a work of Spanish mien, suggesting at first that he might orchestrate some Albeniz piano pieces. Indeed, Ravel was an exceptionally skilled orchestrator; six years earlier, he had famously reworked Mussorgsky's *Pictures at an Exhibition* (see Chapter Six). However, apparently the idea of another such project held little appeal. Instead, he determined to produce something wholly his own. He called it *Bolero*; some observers have insisted that the rhythms are more like that of a fandango or a seguidilla, but Ravel stood by his chosen title. The work premiered November 22, 1928 at the Paris Opera with Rubinstein herself in the solo role as a sultry café dancer enticing her masculine audience, the work's unending crescendo reflecting their growing excitement. A later two-piano arrangement by the composer exists, but it is in its orchestral form that the work has earned its reputation.

Bolero is a set of eighteen variations on an original theme, or perhaps more properly speaking, eighteen orchestrations of that theme, for the theme itself does not change, though the instruments do. After an opening rhythm on the snare drum (a rhythm that will continue unabated throughout the work), the piece proceeds as follows:

- solo flute (in the instrument's low range)

- solo clarinet (also low in the range)

- solo bassoon (startlingly high in its range)

- solo E-flat clarinet (smaller and higher in pitch than the standard B-flat clarinet)

- solo oboe d'amore (between the oboe and the English horn in pitch and tone) muted trumpet and flute (the flute high above and parallel to the trumpet's line)

- solo tenor saxophone (unusual to have saxophones in an orchestra, but Ravel liked jazz)

- solo soprano saxophone (a small, straight, high-pitched saxophone)

- French horn and celesta (the bell-like tones of the latter parallel to the horn's line)

- quartet of oboes, clarinet and bassoon (a combination organ-like in timbre)

- solo trombone (replete with sensuously sliding passages)

- high woodwinds (growing more strident in tone)

With variation thirteen, the strings finally emerge from their place in the background to take the lead for the remaining variations. The crescendo continues to build; the drumbeat becomes ever more prominent, more obsessive. Before long, trumpet accents are added, contributing to the intensity until, in the final moments, the full orchestra is tossed into the mix — trombones and cymbals and all — bringing *Bolero* to an exultant, if abrupt, conclusion.

- Stravinsky: *The Firebird*

Were it not for procrastination, Igor Stravinsky (1882-1971) might never have composed his first important ballet, *The Firebird*. The procrastination in question was not Stravinsky's own; he was only the beneficiary of another colleague's lack of work ethic. The year was 1909. Sergei Diaghilev, grand impresario of the Ballets Russes, was planning a Parisian tour for his company, and asked the composer Anatoly Liadov (1855-1914) for a new work that the dancers could perform while on tour. Liadov accepted the assignment, but did not accept the responsibility. In fact, he composed virtually nothing. Time was quickly running out.

With the date of departure fast approaching, Diaghilev had no new ballet, and no immediate hopes of one being completed. In frustration, he decided to find another composer, one talented enough to complete the job well, but not so popular as to have no time for a last-minute assignment. His choice fell upon the twenty-seven-year-old Igor Stravinsky, son of a famed operatic bass who had tried unsuccessfully to divert his son into legal studies. Stravinsky had not yet made for himself a major career, but occasionally managed to get his orchestral works performed in concert, and some of these Diaghilev had heard. Thinking that the fellow could probably manage dance music, he made the job offer. Young Stravinsky was reluctant to accept, for he felt the project was not well suited to his skills, yet a meeting with Diaghilev, the choreographer, the lead dancer, and the two designers all together, proved reassuring. The composer later recalled in his memoirs, "When the five of them had proclaimed their belief in my talent, I began to believe, too."

Stravinsky set to work at once. His co-creators wanted the ballet to be based upon Russian folk stories concerning the Firebird, a kind of powerful good spirit whose feathers supposedly convey beauty and protection upon the earth. As the ballet developed, other characters were included: Prince Ivan Tsarevich; a group of enchanted princesses, one of whom promptly becomes the prince's love; and the evil sorcerer Kashchei, from whom Ivan must rescue the princesses. It is only through the intervention of the Firebird, whose life he had spared earlier in the ballet, that Ivan is able to accomplish his goals, destroying Kashchei and his followers, and marrying his princess. The folk origins of the tale inspired Stravinsky to use a few folk melodies in his score. Yet most of the ballet, especially the fluttering dance of the Firebird and the memorable wedding march at the ballet's conclusion, was his own creation.

The Firebird ballet was completed by mid-April of 1910 and was promptly sent to Paris, where the dancers were already preparing for the scheduled June premiere. One last roadblock arose when Anna Pavlova, the principal ballerina, refused to dance the role of the Firebird, declaring that she detested the music. Disaster was only averted when another dancer, Tamara Karsavina, stepped into the role, and went on to score a triumph. Stravinsky himself was in attendance at the first performance, as were Claude Debussy, Sarah Bernhardt, and other artistic luminaries. As the composer later remembered, "The first-night audience glittered indeed, but the fact that it was heavily perfumed is more vivid in my memory . . . I was called to the stage to bow at the conclusion, and was recalled several times." It was the first major performance of a Stravinsky work outside of Russia. To receive such acclaim for what was not only the ballet's premiere, but also the premiere of the composer himself, boded well for his professional future.

- Stravinsky: *The Rite of Spring*

Ballet is not always grace and beauty. Sometimes, it's riots in the recital hall, and scandals in the city. At least, that's what Stravinsky found in 1913. The young Russian composer had, in prior years, written several works for the Ballet Russes to perform in Paris. *The Firebird* and *Petrushka* had originated from this partnership, and were very successful, but *The Rite of Spring* was different. Like the others, it was inspired by Russian culture. Unlike them, this newest work was chaotic and percussive, "architectonic," to use the composer's powerful word. A stark portrayal of tribal rites, in which a young girl dances herself to a sacrificial end, *The Rite of Spring* was primitive in subject matter, but startlingly radical in execution. Its premiere became one of the most infamous evenings in the history of music.

It was May 29, 1913, at the Théâtre des Champs-Elysées in Paris. The assembled audience was accustomed to the high quality of Ballet Russes productions, but no one was quite prepared for this piece with its dissonance, its savage, erratic rhythms and abruptly angular choreography. Boos and catcalls began quickly, as did the shouts of support from those who were more adventurously minded (the French Impressionist Claude Debussy was among the work's vocal supporters that night). From that point, what occurred on stage was immaterial; the audience had taken over the evening. Fist-fights and shouting matches erupted between supporters and opponents. Debussy recalled seeing well-dressed ladies bashing each other with their purses, and, at last, the din of the mob overwhelmed the orchestra, until the dancers could no longer hear the music. The furious choreographer, Vaclav Nijinsky, stood at the edge of the stage shouting directions to his beleaguered troops. Stravinsky left the theater in a rage. It can hardly be said that anyone actually "heard" *The Rite of Spring* that night.

The controversy lasted for weeks and months, as newspapers fueled the fire. One Parisian paper, reporting on the riot that had occurred five days earlier, judged this radical score to be "the most dissonant and the most discordant composition yet written. Never was the system and the cult of the wrong note practiced with so much industry, zeal and fury." Later that summer, a London newspaper, after noting that *Rite* "baffles verbal description," valiantly insisted on describing it anyway, finally settling on the word "hideous." When *Rite* finally reached the US, it was no better received. One Boston paper even waxed poetic:

> Who wrote this fiendish *Rite of Spring*?
> What right had he to write the thing,
> Against our helpless ears to fling
> Its crash, clash, cling, clang, bing, bang, bing?

Apparently, a 1920s predecessor of Dr. Seuss had appointed himself as music expert.

Amidst all these attacks, the supportive remarks were rare, but perhaps the most accurate assessment of the work was one apparently not intended as a compliment. Deems Taylor, American composer and music critic (and later host of the first *Fantasia* film), wrote about *Rite* in 1920: "I'm bored with imitations of noises . . . and their monotonous cacophony. Of course, it sounds like cacophony because I'm not used to it, and it probably sounds all alike for the same reason that Chinamen all look alike to me: I'm not well acquainted." Here one of the nation's most experienced men of music admitted that understanding requires familiarity, that he could not comprehend the piece without becoming better acquainted with it. It is unfortunate that the original Parisian audience was less astute than Deems Taylor. Their own confusion, not the piece itself, was to blame for the tumult. Now, roughly a century later, the debate continues, but one thing is certain: no one, on first hearing *The Rite of Spring*, can come away from it without an opinion.

- Prokofiev: *Romeo and Juliet*, op. 64

Sergei Prokofiev (1891-1953) was a Russian-born composer who spent the heart of his career abroad. He departed for Western Europe shortly after the 1917 revolution, and remained abroad for fourteen years. By the time he came back to in his homeland at age forty-one, Prokofiev had become so familiar with the tastes of Western Europe, especially in terms of ballet, that he had to readapt to the preferences of his own countrymen. Apparently, Russians liked long ballets, whereas other Europeans preferred shorter works. In his autobiography, Prokofiev summed up the situation this way: "We [the Russians] attach greater importance to the plot and its development; abroad, it is considered that, in ballet, the plot plays a secondary part, and that three one-act ballets give one the chance to absorb a large number of impressions." Faced with these cultural differences, Prokofiev wrote short, one-act ballets while abroad. Not until his return to his homeland did the composer begin his four-act dramatic masterpiece, *Romeo and Juliet*.

Its path to the stage was rocky. The earliest controversy surrounding the piece was Prokofiev's intention to change the ending. Not for him the deaths of the two protagonists: reasoning that the dead cannot dance, the composer was determined to have a happy ending, with Romeo arriving in the tomb in time to save Juliet. Only when it was pointed out to Prokofiev that the music he had composed for this controversial alteration was not actually joyful sounding did he consider returning to the original ending. Once the choreographer reassured him that Shakespeare's original tragic conclusion could be expressed in dance — one need only have Friar Lawrence or some other character come into the scene and find the lifeless lovers — did Prokofiev acquiesce.

Prokofiev began his *Romeo and Juliet* in the 1930s at the suggestion of the directors of the Kirov Theater, in what was then Leningrad. However, by the time the ballet was finished in 1935, the Kirov was no longer interested in the project. Prokofiev offered it instead to the Bolshoi in Moscow, which at first agreed to stage the work, before the Bolshoi dancers dismissed the piece as impossible for dancing, and *Romeo and Juliet* was again without a venue. With this second rejection, the composer decided to pursue a different route. Instead of aiming for a ballet performance, he converted the score into orchestral suites, hoping that these at least would be heard. The orchestral suites were performed in 1936 and '37. The actual ballet did not reach the stage until 1938 in Brno, Czechoslovakia. Its Soviet premiere waited until 1940.

- Copland: *Appalachian Spring*

For many decades, the ballet was strongly identified with Russia in general and Tchaikovsky in particular. After all, most people, if asked to name a ballet, would mention either *The Nutcracker* or *Swan Lake*, and would be unlikely to look to this side of the ocean for inspiration. Nevertheless, there are numerous American ballets, some of which revolutionized the dance by bringing a New World spirit to the stage. Of those, the best-known offerings are by Aaron Copland (1900-1990), composer of *Billy the Kid*, *Rodeo*, and *Appalachian Spring*. That last work is perhaps the most beloved of all American ballets. Its enduring and endearing qualities were recognized when, in 1945, it won the Pulitzer Prize for music.

Appalachian Spring was commissioned in 1943 by American patron of the arts Elizabeth Sprague Coolidge, who requested a new ballet for the great dancer and choreographer Martha Graham. Graham and Copland were quite familiar with each other's work. They had, in fact, been thinking of collaborating for several years, so this might have been a dream assignment, except for the fact that they did not actually work together on the project. Rather, Graham supplied Copland with an untitled scenario divided into scenes along with notes concerning the approximate length of each scene; the composer completed the ballet while on a concert tour of Mexico and mailed the music to Graham in New York. Years later, Copland recalled the experience: "I got back the day before the premiere and went to the last rehearsal, and the first thing I said to her was, 'Martha, what have you called it?' '*Appalachian Spring.*' [a title taken from a Hart Crane poem] 'Oh,' I said, 'what a nice name.' . . . Since that time, I can't begin to tell you how often people have come up to me and said, 'Mr. Copland, when I hear your score I can just <u>see</u> the Appalachians and <u>feel</u> spring!'"

Graham's scenario concerns a pioneer celebration in the spring in a Pennsylvania farmhouse. As it begins, the dawn comes quietly, ushered in by gentle strings and winds. Each of the ballet's characters enters: the revivalist preacher, the pioneer woman, the young couple due to be married, and the followers of the preacher. There is a lively general dance, then a prayer scene, followed by a gentle *pas de deux* to be danced by the young couple. Their sweet interlude comes to a sudden end, erupting into joyous dance rhythms as the wedding is celebrated. Still, they remain somewhat apprehensive about their new life, and the music at times carries a somber undertone that belies the otherwise festive spirit. Only the rocky strength of their older neighbors and the solid faith of a revivalist meeting (conveyed by Copland's direct quotation of the Shaker hymn, "Simple Gifts") provide reassurance. At last, taking courage from those around them, the bride and groom stand quiet and strong in their new home. Copland's score concludes as serenely as it had begun, ending the day with the same chords with which dawn had been evoked.

When it premiered in Washington D.C. on October 30, 1944, *Appalachian Spring* was scored for a chamber group of only thirteen instruments. That small scale was not Copland's own choice. Rather, it was dictated by the space available at the Library of Congress where the work premiered. Since that time, the ballet has usually been performed by larger musical forces, but, even with a full orchestra, the austere beauty of the work is preserved. Copland noted that he styled the piece after Graham herself, a woman he viewed as "unquestionably very American," saying, "There's something prim and restrained, simple yet strong, about her which one tends to think of as American." Those same quiet adjectives might be applied to *Appalachian Spring* itself, or indeed, to Copland's music as a whole. Rarely has a composer been so thoroughly in touch with the images he sought to portray.

- Khachaturian: *Spartacus*

Son of an Armenian book-binder, Aram Khachaturian (1903-1978) was born in Tiflis (now Tblisi), in the rugged region where Armenia, Georgia, and Turkey come together. This distant corner of the Caucasus boasted a proud folk tradition that would influence the native son's compositions. A self-taught pianist, the boy also played tenor horn in his school band, but did not undertake formal music instruction until he moved to Moscow at age eighteen. He studied at the Moscow Conservatory and by the age of thirty was attracting favorable attention for his colorful, nationalistic works redolent of Armenian rhythms. Khachaturian was no modernist, a fact that may have contributed to his success, since in musical terms, the Soviet government was ultra conservative and actively silenced composers who too closely embraced any new or radical idea. In his ballets *Gayane* and *Spartacus*, Khachaturian glorified the people, specifically peasants and slaves. Such philosophy fit well in the Soviet psyche, even as the music won fans in the West.

Khachaturian's most famous ballet was inspired by the slave revolt which began in Rome in 73 BC; its leader, Spartacus, was a Thracian warrior captured in battle. The rebellion's highpoint — literally and figuratively — was their seizure of Mt. Vesuvius as a stronghold. After two years of unrest, they were finally put down, and the surviving rebels, including Spartacus himself, were crucified along the Appian Way. A scenario for the ballet was drafted in 1933 for the Bolshoi, though no composer took it up. In 1956, it was brought to Khachaturian's attention, and he composed it for the Kirov Ballet. It was not a great success, perhaps as much due to elements beyond the music, since the major differences between that version and the 1968 success at the Bolshoi were revised music, but also new choreography and a restructured story. The revised version, with its contrasting moods of vibrant energy and gentle lyricism, was such a hit in Moscow that the Bolshoi took it on the road to London's Covent Garden the following year. The composer himself had already arranged orchestral suites from the music so as to maximize its audience potential.

Of the piece, Khachaturian would observe that he saw it as an allegory of human rights. Although Soviet authorities approved it for performance, apparently seeing the ballet as relating to the Russian people throwing off their oppressors in the 1917 Revolution, it seems impossible that one could not also regard it as a vision of the Russians under Communism rebelling against those later and no less oppressive leaders. Khachaturian, after all, had spent much of his life under the watchful eye of Stalin, and though he himself rarely attracted negative attention, he had seen friends and colleagues disappear into the night. If that message were his intention here, he managed to keep authorities from noticing it.

- Ginastera: *Estancia*

Alberto Ginastera (1916-1983) was Argentina's answer to Aaron Copland. Both men were devoted to the folk music of their nations and sought to bring that folk spirit to the concert stage. Interestingly, both men wrote ballets on western themes, specifically the Wild West frontiers of their homelands. Copland's was *Rodeo*; Ginastera's was *Estancia*. "Estancia" is the Argentine word for ranch. The ballet tells the story of a city boy in love with a rancher's daughter. At first, the love affair is only one-sided. She thinks he's spineless, at least in comparison with the intrepid gauchos, or cowboys. Yet by the final scene, the hero wins her heart by beating the gauchos at their own game.

This one-act ballet was commissioned in 1941 by the American Ballet Caravan, which was then touring South America. The work was to have choreography by George Balanchine, but the troupe disbanded before Ginastera finished the composition. Its premiere as a ballet had to wait until 1952. In the interim, Ginastera had extracted four dances from the score for use as a concert suite. That version premiered May 12, 1943, at the Teatro Colón in Buenos Aires and it is the form most often heard today.

The suite's first movement opens with the driving rhythms that characterize much of the work, as repetitive motifs rise both in pitch and intensity. Although the emphasis is on strings and brass, woodwinds add occasional decorative phrases. The far gentler second movement begins with lyrical flute phrases floating over string accompaniment, with a high violin solo of similar mood later in the movement. For the third movement, the powerful rhythms return, driven along by strings, brass, and percussion. Woodwinds become more prominent in the final movement, with a sense of frenetic urgency. As the movement nears its conclusion, a repetitive rising phrase with irregular accents takes charge and dominates into the utterly exuberant closing bars.

- Ellington: *The River*

Better known by his enduring nickname "Duke," Edward Kennedy Ellington (1899-1974) grew up in a middle-class black family in Washington DC, at a time when the nation's capital boasted high standards of cultural resources for African Americans. His father's employment, ranging from making blueprints to serving as a butler at the White House, kept the family fairly comfortable, and the boy grew up loving the arts, particularly painting. Music came to him when his protective mother, seeing him get hit with a baseball, determined that piano would be a safer use of his free time than sports. By the time he was in high school, Duke, who had gained his nickname because of certain flair in dressing, was leading a jazz combo and earning pocket change playing in area clubs.

In 1923, he relocated to New York City in hopes of making his way in the jazz community of Harlem; his big break came in 1927, when he and his band were hired at the Cotton Club. Thanks to their affiliation with this most highly regarded of all jazz clubs and the millions who heard them through a regular weekly radio program, Ellington and the band became international stars, making the first of many European tours in 1933. Later, Ellington recalled, "The main thing I got in Europe was spirit. That kind of thing gives you the courage to go on. If they think I'm that important, then maybe our music does mean something." His and the band's reputation lasted well beyond the Jazz Era, with their popularity continuing into the days of rock-and-roll. In fact, Ellington was held in such regard in American music that in 1969, President Nixon awarded him the Presidential Medal of Freedom, the nation's highest civilian honor. Ellington's direct impact on the world of music spanned most of a century and his music is still strongly admired today.

In his ballet *The River*, Ellington successfully blended many of those concepts: the rhythms and harmonies of jazz, the grander scale of fine music, and even dance. The ballet was commissioned in 1970 by Alvin Ailey's dance company, which premiered it the following year. It intends to show the course of a river, starting at the spring where it is born. One might say the same thing of Smetana's *The Moldau* (see Chapter Three), though Smetana was no connoisseur of syncopation and his 'rapids' did not 'giggle,' as Ellington asks his to do: such is the title of one of the ballet's scenes. It may be a less grand ballet than Copland's *Appalachian Spring*, but *The River* is no less essentially American in its musical spirit.

Further Recommendations:

Here is a selection of other interesting marches and dances for which there was not room in the main body of the chapter:

- Michael Praetorius (1571-1621): Proving that not all Renaissance composers were focused on sacred music, Praetorius composed many dozens of courtly dances; his *Dances from Terpsichore* were named for the Greek muse of the dance.

- Wolfgang Amadeus Mozart (1756-1791): His various sets of *German Dances*, mostly composed for light entertainment at the Austrian imperial court, include one with sleigh bells as part of the performing ensemble.

- Joseph Lanner (1801-1843): Another Viennese king of waltzes — contemporary of Johann Strauss Sr., and his strongest competitor, until the rise of Johann Jr.

- Alexander Borodin (1833-1887): A friend of Tchaikovsky, Borodin was so busy as a chemistry professor that he composed relatively little, but his *Polovtsian Dances* from the opera *Prince Igor* earned a devoted following. Devotees of the musical *Kismet* will recognize some melodies, which Broadway borrowed from here.

- Richard Strauss (1864-1949): One of his most frequently performed short works is the racy *Dance of the Seven Veils*, from his darkly dramatic opera *Salome*. Placing it in orchestral programs absolves a producer of needing to find a soprano who can also dance seductively.

- Alexander Glazunov (1865-1936): A junior member of the Russian late Romantic school of composers, Glazunov's contribution to his nation's ballet traditions was the vividly colored *The Seasons*.

- Reinhold Gliere (1875-1956): This Russian's ballet *The Red Poppy*, a tale of downtrodden Chinese workers standing up to their rulers, enjoyed great popularity in the Soviet Union. Beyond those borders, it is mostly remembered for its vibrant *Russian Sailor's Dance*.

- Manuel de Falla (1876-1946): Most prominent Spanish name in ballet, Falla composed two such works — *El amor brujo* (*Love, the Magician*) and *The Three-Cornered Hat* — that are rich with the rhythms of his homeland.

- Darius Milhaud (1892-1974): The Frenchman's ballet *La creation du monde* offers an African flavored creation myth; composed in 1923, it has tinges of jazz.

- Sir William Walton (1902-1983): *Crown Imperial* March and *Orb and Sceptre* March were each composed for royal coronations (1937 and 1953 respectively).

- Morton Gould (1913-1996): His *American Salute* takes the old Civil War marching song "When Johnny Comes Marching Home" and builds it into a colorful set of variations, some friendly to marching, others less so. Yet down in its heart is that familiar marching song.

- Astor Piazzolla (1921-1992): Inventor of "nuevo tango," he composed tango-flavored chamber and orchestral works for such fine performers as cellist Yo-Yo Ma.

- English composer Philip Feeney (b. 1954) has specialized in full-length ballets upon familiar stories, including the *Hunchback of Notre Dame* and *Peter Pan*. He effectively varies the character of his music to reflect the action of the moment, as his great predecessors would have done.

Chapter Eleven
Choral Music

Hallelujah: Handel's bold and declamatory musical statement from his oratorio *Messiah* stands as perhaps the most familiar of all choral works. It happens to be sacred and two and a half centuries old, but those facts have not decreased its popularity over the years. Moreover, as we'll find, there is much choral music not intended specifically for worship, even some that is recent and some crafted with the internet in mind.

Music has been part of religious expression from earliest history, though how it sounded in those days, one can only guess, as tribal cultures didn't seek to preserve it. As for written-down-and-preserved music, sacred music was the first to be put to paper in Europe, back in the Middle Ages. For centuries, that was the only music preserved, as the ability to capture music had been developed within the Catholic Church, which had little interest in documenting secular music. So the earliest written music in Europe was exclusively Catholic. With the advent of the Reformation in the early 1500s, the Catholic Church began to have competition, both musical and spiritual, from the Protestant Church, which became another font of fine music. At this point, composed expressions of piety grew to become more elaborate and more expansive artistic works, rather than just musical settings of brief Biblical verses and prayers.

Throughout this time, of course, there were other religions, some of which had a toehold in Europe itself. However, in these early centuries, these non-Christian religions didn't set out to make a musical mark, so they are not represented in the sacred music that is still heard outside their own worship services. With Felix Mendelssohn in the early 1800s, a Jewish influence might have appeared, for his family had been Jewish. However, Mendelssohn himself was raised Protestant and championed the great sacred music of Bach; in his own sacred music, he drew on both Old and New Testament topics. The American composer/conductor Leonard Bernstein was more determined in expressing Jewish points of view. Some recent works by current composers blend diverse religious views into single compositions.

The majority of the works in this chapter are from the sacred tradition. A few are secular works that still make use of a full choir with or without instrumental accompaniment. Those without instruments — that is, only voices — are said to be 'a cappella,' a term that originally meant 'in the chapel style,' but in practical usage, does not presume sacred purpose. One could just as well apply 'a cappella' to barbershop quartet pieces as to Renaissance hymns. Secular choral works tend to be a more recent trend. Johann Sebastian Bach (1685-1750), long employed by the church, wrote only a few; Eric Whitacre (b. 1970) has written many.

- Allegri: *Miserere Mei*

Gregorio Allegri (1582-1652) was a successful and respected artist in his day, serving some three decades as singer and composer for the papal choir, first for Pope Urban VIII, then for Innocent X. His compositions show an unsurpassed mastery of counterpoint: those intricate techniques for combining diverse melodies for simultaneous performance. However, though his reputation in his own time was secure in Italy, and especially at the Vatican, his reputation today is largely due to the genius of young Wolfgang Mozart, who at age fourteen was touring Italy with his father Leopold.

At Easter, the Mozarts found themselves in Rome and attended services at the Sistine Chapel, then less a tourist site than the Pope's preferred chapel. There, they heard a performance of Allegri's *Miserere Mei*, using text from Psalm 51. Composed for Urban one-and-a-half centuries earlier, it had never been published, as the Vatican wished to retain the piece as its own property. Young Mozart was so impressed by the piece – twelve minutes of intricate Renaissance polyphony, accented by an astonishingly high descant soprano line – that back at their hotel that afternoon, he wrote it all down from memory, not just the lead melodies but every layer of the music note for note. Then in a rare moment of doubt, he took his hand-written copy back to the next service so as to hear the music once more and double-check his work. Chapel ushers were not amused to find a copy of music owned by the Vatican in the hands of an adolescent Austrian and confiscated his work. Yet all they cost the boy was time: now he'd heard it twice, and writing it out again was that much easier.

Had young Mozart not been impressed by the *Miserere*, he wouldn't have troubled himself about it; had he not troubled himself, the world beyond the Vatican would not have known of this impressively ethereal score. It is virtually the only Allegri composition still performed today, but its magic and mystery prove that the man knew his business well.

- Tallis: *Spem in alium*

The English Renaissance composer Thomas Tallis first appears in the written record in 1532 as an organist in Dover. A subsequent stint at Waltham Abbey ended with the dissolution of that institution in 1540, at which point he made his way to Canterbury Cathedral. Soon thereafter, he found employment with the royal household, serving under each of the Tudor monarchs from Henry VIII to Elizabeth I until his death in 1585. That he held his post throughout those turbulent years may be a tribute to his political skills as much as his musical abilities.

During Henry's reign, Tallis was amongst the first composers to write for the new Anglican Church, yet also composed for — and earned accolades from — the Catholic Mary. Yet it was for the Protestant Elizabeth that he would produce his single greatest achievement: the motet *Spem in alium*, to a text musing upon God as the hope of all mankind. According to some historians, the piece was presented at court on the occasion of the queen's fortieth birthday in 1573. If so, one wonders how many of the courtiers had enough musical training to appreciate fully Tallis' astonishing achievement: dividing his choristers into eight separate choirs, each of five voice parts, then devising intricate interactions amongst these musical forces. Note that with the numbers eight and five in that previous sentence, the total number of voice parts is forty, supporting the notion of the work's association to the queen's birthday. The result, a ten-minute panorama of shifting tone colors, is a *tour de force* of Renaissance polyphony, unsurpassed in the English repertoire.

- Palestrina: *Pope Marcellus Mass*

Born in the Italian community of Palestrina, located about twenty miles east of Rome, the composer remembered to history as Giovanni da Palestrina (about 1525-1594) received his music education as a boy chorister in Rome itself. By the time he was twenty, he was back in his home town as church organist, and might have remained there until the end of his days. However, in 1550, the local bishop became Pope Julius III and asked the organist to accompany him to Rome. Palestrina would serve in the musical staff of Julius, then Marcellus II, then several more popes through nearly the end of the century, remaining in Rome until his death. That a man twice-married yet was able to serve on the Papal staff for so long says much for his music: for the sake of the music, these popes were willing to overlook the fact that Palestrina, unlike almost any other man at the Vatican, never became a priest.

Palestrina composed about five-hundred sacred works, including over one-hundred masses. At the urging of the church, which in the 1550s and 1560s was much occupied with reforming the way in which the church's message was delivered, he strove to make the texts of his works more easily understood, so as not to obscure the religious message with musical details. Highly regarded, even revered, during his lifetime and after, Palestrina and his works were studied for centuries as an example of how to write polyphonic choral music with much use of counterpoint, even after that type of intricate musical layering was no longer in favored use.

The *Pope Marcellus Mass* is named for Palestrina's second papal employer, Marcellus II, who, in fact, ruled for less than a month in 1555. As the mass was not completed until nearly a decade later, Palestrina must have chosen the title as a belated tribute; the mass would not have been lying on his desk unused all those years. Tales have been told that Palestrina wrote it to persuade the authorities debating church policy at the so-called Council of Trent that he — and, presumably, other composers as well — should still be permitted to compose polyphonic music as long as the words were still clear. In fact, this mass does not differ markedly in style from what Palestrina had composed in earlier years, so the story seems unsupported. Here, his choir of six voice parts — soprano, alto, tenor I, tenor II, baritone, and bass — is deftly managed for maximum effect, with much interplay between the voices so that a melodic element will begin in one part before moving gradually to the others. Even if one did not know the Latin text, one could scarcely avoid being moved by the changing effects.

Incidentally, in Palestrina's time, and working as he did at the Vatican, his sopranos and altos would have been boy choristers. During the Renaissance, the Vatican did not support the idea of mixed choirs, though in performances of Palestrina's music today, one would customarily allow both men and women.

- JS Bach: *St. Matthew Passion, BWV 244*

Johann Sebastian Bach's longest and most elaborate work, the *St. Matthew Passion*, is one of hundreds of sacred pieces written during his long tenure as Kantor at the St. Thomas Church in Leipzig. Bach's responsibilities there ranged from playing the organ to teaching Latin to the choir boys, in addition to writing new works for every service and celebration. Frequently, deadlines forced Bach to recycle old music under new titles, but the *St. Matthew* earned his undivided attention. The entire score, lasting nearly three hours, was newly composed. An early version of the score, dated 1736, was exactingly copied, in two colors of ink, with red ink devoted to the Gospel texts. At some point, the score was damaged and Bach himself repaired it with extraordinary care: clear proof of the importance he placed on this work.

The story for the *St. Matthew* was taken mostly from the gospel of that name, but the actual verses which Bach set were provided by several contemporary poets. His principal contributor was one Christian Friedrich Henrici, a poet who wrote under the name of "Picander." This same author had also supplied the text for Bach's secular *Peasant Cantata*. Apparently, the two men worked together well, and, while Picander's verses are not particularly profound, their images, rhymes and meters are well-suited to musical adaptation.

The earliest verified performance of the St. Matthew Passion was Good Friday, April 15, 1729, at St. Thomas in Leipzig. At least two revivals of the work took place during Bach's life. However, at his death in 1750, the *St. Matthew*, along with most Bach compositions, was utterly forgotten, and it might have been lost forever, except for a fortunate coincidence. Some sixty years later, Felix Mendelssohn (1809-1847), who himself lived in Berlin, was given the manuscript to the *St. Matthew*. Somehow, the music had come into the hands of Mendelssohn's teacher, Karl Friedrich Zelter, formerly of Leipzig, who knew the young man's interest in Baroque music, but tried to dissuade his twenty-year-old prodigy from staging the long-neglected masterpiece. However, Mendelssohn, barely twenty years of age, was devoted to idea and could not be stopped. On March 11, 1829, at the Berlin Singakadamie, he led a four-hundred member chorus and a full orchestra in the *St. Matthew's* nineteenth century premiere. As Mendelssohn's sister Fanny reported, "The crowded hall looked like a church . . . Everyone was filled with the most solemn devotion." The sacred music of Bach was at last restored to the public.

The *St. Matthew Passion* is divided into two parts. The first part concerns Christ's betrayal, the Last Supper, and His prayers and arrest in Gethsemane. The second part presents the rest of the story, through the Crucifixion, death and burial. Incidentally, "Passion" has nothing to do with the common contemporary sense of the word. In the old parlance, a "Passion" was a musical setting of Biblical texts relating to the suffering and crucifixion of Christ. Such Passions were known as far back as the fourth century, and by the thirteenth century had become semi-dramatic works as Bach's would be. Composing Passions was especially popular with German Protestant composers, such as Bach; Italian and French composers were more likely to produce simple and literal settings of the Biblical texts.

- Handel: *Messiah*

American audiences are accustomed to hearing the great oratorio *Messiah* at the Christmas season, and supporters of this timing like to point out that one of its most popular choruses sets the Biblical text "For unto Us a Child is Born." However, the composer would be surprised by such notions. Indeed, the work begins with Christmas, but then proceeds to Easter, the Resurrection, and ultimately Judgment Day. Moreover, the work was first performed at the Easter season. So it is not specifically a Christmas piece, but as long as one listens, Handel would not have minded one's timing. He once remarked to the English king that through his music, he hoped to make people better, and one supposes that a person can be made better at any season.

Early in 1741, George Frideric Handel (1685-1759) was invited by the Lord Lieutenant of Ireland to come to Dublin for a series of subscription concerts. Around the same time, he received a libretto for a sacred oratorio compiling Old and New Testament verses concerning Christmas and Easter. The text was assembled by the composer's friend, Charles Jennens, a wealthy supporter of the arts. Typically a quick composer, in this instance Handel exceeded any possible expectation. He began the new oratorio August 22, 1741, and finished the entire score — all 259 pages of it — in twenty-two days. Shortly thereafter, he was on the boat to Ireland.

Messiah's premiere took place in Dublin the following spring, after the subscription concerts had attracted sufficient attention. Publicity for the impending event would draw the admiration of any Broadway producer today. Handel craftily announced the new piece before the end of his preceding concert series, to capitalize on his popularity. Then, he revealed that all those buying advance tickets would be admitted to a rehearsal. The masterful touch, though, was a newspaper advertisement placed the day of the performance, asking ladies not to wear hoops and gentlemen to leave their swords at home, so as to make room for anticipated crowds. That first performance, April 13, 1742, was filled to the walls: a stunning success. Dublin insisted on, and received, a second performance. At last, Handel had another masterwork with which to tackle the fickle London stage.

Londoners had always been skeptical of religious works being staged in popular theaters. That concern had led to the failure of some earlier Handel oratorios, viewed as scandalous and sacrilegious. The Bishop of London, it seems, was not prepared to forgive a work just because its music was marvelous. At first, this conservative faction had the upper hand against *Messiah*. The first London performance, in 1743, did poorly, and presentations in '45 and '49 were also financial losers. Not until the Bishop's death in 1749 could Handel overcome his opposition. *Messiah* was performed three times in the spring of 1750, repeatedly to sell-out houses, and it was staged twice yearly in London until Handel's own death nine years later.

Handel's score calls for a typical Baroque orchestra of a few dozen players, along with a small, though skillful, chorus. Not until after his death did immensely scaled performances become popular. As early as 1784, in a festival commemorating the composer's centenary (a year premature, as it turns out), Westminster Abbey presented it with 60 sopranos, 48 counter-tenors, 83 tenors, 84 basses, six flutes, 26 oboes, 26 bassoons, one double-bassoon, twelve horns, twelve trumpets, six trombones, 157 strings, assorted percussion and an organ. More would follow. Some nineteenth-century performances brought thousands to the stage. The power and impact of such massive performances cannot be argued, and Handel himself was such a showman that he might well have enjoyed the spectacle. Still, there is much to be said for the original scoring. With a Baroque orchestra and a skilled conductor, *Messiah* shines with the clarity of a Christmas morning. It doesn't need a crowd to have an impact.

- Haydn: *The Creation*

When music lovers think of oratorios, Handel's *Messiah* probably comes first to mind. Yet Joseph Haydn (1732-1809), also composed oratorios, and not without his predecessor's influence. In the 1790s, Haydn made two extended visits to London where he heard *Messiah* performed at St. Margaret's Chapel. Returning from the second of these trips in 1795, he brought with him a libretto (that is, a written text for singing) telling the story of the Creation as related in Milton's *Paradise Lost*; supposedly, the libretto had been written for Handel who never found the chance to use it. Haydn was content with the subject, but not being comfortable in English, agreed with his patron Baron Gottfried van Swieten's proposal that the piece should be reset in German, a task that the Baron undertook personally. Swieten was musically minded; in the previous decade, he had been a great supporter of Mozart and dabbled at his own compositions. So along with his translation, he included suggestions as to how the music might best evoke the powerful images. Some of these hints Haydn followed, others not. It seems he was willing to humor his supporter when necessary, but always remained guided by his own instincts.

Haydn conducted the oratorio's premiere in April 1798 at the Viennese palace of Prince Schwarzenberg. The work was well received, yet a later performance would attract even greater attention. On March 27, 1808, just prior to composer's seventy-sixth birthday, an impressive crowd assembled at Vienna University to witness *Die Schöpfung* (*The Creation*) as conducted by Antonio Salieri (1750-1825) with Haydn himself seated at the front of the orchestra. One observer recalled that, when applause erupted at the music accompanying the phrase "and there was light," the composer raised his hands toward the heavens, declaring, "It came from there!" Indeed, it is one of the most evocative moments in the piece, but there are many others as well. Haydn's stark opening chords portray masterfully the chaos that preceded the Creation, and each further step of the Creation process is shaded with picturesque tones. From light, to water, to fields and flowers, to the beasts of land and sea and air, culminating at last in a marriage duet for Adam and Eve, Haydn paints a scene for the ears no less colorful than Michelangelo's portrayal of the same images in the Sistine Chapel.

- Mozart: *Ave verum corpus*, K. 618

Completed not quite six months before the composer's premature death in 1791, the brief motet on the text *Ave verum corpus* is Mozart's last sacred work, other than the famed Requiem that he did not live to complete. It was written for Anton Stoll, choirmaster in the town of Baden, where Mozart's wife Constanze often visited the spa. At the time, Mozart had not completed any sacred music since his Mass in c minor of eight years earlier, yet he was well-familiar with the demands of writing for the church. His formative years had been spent on the staff of the prince-archbishop of Salzburg, for whom the teenager composed over a dozen masses and various shorter works. However, few of Mozart's many sacred works date from his last decade, spent in Vienna. Although his friends describe him as genuinely pious, the composer seems to have found professional reasons to shift his focus away from sacred music, for in Vienna, music for the concert hall was simply more lucrative. The *Ave verum corpus* reveals that this long silence in the field had not caused Mozart to lose his touch for sacred music. It is a work of gentle and serene beauty well worthy of Mozart's name.

- Mozart: Requiem in d, K. 626

Mozart's Requiem is the object of many misconceptions. To clear up these erroneous beliefs, let it be stated unequivocally that the composer Antonio Salieri (1750-1825) had nothing whatsoever to do with the commissioning of the work, nor did he help Mozart to write it, and, contrary to Hollywood, there never was a ghostly stranger at the door with an anonymous commission. Mozart knew perfectly well who had requested and paid in advance for the Requiem. He even signed a contract for it, witnessed by an attorney. The only unusual part of the affair was that Mozart was neither to make copies of the score nor to reveal his involvement in it, and that the first performance was reserved for the man who commissioned the piece, Count Franz Georg von Walsegg-Stuppach. The Count, it seems, pretended to some compositional ability, and liked to pass off the work of others as his own. The new requiem, intended as a tribute to the Count's wife, was part of this same game. Any further mystery about the transaction is purely the creation of overly imaginative historians.

The Requiem dates from late in 1791, the last few months of Mozart's life, when he was already deeply entrenched in two new operas: *The Magic Flute* and *La Clemenza di Tito*. Three assignments together were too much for a man suffering from a succession of debilitating fevers, but Mozart needed funds too badly to refuse any offer. Most of his failing strength went into the operas, both of which were completed and staged. As for the Requiem, he dabbled away at it when strength permitted, and several friends came to his apartment December 4 to sing through the score-in-progress. Yet his condition worsened, and by the time of Mozart's death early the next morning, he had finished only the Introit. The Kyrie, Sequenz, and Offertorium were sketched out. The last three movements — Benedictus, Agnus Dei, and Communio — remained unwritten, and nearly all the orchestration was incomplete.

Mozart's widow Constanze faced a difficult decision. Without a finished score, she would have to refund the Count's money, which was already spent. But who could complete it? She asked several composers to help. Most refused, apparently fearful of the task of matching Mozart's skill. The task finally fell to Mozart's twenty-five-year-old composition student, Franz Xavier Süssmayr (1766-1803), who had several qualifications for the assignment. He claimed that Mozart had discussed the work with him, thus, theoretically, he could proceed according to the original plan. Also, since his handwriting resembled Mozart's, it was hoped that the Count would not notice the difference. Unfortunately, Süssmayr had not half his teacher's talent. Despite working from Mozart's sketches and orchestrations, and drawing upon earlier material in the Requiem for the sections that had to be written from scratch, his contributions to the Requiem include harmonic errors and ungraceful details never committed by his mentor. Still, it would have to do. Constanze delivered it to the Count, and held her breath.

The Count was not fooled for long. Perhaps the mistakes were a give-away, or maybe he heard something through the grapevine. What is certain is that the Requiem was performed in Vienna shortly after Mozart's death, as a benefit for his widow and two young sons (not, as the film *Amadeus* would have it, one son). That performance violated the terms of the original contract, and the Count was barely restrained from filing suit against Constanze. Despite his fury at the progress of events, he should have been grateful, for it is the debate around the Requiem that has preserved his name. Had there been no hint of scandal, Count Walsegg-Stuppach would have long ago vanished from history.

- Beethoven: *Choral Fantasy in c, op. 80*

On December 22, 1808, Viennese devotees of new music made their way to the Theater-an-der-Wien for a lengthy all-Beethoven concert. The program included both his Fifth and Sixth Symphonies, as well as the concert aria, *"Ah, perfido"*, two movements from the Mass in C major, the Fourth Piano Concerto, and, last but not least, the *Choral Fantasy*. The Symphony no. 5 was discussed in Chapter Two; let us now consider the *Choral Fantasy*.

Although all the other works had been written in preceding months and years, the *Choral Fantasy* was completely new, quickly composed in a few weeks before the concert. It was specifically intended as a grand finale to the mammoth program, and its unusual scoring for piano, chorus, and orchestra arose from the requirements of the other pieces. Since a piano was there for the concerto and a choir had been hired for the mass, it seemed sensible to bring them all together with the orchestra for this concluding work. The title might have startled audience members, who at that time were accustomed to a "fantasy" being a solo keyboard work. Indeed, that is how the work begins: with a lengthy solo piano passage that Beethoven himself improvised at the premiere, despite the fact that, by this time, his hearing had almost completely failed. In the *Fantasy*'s second section, the orchestra joins in, creating a concerto-like mood. The chorus is saved for the grand finale. Initial public reaction to the piece has not been recorded, but coming as it did as the closing work of such a musical marathon, it was probably met by sighs of relief.

Many scholars have pointed out the similarities between this work and Beethoven's Symphony no. 9, known as the *Choral Symphony* (see Chapter Two) which it preceded by sixteen years. Indeed, there are strong similarities between the two works' principal melodies. Another parallel lies in the philosophies expounded by the two texts. The Symphony, based on a poem by Schiller, praises the brotherhood and goodwill that arise from shared joy. The *Fantasy* speaks of similar delights, proclaiming in its concluding measures, "When love and power unite, God's grace descends on all mankind." The identity of the Fantasy's librettist is uncertain. Some sources cite Georg Friedrich Treitschke, who also provided the text for Beethoven's only opera, *Fidelio*. Yet Beethoven's student Carl Czerny insisted that another poet, Christoph Kuffner, should be credited. Neither Treitschke nor Kuffner would make a strong mark in Germany's literary history, yet any man who inspired Beethoven to create this magnificent work deserves to be remembered.

- Mendelssohn: *Elijah*, op. 70

Felix Mendelssohn (1809-1847) was a composer with a taste for the past. This, after all, is the man who at the grand age of twenty launched a personal mission to revive interest in the grand religious scores of Bach, personally conducting them in their first public performances since the Baroque master's death. So if any composer of the 1800s was going to compose oratorios, Mendelssohn would be the man. He completed two such works, first *St. Paul* in 1836 and a decade later *Elijah*. Each shows his mastery of this old field of oratorio: the task of presenting a religious story with voices and instruments but without props and costumes.

Elijah exists in part because of the success of *St. Paul*. The earlier work had premiered in Düsseldorf, in the composer's native Germany, but his music also enjoyed a devout following in England. Not long after *St. Paul*'s German premiere, it made its way to England and was presented in Birmingham to great success. A determination arose in that city to have Mendelssohn write another oratorio especially for Birmingham; *Elijah* would be the result.

Because of the composer's busy conducting career, some years passed before realization of the dream. He would not complete *Elijah* until 1846, and it would premiere that summer in Birmingham, with subsequent performances in London with the composer himself conducting. At the London performance, the audience included the German-born Prince Albert, who was so favorably impressed that he sent to Mendelssohn a gift inscribed, "To the noble artist." Other than a single string quartet, *Elijah* would be Mendelssohn's last major composition; the composer, though still a young man, would live only one more year, brought low by a series of strokes at the age of thirty-eight.

Although Mendelssohn himself was more strongly drawn to the music of Bach, the flavor of *Elijah* is closer to that of Handel, in its dramatic elements that draw listeners into the story. The title character's role is given to a baritone or bass, though there are also three other main soloists and prominent passages for the chorus. The text comes from various books of the Old Testament, especially though not exclusively the first book of Kings. Having based his first oratorio *St. Paul* on the New Testament of the Protestant religion in which he had been raised, here Mendelssohn turns back to the Jewish heritage of his grandfather, the influential philosopher Moses Mendelssohn, in presenting the story of one of the most dynamic figures of the Old Testament. Although the work's initial text was drafted in German, it is often sung in English translation, and was so performed even during Mendelssohn's day. So strongly are the characters portrayed that one can regret the fact the only operas from this composer all date from his teenage years and none survive complete. Any man who can bring such dramatic effect from the human voice might have produced a masterful opera, had he only found time to do so.

- Verdi: Requiem

When a composer of grand opera discovers sacred music late in life, one might presume he has begun to think of eternity. Having devoted his career to the portrayal of passions, he now is determined to atone for those "sins". Indeed, Giuseppe Verdi (1813-1901) was past sixty when he composed his only Requiem. Though his father Carlo had lived to be ninety-two, the master composer had no way of guessing how much time remained to him. Moreover, the musical world was in a state of flux. Verdi's most famed masterpieces, *Rigoletto, Il trovatore,* and *La Traviata,* were two decades in the past, and Richard Wagner — whom one might call an upstart, were he not exactly Verdi's age — was vigorously rocking the operatic boat. With new styles taking hold, Verdi might have imagined that the end of his musical world was in sight.

The problem with such an analysis is that, in 1874, Verdi was in fine health and would remain so nearly to the end of his days (over a quarter century away). It is impossible that he could have viewed his Requiem as a culmination of his career. Furthermore, no one who knew him well viewed him as conventionally religious. "He knew that Faith was the sustenance of hearts," observed his librettist Arrigo Boito. "In the ideal moral and social sense, he was a great Christian, but one should take care not to present him as a Catholic in the political and strictly theological sense of the word." Soprano Giuseppina Strepponi — for ten years Verdi's live-in companion and eventually his second wife (his first had died when the composer was young) — took a similar view: "There are some virtuous natures that need to believe in God; others, equally perfect, that are happy not believing in anything, and simply observing rigorously every precept of strict morality."

So religious belief was not Verdi's inspiration. Rather, this most magnificent of all sacred works — by turns heart-stirring and heart-breaking — was intended as a memorial to a departed hero, the poet, playwright, and novelist Alessandro Manzoni. The leading Italian writer of the 1800s, Manzoni played the role in his nation that Goethe had for an earlier generation of Germans: that of a country's literary soul, a man who vividly expressed the dreams, hopes, and fears of an entire people. Verdi was only sixteen when he first encountered Manzoni's writings, particularly the novel *I promessi sposi* (*The Betrothed*) which he once described as "a consolation for humanity." Nearly forty years later, in 1867, he finally met the man himself. After the visit, he recalled to a friend, "I would have gone down on my knees before him if we were allowed to worship men. They say it is wrong to do so, although we raise up on altars many who have neither the talent nor the virtue of Manzoni and indeed are rascals."

On May 22, 1873, when Manzoni passed away at a great age, all Italy mourned. In a letter to his publisher, Verdi expressed a wish to write something in memory of the great man. The result would be his Requiem. Determined to conduct the work himself on the first anniversary of Manzoni's death, Verdi arranged with the city of Milan, where Manzoni had lived and where many Verdi operas had premiered, that the premiere would take place there in St. Mark's and that the city would pay the performers. He spent the fall and winter devoted to composition, and the Requiem premiered on schedule to massive public acclaim. That first performance at St. Mark's was followed by three more at the La Scala Opera House.

Although the Italian people received Verdi's memorial tribute with enthusiasm, some critics — mostly German ones — were less open-minded. They claimed Verdi had not written a requiem at all, but only an opera to a sacred text, and delighted in pointing out that the soprano and mezzo-soprano soloists had most recently appeared in the leading roles in *Aida*. However, their criticism seems misguided. Of course Verdi hired opera singers: they were the singers he knew and, not incidentally, the only ones sufficiently gifted to sing his challenging music. Moreover, if some of the choruses seem more dramatic than reverent, then one can fairly ask what, after all, is more dramatic than the passing of a national hero, a man whose death deeply shook a nation? With Manzoni on his mind, Verdi produced a Kyrie that weeps heart-felt tears, an Agnus Dei that soothes like a caress, a Sanctus that rejoices as over an epic battle, and a Dies Irae that rages with a fury unsurpassed in all the sacred literature. It is a sacred work of astonishing grandeur and power.

- Brahms: A German Requiem, op. 45

The reputation of Johannes Brahms (1833-1897) today stands largely upon his symphonies and chamber music. In those instrumental realms, he is often lauded as the greatest master of his age, as an inspired composer who, more than any other, perfected the balance of Romantic emotion and Classical structure. Indeed, those grandest of Brahms' creations are triumphs of the musical art, but it is worth noting that, in terms of his overall output, instrumental works stand firmly in the minority. It is music for the human voice that appears most frequently in his catalog. From touchingly simple songs to deeply moving sacred compositions, Brahms demonstrated a thorough knowledge of the human voice, derived in part from experience as a conductor of women's choirs. The familiar Brahms' *Lullaby* (see Chapter Seven) shows only a fraction of his true expertise in the realm of vocal expression.

A German Requiem was Brahms' reaction to two deep emotional blows, the first suffered in young adulthood, the second nearly a decade later. In July 1856, only two months after his twenty-third birthday, death touched Brahms for the first time in the passing of his good friend and mentor, the composer and music journalist Robert Schumann. Soon, Brahms was at work on what he called a cantata of mourning. Despite the composer's youth, this was far from his first choral music. Brahms had already completed a large variety of vocal pieces, some a cappella, others with instrumental accompaniment. Yet at this early point in his career, an entire cantata may have seemed a daunting task. By 1861, he had completed only two movements, and went no further.

It took a second shock, the death of his mother in February 1865, to bring Brahms back to the task. Deciding to make of the score a more expansive requiem, he set to work again, completing four more movements by the summer of 1866. This initial version of the Requiem premiered December 1, 1867 in Vienna to limited acclaim. Later revisions, ultimately resulting in a total of seven movements, rather than the previous six, enjoyed more success, and in 1868 and '69, the Requiem was heard in twenty German cities. "Now I am consoled," Brahms told his friends. "I have surmounted obstacles that I thought I could never overcome, and I feel like an eagle, soaring ever higher and higher." The composer's father was rather more succinct in his praise. After a Bremen performance, the elder Brahms remarked, "It went off rather well."

Typical requiems are settings of the Catholic mass for the dead. Yet Brahms, as a Protestant, took a different approach.

Rejecting the usual Latin texts, he chose his own verses from Luther's German translation of the Bible, selecting New and Old Testament passages that would not only mourn the dead, but also comfort the living. In Brahms' Requiem, unlike those of Verdi or Mozart, fire and brimstone are utterly absent. Instead, the choir sings of the comfort to be found in God and in the ultimate Resurrection, proclaiming, "O death, where is thy sting? O grave, where is thy victory?" It is a message of consolation relevant for listeners and performers alike. In the composer's own words, "I had the whole of humanity in mind when I wrote this music."

- Fauré: *Cantique de Jean Racine*

In the course of a lengthy career, Frenchman Gabriel Fauré (1845-1924) became one of his nation's foremost composers of choral and sacred music. Certainly, his years of experience as organist and choirmaster contributed to that development, but one of Fauré's most exquisite choral works predates his years of work for the church. The *Cantique de Jean Racine* was written in 1865, when its twenty-year-old creator was studying music at the Ecole Niedermeyer in Paris. Written for a student competition, the piece was first rejected by examiners, on the grounds that, whereas the contest's rules specified a Latin text, Fauré had set French words. Fortunately, other panel members, composer Camille Saint-Saëns (1835-1921) among them, insisted the work be considered, and it eventually earned first prize. When Fauré published his score eleven years later, he dedicated it to another of his elder colleagues, composer/organist Cesar Franck.

The *Cantique* is a setting of verses by the seventeenth-century French poet and dramatist, Jean Racine. Although not a standard church text, the poem is filled with the imagery of worship. It begins with these lines:

"Word, equal of the Almighty, our sole hope
Eternal day of earth and heaven,

As we break the silence of peaceful night,
Divine Savior, cast thine eyes upon us."

In its hushed, ethereal beauty, Fauré's score is the equal of the images it invokes.

- Orff: *Carmina Burana*

Born to an old Bavarian military family in Munich, Germany, Carl Orff (1895-1982) rejected his family's background in favor of music. He learned the piano, organ, and cello as a boy, and took up composition as well. He did spend a few years in the army in his early twenties, but by 1919 was back in Munich teaching music. Soon, he would co-found an institution devoted to gymnastics, music, and dance, and before long his definitive text on music teaching, the Orff Schulwerk, would be underway. He also led the Munich Bach Society for four years in the thirties, where he evidenced his respect both for the German master Bach and for the Italian opera master Monteverdi. Orff was also busy in the operatic world, producing numerous Greek and Italian inspired stage works starting in the 1920s. In the postwar years beginning in 1948, he worked with German broadcasting on a five-year series of educational radio programs derived from the theories of his Schulwerk.

"With *Carmina Burana*, my collected works begin." With those jubilant words, Orff destroyed most of his earlier compositions, determined to be judged instead on the reputation of this particular creation. He could not have chosen better. The mix of grandeur and delicacy that inhabit the "scenic cantata," to borrow the composer's own phrase, have remained unmatched, either by Orff himself or by any other composer, in all the years since its debut in Frankfurt in 1937.

Orff drew his text from a thirteenth-century anthology of plays, poems, songs, and satires, written in Latin and Medieval German, and unearthed in 1803 at the Bavarian monastery of

Benedictbeuren, hence "Carmina Burana," or roughly, "Songs of Beuren". Some of the texts were religious, others licentious. Taken together, they vividly portrayed diverse views of an earlier age and helped to dismiss the popular notion that all literature of that period was prayerful. Neither performers nor listeners will get far into this work armed only with Church Latin or schoolbook German. Vocabulary and spelling range significantly further than either of those backgrounds would serve.

The composer does not treat his three vocal soloists quite equally. The tenor has only one solo number — the swan song in Part Two — though its extreme range and difficulty may make up for the lack of time in the spotlight. All the soprano's solos are in Part Three, as if Orff felt that he could not treat its theme of "Court of Love" without a prominent female presence. Her music is arranged conveniently in that the highest parts are the last ones: once she moves up in her range, she need not come back down again. As for the baritone, he earns the most attention, with one solo in Part One, two in Part Two, and three in Part Three. Some of his music is sweet and lyrical; more often, he is written gruff and assertive. Thus, a performer of flexible voice is required.

Beyond the soloists (and, for that matter, the large orchestra), there is a mixed chorus (that is, both men and women) and also a children's chorus. The men and women of the mixed chorus are often separated vocally, so that one or the other — but not always both — will dominate in a single movement. As for the children's chorus, its music all occurs in Part Three, and often is given lines to sing so suggestive that one might not think them appropriate for young performers. Fortunately for choral directors, those lines are in Latin, so the music can be presented to young singers as random syllables to be articulated clearly, but not necessarily understood.

Most famed of all the movements of *Carmina Burana* is its opening, repeated at the close: *O Fortuna*. It offers the ancient idea of the wheel of fortune that carries a person up to triumph and then sends that person swirling downward again. Its first measures are amongst the grandest statements in all the choral literature, but soon yield to quieter, almost whispered phrases, as if the chorus were fearful that fortune's dark eye might turn its way. Those two moods, appearing in close order here, recur throughout the work: Orff alternates between grandeur and reflection, ever imagining a varied tapestry of choral and orchestral sound and making the most of his musical forces.

- Randall Thompson: *Alleluia*

In the years from 1898 to 1900, New York City and its member boroughs gave to the realms of American classical music three men who in different ways forever influenced the American style of composition. The eldest of the three, George Gershwin (1898-1937) would prove that jazz and classical music could co-exist. The youngest of the three, Aaron Copland (1900-1990), also envisioned a musical union, but for him, it was folk music that deserved a share of the classical spotlight. The third native New Yorker has a profile rather lower than those of Gershwin and Copland, but he, too, has played a critical role. His name is Randall Thompson (1899-1984), and no composer has ever exceeded Thompson's contributions to American choral music.

Thompson was twice-over a graduate of Harvard, earning a BA in 1920 and an MA in 1922. He later returned to join the Harvard faculty and during his years there — nearly two decades — counted Leonard Bernstein amongst his students. Thompson's academic efforts would also see him on the faculties of Princeton, Wellesley, the Curtis Institute of Music, and the University of California at Berkeley, yet somehow he also found time to compose. His catalog includes three symphonies, two string quartets, and much choral music, both secular and sacred. It is in the last of these categories that Thompson's most frequently performed work is found.

His a cappella hymn *Alleluia* was composed not specifically for the church, but rather for the opening of the Boston Symphony's

Berkshire Music Center at Tanglewood in 1940. The symphony's conductor, Serge Koussevitzky, wanted something stately to launch opening ceremonies. His choice fell upon Thompson in part because Harvard students were scheduled to sing. They must have been gifted sight-readers, as Thompson only finished the music the morning of the ceremony: July 8, 1940. Ever since then, his *Alleluia* has served as the opening music for the summer season at Tanglewood, and also has graced many choral programs. By turns serene and joyous, it captures the essential elegance of Thompson's compositional voice.

- Finzi: *In Terra Pax*, op. 39

Despite his Italianate name, composer Gerald Finzi (1901-1956) was born in London. His father, whose own ancestors had come from Italy in the 1700s, was a businessman who arranged music studies for the boy starting when Gerald was only 13. This first burst of musical exploration ended when his teacher died in combat during World War I. The wartime passing of three elder brothers turned young Finzi to an introspective slant of mind, which can be perceived in his thoughtful and reflective compositions. He resumed composition studies, and came to know Holst and Vaughan Williams, each about thirty years his senior. Before long, Finzi was teaching composition at the Royal Academy of Music.

After his marriage in 1933, Finzi moved from the hectic scene of London to the hills of Hampshire, where the quiet atmosphere allowed time to compose. There he produced especially choral works and songs, though his catalog also included orchestral compositions and concertos. Another war led to several years back in London, where Finzi served at the Ministry of War Transport, which again took him away from composition for a time. However, after World War II, he resumed his musical activities for the few years that remained to him. Already ill with Hodgkin's disease, Finzi died of the effects of a bout with chicken pox.

Finzi's last work was the Christmas choral piece *In Terra Pax*. Fifteen years earlier, he had written another work on the same topic, the *Dies Natalis* for England's Three Choirs Festival. *In Terra Pax*, however, was not written on commission, but rather because of Finzi's own impulse. He had come across the poem *Noel: Christmas Eve, 1913*, by Robert Bridges, and conceived of setting it together with familiar Nativity verses from the Gospel of St. Luke. Bridges' text serves as the framework of the piece, and is sung by a baritone solo. When the scene shifts to Luke, the chorus enters, and the single angel voice, given those familiar "Fear not" lines, is cast as a soprano. For the "multitude of the heavenly host," the chorus takes charge again, before yielding to the baritone for more Bridges. However, the work closes with a choral reprise of "On earth peace, good will toward men."

In Terra Pax is alternately serene and powerful, as the text demands. Despite his illness, he was clearly moved by the imagery, and by childhood memories of bells ringing across wintery fields. He leads one to recall that for centuries, England had had a strong tradition of sacred music, a field that inspired its finest composers, including, in this instance, Finzi.

- Bernstein: *Chicester Psalms*

In his time, Leonard Bernstein (1918-1990) was the biggest name in American classical music, routinely greeted at airports by paparazzi and doting fans. Even now, over two decades after his death, he still has more recordings in print than any other American-born conductor. It was mostly on that conducting — dramatic, emotional, and highly person in style — that his popular reputation rested. That he was also a skilled pianist and a composer of diverse interests would come as a surprise to those who, if asked to name a Bernstein composition, would produce a list that began and ended with *West Side Story* (see Chapter Nine). However, in addition to the travails of Tony and Maria, he also composed three symphonies (see Chapter Two), a violin concerto, various chamber works and songs, several operas (notably *Candide*), and a pair of sacred works for chorus and orchestra. In 1971, he composed a Mass at the request of Jackie Kennedy for the opening of the Kennedy Center. Six years earlier had been the *Chicester Psalms* for the Chicester Cathedral in southern England. Bernstein himself conducted the work's premiere July 15, 1965, with the New York Philharmonic and the Camerata Singers.

Sung in Hebrew, the *Chicester Psalms* set the complete texts of Psalms, 100, 23, and 131, together with a few verses from Psalms 2 and 133. The first movement begins in a fearsomely commanding mood that soon gives way to bright jubilation, buoyed with more brass and percussion than one typically finds in a sacred work. However, Bernstein was imagining a concert piece, not something specifically for either the church or the synagogue, and he was, after all, a man with a great flair for theater. By contrast, the second movement is sweetly reflective, its opening devoted to boy alto soloist with harp accompaniment. As long as the text of Psalm 23 continues, a restful mood predominates, but with Psalm 2's lines, brisk determination returns, though the movement concludes with lyric beauty. The third and final movement opens with a poignant string prelude, distantly dissonant, and trumpet phrases recalled from earlier in the work. Before long, a graceful theme emerges, first for low strings and the men of the chorus, then joined by high strings and the women of the chorus. Focus shifts repeatedly from voice to instruments and back, and even the brass get to prove they can carry a song-like theme. Ultimately, the music floats to a prayerful conclusion.

- Tavener: *Song for Athene*

The modern composer John Tavener — not to be confused with the Elizabethan composer John Taverner (slightly different spelling and radically different dates) was born in 1944 into a musical environment. His father, a church organist in Hampstead, ensured that the boy would have early musical training and that his first sacred compositions would be performed at the church. While still in his teens, young John was conducting church choirs and playing organ in Kensington. Studies at the Royal Academy of Music would follow. With such a background, it is no surprise that Tavener's music is frequently of sacred content and often scored for a cappella choirs. Although his religious upbringing was Presbyterian, Tavener became fascinated with the Eastern Orthodox Church in his early thirties and has written much music drawing upon that influence, with open choral textures that will remind some listeners of Russian church music. Such is the spirit of his most familiar work, the one that concerns us here.

Composed in 1993 and renowned four years later when it was included in Princess Diana's funeral ceremony, *Song for Athena* was originally composed as a tribute to a young friend of the family who had died in a cycling accident. The title carries the young lady's name more than that of the Greek goddess, and the chosen text combines phrases from the Orthodox liturgy with lines from *Hamlet* (beginning "Life, a shadow and a dream") which Tavener had heard young Athena, an aspiring actress, recite in Westminster Abbey. After the work was used so prominently for Diana's funeral, Tavener decided to write another piece specifically in the princess' memory. That later tribute, titled *Eternity's Sunrise*, drew its text from the poetry of William Blake, whose words have appeared frequently in Tavener's works. His reputation in England is such that he was knighted in 2000.

- Rutter: composer of carols (and much more)

Technically speaking, a "carol" is a dance-like song for singers without instrumental accompaniment, written in several verses with a recurring refrain; that was how the term was first used back in the Middle Ages. It was often sacred in subject, though not necessarily for the Christmas season. Over the centuries, however, "carol" has come to mean Christmas, and though instruments may be allowed, a cappella is best suited for door-to-door singing at the holiday season. Dance-like rhythms are not always present — few of us could find a useful way to dance to "Hark the Herald Angels Sing" — but other carols, particularly those of folk-like mood, like "Bring a Torch" or "Here We Come a Wassailing," are sufficiently bright in spirit to remind one of the origin of caroling. With such bouncy rhythms, one might be hard pressed to sit quite still.

English composer John Rutter (b. 1945) clearly did not invent the idea of carols, but he has been a busy contributor to the field, both with arrangements of ancient melodies and many new compositions of his own. Born in London, he was educated at Cambridge and has long been associated with the Cambridge Singers, which he founded and conducts, principally in recordings, although they make occasional concert appearances. His many dozens of carol settings have become favorites on both sides of the Atlantic, and offer a tuneful cheer much appreciated by all, especially at the holiday season, with professional performers and amateur choirs alike.

Of his long association with music of the Christmas season, Rutter observed in an interview with this writer, "I don't really mind. This was the first kind of music I remember really liking when I was a kid, so to be identified with it is fine." If one must be typecast, let in be in a place for which one has affection, as Rutter does. However, he has also composed a remarkable Requiem, a two-piano concerto on Beatles themes, and some imaginative musical "fables" for narrator, chorus, and orchestra. Rutter is a composer of diverse talents.

- Whitacre: *Lux Aurumque*

Born in Reno, Nevada, composer Eric Whitacre (b. 1970) has made more thorough use of digital resources in his music than any other composer to date. Having developed an early interest in choral music through singing in his college choir, he began composing a great quantity of large scale vocal works, often a cappella. His music attracted favorable attention on five continents, and he found himself much in demand as conductor and choral clinician in choral festivals. Late in 2009, he had the idea of reaching out to amateur choral singers around the world, tapping into the wide-spread enthusiasm for singing that had originally led him to choose a music career for himself. He launched his Virtual Choir project, offering to distribute digitally copies of the music for his *Lux Aurumque* and then accept amateur video recordings of persons singing their chosen voice part. From these submissions, he compiled his Virtual Choir, pasted all the selected videos together into a patchwork of visual images and let these various voices — virtually all unknown to one another — blend in harmony. The resulting recording, posted on YouTube in March of 2010, received over one million viewers in only two months, and is still available for viewing.

At this writing, Whitacre is now at work on his second Virtual Choir project, centered on his composition *Sleep*, which itself is a meditation on the Robert Frost poem "Stopping by the Woods on a Snowy Evening." That he was savvy enough to make advantageous use of the internet is clear. However, there is also the fact that his music proved itself worthy of such wide attention. His compositions — including both secular and sacred works — are lush and tonal, hauntingly rich in harmonies. Although not so complicated in technique as to preclude performance by amateurs, his music yet requires perfect intonation to make the textures fit. One who cannot reliably sing in tune need not bother with Whitacre's music; one who delights in fine singing will find much to enjoy, either as a performer or as a listener. Best of all: one needn't go online to enjoy his music. Whitacre's CD recordings are widely available and critically acclaimed.

Dating from 2000, and so barely a twentieth century work, Whitacre's *Lux Aurumque* (*Golden Light*) is a setting of a poem by the poet Edward Esch. Esch's text — of angels singing to a babe as golden light beams — had been written in English, but Whitacre decided to have it translated into Latin for his setting. The change brings softer consonants and broader vowels into the text, arguably more conducive to singing, even beyond the question of giving it a more ancient feel, despite the fact that Esch is a contemporary writer. Set for a cappella voices — with no instrumental accompaniment — the piece is serene and spacious in mood, with occasional high-floating descant phrases that seem reminiscent of how, centuries earlier, the Renaissance composer Allegri set his *Miserere Mei*. Brief strong passages appear, seeming more vividly colored that those that surround them, but the ultimate mood is one of restfulness.

Further Recommendations:

Here is a selection of other interesting choral works for which there was not room in the main body of the chapter:

- Johann Sebastian Bach (1685-1750): Working nearly thirty years for the St. Thomas Church in Leipzig, Germany, Bach composed several hundred Lutheran cantatas for use in regular Sunday services. Especially notable amongst these are Cantata no. 80, which features the famous hymn "Ein feste Burg," and Cantata no. 140, known in English as "Sleeper's Awake."

- George Frideric Handel (1685-1759): For the coronation of England's King George II in 1727, Handel composed a set of four coronation anthems to be performed as part of the service. Grandest of the four is *Zadok the Priest*, with its bold declarations of "God Save the King."

- Ludwig van Beethoven (1770-1827): His oratorio *Christ on the Mount of Olives* includes a particularly glorious Alleluia movement, which except for the larger scope of its orchestra might almost be borrowed from Handel, were one to judge by the rich writing for its chorus.

- Charles Stanford (1852-1924): In earlier generations, English composers were fond of writing so-called "part songs:" small scale pieces for a cappella chorus, which might be tackled by reasonably talented amateur choirs. Stanford's *The Blue Bird* is a serene example of the field.

- Ralph Vaughan Williams (1872-1958): His *Serenade to Music* sets text from Shakespeare's *The Merchant of Venice*, in which two characters muse upon the power of music. Vaughan Williams scored the piece for orchestra, multiple choirs, and sixteen vocal soloists, writing the names of each individual soloist into the score.

- Sergei Rachmaninoff (1873-1943): *The Bells* sets a Russian translation of the Edgar Allen Poe tale, with much evocative portrayal of bell effects, even in the voice parts. Consider also his grand and reverent *Vespers*, intended for the Russian Orthodox Church.

- Francis Poulenc (1899-1963): The Frenchman — descendant of the family that invented and first marketed Maalox; look for the name on the label at the pharmacy — chose music over business and wrote in almost any imaginable genre of composition. His choral works include a set of four a cappella motets written for the Christmas seasons of 1951 and 1952.

- Samuel Barber (1910-1981): Having observed that the melodies of his widely-beloved *Adagio for Strings* would suit themselves well to singing, Barber adapted the work as a choral piece to the text of the *Agnus Dei*.

- Ariel Ramirez (1921-2010): The Argentine composer's folk-flavored *Misa Criolla*, from 1964, benefited from the Vatican declaring that no longer need all Catholic sacred music be sung in Latin. The music is sufficiently well-crafted that each of the legendary Three Tenors — Carreras, Domingo, and Pavarotti — saw fit to include it in their repertoires.

- Paul McCartney (b. 1942): Not a religious work, but rather the story of a boy growing up in northern England, McCartney's *Liverpool Oratorio* was a collaboration with the conductor/composer Carl Davis and makes fine use of McCartney's long-proven facility for imagining singable tunes.

- Morten Lauridsen (b. 1943): Honored with the National Medal of Arts by President George W. Bush, Lauridsen is especially known for his choral music. Seek out his *Mid-Winter Songs* on poems by Robert Graves, or other choral cycles using texts by Rilke and Lorca. There are also many sacred works.

- Karl Jenkins (b. 1944): Written for the UK Millennium Commission and premiered in 1999, the Welsh composer's *The Armed Man: A Mass for Peace* blends influences from various world views — from Catholic to Islamic — with the melody of an early Renaissance folk song, "L'Homme armé" (The Armed Man). More than simply a mass, it explores views of war and peace.

- Scottish composer James MacMillan (b. 1959) began his music career as a church choir director, and has continued to write choral music when professional obligations allow. His *Strathclyde Motets*, named for Scotland's Strathclyde University Choir, blends a cappella textures, as Renaissance composer would have used them, with somewhat more modern harmonies to impressive effect.

Chapter Twelve

Coda

Composers call it a "coda:" the final minutes or moments of a composition (or of one of its constituent movements) that serve to bring it to a close. The goal is to make things sound finished, in the way that the great burst of rockets at the end of a fireworks show finishes that program. Like those fireworks, codas are often bold and flashy, though sometimes more understated. It seems to depend on whether the composer wishes to ride off into the sunset in a blaze of glory, or prefers to stroll away in a thoughtful mood. The music at the top of this page is the string parts from the very end of the coda to the last movement of Beethoven's Symphony no. 9, the "Choral," possessing one of the punchiest of all conclusions. By contrast, that same composer's Symphony no. 6, the "Pastorale," seems to close with the gentle fading of the day. Thus, even Beethoven, who could teach most of us things about music, saw more than one way to end a work.

For the coda of this collection of musical essays, I would like to sum up with thoughts about what classical music is and why it still matters, even in the twenty-first century (and beyond). As I hope I've managed to make clear in the preceding pages, it is music written by real people with real lives, using music to reflect their view of the world at their time in history. Since those times, those views, those lives, and those people vary widely, it is therefore music of great variety, giving us perspective into both past and current humanity.

How better to understand life in Vienna in the 1780s than by listening to Mozart (1756-1791), and hearing how the man expressed himself and how his listeners (some of them also his employers) expected to spend their leisure time? How better to grasp the differences between that Vienna and the Vienna of a bit more than a century later than by turning to Schoenberg (1874-1951)? Add in-between generations with Beethoven (1770-1827), Brahms (1833-1897) and Mahler (1860-1911), and one has a panorama of insights into that locale, and how those people lived their lives. Schoenberg's darker world view, compared to those of his predecessors, says much about how World War I changed people's attitudes in Austria, and in the world at large. It is a lesson in world history made alive by music.

Closer to home, consider the music of Nebraska-born Howard Hanson (1896-1981) and that of Brooklyn-born Jennifer Higdon (b. 1962). For these two, gender is less the difference than time and place; yet across those times and places, certain ideas recur. In an interview with this writer, Ms. Higdon observed, "Part of my job as a composer is to talk to the audience through my music . . . There is so much demanding our attention these days. A much faster paced world compared to Beethoven's time. It's important to address that, to stay in touch." Indeed, our world today is faster paced — sometimes regrettably so — but even Beethoven needed to "talk to the audience" with music, and to "stay in touch" with his world. His music brings us close to that world, and the music of skilled composers today expresses the world in which we are living.

That the subject is "classical" music of today, rather than popular music, shifts the equation only in a positive direction. Classical composers can take advantage of a broader canvas and more strongly expressive tools. That's part of why such men as Gershwin (1898-1937) and Ellington (1899-1974) took steps in the direction of the classical concert hall: they had excelled at popular music, and Ellington would live long enough to play both sides of that fence for decades, but both men were searching for something more than what they got from three-minute tunes. The expansive possibilities of classical music and its more disciplined structures make it a richer, stronger experience. Even a short solo piano piece can be kaleidoscopic in its effect. Moreover, when Mozart and Beethoven and Company were writing it, it was popular music of the day. Were their audiences cleverer than we are? I think not.

Audiences, too, can find that "something more" in classical realms. As composers put more into it, we can gain more from it, finding something new at each exposure. That's why great works of the past are still performed today. It is highly unlikely that anyone will ever discover every last nuance of Beethoven's Symphony no. 9, leaving nothing else there to find; further exposure and further hearings are immeasurably valuable, particularly as our own experiences change us, so that we bring something new to the work each time we approach it.

Music of such complexity has unending rewards of adventure, especially for the performer, but also for the listener. Admittedly, complexity can be such that a casual listener cannot absorb it all at once, so the trick is to listen for one aspect at a time, then go back again to find something else. As one can re-read a favorite novel or re-watch a favorite movie and find some effective line of dialog or visual image that one hadn't remembered from the previous time, so great music always has something to give. Long after the composers have gone, the music itself is still alive.

Composers of today are in a similar situation to those in the past. They use their music to express their ideas to their audiences, hoping that later audiences in future years will still have ears for those ideas. There are easier ways to make a living, but there are few that are equally satisfying.

Which composers of today are destined to be regarded in the future as the Mozarts and Beethovens of our time? One cannot be sure. Certainly, there are some for whom this writer is hoping, as their music seems to her rich enough as to deserve that lasting existence. Many of those persons are in this book. Others are not here only because space began to run short. Moreover, it's entirely possible that one of the next Mozarts is new enough on the scene as to be currently seeking first attention for his/her music and has yet to come to public notice. If we stay attentive, we can always expand the list of possibilities.

Great music speaks on many levels. If we keep in mind how it came to be that way — as opposed to some other way that the composer decided not to use — we can gain perspective on that music, the world in which it came to be, and even ourselves. Just because Mozart wrote it over two centuries ago doesn't mean that it can't still be richly rewarding today. Shakespeare lived even longer ago, but isn't *Romeo and Juliet* still a touching story?

As Friedrich Nietzsche (1844-1900) famously observed, "Without music, life would be simply a mistake, a strain, an exile" ("Das Leben ohne Musik ist einfach ein Irrthum, eine Strapaze, ein Exil."). One does not often hear the "simply," "strain" and "exile" parts of the quotation, but there they are in the original German, if one lets him finish his sentence. Great music is one of the marvelous creations of mankind, as rich as an enduring work of literature, each always deserving another look. Given that second — or twentieth — hearing, great music has much to give. All we need to give is our attention.

Appendices

I. Glossary

- **A cappella** — voices without instruments; original meaning was "in the style of the chapel," as in the Renaissance, church music was performed in this fashion
- **Age of Reason** — during the Baroque Era, an intellectual movement that emphasized logic, discipline, and structure
- **Allegro** — a quick and lively tempo (speed at which the music is performed)
- **Andante** — a slower tempo (speed at which the music is performed)
- **Arpeggio** — playing the several notes of a chord sequentially, rather than simultaneously
- **Art song** — a short musical setting of a poem, generally for one singer and one pianist, though some art songs may add more accompanying instruments; synonym of "lieder"
- **Atonality** — not emphasizing particular tones in a composition so that it does not have an aural center of gravity; the opposite of "tonal"
- **Avant garde** — the radical, progressive, cutting-edge of music, a term especially in use since the beginning of the twentieth century

- **Baroque Era** — a time in European history,1600-1750, in which the royal courts were supremely powerful and music tended to be highly detailed
- **Cadenza** — a totally solo portion of a concerto in which the orchestra waits while the soloist plays on; in the 1700s and 1800s, the soloist was expected to improvise
- **Canon** — A compositional form in which different layers of the music are based on the same, ever-changing melody, though at any one moment, those different layers are playing different portions of the melody; popular in the Baroque Era
- **Cantabile** — a smooth and song-like style of playing
- **Cantata** — a multi-movement composition for chorus and orchestra usually intended for liturgical use in the Protestant Church; especially identified with JS Bach
- **Chaconne** — a compositional form in which a repetitive bass line underlies an array of varying melodies, emphasizing relationships between those themes; especially popular in the Baroque Era
- **Chamber music** — music for small groups of players (duets, trios, quartets, etc.) playing "one to a part," so that each player makes a unique contribution to the composition
- **Classical Era** — a time from 1750-1820 or so, when the royal courts were declining in influence and composers were increasingly composing for general audiences; music tending to be simpler in structure than formerly
- **Clavichord** — a very quiet and delicate keyboard instrument popular in the Baroque Era, especially for use in the home; even lighter in sound than a harpsichord
- **Coda** — the final minutes or moments of a composition (or of one of its constituent movements) that serve to bring it to a close
- **Coloratura** — a very high singing voice nimble enough to be able to sing many different pitches quickly; usually applied to sopranos

- **Commission** — a request to a composer that he/she write a composition in return for payment, usually requesting a particular type of music for a particular occasion
- **Concert overture** — a one-movement piece of program music
- **Concerto** — a multi-movement instrumental composition in which one or more soloists are contrasted with a full orchestra
- **Consonance** — the sense that certain combinations of notes blend well; opposite of "dissonance"
- **Continuo** — the accompanying foundation of a Baroque Era work, generally played by harpsichord and one other low-pitched instrument
- **Counterpoint** — techniques for combining diverse melodies for simultaneous performance; especially important in music of the Baroque Era
- **Countertenor** — a particularly high male singing voice, higher than a tenor
- **Development** — a contrasting middle section of a composition in which material derives from fragments of the original themes; especially associated with "sonata form"
- **Dissonance** — the sense that certain combinations of notes do <u>not</u> blend well; opposite of "consonance"
- **Dynamics** — how loud or soft the music is played
- **Expressionism** — a style especially identified with the Second Viennese School, emphasizing musical expressions of dark, perhaps violent emotions; influenced by the theories of Sigmund Freud
- **Form** — the structure or blueprint of a composition, determining in what order its main components occur
- **Fugue** — a compositional form in which several simultaneous and equally prominent melodies are combined into a single tapestry of sound; especially associated with the Baroque Era, though not unknown in later years

- **Harmony** — combinations of simultaneous notes, often as accompaniment to a melody; the three-dimensional aspect of music
- **Harpsichord** — a keyboard instrument popular in the Baroque Era and before the piano; keys are laid out the same as a piano, but the mechanism inside the instrument plucks the strings, rather than striking them with a hammer, leading to a more delicate sound
- **Impressionism** — a movement of the late 1800s/early 1900s emphasizing softer, subtler edges and structures in music; related to the artistic movement of the same name
- **Improvisation** — spontaneous creation of music, even in front of a live audience
- **Incidental music** — a set of short pieces to accompany performance of a play
- **Inversion** — turning a musical theme upside-down, so that where it formerly rose in pitch, it now falls, and vice versa.
- **Jazz** — American popular music style originating in the 1920s and emphasizing improvisation and syncopation; influential even in the classical world; especially associated with Gershwin and Ellington
- **Key** — the central set of notes upon which a composition is based, giving it a particular character; "major" keys generally sound bright and cheerful, "minor" keys dark and somber
- **Legato** — smooth and connected notes; the opposite of "staccato"
- **Leitmotif** — a melodic fragment used to convey plot content in a composition, especially in Wagnerian opera
- **Librettist** — the person who writes the text of an opera or operetta
- **Libretto** — the text of an opera or operetta
- **Lieder** — a short musical setting of a poem, generally for one singer and one pianist, though some art songs may add more accompanying instruments; synonym of "art song"

- **Medieval Era** — roughly 450AD to roughly 1450AD; a time in history and music in which the Catholic Church was strongly influential in Europe
- **Meter** — the pattern of accented and unaccented beats in a composition. For example, 1-2-3, 1-2-3, as opposed to 1-2, 1-2, 1-2
- **Minimalism** — a musical style of the late 20th century in which a hypnotically steady beat is prominent, with small, subtle changes to melodic fragments; especially identified with Philip Glass
- **Minuet** — originally a triple-meter (1-2-3, 1-2-3) ballroom dance of the 1700s; becomes a popular form for composition in the late 1700s
- **Motif** — a fragment of a melody upon which larger musical structures may be built; one exceptionally famous motif is represented in the first four notes of Beethoven's Symphony no. 5
- **Movement** — a self-contained chapter of a more extended composition
- **Nationalism** — expressing pride in one's nation or ethnic group through one's music; especially prevalent in the mid to late 1800s in Eastern Europe
- **Neo-Classical** — a movement in the early 1900s in which some of the ideas of the late 1700s were revived, though perhaps with more modern harmonies
- **One to a part** — each player makes a unique contribution to the composition, with no simultaneous duplication whatsoever
- **Opera** — a musical drama with singers and orchestra
- **Opera buffa** — a type of comic opera especially popular in the late 1700s and early 1800s
- **Opera seria** — a type of serious opera especially popular in the early 1700s
- **Operetta** — light opera with spoken dialog; a predecessor of modern musical theater
- **Oratorio** — a multi-movement composition for singers and orchestra, generally telling a Biblical story, though

without sets or costumes, so not an opera; especially associated with Handel

- **Ostinato** — a steady, repeated rhythm at an unchanging pitch level, neither rising nor falling in pitch
- **Overture** — an instrumental introduction to a large-scale stage work, such as an opera; distinct from a "concert overture"
- **Pas de deux** — literally "steps for two": a scene for two ballet dancers, usually a man and a woman
- **Pitch** — the highness or lowness of a sound
- **Pizzicato** — plucking of the strings on an instrument
- **Polyphony** — the practice of having several simultaneous and equally important melodies; especially important in the Baroque Era, though not unknown in later times
- **Polytonality** — the practice of having several simultaneous keys, so that sometimes one section of the orchestra seems to clash with another section
- **Post-Romantic Era** — a time from 1890 to 1910 or so, in which music was moving away from the expectations of the Romantic Era, becoming even more free from any expectation
- **Program music** — instrumental music with a story to tell or a scene to paint; includes "tone poems," "symphonic poems," "concert overtures," and "program symphonies"
- **Program symphony** — a multi-movement work of program music; such as Berlioz' *Symphonie fantastique*
- **Punteado** — a guitar technique in which the player plucks a set of notes
- **Quarter-tones** — pitches between the standard notes on the piano, generally reachable only by the singing voice or string instruments; popular with certain highly progressive, avant garde composers of the early twentieth century
- **Rasgueado** — a guitar technique in which the player strums a set of notes

- **Recitative** — a half-singing/half-speaking kind of monologue or dialog in an opera, using the rhythms of every-day speech but set to particular musical pitches
- **Reformation** — the religious revolution beginning in 1517 as part of which the Protestant Church broke away from the Catholic Church
- **Renaissance Era** — after the Medieval Era but before the Baroque Era, therefore about 1600-1750; increasing power of the royal courts and a greater tendency toward secular music
- **Romantic Era** — a time from 1820 to 1890 or so, in which music was moving away from the expectations of the Classical Era, generally (though not always) becoming bigger, more dramatic, and more personal in its expression
- **Rubato** — a flexible tempo, permitting slight variances in pacing; especially identified with Chopin's piano music
- **Scherzo** — a form for composition having a forceful triple meter (1-2-3, 1-2-3) and usually two distinct melodies; one heard at the beginning and the end, the other in the middle
- **Score** — all the notes of a composition, with all its many parts, on the printed page
- **Second Viennese School** — a group of early 20th century composers who tended to be interested in radical, progressive, avant garde ideas; included Schoenberg and Berg
- **Serialism** — the practice of using every note within an octave with exactly equal frequency; especially associated with the Second Viennese School
- **Singspiel** — light opera with spoken dialog; similar to operetta, though in the late 1700s/early 1800s, German-speaking composers called it "Singspiel," not operetta.
- **Sonata** — a chamber work for one or two players, generally including a piano
- **Sonata form** — a pattern for composition in which a movement will have at least two main melodies of

contrasting character; these melodies will be stated at the beginning and the end of the movement, with the middle given to contrasting material derived from motifs (fragments) of the original themes; this middle section called the "development"

- **Staccato** — short and separated notes; the opposite of "legato"
- **Sturm und Drang** — an artistic movement just before and after 1800 that led to stronger, more dramatic compositions; especially associated with Beethoven; literally "storm and stress"
- **Symphonic poem** — a one-movement piece of program music
- **Symphony** — a multi-movement instrumental composition distinct from a concerto in that a symphony has no featured soloist
- **Tempo** — how fast or slow the music is played
- **Timbre** — the general quality or color of a sound, whether vocal or instrumental
- **Tonal** — the practice of emphasizing particular keys in a composition so as to give it an aural center of gravity; the opposite of "atonal"
- **Tone poem** — a one-movement piece of program music
- **Triplet** — fitting three notes of equal length into a single beat of the music
- **Variations** — taking a basic melody and steadily changing it (perhaps its rhythm or its key) so as to create different views of that original melody
- **Vocalise** — a piece for singing in which there is no specific text, only syllables to be sung

II. Composer Pronunciation Guide with Phonetic Spellings

Obvious names (such as John Adams) are not included. Although pronunciations are provided for all the last names given below, pronunciations are only given for first names that might prove problematic. The exception here is Ralph Vaughan

Williams, for whom the first name is actually more unusual in pronunciation than the last. Accented syllables are written in CAPITAL letters.

This list includes two foreign sounds that are often difficult for English speakers:

- German "ch" The German "ch" (as in Johann Sebastian Bach, Richard Wagner, and Richard Strauss) is pronounced like the "h" in "hue".

- French "G". The French "G" (as in Georges Bizet) has a sort of buzzing "zh" sound.

Adam, Adolphe	ah-DAHM	ah-DOLF	(He's French, not German.)
Albeniz, Isaac	al-BAY-nith	EEE-thak	(Castilian Spanish has a lisp.)
Allegri, Gregorio	al-LEG-ree	greg-OREO	
Bach, Johann Sebastian	BAHCH	YO-han se-BAS-tian	(German CH as above)
Balakirev, Mily	bal-ah-KEER-ev	MEEL-yee	
Bartók, Bela	BAR-tock	BAY-lah	
Beethoven, Ludwig van	BAY-tow-ven	LOOD-vig van	
Berlioz, Hector	BEAR-lee-ohz		
Bernstein, Leonard	BURN-styne		(Not "BURN-steeeen")
Bizet, Georges	bee-ZAY	Zhorzh	
Bloch, Ernest	bloch		(German CH as in Bach)
Boito, Arrigo	bo-EE-to	ah-REE-go	
Brahms, Johannes	BR-AH-MS	yo-HAN-es	
Bruch, Max	BREWCH		(German CH as in Bach)
Canteloube, Joseph	can-tah-LOOB		
Catán, Daniel	ka-TAHN		
Chopin, Frederic	SHOW-pan ·		
Copland, Aaron	COPE-land		(rhymes with "hope-land")
Couperin, François	coop-er-AN	fran-SWAH	

Debussy, Claude	day-byu-SEE		
Delibes, Leo	duh-LEEB	LAY-oh	
D'Indy Vincent	dahn-DEE	VIN-sahn	
Donizetti, Gaetano	DO-nih-ZET-tee	gay-TAH-no	
Dvořák, Antonín	duh-VOR-zhak	AHN-tow-neen	(Czechs roll the r.)
Fauré, Gabriel	faw-RAY	GAHB-ree-el	
Gershwin, George	GURSH-win		
Glazunov, Alexander	GLAH-zoo-nawv		
Golijov, Oswaldo	GO-lee-awv		
Grofé, Ferde	grow-FAY	FAIR-day	
Handel, George Frideric	HAN-dull		
Haydn, Joseph	HY-din		(Not HAY-din)
Hindemith, Paul	HIN-day-mit		
Hovhaness, Alan	hoe-VAHN-es		
Hummel, Johann Nepomuk	HUM-el	YO-han NEH-po-mook	
Joachim, Joseph	YO-ah-cheem		(German CH as in Bach)
Kabalevsky, Dmitri	KA-ba-LEV-ski		
Khachaturian, Aram	CATCH-a-TUR-ee-an	ah-RAM	
Köchel, Ludwig	KUR-schel	LOOD-vig	(Barely an r sound.)
Lehar, Franz	LAY-hahr		
Leoncavallo, Ruggiero	LEE-on-ca-VAHL-oh	ru-JAIR-oh	
Ligeti, György	LIH-get-ee	gee-OR-gee	
Liszt, Franz	list		
Mahler, Gustav	MAH-ler		
Marsalis, Wynton	mar-SAL-is		
Mascagni, Pietro	mas-KAHN-yee	pee-ET-ro	
Massenet, Jules	mass-uh-NAY	ZHUUL	
Mendelssohn, Felix	MEN-del-son		
Menotti, Gian-Carlo	men-OT-ee	JOHN CAR-lo	
Messiaen, Olivier	messy-AHN	oh-LIV-ee-ay	

Milhaud, Darius	mee-YOH	DAR-ee-us	
Monteverdi, Claudio	MON-teh-VAIR-dee		
Mussorgsky, Modest	mus-SORG-ski	MOH-dest	
Mozart, Wolfgang Amadeus	MOAT-zart	VULF-gahng ah-mah-DAY-iss	
Offenbach, Jacques	OFF-en-bahk	ZHAHK	
Pachelbel, Johann	PACH-ih-bell	YO-han	(German CH as in Bach.)
Paganini, Nicolo	PA-ga-NEE-nee	NICK-oh-low	
Palestrina, Giovanni	PAL-es-TREE-nah	JEE-oh-VAH-nee	
Piazzolla, Astor	pee-ah-ZOH-lah	AS-tor	
Ponchielli, Amilcare	PON-key-ELL-ee	AH-mil-CAR-ey	
Poulenc, Francis	poo-LAHNK	frahn-CEES	
Praetorius, Michael	pray-TOR-ee-us		
Prokofiev, Sergei	pro-KOH-fee-ev	SAIR-gay	
Puccini, Giacomo	poo-CHEE-nee	JAH-ko-mo	
Purcell, Henry	PURR-sell		
Rameau, Jean-Philippe	rah-MO	ZHAHN fee-LEEP	
Rautavaara, Einojuhani	RAOW-tah-VAR-ah	EI-no-you-HAH-nee	(RAOW rhyming with 'ow'.)
Ravel, Maurice	rah-VELL		
Respighi, Ottorino	res-PEE-ghee	auto-REE-no	
Rimsky-Korsakov, Nicolai	RIM-ski KOR-sa-kov		
Rodrigo, Joaquin	ro-DREE-go	wah-KEEN	
Rorem, Ned	ROAR-em		
Rota, Nino	ROW-tah	NEE-no	
Rózsa, Miklós	ROW-zha	MEE-clowzh	
Salieri, Antonio	SAL-ee-AIR-ee		
Sarasate, Pablo de	SAIR-ah-SAHT-eh		
Schoenberg, Arnold	SHOON-bairg		
Schubert, Franz	SHOO-bairt		
Schumann, Clara Wieck	SHOO-mahn	KLAIR-ah VEEK	
Schumann, Robert	SHOO-mahn		
Scriabin, Alexander	scree-AH-bin		
Shostakovich, Dmitri	SHOS-ta-KO-vitch		
Sibelius, Jean	sih-BAY-lee-us	ZHAHN	

Smetana, Bedrich	SMET-an-nah	BAYD-rik	
Sousa, John Philip	SUE-sah		
Strauss, Richard	SHTR-OW-ss	REE-chart	(German CH as in Bach)
Stravinsky, Igor	stra-VIN-skee	EE-gor	
Suk, Josef	SOOOK	YO-sef	(long ooo – not "suck")
Tchaikovsky, Peter	chy-KOV-skee		
Vaughan Williams, Ralph	RAFE		(rhyming with "safe")
Verdi, Giuseppe	VAIR-dee	juh-SEP-ee	
Vivaldi, Antonio	vih-VALL-dee		
Wagner, Richard	VAHG-ner	REE-chart	(German CH as in Bach)
Waldteufel, Emil	VAHLD-toy-full		
Weber, Carl Maria von	VAY-burr		
Ysaÿe, Eugene	ee-SIGH	you-ZHAYN	

III. Source List

Note: Some information about recent and current composers and their works I obtained from interviews with the composers themselves and with respected interpreters of their works, either for my radio programs or in live interviews with audiences prior to concerts. These include John Adams, John Cage, Carlisle Floyd, Jennifer Higdon, Libby Larsen, Edgar Meyer, John Rutter, Joan Tower, and the Takács Quartet (this last ensemble for their perspective as Hungarians on the music of Bartók – I spoke with the original members of the Quartet, before membership changes brought non-Hungarians to the ensemble.). Philip Glass I have not personally interviewed, but have transcribed interviews he has given with other members of the media, who are credited where those interviews come into play.

Further Note: many of the German sources I read in the original German, and translated myself when translations of quotations were needed.

Last note: Some current composers make a point of maintaining their own websites in which they comment upon their own lives and music; if the composer himself is supervising the site, it can be considered authoritative. These include Michael Daughtery, Jay Greenberg, Jake Heggie, Karl Jenkins, Michael Torke, and Eric Whitacre.

- Adami, Giuseppe: editor. *Letters of Giacomo Puccini*. Vienna House: New York. 1973.

- Adams, John. *Hallelujah Junction: Composing an American Life*. Farrar, Straus and Giroux: New York. 2008

- Altmann, Dr. Wilhelm. *Richard Wagners Briefe*. Breitkopf und Härtel. 1905.

- Barrie-Jones, J. The *Correspondence of Camille Saint-Saëns and Gabriele Fauré*. Ashgate Publishing. 2004

- Behague, Gerard. *Heitor Villa-Lobos: The Search for Brazil's Musical Soul*. Institute of Latin American Studies, University of Texas, Austin. 1994.

- Burney, Charles. *A General History of Music*. Dover Publications: New York. 1957. First published 1789.

- Carr, Jonathan. *Mahler: A Biography*. Overlook Press: Woodstock and New York. 1997.

- Deutsch, Otto Erich. *Schubert: Erinnerungen von seine Freunden*. Breitkopf und Härtel: Leipzig. 1958.

- Dvořák, Otakar. *Antonín Dvořák, My Father*. Written 1961; published 1993 by Czech Historical Research Center of Spillville, Iowa. Edited by Paul J. Polansky, translated by Miroslav Němec.

- Eaglefield-Hull, A., editor. *Beethoven's Letters*. Letters translated by JS Shedlock. Dover: New York. 1972.

- Ellington, Edward Kennedy "Duke". *Music is My Mistress*. Da Capo Press. 1976.

- Gottlieb, Jack. *Working with Bernstein*. Amadeus Press: Milwaukee. 2010

- *Gramophone Magazine*. Various editors over many years. London. In print since 1923, and a fine source of first-hand composer information, including interviews both with current and with now long-departed composers.

- Hanslick, Eduard. *Musikkritiken*. Philipp Reclam: Stuttgart. 1972.

- *Harvard Magazine*, July 2001 (information regarding alumnus Randall Thompson).

- Hildesheimer, Wolfgang. *Mozart*. Suhrkampf Verlag: Frankfurt am Main. 1977.

- Hilmes, Oliver. *Cosima Wagner: The Lady of Bayreuth*. Translation by Stewart Spencer. Yale University Press: New Haven and London. 2010.

- Hoffmann, E.T.A. *Kreisleriana*. Philipp Reclam: Stuttgart. 1986.

- Holst, Imogen. *Holst*. Faber and Faber: London and Boston. 1974.

- Honolka, Kurt. Translated by Anne Wyburd. *Dvořák*. Haus Publishing Limited: London. 2004

- Kennedy, Michael. *Master Musician: Britten*. Dent: London 1981.

- Kennedy, Michael. *Richard Strauss: Man, Musician, Enigma*. Cambridge University Press: Cambridge and New York. 1999.

- Mahler, Alma. *Gustav Mahler: Erinnerungen und Briefe*. Verlag Allert de Lange: Amsterdam. 1940.

- Morgenstern, Sam. *Composers on Music: An Anthology of Composers' Writings from Palestrina to Copland*. Pantheon Books: New York. 1956.

- Musgrove, Michael. *A Brahms Reader*. Yale University Press: New Haven and London. 2000.

- Neumann, Werner: editor. *Bach Dokumente: Herausgegeben vom Bach-Arkiv Leipzig*. Bärenreiter: Kassel — Basel — Paris — London — New York. 1963.

- New York Philharmonic digital archives. http://archives. newyorkphil.org

- *New York Times* microfilm archives: various reviews of premieres of major works.

- Newman, Ernest: translator. *Memoirs of Hector Berlioz from 1803 to 1865*. Dover Publications: New York. 1932.

- Nichols, Roger: translator and editor. *Debussy Letters*. Faber and Faber: London and Boston. 1987.

- Orlova, Alexandra. *Tchaikovsky: A Self-Portrait*. Oxford University Press: London. 1990.

- Pleasants, Henry: translator and editor. *Hanslick's Music Criticisms*. Dover Publications: New York. 1950.

- Pleasants, Henry: translator and editor. *Schumann on Music: A Selection from the Writings*. Dover Publications: New York. 1965.

- Pollock, Howard. *George Gershwin: His Life and Work*. University of California Press: 2006.

- Prokofiev, Sergei. *Prokofiev by Prokofiev: A Composer's Memoir*. Doubleday and Company: New York. 1979.

- Rimsky-Korsakov, Nikolai. *My Musical Life*. Translated by Judah A. Joffe. Vienna House: New York. 1972.

- Ross, Alex. The Rest is Noise: Listening to the Twentieth Century. Picador: New York. 2007.

- Sadie, Stanley, editor. *Grove's Dictionary of Music and Musicians*. MacMillan Publishers: London. 1980. 2001.

- Schindler, Anton Felix. *Beethoven as I Knew Him*. Translated by Constance S. Jolly. Dover Publications: New York. 1996.

- Schonberg, Harold C. *The Great Pianists: From Mozart to the Present*. Simon and Schuster: New York. 1987.

- Schumann, Robert. *Schriften über Musik und Musiker*. Philipp Reclam: Stuttgart. 2010.

- Secrest, Meryl. *Leonard Bernstein: A Life*. Alfred A. Knopf: New York. 1994.

- Selden-Goth G. *Felix Mendelssohn: Letters*. Elek Publishers: London. 1946.

- Seroff, Victor Ilyich. *Dmitri Shostakovich: The Life and Background of a Soviet Composer.* Books for Libraries Press: Freeport and New York. 1970.

- Siblin, Eric. *The Cello Suites: J.S. Bach, Pablo Casals, and the Search for a Baroque Masterpiece.* 2009. Grove Press, New York.

- Slonimsky, Nicolas. *Lexicon of Musical Invective: Critical Assaults on Composers since Beethoven's Time.* University of Washington Press: Seattle and London. 1953. 1994.

- Solomon, Maynard. *Beethoven.* Schirmer Books: New York. 1998.

- Solomon, Maynard. *Mozart: A Life.* Harper Collins: New York. 1995

- Spaething, Robert. *Mozart's Letters, Mozart's Life: Selected Letters Edited and Newly Translated.* Norton and Company: New York and London. 2000.

- Strauss, Dr. Franz. *Richard Strauss Briefwechsel mit Hugo von Hofmannsthal.* Berlin. 1925.

- Stravinsky, Igor. *Igor Stravinsky: An Autobiography.* W.W. Norton and Company: New York and London. 1936.

- Tchaikovsky, Modest. *The Life and Letters of Peter Ilyich Tchaikovsky.* Translated by Rosa Newmarch. Vienna House: New York. 1973.

- Thomas, Nancy G. and Jaffe, Jane Vial, editors. *Kurt Oppens on Music: Notes and Essays for the Aspen Music Festival 1957-1995.* Science/Art Press: Aspen, Colorado. 2009.

- Vaughan Williams, Ursula. *R.V.W: A Biography of Ralph Vaughan Williams.* Oxford University Press: London. 1964.

IV. Acknowledgements

Many thanks to my professional colleagues who pre-read chapters of this book and offered helpful suggestions:

Lorrie Evans	Pat McNulty
Dr. Michael Kornelsen	RJ Miller
Timothy Krueger	Dr. Bradley Thompson
Dr. Brandon Matthews	Dr. Trudi Wright

Extra thanks to RJ for using his skills as a composer to tidy up my originally hand-written music headers for the chapters. My music handwriting is good; his computer's is much better.

Thanks to graphic artist Wayne Rigsby of Gearbox Creative, Inc., for the cover art.

Also, thanks to my family: Rick, Colin, Conor, and even Ferdi and Lena, for letting me talk about music, identify classical bits that go by on the television, and spend hours at the computer. Ferdi, the Sheltie, sings along with live music. Lena, the cat, can sleep through anything except Charles Ives and John Cage, who seem to make her nervous — but Philip Glass she quite likes.

V. Author Biographical Notes

With degrees in history and humanities, Betsy Schwarm has worked in classical music for about twenty-five years in various capacities, including:

- Classical radio announcer/producer, especially at KVOD, "The Classical Voice of Denver"

- Music department faculty at Metropolitan State College of Denver

- Pre-performance speaker for the Colorado Symphony, Opera Colorado, the Newman Center for the Performing Arts, the Colorado Music Festival, the Bravo Vail Valley Festival, and other organizations

- Program annotator for the Cleveland Orchestra, the Huntsville Symphony, the Philharmonic Society of Orange County, the Phoenix Symphony, Opera Colorado, and other organizations

- Recording engineer for the Central City Opera

- Freelance reporter with National Public Radio

This book represents about ten percent of Ms. Schwarm's catalog of concert program notes for classical works. To see the full list, please visit her website: www.classicalmusicinsights.com.

Index